Lestevenon de Berkenroode

M
I } Rüppell
N

©

27740

THE MEMOIRS OF CHARLES-LEWIS, Baron de POLLNITZ.

BEING

The OBSERVATIONS He made in his late TRAVELS from *Prussia* thro'

GERMANY,	FLANDERS.
ITALY,	HOLLAND,
FRANCE,	ENGLAND, &c.

In LETTERS to his FRIEND.

Discovering not only the PRESENT STATE of the Chief CITIES and TOWNS;

BUT

The CHARACTERS of the PRINCIPAL PERSONS at the Several COURTS.

In TWO VOLUMES.

The SECOND EDITION, with ADDITIONS.

LONDON:

Printed for DANIEL BROWNE, at the *Black Swan*, without *Temple-Bar*. M.DCC.XXXIX.

To the Right Honourable

PHILIP, *Lord* HARDWICKE;

Baron of *Hardwicke,* in the County of *Gloucester;*

LORD HIGH CHANCELLOR of *Great Britain;*

AND

One of the LORDS of His Majesty's most Honourable PRIVY COUNCIL.

MY LORD,

THE good Reception these Memoirs, which I most humbly offer to your Lordship, have met with Abroad; and the Protection and Favour the *Author* has obtain'd at one of the Chief Protestant Courts of EUROPE; encourage me, tho' with the profoundest Submission, to intreat your Lordship's favourable Acceptance of this *Translation.*

'Tis,

DEDICATION.

'Tis, my Lord, the only Homage I am capable of paying your Lordship, and the best Testimony I can give with what Zeal and Pleasure I join in the Congratulation of the Public for that illustrious Regard paid to your Lordship's Merit, and Their Wishes, by his SACRED MAJESTY, this Day in Council.

That your Lordship may very long enjoy a sufficient Portion of Health, equal to the Abilities of your Great Mind, for supporting you under that vast Weight of Service which you have now taken upon you for your King and Country, is the hearty Prayer of all good ENGLISHMEN; and particularly of Him, MY LORD, who has the Honour to subscribe

YOUR LORDSHIP's

Most Devoted,

Most Obedient, and

Most Humble Servant.

PREFACE,

By the TRANSLATOR.

THE Author of these *Memoirs*, who is a Person of an honourable Family in *Prussia*, and confess'd by all that know him to be a Gentleman of extraordinary Talents, is one that may be truly said to have seen the World; he having not only travell'd twice thro' the principal Parts of *Europe*, but by his Acquaintance with People of the first Rank, and a diligent Inquiry and nice Inspection into Men and Things, attained to that Knowledge of Both, which is of such Service and Entertainment to Mankind in the general, and so particularly necessary for All who attend to what is doing in high Life.

He has succeeded very happily in the right Narrative Stile; and the *French* Language, in which he wrote the following Letters, seems to be as natural to him as if it was his Mother-Tongue. But the Thing which has most contributed to the Demand for these Memoirs, is the Multitude of Characters that the Baron has interspers'd, not only of the Deceas'd, but even of Perſons that are ſtill living, and diſtinguiſh'd by the exalted Spheres in which they move.

That every one of thoſe Characters is equally juſt, or that every Circumſtance relating to them is told with the utmoſt Exactneſs, is not to be imagin'd: For ſuppoſing the Author to have been ever ſo circumſpect and impartial, how was it poſſible for him to take the true Likeneſs of every one, in ſuch a Variety of Perſonages of both Sexes, and to be perfectly ſure of every Particular that he mentions; ſince he could not be Eye-Witneſs of every thing, and muſt be oblig'd for many to Information from other Perſons, of whom, 'tis no wonder if ſome were prejudic'd? But to do the Baron Juſtice, it muſt be allow'd, that he no where fails in that Reſpect and Decorum to Princes which are their due; and that he has not diſcover'd a predominant Paſſion for Satire: becauſe where he has painted in the ſtrongeſt Colours, and repreſented his Subjects in the moſt diſadvantageous Light, they were ſuch whoſe Follies or whoſe Vices were too flagrant and notorious to be either conceal'd or diſguis'd: And, conſidering the Groupe of Courtiers whom he has crouded into his Canvaſs, the Reader will rather be ſurpris'd to meet with ſo few Imperfections in his Characters, and ſo many excellent Qualities. By this means, his Memoirs have, upon the whole, done Honour to his Underſtanding, without offending his Conſcience, or hurting his Fortune;

PREFACE.

tune; he being, at this very time, upon a handsome Establishment at the Court of *Prussia*.

It cannot possibly escape the Observation of the Reader, that the Baron, when he wrote these Letters to his noble Friend, was a profess'd Member of the Church of *Rome*; but that nevertheless, he was not such a Bigot to its Constitution, nor such a Believer in the Legends of its Writers, or the pretended Miracles of its Saints, as to incur the Character of a blind and furious Zealot; it appearing on the contrary, from several Declarations of his Mind in the following Pages, that he did not want Charity either in his Nature or Principles for those from whom he differ'd in religious Sentiments. Such a Catholic Spirit, assisted by his good Sense, made it, no doubt, much easier for him, after reflecting upon the Fopperies and Impostures which he had seen in that Church during his Travels, to abjure the *Romish* and to embrace the *Protestant* Religion, which he did accordingly with great Devotion last Summer, at *Berlin*; after which, his *Prussian* Majesty was pleas'd to distinguish him with peculiar Marks of his Favour and Esteem, by declaring him one of the Gentlemen of his Bedchamber, and Chief Cup-Bearer of his Court; and he has very lately given him a considerable Prebend.

To the new Edition of his Memoirs, from which the following Sheets are translated, there's not only a great number of material Additions in the Body of the Work, as is observ'd by the Editor

tor of it, at *Amsterdam*, but several new Notes: In this Translation, these Notes are likewise considerably augmented, for the sake of continuing the Thread of the History to the present Time, by the Notice taken of certain remarkable Alterations, or other curious Particulars that have happen'd to the Persons or the Places mentioned, since 1734, when the said Edition was publish'd.

One great Defect for which the foreign Editor has been very much blam'd, was the want of a Table to these Memoirs; which, if not absolutely necessary in a Work of this kind, wherein so many Persons and Facts are mentioned, cannot be necessary for any Book whatsoever that comes from the Press. To supply this Defect, the Translator has added an Alphabetical Index to each of the two Volumes; which Indexes are the more copious, that the Reader might know where to turn in an Instant for some Account of the Characters, Conduct, or Familys of those public Personages, whose Names so often occur in the News-Papers.

THE

THE AUTHOR's PREFACE TO THE FIPST EDITION.

THERE are very few Books without a Preface; and that there are so, is in a great measure owing to the Fancy of the Bookfellers, who think them to be absolutely necessary, and too often judge of the merit of a Copy by the Flights of its Preface, and the infinuating Tone of the Author's Voice in reading it. I had the misfortune to fall into the hands of one of these Bookfellers, so fond of Prefaces, whom nothing would serve but he must have one at the Head of my Memoirs. My telling him that I did not know what to put into a Preface, signify'd no more than if I had been talking to a Post; for he threatned to get a Preface compos'd by an Author who wrote for Wages. This startled me, and I trembled for the fate of my Book, not doubting that a Preface written by a Man of Letters, who made it his profession to compose such marvellous Pieces, would altogether eclipse the few Excellencies in this Work of mine. What, said I to myself, the Sale of my Book then must depend only on the Goodness of the Preface, which, when the Readers compare with the Book it self, they will say, O! what a wonderful Man is the Author of the Preface! What a pitiful Writer, the Compiler of the Memoirs! No, said I again to my self, I am resolv'd that the Preface and the Book shall run the same risk; and since

Chance

The Author's Preface

Chance has enter'd me an Author, I'll play out the whole part of one.

I am told that the Design of a Preface is to give the Publick an account, in the first place, of the Reasons that have engag'd the Author to compose his Work; that then he is to inform the Publick, that 'tis in meer Complaisance to his Friends, and because there are mangled Copies of his Manuscript abroad, that he has been determined to put it to the Press; and finally, that he is to conclude with a sort of Petition, wherein he is to beg the Reader's Indulgence for his Productions. This, I have been assured, is the Plan of a Preface; let us now see how well I can execute it.

As to the first Article, viz. what Motives I had to write, I sincerely own that when I set Pen to Paper, I meant nothing more than to amuse my self. I was the farthest in the World from thinking that I should one day be overtaken with the Temptation of setting up for an Author. I wrote Letters to a Friend of mine, purely to divert him with an Account of such things as came in my way; the Minutes of which Letters I preserved till I had insensibly formed a Volume of 'em; and having nothing else to do, I augmented and digested them in the manner that I now give them to the Publick. The truth is, that my Friends have not used the least Importunity with me to commit my Manuscript to the Press, nor was it possible for any spurious Copies of it to get abroad, because no body ever saw it till I put it into the hands of the Bookseller.

But I shall be ask'd, what possess'd me to commence Author, and how came I to be so idle as to put my Name at the Head of a sorry book? I must answer again, that it was downright Indolence. As to my Name, it would have been very difficult to have concealed it from Persons to whom I have the greatest Obligations. I should have been suspected to have been the Author of these Memoirs at certain Courts, for which I have a Respect both by Inclination and Duty; and perhaps,

if

if I had left this Copy to the wide World, as some do those Foundlings which they are asham'd to own, such Passages might have been foisted into it, as would have been father'd upon me, in spite of all Protestations of my Innocence.

As to the Book itself, I am apt to think there is nothing in it that any Person whatsoever ought to take offence at. When I speak of Sovereign Princes, 'tis with the Reverence due to the Lord's Anointed; *and I also endeavour to honour them in their Ministers, being taught by my Religion that I ought to honour God in his Saints. I have done my utmost to paint the true Characters of People in Place, and can safely say, that my Authorities are not meer hear-says or scraps out of News-Papers; for, thank to God, my Birth and Fortune have put me in a capacity to see, hear, and judge for myself.*

It will be thought perhaps, that when I speak of Nations in general, I judge too rashly. It may be so; this being an Article especially in which all Men do not think alike. The French *have a quite different Idea of the* Germans *from what the* English *have, and the* English *do not pass the same Verdict on the* French *as the* Swedes *do. 'Tis the same in private Life. Every one makes his own Condition the Standard of his Judgment. The Man of Quality, the Citizen, the Soldier, the Merchant, have all different Ideas. The Traveller judges of the Nation where he is, by the Company he keeps. A* Frenchman *who in* Germany *converses with none but those of the second Class, will say that the* Germans *are honest People, but clownish; whereas another, who keeps company with Persons of Quality, or those in Offices, will agree, that the* Germans *are more polite than they have been painted by certain* French *Writers, who have been transplanted to* Germany *either by their Distresses, or by meer Chance. So, a* German, *who, when he is at* Paris, *sees no better Company than the Marchionesses of the*

Suburb

Suburb of St. Germain, *imagines that all the Women both at Court and in the City are like them. In fine, a Foreigner who takes up his Residence in the City of* London, *will entertain a different Idea of the* English *from what another shall do who lodges at* St. James's *end of the town. They are, as one may say, so many different Nations in one and the same State, which stand in little relation to one another, and sometimes attribute Virtues and Vices to each other without due Consideration. A Foreigner therefore can form a solid Judgment of none but those with whom he is conversant; and if he has the good luck to pitch his Tent well, he entertains an advantageous Opinion of the Nation in general. Let Foreigners, when they return home, after having kept such various sorts of Company, sit down to draw the Characters of the Nations they have seen, I do but think what a strange difference would appear in their Descriptions! The Judgment therefore which I make of People, is founded upon the Company I kept, and upon what I heard from such Inhabitants of the Country as appear'd to me to be altogether unprejudiced, and were pleased to honour me with their Information. I do not say but, after all, I may have been mistaken; for I do not pretend to have painted things in any other light than as they appear'd to me. If, nevertheless, any particular Person thinks himself particularly intended when I speak of the Inhabitants of any Province or Town in general, I beg him to remember, that I confess in my Memoirs there are worthy People in all parts of the World, and 'tis not my fault if his Conscience does not permit him to rank himself in that number.*

No doubt I shall be reproach'd for relating too many Trifles, and passing too lightly over things of greater Importance. To speak freely again, I will make no difficulty to own, that, if when I began these Memoirs, I had ever thought of printing them, the desire of promoting their Sale might perhaps have put me upon in-

serting

serting a great many Nothings which I omitted, as not thinking it worth while to charge my Memory with 'em. The far greatest part of what the World reads is Trifles, and a History will make its fortune not by the instructive Facts that are in it, but by the Romantic Turn the Author gives it. Besides, I am not so vain as to write with a design of Instructing; for what could I relate in my Travels which others have not done before me in better Terms? To talk of Learned Men, to make a Catalogue of Books and MSS. that are to be met with in Libraries, to ransack the Cabinet of the Curious, to publish Inscriptions, to treat of antique Medals, to affirm that I have seen an Otho of Brass, which is known to be but of Silver, what a Posse of Men of Learning would rise up against me! Whereas, now I fear nothing; the Learned don't read Trifles, or if they do, they scorn to criticise them. I shall to them remain unknown, or at least, my Meanness will be my Protection against their Indignation.

I would fain be as secure against the Criticism of those, who reading for the sake of their amusement, require an exact, elegant Stile in Trifles, that is, adorn'd with the Flowers and Garlands of Rhetorick. But how shall I gain their Indulgence? If I own to them that I could do no better, they will say to me, and justly enough, Alas! then what made you write? To which I shall answer, as I said before, that it was meerly for want of something else to do. If they will but forgive me this time, I assure them that I not only will never relapse into the same error, but that I shall not be sorry if they disdain to take Notice of my Book: And if the reading of these Memoirs inclines them to sleep, I shall think my self very well rewarded for having contributed to their Repose.

After all, I am more particularly obliged to ask pardon of the French than any other Nation: 'Tis in their Language I have presumed to write, and they are my proper Judges. Such is their Politeness and their

Readiness

xiv *The Author's* PREFACE.

Readiness to assist Foreigners, that I doubt not of Mercy. And in return, I promise them, that if a Frenchman *ever vouchsafes to write in the* German *Language, I will forgive him any Errors that he may commit.*

ADVERTISEMENT by the EDITOR.

N.B. "THESE Memoirs went off so quick, that before they had been out scarce six Months, the *French* Booksseller was oblig'd to prepare for this *Second Edition*; to which, there are considerable Additions both in the Body of the Work and in the Notes, of curious and interesting Facts and Characters, and the principal Alterations that have happen'd at the several Courts, since the first Edition.

"There is added in particular, a very circumstantial Account of the present Elector of *Saxony*'s Family, his Ministers, and Officers; and in short, of the Chief Persons of both Sexes belonging to his Court and Houshold. This is prefix'd in the Original, at the Head of the Memoirs; but the Translator thought it more regular as well as more consistent with the Method observ'd every where else by the Author, to place it at the End of his Description of the City of *Dresden*. The Baron has dedicated that Account to the present Elector (*Augustus*, King of *Poland*) and introduc'd it with the following Preface."

PRE-

PREFACE,

To the Second Edition.

THE Present State of the Court of Saxony, which is added to this Edition, has no need of a Preface to recommend it, the very Title shewing that 'tis what concerns every Saxon especially to be acquainted with.

All Subjects have a desire to know something of their Sovereign; and private Men in every State have this Curiosity, with respect to their Ministers and Courtiers. These are the Characters which I have ventured to draw, tho' I own, that I don't think I have always hit the Life, for want of that Penetration and Delicacy of Imagination which Nature, to me a Step-Mother, has deny'd me; and also because it would have been necessary for me to have stay'd longer than I did at Dresden. Three Months Residence at so great a Court, are hardly sufficient to make a Man acquainted with it, were his Fund of Knowledge even as deep as mine is shallow. Then what a Presumption would it be for me to think I have attained to it!

I must not dissemble, that this Book with all its Imperfections, has cost me more trouble in composing than one much larger would have done upon a Subject that had been more familiar to me. There was a necessity for me to make Inquiry into many Particulars, and to get some of my Information from a private hand. I own my Obligation to the Civility of M. Konig, the Counsellor of the Court, for the Intelligence I wanted

relating

relating to some of the Court-Nobility. If I had been so happy as to have found out but one or two Persons more as active for me as he was, my Work would have been more correct and more extensive. Such as it is, I intreat the Reader to accept it, and to forgive any Errors in it, in consideration that I am the first who has ventured to treat of such a Subject. I own, there is a certain degree of Rashness in the Undertaking, but the noble Motive that has induc'd me to it, seems to plead for my excuse.

All Saxony knows in general, that 'tis govern'd by a Sovereign, gracious, and vigilant to render it happy. It were needless to set the King's Virtues and Actions before their Eyes, which the People already admire, and pray for him. But as this Great Prince does not want those who envy his Glory, they are the Persons whom I have chose to make asham'd of themselves; and have endeavoured, if possible, to reclaim others whom a fatal blindness keeps at a distance from his Majesty's Person **.

All that ever had the honour of approaching Augustus III. will agree with me that he adorns that Throne, upon which a respectful Nation has plac'd him; and that whatever I have said of this Monarch is short of what might be mention'd. How is it possible to give the true Portraiture of a King born without Vice, by Principle virtuous, and religiously good? To admire him in silence is the only way to please him, which I know too well, not to conform to it; and therefore I have not presum'd to expatiate so far in his Praise as the Sublimity of the Subject demands.

The same Aversion of the Queen to Praise, has confin'd me within the same bounds. How many Virtues have not I been forc'd to smother? What Thoughts have

---

* The Reader will please to observe, that this Preface was written during the late Distractions in *Poland*, before the Malecontent Lords had reconcil'd themselves to their Allegiance to their lawful Sovereign.

have not I sacrific'd, left I should offend the noble Modesty of that August Princess, who with a Simplicity attending her Grandeur, makes her Glory to consist in being humble in the midst of Honours?

I believe no body will dispute the Truth of what I have advanc'd relating to the PRINCE ROYAL *and* ELECTORAL, *the* PRINCES HIS BROTHERS, *and the* PRINCESSES HIS SISTERS. *The hopes I have raised of what may be expected from* THEIR ROYAL HIGHNESSES, *will surely be confirm'd by Time, and by all those who have access to them.*

The Actions of the Duke John-Adolphus *of* Saxe-Weissenfels *are so well establish'd that I have not thought fit to anticipate History, by which they are to be consecrated: And for the same reason, I have but just touch'd upon the amiable Qualities of his Mind, which are rever'd both by the Court and the Army.*

As to the Princess of Saxe-Weissenfels, *I frankly own, that as I had not the honour of paying my Court to her, what I have said of her Virtues has no other Authority than the Voice of the Publick, which can never speak enough in her Praise.*

I have been more copious in treating of the Ministers; and what I have said of them is so true, that they who know them not may thereby form a just Idea of what they are.

I have taken as much notice of the principal Lords and the most distinguish'd Ladies of the Court, as the little time I had for this Work, and the Limits to which I was confin'd, would permit. I flatter myself they will forgive the Freedom with which I use them; and hope I have preserv'd a Decency in my Language which will secure me from Reproach.

a   A D-

ADDENDA to Vol. I.

PAP. 15. M. *Beausobre*, Minister of the Gospel at *Berlin*, and Author of several learned Treatises, died in *May* 1738.

P. 26. The Princess of *Brandenburg-Schwedt*, fourth Daughter of the King of *Prussia*, was deliver'd of a Daughter in *April* 1738.

P. 27. The Count *de Truchses-Walbourg*, Major-General in the Service of the King of *Prussia*, died at *Berlin* in *April* 1738.

P. 34. In *July* 1738, his *Prussian* Majesty, together with the Prince Royal and Prince *William*, made a Tour to *Holland*, and paid a Visit to his most Serene Highness the Prince of *Orange*.

P. 66. His Excellency Baron *Hattorf*, Secretary of State for the Affairs of *Hanover*, died in *August* 1737.

P. 70. *Christina-Louisa*, Princess of *Œtingen*, died in 1736.

P. 72. *Philippina-Charlotte*, Duchess of *Brunswic-Wolfembuttle*, and third Daughter to the King of *Prussia*, after having had two Sons by Duke *Charles* her Husband, viz. the first born in 1735, and the other, who is called *George-Francis*, in 1736, was deliver'd also of a Daughter in *September* 1737, who in the Month following was baptiz'd by the Names of *Christina-Sophia-Maria*.

P. 105. M. *de Miltitz*, who was Tutor to the present King *Augustus* when he was Electoral Prince of *Saxony*, died in *March* 1738.

P.

Addenda to Vol. I.   xix

P. 113. The Princess Royal of *Poland* was married in *July* 1738, to Don *Carlos* King of *Naples* and *Sicily*.

P. 130. The Count *de Sulkowski* in *January* 1738 fell under some Disgrace, so that his Majesty order'd his Papers to be seal'd up, and excused him from farther Attendance on him, but was willing he should keep the Title and Rank of Minister of the Cabinet, and General of the Foot, with 6000 Crowns Pension.

P. 140. *Adolphus de Bruhl* was in *January* 1738 appointed Grand-Master of the Horse, at the *Saxon* Court, in the room of the Count *de Sulkowski*.

P. 142. The Count *de Moschinski* died in *September* 1737.

P. 147. The Count *de Diedrichstein* died at *Prague* in *September* 1737. He was Baron of *Hollenbourg, Finckenstein, Dahlberg* and *Landskroon*, Hereditary Great Huntsman of *Styria*, Hereditary Cup-Bearer of *Carinthia*, Knight of the Order of St. *John* of *Jerusalem*, Grand Prior in *Bohemia, Moravia, Silesia, Carinthia, Styria, Tirol, Austria* and *Poland*, Bailiff of the aforesaid Order, and Commander of the Commanderies of *Little Oels, Furstenfeld* and *Mosling*, a Privy-Counsellor of the Emperor, and Governour-General of the Kingdom of *Bohemia*.

P. 168. The last Duke of *Saxe-Merseburg* mention'd in the Note of that Page, died in *May* 1738.

P. 182. In *April* 1738, the Emperor appointed the Prince of *Saxe-Gotha* Lieutenant Velt-Marshal of his Armies; and in *September* following he solicited the Diet of *Ratisbon* for the Post of second Velt-Marshal General of the Empire, in the Disposal of the Protestant States, vacant by the Death of the Baron *de Wutgenau*.

Addenda to Vol. I.

P. 182. *Augusta* Princess of *Wales* was deliver'd of a Princess on the 31st of *July* 1737, who was baptized after her own Name; and on the 24th of *May* 1738, she was deliver'd of a Prince who was baptiz'd *George-William Frederic*.

P. 208. The Margravine of *Brandenbourg-Culmbach*, Mother to the Queen of *Denmark*, died at *Copenhagen* in *August* 1737, in the 70th Year of her Age, very much lamented.

P. 220. Count *Philip Kinski* was made Chancellor of *Bohemia*, in *May* 1738, in the room of the late Count *de Collowrat*.

P. 233. The Archduchess, Wife to the Duke of *Lorrain*, had a Daughter, born *January* 25, 1737, and another born in *September* 1738.

P. 264. The eldest Son of the Duke *Ferdinand* of *Bavaria*, died in *April* 1738.

P. 266. The Count *Maximilian de Fugger* died at *Vienna*, in *January* 1738.

P. 266. The Count *de Thirheim* died in *January* 1738, at *Lintz*, the Capital of *Upper Austria*.

P. 285. *Charles-Alexander* Duke of *Wirtemberg-Stutgard*, died on the 1st of *March* 1737, and was succeeded by his eldest Son *Eugene-Lewis* the present Duke, who was born the 30th of *January* 1728.

P. 298. The Margrave of *Baden-Dourlach* died the first of *May* 1738, at *Carelsruhe*, who having no Issue living, is succeeded by *Frederic* of *Witgenstein*, who is marry'd to the Princess *Augusta-Amelia-Albertina* of *Nassau-Siegen*. The Deceased was 58 Years and near 11 Months of Age, being born the 17th of *June* 1679. He was a General in the Emperor's Army, and Great Master of the Artillery in the Circle of *Suabia*. By his Wife, a Daughter of the Duke of *Wirtemberg-Stutgard*, he had four Children, who are

all

all dead. When he laid the Plan and Foundation of the City and Castle of *Carelsrube*, he gave equal Liberty of Conscience to the Lutherans, Calvinists, and Roman Catholics.

P. 321. The Cardinal *de Schonborn* died in *August* 1737.

P. 335. The Baron *de Beveren*, Grand Marshal at the Elector Palatine's Court, died there in *January* 1738.

P. 357. In *January* 1738, the Prince of *Hesse-Hombourg* was married to the Velt-Marshal *Trubetskay*'s Daughter.

P. 362. After the Death of the Count of *Hanau* without Issue, the Succession was awarded to the Prince of *Darmstad* as next Heir, on condition of his paying 200000 *l.* by way of Compensation to the House of *Cassel*.

ADDENDA to Vol. II.

PAG. 14. Cardinal *Biffi* died in *August* 1737.

P. 44. Cardinal *Olivieri*, Secretary of the Pope's Briefs, died at *Rome* in *February* 1738.

P. 61. Prince *James Sobieski* died in *December* 1737.

P. 136. On the 28th of *June* 1737, the Great Duke of *Tuscany* died in the 67th Year of his Age, and was succeeded by *Francis* Duke of *Lorrain* (who married the Emperor's Daughter) for whom possession was immediately taken of the Duchy by the *German* Forces.

Ferdinand,

Ferdinand, Duke of *Courland*, who is mentioned in the same Page, died in 1737; and the Nobility assembling at *Mittau* elected Count *Biron*, a Native, to succeed him.

P. 150. The Affairs of *Corsica* are very much alter'd since the first Edition of these Volumes. Baron *Theodore* having left the Island, and promis'd to return soon with Succours, went to *Amsterdam*, where he was confin'd for Debt; but being soon discharg'd by the Interest of some foreign Power, he proceeded to *Paris*, and thence to *Marseilles*, in order, as he gave out, to put himself again at the Head of the *Corsicans*: But during this the *French* having undertaken to be Mediators betwixt the *Corsicans* and *Genoese*, have, with the Approbation of both, sent a General thither with some Troops, and the *Corsicans* have agreed to send over a dozen of their chief Men to the Court of *France* as Hostages for their good Behaviour; but since this, *Theodore* has set his Foot again upon that Island.

P. 257. The Duke of *Liria*, Son and Successor to the late Marshal Duke of *Berwic*, died at *Naples* in *May* 1738.

P. 260. The Marshal *d'Estrees* died the 5th of *December* 1737.

P. 309. The Marshal *de Wrangel*, Governour of *Brussels*, died in *August* 1737, in the 87th Year of his Age.

P. 332. The Succession to the Duchies of *Juliers* and *Berg*, is an Affair which has been very much canvass'd for several Months past, between the Elector Palatine and the Courts of *Prussia* and *Saxony*. The maritime Powers of *Great Britain* and *Holland* have proposed an Accommodation, with regard to the Succession, into which the Elector Palatine is willing to enter; but the Courts of *France*, *Prussia* and *Saxony* don't concur

cur with it; and *France* has guarantee'd the actual Poffeffion of thofe Duchies to the Prince of *Sultzbach*.

P. 447. On the 20th of *November* 1737, *Wilhelmina-Carolina* Queen of *Great Britain* died of a Mortification in her Bowels; and on the 17th of *December* following fhe was privately interr'd in *Weftminfter-Abbey*.

BOOKS lately published,

1. THE Third and Fourth Volumes of the MEMOIRS of CHARLES-LEWIS BARON DE POLLNITZ; being the Observations he made in his late Travels from Prussia thro' Poland, Germany, Italy, France, Spain, Flanders, Holland, England, &c. discovering not only the present State of the chief Cities and Towns, but the Characters of the principal Persons at the several Courts.

2. CYCLOPÆDIA; or, An Universal Dictionary of ARTS and SCIENCES: Containing, An Explication of the Terms, and an Account of the Things signified thereby in the several Arts, both Liberal and Mechanical, and the several Sciences, Human and Divine: The Figures, Kinds, Properties, Productions, Preparations and Uses of Things, Natural and Artificial: The Rise, Progress, and State of Things, Ecclesiastical, Civil, Military and Commercial; with the several Systems, Sects, Opinions, &c. among Philosophers, Divines, Mathematicians, Physicians, Antiquaries, Critics, &c. The Whole intended as a Course of Antient and Modern Learning, extracted from the best Authors, Dictionaries, Journals, Memoirs, Transactions, Ephemerides, &c. in several Languages. By E. CHAMBERS, F.R.S. The Second Edition, corrected and amended, with some ADDITIONS. In Two Volumes, Folio.

3. BAYLE's GREAT HISTORICAL and CRITICAL DICTIONARY, the second Edition, carefully collated with the several Editions of the Original; in which many Passages are restored, and the Whole greatly augmented; particularly with a Translation of the Quotations from eminent Writers in various Languages: To which is prefixed, the Life of the Author, revised, corrected and enlarged, by Mr. Des Maizeaux, Fellow of the Royal Society; compleat in 5 Volumes, Folio.

4. A Tour thro' the whole Island of Great Britain, divided into Circuits or Journies, giving a particular and entertaining Account of whatever is Curious, and worth Observation, viz. 1. A Description of the principal Cities and Towns, their Situation, Government and Commerce. 2. The Customs, Manners, Exercises, Diversions, and Employment of the People. 3. The Produce and Improvement of the Lands, the Trade and Manufactury. 4. The Sea-Ports and Fortifications, the Course of Rivers, and the Inland Navigation. 5. The public Edifices, Seats and Palaces of the Nobility, and Gentry. Interspersed with useful Observations. Particularly fitted for the Perusal of such as desire to travel over the Island. The second Edition, with very great Additions, Improvements and Corrections, which bring it down to the beginning of the Year 1738, in three neat Pocket Volumes. *Price, Nine Shillings.*

All printed for D. BROWNE, without *Temple-Bar.*

MEMOIRS

OF THE

Baron de POLLNITZ.

In SEVERAL LETTERS to Mr. *L. C. D. S.*

LETTER I.

SIR, *Berlin, June* 6. 1729.

FROM *Breslaw* to *Berlin* 'tis 40 *German* Miles of very even Country, well peopled and cultivated. There are I know not how many little Towns in the Road, not worth mentioning.

The first Place of any Importance is CROSSEN. This City is the Capital of the Dutchy from whence it has its Name, which formerly made a Part of *Silesia*, but is now annex'd to the Electorate of *Brandenburgh*. There's a Bridge at *Crossen*, by which we pass the River *Oder*, defended by Fortifications. The Town is situate in a pleasant fruitful Country. The Houses, which are all of Brick, are uniform, and the Streets as strait as a Line. The chief of them

VOL. I. B terminate

terminate in a great Square in the middle of the Town, where there is a Statue of the King of *Prussia*. The River *Oder* is of great advantage to the Commerce of *Crossen*, which carries on a considerable Trade in Linnen-Cloth and Earthen Ware.

Going out of *Crossen*, we pass this River by a Bridge, as we do a second time over to FRANCFORT, a considerable City of the Marquisate of *Brandenbourg*, famous for its Fairs, and its University. This City has stood the Shock of various Revolutions. It was put under the Ban of the Empire by the Emperor *Charles* IV. for having disobey'd his Orders; and the Inhabitants to make him easy were forc'd to pay him down 12000 Marks of Silver, which at that time was an immense Sum. In 1631 the *Swedes* besieg'd and took it by Storm, when they put all the Inhabitants to the Sword in reprisal for the Massacre of 2000 *Swedes*, whom the Emperor's General Count *Tilly* had inhumanly put to death in the City of *Brandenbourg*. By the Peace of *Munster*, or *Westphalia*, which establish'd the Tranquility of the Empire, *Francfort* was restor'd to the Elector of *Brandenbourg* its lawful Sovereign.

Here is a University founded by *Joachim* I. (Margrave of *Brandenbourg*) in 1506, which is very much frequented by the *Silesians*, and by the *Hungarian* Protestants.

There are two Fairs a Year at *Francfort*, which render it a trading City, and its Commerce consists in Linnen-Cloth, and Fells.

'Tis ten Miles from *Francfort* to *Berlin*, and a flat sandy Country. The Road leads thro' *Munchenbourg*, a little Town chiefly inhabited by the Descendants of *French* Men, who left their Country upon the Revocation of the Edict of *Nantes*.

The nearer one comes to the Capital of *Brandenbourg*, the more sandy is the Soil, yet the Country produces plenty of Corn and Fruits.

BERLIN

BERLIN is the common Residence of the King of *Prussia*, and one of the largest, best built, and best govern'd Cities in all *Germany*. The Streets are spacious, strait, neat and well pav'd. The Situation is advantagious; for tho' it lies in a very sandy Soil, yet it is encompass'd with agreeable Gardens producing Fruits and excellent Pulse, and its Commerce is much improv'd by the River *Spree*, which passes thro' the City, and has a Communication with the *Havel*, the *Oder*, and the *Elbe*.

The *French*, who for the sake of Religion became Refugees, have contributed in an extraordinary manner to the Establishment and Aggrandisement of *Berlin*, by the establishing of all sorts of Manufactures, and the introducing of Arts into it; and it may be said of them, that they have omitted nothing to testify their Gratitude to the Elector *Frederic-William* and his Posterity, for the generous Reception which he gave them in his Dominions.

Berlin is divided into five Wards exclusive of the Suburbs, which are very extensive. I will run thro' these Wards in the Order of their Situation: But before I do this, I propose to shew you what is most remarkable in the Suburbs; where the Houses are generally of Timber, but so well plaister'd that they seem to be of Stone; and the Streets are broad, lightsome and strait.

In the Suburb of *Spandau* the Queen has a delightful House and Gardens. The House is called *Monbijou*; a very proper Name for it, because 'tis really a Jewel. 'Tis a Pavilion, the Apartments of which are laid out with Art, and furnish'd with great Judgment and Elegance. The Gardens are charming, and lie finely open to the River. This House was built by the Countess *de Wartemberg*, Wife to the Prime Minister of King *Frederic* I. As her Husband's Power and Favour were at that time so great, that he did whatever he pleas'd, all the

King's

King's Workmen and Architects us'd the utmost Diligence to serve her well. But she did not enjoy this fine House long; for it was scarce compleated when the King removed the Count from all his Employments, and banish'd him to *Francfort* on the *Maine*. However, he settled a Pension upon him and his Lady of 24000 Crowns, and the Countess by way of Acknowledgement gave the King this House, which of all the immense Treasure that she had amass'd, was the only Piece that she cou'd not carry with her. The King gave this House to the Princess Royal now Queen, who has added great Embellishments to it, and brought it to its present State of Perfection.

In the Suburbs of *Stralau* is the House and Gardens of *Belvedere*, belonging to the King. *Rollé* Superintendant of the Finances to the Elector *Frederic-William*, caus'd this Garden to be made, in which he laid out considerable Sums; and as this Minister was at other very great Expences, it so impair'd his Fortune, that he was oblig'd to throw up all and retir'd to *Holland*; and being very much in debt to the Elector, his Garden was forfeited to that Prince, who made a Present of it to M. *de Fuchs*, one of his Ministers. King *Frederic* I. purchas'd it of the latter, and after having embellished it, made a Present of it to the Queen his third Wife; but that Princess's ill state of Health obliging her to retire to *Mecklenbourg* her Native Country, *Belvedere* became neglected.

Near this Royal House is the magnificent Gardens of *Craut*, who from a Boy behind the Counter rais'd himself by his Industry to the Post of Paymaster General of the Army, and at length to that of Minister of State. He was to have been call'd to account in his last stage of Life, but he cunningly diverted that Storm by feigning himself Lunatic; and dying, he left an immense Estate, part of which

fell

BERLIN.

fell to the King by way of Restitution, and the rest to his Nephew, who makes a grand Figure at *Paris*.

I enter'd *Berlin* thro' that call'd the Gate *Royale*, which has had that Name ever since the Day that *Frederic* I. made his Entry there, after his Coronation at *Koningsberg* in *Prussia*. This Gate is defended by a Half-Moon, and two Bastions fac'd with Brick, and fronts that call'd the Street *Royale*; one of the longest and most frequented in all the City. There are very fine Houses in it, particularly that of M. *de Catsch*, a Minister of State, that of *Grumkau*, and the Post-House, which last Building was begun by order of the late King, for his Favourite the Connt *de Wartemberg*, who was hereditary Post-Master.

Thro' the Street *Royale* there run fine, spacious and beautiful Streets. The first is call'd *la Rue du Cloitre*, in which we see the Royal Manufactory. *Frederic* I. who bought it of the Heirs of the Marshal *de Flemming*, established an Academy of Nobles there; so that, on the Payment of three hundred Crowns, they had Lodging, Provision, and Instruction in every thing that it's natural a Man of Quality shou'd know. This Establishment existed a few Years, but sunk at last meerly thro' the Neglect of Persons whose Business 'twas to take care of it. The present King has chang'd this Fabrick into a Work-house, and allowed Lodgings in it for several Woollen Manufacturers.

Adjoining to the Royal Manufactory, there are public Warehouses, which were established and built by the late King; and being destroyed by Fire, the present King caus'd them to be rebuilt. Opposite to the Warehouses stands the House of M. *de Creutz*, Minister of State; which has fine Apartments, and is very neatly furnish'd. Higher in the same Street there's the House of M. *Duvaine*, a *French* Man by Birth, and Lieutenant-General of his *Prussian* Majesty's Forces: And contiguous to his House, which makes a fine Appearance, is the *Calvinists* new Church, a Structure rais'd after the Model of *Grunberg*, an Architect who had before acquir'd a Reputation, which did not suffer by his Contrivance of this great Fabrick: The Front of it is magnificent, but the inside plain, as are all the Churches of the *Calvinists*, which you know don't admit of Images. The subterranean Places or Catacombs, for interring those that worship here, are worth seeing. Several Persons have been interr'd there of great Note, particularly *Casimir de Colbe*, Count *de Wartemberg*, Prime Minister, Great Chamberlain, Master of the Horse, Post-Master General, Protector of all the Academies in the Dominions of the King of *Prussia*, and Knight of the Order of the Black Eagle. Being banish'd in 1711, to *Francfort* upon the *Maine*, where he died the Year following, he order'd that his Corpse shou'd be carry'd to *Berlin*; and his Will was accordingly fulfill'd. He was so dear to King *Frederic* I. that he was very loth to part with him; but was, as it were, compell'd to it by a Cabal, who oppos'd his Ministerial Authority; tho' he was provok'd at the Insolence of *Wartemberg*'s Wife, and at his mean Submission to her. The King made an Offer to him afterwards, by the Count *Christophle de Dohna*, (who was then his Ambassador at *Francfort*, for the Election of the Emperor,) to come and resume his Employments, on condition that he wou'd not bring his Wife with him; but *Wartemberg* refus'd, saying, he was engag'd in honour not to forsake her. Perhaps he was very glad of this Excuse for not returning, because he had once experienc'd the Vicissitude of Fortune, and knew well that he had been too powerful a Man not to be hated. King *Frederic* I. who was desirous

sirous to see his Funeral pass by, cou'd not refrain Tears; which undoubtedly was the greatest Character that he cou'd give of his Minister.

Next to the Count *de Wartemberg*'s Tomb, is that of *Henrietta de Pollnitz*, Wife to *Francis* Count *de Dubamel*, the *Venetians* Generalissimo. Her Husband dying in the *Morea*, this Lady return'd to *Venice*, proposing to go and end her Days at *Berlin*, where she was born; but while she was performing her Quarantain she died, after desiring her Body to be carry'd to *Berlin*; which was accordingly done by two of her Nephews, and one of her Nieces, whom she made her Heirs. There is also the Tomb of the Count *de Denhoff*, Lieutenant-General of the King's Armies, Knight of his Order of the Black-Eagle, Minister of State, Governour of *Memel*, and Ambassador at the Treaty of *Utrecht*, where he acquired a high Reputation among the foreign Ministers. The Marshal *de Villars*, who had known him at *Vienna*, when he the Marshal resided there in the quality of Minister, to take care of the Affairs of *France*, said to me one day, speaking of the Count *de Denhoff*, that the King of *Prussia* cou'd not do enough to reward the Count's great Merit. *If he wou'd have been rul'd by me*, added he, *he wou'd have been in the Service of the King my Master*.

The second Street that crosses the Street *Royale*, is the *Jews* Street, which runs into the Square *Molcke-Marck*; where the Hotel *de Schwerin* makes a fine Appearance. Within a few Houses lower down, there's a Manufactory of Gold and Silver Lace, which one *Schindler* has established with good success: This House belong'd to the Wife of M. *de Wensen*, Marshal of the Court to King *Frederic* I. but she resign'd it as part of Payment of a Fine, to which her Husband had been condemn'd by the Count *de Wartemberg*, then prime Minister;

who confin'd M. *Wenfen* in *Cuftrin* Caftle, becaufe he had prefum'd to reprefent to the King that the Table of the prime Minifter, which was ferved by his Majefty's Cooks and Butlers, was more expenfive than his Majefty's own Table. *Wenfen* however, upon the Payment of this Fine, obtain'd his Liberty, and was banifh'd to his Lands in the Dutchy of *Zell*.

In the middle of *Molcke-Marck* is the Statue of *Frederic* I. Father to the prefent King, with a Crown on his Head, and a royal Mantle on his Shoulders. The Statue was caft by order of *Frederic* I. himfelf, who intended to have it plac'd in the Court of the Arfenal; but dying before it cou'd be brought about, the King his Son caus'd it to be fet up where it now ftands, which is indeed a much better Place for it.

The *Spandau* Street, which is the third that croffes the Street *Royale*, contains the Town-Houfe, and other fine Buildings: The Street *St. Efprit* is altogether as beautiful, as is the Kay, which fronts the Caftle or Palace of the King. Upon this Kay we fee the Houfe of the Baron *de Vernefobre*, whofe Anceftors being *French* Proteftant Merchants, fettled at *Koningfberg* in *Pruffia*. He was in *France* at the time of the *Miffiffippy* Plague, which, tho' fo fatal to others, prov'd fo fortunate to him, that he gain'd feveral Millions of Livres, with which he came and fet up at *Berlin*, where he has taken to building, having purchas'd the Eftate of *Hohenfibn* from Monfieur *de Borftel*, one of the beft Gentlemen of the Country, procur'd himfelf the Title of Counfellor of State, and cuts a Figure now among Perfons of Quality.

The Churches of St. *Mary*, St. *Nicholas*, and that belonging to the Garrifon, are as magnificent as any of the Proteftant Churches. St. *Mary*'s has a beautiful Spire. When *Frederic* I. made his royal Entry here, at his return from his Coronation, a Man afcended to the Globe of this Spire, and faluted

luted the new King by flourishing a pair of Colours. The Church of the Garrison was founded by the late King, but was very much damag'd some Years ago by the blowing up of a Magazine of Gun-Powder in the Neighbourhood, just as they were removing it to a safer Place. King *Frederic William* has caus'd it to be rebuilt with more Magnificence than before. The Organs are very fine, and the Galleries very well contriv'd.

That Ward of *Berlin* which I have now run through, is separated from that of *Coln* or *Cologne* by the River *Spree*, over which there are four Bridges, whereof there is one of Stone, call'd the *Pont-neuf*. *Frederic* I. in imitation of the *Pont-neuf* at *Paris*, famous for the Statue of *Henry* IV. caused the Equestrian Statue of his Father, the Elector *Frederic-William*, to be erected upon this Bridge, with very great Pomp and Splendor; for no Prince in *Germany* strove more than he did to copy *Lewis* XIV. in Magnificence and every thing else. When this Statue was dedicated, the Count *de Lottum*, who was then Grand Marshal of the Court, accompanied by most of the Courtiers on horseback, and by the City Companies, assisted at the Ceremony, which was performed with an *Apparatus*, till then unknown in *Germany* upon the like Occasions; but had been practised at *Paris*, when the Statue of *Lewis le Grand* was erected in that City.

This entire Monument was design'd by one *Jacobi*, who after several Years Labour and constant Application to it, has brought it to its present State. This skilful Operator has represented the Elector in a *Roman* Dress, and in an heroic Stature; that is to say, above the natural Size. The Statue is placed on a magnificent Pedestal of white Marble. At the four Corners of the Base, are placed as many Slaves in Brass, who seem as if they were chain'd to it.

When

When one has pass'd the Bridge, the King's Palace offers itself to view; a great and stately Fabric, which *Frederic* I. began in the Year 1699, and a worthy Monument of that Prince's Magnificence, who was of Opinion, that of all the Sums expended by Sovereigns, those which they lay out in Buildings are least liable to Censure. And indeed Magnificence is well bestowed, and even Profusion seems justifiable in Architecture, because grand Edifices are the principal Ornament of any State.

The Palace has been the Workmanship of several Architects; the Name of the first was *Schluter*, but he not giving Satisfaction was dismiss'd, and went into the Service of the Czar *Peter Alexiowitz*. Whatever he did is extremely incumber'd with Ornaments which have not a due Proportion. His Successor was *Eosander*, a *Swede*, who is a Lieutenant-General in the Service of the King of *Poland*: He was oblig'd in some measure to pursue what *Schluter* had begun; so that if he has not come off well every where, he has at least that for his Excuse. The third was *Bot*, a *Frenchman*, and now General Officer in *Poland*; who without dispute was a much better Artist than the others. Every thing that he has done is more simple, yet more grand, noble, and complete.

These three Architects having gone upon different Plans, you will easily imagine that the Fronts are not perfectly regular; yet for all this, had the Palace been finish'd according to the Models approv'd of by the late King, it wou'd have been inferior to no Edifice for Grandeur and Magnificence, except the *Louvre* of *Paris*. King *Frederic-William* does not think fit to carry on this Building, but leaves that Honour to his Son, the Prince Royal.

As to giving you all the Particulars of this vast Palace, you will be so good as to excuse me: Be sa-

satisfied if I only tell you, that it consists of four Stories: The Apartments are large, have fine Cielings, and are royally furnish'd. In no part of the World did I ever see such a prodigious quantity of Plate, Tables, Stands, Lustres, Chandeliers, Screens, Looking-Glass Frames, Couches, Arm-Chairs, all of Silver. The late King left Plate to the value of two Millions eight hundred thousand Crowns, not reckoning the Fashion. In that call'd the Knights Hall, there's a Beaufet which takes up one intire side of the Room, where there are Cisterns and Basons Silver gilt, of an extraordinary Size.

The Furniture of the grand Apartment is very rich; there's a fine Gallery adorn'd with Pictures, the Cieling of which was painted by one *Peine*, a *Frenchman*, who in divers Compartments has skilfully represented the principal Actions of King *Frederic* I. At the End of this Gallery there's a Saloon, which was formerly magnificent to the last degree, being wainscotted, if I may so call it, with Amber: But the late Czar coming no *Berlin* in his return from *Holland* and *France*, and not a little admiring this Furniture, which was the only thing of its kind, the King made him a Present of it: so that what had been amass'd with great Care and Cost by several Electors, fell in one Day into the hands of a Nation, which, no longer ago than the beginning of the present Century, was reckon'd Barbarian.

The Palace had fine Gardens belonging to it before they were destroy'd, and converted into a Place of Arms, and a Parade for the Guards.

Hard by the Palace are the King's Stables, a very grand Building, facing the great Street. The Architecture without is *Gothic*, but the inside is more magnificent; the Stables are broad and spacious, very

very lofty, and very lightsome: the Mangers are of Stone, and the Pillars which mark the Stands for the Horses, are of Iron, and adorn'd with the King's Cypher, gilt: Over the Mangers are several great Pictures of the finest Horses that ever came out of his Majesty's Studs. The Backside of the Stables projects towards the River *Spree*, to which they can lead the Horses by a Stair-Case without Steps, built in the form of a Horse-Shoe.

The Main Body of the House contains grand Lodgings for the Master of the Horse, and the Officers under him. Over the Stables are great Rooms where they keep a deal of fine Furniture, both for the Horse and Mule; magnificent Sleds, with convenient Harness, adorn'd with Bells of Silver, or Silver gilt; a great number of fine Arms; the rich Accoutrements of the Horse which serv'd *Frederic* I. on the Day of his public Entry; all the Ornaments of the Bridle, the Breast-Leather, and Crupper, as well as the Bits and Stirrups, being of Gold adorn'd with Brilliants.

Over the Riding-House is the great Theatre, where, in the late King's time, Interludes and Comedies us'd to be acted before the whole Court; but the Opera of *Roxana* and *Alexander* was the last that was acted on it. It was play'd in 1708, upon the Marriage of King *Frederic* I. with *Sophia* of *Mecklemberg*. In 1706, an Interlude was acted there, on account of the Arrival of the Princess Royal, now Queen; intitled, *Beauty triumphing over Heroes*; at which the Markgraves *Frederic-Albert* and *Christian-Lewis*, the late King's Brothers, danc'd, with all the young Courtiers.

As we go farther down the great Street, we come to the Fish-Market, where is the Hotel of the City of *Cologne*, and *Dorffling*'s Hotel occupied by the Count *de Finck*. This Family is oblig'd for its Rise to the Marshal *Dorffling*, who from an Apprentice

tice to a Taylor rais'd himself by his Valour and Merit to the highest Posts in the Army. The Story goes, that when he had serv'd his Apprenticeship at *Tangermunde*, having a mind to go to *Berlin*, he came to a part of the Country where he cou'd not proceed without crossing the *Elbe*, but not having wherewithal to pay his Passage, the Ferry-Men refus'd to carry him over; which so vex'd him, that he threw his Knapsack into the River in a Pet, curs'd the Trade of a Taylor, and went back to *Tangermunde*, where he lifted himself a Soldier. There being a War at that time all over *Germany*, it was no difficult matter for the young Warrior to find an Opportunity to shew his Courage; and he signaliz'd it in such a manner, that his Officers, who were all in love with him, strove to advance him, and therefore made him known to the Elector *Frederic-William*. This Prince who lov'd, rewarded, and was a good Judge of Valour, did not depend upon what Fame reported of him; but in order to see his Officers and Soldiers fight with his own Eyes, conducted them himself to the Enemy, and very soon took notice of *Dorffling*. He saw him at every part of the Field where there was Honour to be won: He saw he was a sensible industrious Fellow, that he hated Parties and Cabals, and that he had that *Germanic* Probity which was the distinguish'd Virtue of our Forefathers, but which we now content ourselves with admiring. The Elector observing such a Stock of Virtue in *Dorffling*, thought him deserving of his Favour, advanc'd him to the tip-top Employments, and made him very rich. Envy, which is as old as the World itself, and which like that, never stands still, made several of the Courtiers jealous of the Fortune or rather the Merit of *Dorffling*, and there were some who did not stick to say, that if the Marshal came to be ever so great a Nobleman, he wou'd always retain the Air of a Taylor. This

being

being carry'd to *Dorffling*, *True enough*, said he, *I was a Taylor, and I have cut out Cloth; but now*, said he, clapping his Hand to the Hilt of his Sword, *I have an Instrument in my Hand, with which I'll cut off the Ears of any Man that slanders me.*

This brave Fellow liv'd to a great Age, and left a Son who was one of the King of *Prussia*'s Lieutenant-Generals, and Colonel of a Regiment of Dragoons, but died without Issue. He had not quite the Vivacity of his Father, but he had his Honour and Integrity.

Going out of the Fish-market, as we turn to the right, one perceives the *Lutheran* Church of *St. Peter* *, which is a considerable Structure; and then we come into that call'd the *Fryars* Street, the Houses of which are all well built. In this Street stands the Palace where the *Aulic* Council meets, which in *France* they call the *Parlement*; 'tis here that all Civil Causes are try'd, and from thence there lies an Appeal to the King's Council.

Beyond the Palace there is a Square, on the Right side of which there's a Church with a Cupola which belongs to the *Calvinists*, and is look'd upon as the Cathedral of *Berlin*: For you know that the late King made two Bishops, one in *Prussia* and the other at *Berlin*, and they were the Prelates that crown'd him. They are since dead, and the present King lets their Sees lie vacant. In this Church is the Tomb of the Royal Family. There's a great Row of Buildings over against it, which consists of several uniform Houses belonging to Mer-

---

* This Church being destroy'd by Lightning in 1730, is magnificently rebuilt. The 21st of *August* 1734, the new Spire of it, which had been 4 Years erecting, and was carry'd up to the Height of about 190 Feet, fell at 9 o'clock at Night upon the Roof of the Church, whereby that and the neighbouring Houses suffer'd very great Damage. How it happen'd, no body yet knows; some say it was caus'd by Thunder, others by an Earthquake, and some will have it that it fell down of its own accord.

chants,

chants, and supported by stately Arches with Shops under them, where are sold all sorts of Goods. Turning round by that Piazza, brings one to a second Branch of the River, which divides the Ward of *Coln* from that of *Werder*. This River, which has three wooden Bridges over it, is confin'd in a Canal lin'd with Freestone, and form'd by two fine Kays.

The most considerable Edifices in the Ward of *Werder* are the Royal Custom-House, so commodiously situate that Boats can come up close to it: The *French* School, and their Church, which is serv'd by able Ministers; some of whom, as the late M. *Lenfant* (Author of the celebrated *History* of the *Council of Constance*, &c. and Chaplain to the King of *Prussia*) M. *de Beausobre* and M. *Jacquelot*, &c. have acquir'd a Reputation in the Republic of Letters. The Royal Hunting-House is a large magnificent Structure for lodging the great Huntsman and all his inferior Officers: There too is the great Dog-Kennel and the Magazines for all the Hunting Equipage. Near this place is the Hotel or Palace for Ambassadors, where are likewise entertain'd such Foreign Princes as are not of a Rank high enough to be accommodated in the King's Palace. This Hotel belong'd formerly to the Baron *de Danckelman*, Prime Minister to King *Frederic* when he was only Elector, and being built by the said Minister at a time when he was such a Favourite that he did almost what he pleas'd, he spar'd no Cost to render it a Mansion worthy of his high Station. I was assur'd by Persons of Credit then alive, that after it was built, the late King had a Desire to see it, upon which ocasion M. *de Danckelman* made a great Entertainment for him; and that while the Queen and the whole Court were dancing, the King retir'd into his Minister's Closet, to have a private Conference with him; and looking very earnestly on a certain Picture

ture there, M. *de Danckelman* told him, that Picture and all that he saw would soon be his Majesty's. The King not knowing what he meant, desir'd his Minister to explain himself; whereupon he made answer, 'That he shou'd very shortly incur his 'Displeasure; that his Fall wou'd be attended by 'the Forfeiture of all his Estate; that he should be 'arrested and committed to the *Spandau* Prison; 'and that there he should be confin'd ten Years, at 'the Expiration of which his Innocence wou'd 'be made to appear, his Estate wou'd be restor'd 'to him, and he shou'd be taken again into his 'Majesty's Favour.' The King, who was at that time very fond of his Minister, and did not think he cou'd ever do without him, ridicul'd what he had said as the Surmise of a Visionary, and was going to swear by the New Testament then upon a Table in the Room, that this sad Prophecy wou'd never come to pass. But the Minister held his Hand, and begg'd him not to take an Oath which it wou'd not be in his power to keep.

I tell you this Story just as I had it from a Lady of Quality to whom the King himself told it: But in short, let the Story be as it will, 'tis very certain that M. *de Danckelman* was disgrac'd, committed Prisoner to *Spandau*, and from thence remov'd to *Peitz*, without any Companion but his Wife, who generously desir'd to suffer Imprisonment with him. His Confinement lasted much longer than he had prophesy'd, and when at length he obtained his Release, he was not restor'd to his Employments, nor even to his Estate. 'Tis said indeed that the present King, who on his Accession to the Crown sent for M. *de Danckelman* to *Berlin*, offer'd him the Ministry; but that the Baron excus'd himself by reason of his great Age and his tedious Imprisonment, which had made him lose the Connection of Public Affairs. This Minister died

lately

lately, having lived to the Age of fourscore. His remarkable Disgrace, and fifteen Years Confinement in a Prison, had not sunk his Spirits, nor shock'd his Constancy of Mind; and one shall scarce meet with an Instance in History, either before or since, of more Merit and more Misfortune in one and the same Person. He was a passionate Admirer of Learned Men, and a Rewarder of Virtue. In a word, by the Disgrace of this Great Man, the State lost a faithful disinterested Minister, and Men of Learning lost a *Mecænas*, full of Zeal and solid Knowledge, who never fail'd to support by his own Authority, and to procure a Reward from his Master, for all Persons that apply'd to him with any Proposal that was useful and uncommon.

To go from the Ambassaors Hotel to the New Town, one must pass before the House belonging to the Governour of *Berlin**, who is at present the Marshal Count *de Wartensleben*; a Nobleman whose Virtues, long Services, and great Age, challenge Veneration. The House he lives in was built by order of the Elector *Frederic-William*, for the Reception of the Marshal *de Schomberg*, who resign'd the Battoon of the Marshal of *France* to *Lewis* XIV. after that Prince had revok'd the Edict of *Nantes*, and came with a numerous Retinue of Gentlemen, to desire Employment under the Elector. Accordingly that Prince gave him the Command of his Troops; but the Marshal quitted that Employment, to accompany the PRINCE of ORANGE to *England*, in his famous Expedition against his Father-in-Law; and he likewise attended that Prince to *Ireland*, where he acquir'd great Glory, but was kill'd in passing the River *Boyne*.

* This House is no longer the Governour's; for the King, who has caused great Additions to be made to it, has given it to the Prince Royal, and it goes by the Name of the *Prince Royal's Palace*. The Governour lives at present in the Street *Royale*, the King having purchas'd the fine House of *Catsch* there purposely for the Governour's Residence.

The *Governour's House* is separated by a great Square from the *Arsenal*, which is one of the compleatest Fabrics in *Europe*, and was built according to a Model design'd by *Bot*, whom I mention'd to you before; which skilful Architect has, upon this occasion, equalled any thing that was ever done by the famous *Bernin*.

The intire Structure consists of four main Bodies of Building, which form a spacious Quadrangle in the middle. The lower Story is of Rustic Architecture, with arch'd Windows. There are three great Porticoes at the Entrance to each Front. Over the principal Gate there's the Picture of the late King, in a great Medal of Brass. The four Cardinal Virtues of a Gigantic Size, are plac'd on Pedestals by the Portico, and seem to look towards the King's Effigies, which is supported by Fame and Victory. The *Corinthian* Order prevails throughout the first Story, and is very artfully executed. A Gallery or Balustrade runs round the whole Edifice, and is adorn'd with Trophies and Statues, particularly a very perfect one of *Mars*, sitting upon a Heap of Arms of different sorts; and the Decoration of all together is noble and majestic. Studs of Iron in form of Cannon are plac'd at proper Distances, and support Iron Chains, hung in Festoons, which hinder People from clambering up to the Windows.

The Inside of this *Arsenal* is as magnificent as the Outside. The lower Rooms are stor'd with a great number of Brass Cannon. The Walls and Pillars that support the Arch are garnish'd with Cuirasses and Helmets. In the upper Story there are several Rooms full of Arms, rang'd in such Order as can never be enough admir'd.

Behind the *Arsenal* there's the House of the General of the Ordnance, which also contains the Foundery, where Men are continually at work.

Besides this *Arsenal*, there are several others in *Berlin*, where they keep Field-Pieces, Iron Cannon, and

and all that belongs to the Train of Artillery. 'Twas the late Margrave *Philip**, Brother to *Frederic* I. who when he was Great Master of the Ordnance began to put the King's *Arsenals* into a good State. But King *Frederic-William* has finish'd what his said Uncle began, and has put the Artillery on such a footing, that 'tis a question if any *Arsenal* in *Europe* is on a better Regulation.

A Rampart and a Ditch separate the *Werder* from the *Dorothy-Stadt*, or new Town, which is for most part inhabited by *French* Families. It had the Name of *Dorothy-Stadt* in honour of the Electress *Dorothy* of *Holstein-Glucksburg*, the second Wife of *Frederic-William*, who with her own Hand planted the first Lime-Tree of the seven great Rows which divide this Ward into two Parts. The middlemost Row, which is the widest, is inclos'd with Ballustrades, and forms a pleasant Grass-Walk for Foot Passengers. The Walks on each side are pav'd, and serve as a Ring for the Coaches. Nothing is more beneficial and agreeable than taking the Air in this Place, where you may have any thing that can be desir'd in a City. At the end of one of these Walks is a Gate which opens to the Park, the Walks of which being above a League in length, form a fine Point of View.

On both sides the Lime-Tree Rows, are Houses, among which the Palace of Madame the Margravine, Dowager † to the Margrave *Philip*, Brother to the late King, is one of the best. The late Mar-

---

* This Prince died at *Schwedt*, Dec. 19. 1711. He left two Sons, one of whom was marry'd in 1734, to the Princess *Dorothea Sophia* the King of *Prussia*'s fourth Daughter, then about fifteen Years of age. So that his Majesty, who had six Daughters, married four of them within the space of four Years, and has now but two more to dispose of.

† Her Name is *Jean Charlotte*, and she is the youngest Sister of Prince *Leopold* of *Anhalt Dessau*, being the Daughter of the Prince *John-George* II. by *Henrietta Catherine*, Daughter of *Frederic-Henry* Prince of *Orange*.

grave purchas'd this Palace (which at that time was inconsiderable) of the Wife of *Weiller* Colonel of the Artillery, who had thrown up his Employments, Wife, Children and all, to go with a Lady of Quality, that was in love with him, to *Vienna*. This Gentlewoman pass'd for a modern *Sappho*, and every body talk'd of her Virtue and good Sense. But being a Slave to the Follies of Love, and asham'd to let them be seen at *Berlin*, where she was counted an Oracle, she resolv'd to quit the Place of her Birth, and engag'd her Lover to leave all and follow her.

The Margrave made considerable Augmentations to this House, and render'd it very commodious. The Furniture of the Palace also is rich, and worthy of the Princess who resides in it.

Opposite to the Margravine's Palace is a Building which was formerly call'd the King's Little Stables, but has been metamorphos'd into Caserns for the Gendarmery; they discover the Magnificence of *Frederic* I. who caused them to be built. The Apartments that run over the Stables are occupied by the Academy of Painters, and that of Arts and Sciences. Behind the Stables there's the Observatory, with a great number of Astronomical and Mathematical Instruments, of which there are many of a new Invention.

Frederic-Stadt, which is the fifth Ward of *Berlin*, communicates with the New Town and the *Werder*. This is one of the pleasantest Wards in the whole City, the Streets being spacious, strait, and planted with Lime-Trees*.

Perhaps

---

* Since the Original was publish'd, this Ward has been lengthen'd two thirds. There is one Street so long, that in this respect there are few that equal it: 'tis as strait as a Line; and terminates in an Oval, surrounded with very fine Houses. A new Ward is also erected at the End of that call'd the New Town; from whence it ranges behind *Frederic-Stadt*. Here most of the chief Nobility are building Hotels or Palaces, rather than Houses.

Perhaps I have dwelt too long upon the Metropolis of the Electorate of *Brandenburgh*; but I thought that as there had been no true Account yet given of this City, you wou'd not be sorry to have it from me.

The next day after my Arrival here, I had the Honour to see the King, who was then seeing his Soldiers mount guard. He is a Prince of a middling Stature, and in very good Plight of Body: His Air commands Respect; yet, when he pleases, no Prince in the World can be more gracious. I heard him speak to his Officers in such a kind manner as cou'd not but charm them; I admir'd his Genius for military Discipline, and perceiv'd that with the Glance of an Eye he cou'd discover the least Fault committed against that wonderful Exactness which is introduc'd in the Evolutions of his Troops. After the Guards had perform'd their Exercise, the King stay'd to see them file off. I never yet saw Troops march with more Order and State, so that it seem'd as if they were all mov'd by one Spring. All the Soldiers are young, of an even Stature, and the cleverest Fellows that Nature ever form'd: they are well cloth'd, and have such an Air of Neatness, that even the private Centinels might all pass for Officers. I remember you was prejudic'd against their Clothing; their Clothes you said were too strait, and too short. I was of your Opinion once, and think so still, when I happen to see one of their Officers and Soldiers singly among us, who wear Night-Gowns rather than Coats; but when I see a whole Body of *Prussians* together, I am of another Opinion, and think their Dress gives them a warlike Air which other Troops have not. You will tell me perhaps, that the Clothing of the *Prussians* is good in a Garrison, but that in the Field their Garments are

In a word, if the Number of the Inhabitants of *Berlin* was proportionable to that of the Houses, it would be the finest, and the most flourishing Town in all *Germany*.

not wide enough to cover the Soldiers in the Night. I answer, that the *Prussian* Soldiers are in no danger of not being cover'd, because when they are in the Field, every Captain is to carry as many Coverlids, as there are Comrades in his Company. But you'll say, this must be a very great Incumbrance, and take up a deal of Equipage. 'Tis true, it may require two Sumpter Horses in a Company, but a Soldier fares the better for it; because when he goes wet into the Camp, he can get his Clothes dry'd in the Night while he is under his Coverlid. After all, the Incumbrance is no greater at present, for those Troops, than it was at the time when all the *Prussian* Infantry had Cloaks, which the Soldiers wore, was the Weather ever so hot, folded over their Shoulders, and ty'd both before and behind by their Belt. If they had any hasty March to make, such as I saw they made in *Flanders* in 1708, when they went to attack the *French* near *Audenarde*, the *Prussians* left their Cloaks behind with a Guard, and when the Battle was join'd, the Captains were oblig'd to send for their Cloaks. In short, what makes me think the *Prussian* Clothing the most convenient for a Soldier, is, that most of the *German* Princes are now come into it, and like it well: The Troops of *Saxony*, and *Brunswic* in particular, are cloth'd like those of *Prussia*.

The *Prussian* Troops, which are new cloth'd every Year, have Breeches of Woollen Cloth for the Winter, and of Linnen for the Summer; and they are allow'd Shirts, Necks and Spatterdashes: Their Pay is good and regular; the Soldier is compell'd to do his Duty, but when he does it, enjoys more Liberty than in the Service of any other Nation: so that were I to carry a Musket, I fancy it wou'd be in the Service of *Prussia*, where such a strict Discipline is observ'd, that the Soldier is no Swearer, and is not allow'd to game, and where in a word he does not

abandon

abandon himself to Licentiousness. On Sundays and Saints Days they are requir'd to go twice a day to hear a Sermon: The Catholicks have the liberty of going to Mass. In short, good Manners are introduc'd and observ'd in those Troops to such a Nicety, that you would wonder at it.

All the Infantry is cloth'd in blue. It depends on the Colonel of every Regiment, to order what Waistcoats and Trimming he pleases for the Clothes. The Horse and Dragoons wear white, but the Houshold Troops blue, with Campaign Coats of Gold Lace. The Hussars Clothing is red, but the Garbs of the Officers both of Foot and Horse are plain, and only differ from the Apparel of the Soldiers in the fineness of the Cloth; tho' there are some Regiments whose Waistcoats are bedaub'd all over with Gold or Silver Lace.

The Colours, which are uniform in all the Regiments, are white, with the King's Device, representing an Eagle flying towards the Sun with this Motto, *Nec Soli cedit.* There's such a Uniformity preserv'd in all things throughout the Army, even in their Guns, Swords, Bayonets, &c. that in every Regiment they wear the very same, even to their Shoe-Buckles.

The same Regularity is observ'd in the Horse and Dragoons, which ride both upon black Horses; and indeed they are not permitted to have any others, the Officers themselves being not exempt from this Rule, when they are at the head of their Squadrons or Companies. The Housings and Equipage of the latter are of the same Pattern, and extremely rich. All the Horse wear Buff-Coats, and underneath Cuirasses. They perform their Exercise on Foot like the Infantry, and with the same Exactness. The Kettle-Drums and Trumpets of all the Horse are of Silver.

There is not a Captain in all the *Prussian* Army but has at least ten supernumerary Men; so that these included, the King's Forces amount to near 100000, all pick'd Men. You cou'd not but admire if you were to see how they behave; insomuch that whenever they take the Field, 'tis pity but Fortune shou'd favour them.

Not many Days after my Arrival here, the King being gone to visit his Kingdom, I had the Honour of waiting on the Queen. This Princess, whose Name is *Sophia-Dorothea*, is Sister to the present King of *Great Britain*, being the Daughter of *George* I. the late King, and of *Sophia-Dorothea* Princess of *Brunswic-Zell*. And she does every thing that is worthy of her August Extraction; for surely never did Daughter more resemble a Father; she has the same Benignity and Wisdom, the same Equity and Justice, and Sweetness of Temper. Like him she knows the Charms of a private Life, and Friendship, on a Throne: Like him she is ador'd by her Subjects and her Domestics, and is the chief Blessing and Darling of both. To extend Goodness and Affability farther, were impossible; there being no Foreigners but what are charm'd with the gracious Manner in which this Princess receives them. To a thousand Virtues worthy of Veneration, she has added the singular Talent of speaking the Language of several Countries which she never saw, with as much Delicacy as if they had been her Mother Tongues. The *French* Language especially, is so familiar to her, that one wou'd take her to be a Princess of the Royal Family of *France*; and the Grandeur and Majesty that accompany all her Actions, induce those even who don't know her, to be of Opinion that she was born to reign.

That which still more endears this Queen to her People, is the Care she takes of the Education of her Family; which consists of four Princes, and six Princesses. The eldest of the Sons is stil'd the

Prince

Prince Royal*. This young Prince is handsome, charms every one by his Kindness and Good-Nature; and loves Reading, Musick, the Arts, and Magnificence: His Sentiments, his Behaviour, and his Actions, make it probable, that if he comes to the Crown, his Reign will be one of those mild and peaceable Reigns, which procure Kings that Love of their People, wherein consists their true Glory. The Care of the Prince Royal's Education was committed first of all to Madam *de Camke*, one of the Queen's Ladies of Honour, and Governess of the Children of *Prussia*. But this Lady left the Charge of the latter to the Sub-Governess, Madam *de Rocoule*, and her Daughter Madamoiselle *de Montbail*. Madam *de Rocoule* had also the honour to be Sub-Governess to the King; so that she was no Novice in the forming of young Princes. As she talks nothing but *French*, she has taught it to the King's Children; who speak it with as much ease as they do the *German* Language. At seven Years of Age the Prince Royal was taken out of the Hands of the Women; and the Count *de Finck* of *Finckenstein*, Lieutenant-General of the King's Forces, a Knight of his Order, and Colonel of a Regiment of Horse, was appointed his Royal Highness's Governour; and the Baron *de Kalestein* was made Sub-Governour. The King's Choice of both these Gentlemen was universally applauded.

The eldest of the King's Children is *Frederica-Sophia-Wilhelmina*, the Princess Royal; who was born in 1709. I was at *Berlin* at the Ceremony of her Baptism, which was performed in the Chapel of the Castle, in presence of *Frederic* IV. King of Den-

---

* He married (in *June* 1733,) the Princess *Elizabeth Christina* of *Brunswic-Lunenburgh*, and *Bevern*, Daughter of *Ferdinand Albert* Duke of *Brunswic-Lunenburgh*, and *Bevern*, Field-Marshal General of the Armies of the Emperor and Empire; and Presumptive Heir to the Duke Regent of *Brunswic-Lunenburg Wolfembuttle*.

Denmark, Frederic-Augustus King of *Poland*, and *Frederic* I. King of *Prussia*. The Birth of this Princess, and the Circumstances of three Kings and a Queen attending at her Baptism, gave occasion to a great many Copies of Verses. All the Poets said that the Presence of these three Kings, was a Sign that she wou'd one day have Possession of three Crowns. They had then in view the Crowns of *Great Britain*, that were to devolve to the Family of *Hanover*; in which there was a young Prince *, who, it was then imagin'd, was to be in time the Husband of this Princess. Whether this Match will ever take place, and whether the Princess will be Queen, I can't say; but if she is not, Fortune will not do Justice to her Merit.

The Princess *Frederica-Louisa*, the King's second Daughter, is lately married to the Margrave of *Brandenburgh Anspach*. 'Tis said that his Majesty's third Daughter, the Princess *Philippina-Charlotte*, is promised to † *Charles*, hereditary Prince of *Brunswic Bevern*, Nephew to the Empress Regent.

The other Princes and Princesses, the King's Children ‖, are as yet too young to furnish any Particulars for their Character. In a word, put them all together, they form a very fine Family.

The Margravine, Dowager of the Margrave *Philip*,

---

* This was his Royal Highness, now Prince of *Wales*. All *Europe*, in short, thought, as did the Poets of that Time; and every one in general mark'd out the Princess for this Prince. It was then too the Desire of both the Queens; and the Princess herself seem'd to have been brought up in that Notion. But when 'twas least of all expected, certain Reasons of State cancell'd all these Views; and the King of *Prussia* thought fit to marry his eldest Daughter in 1731, to the Hereditary Prince of *Brandenburg-Bareith*: as King *George* II. of *Great Britain*, in 1736, thought fit to marry his eldest Son to her Highness, *Augusta*, youngest Sister of the present Duke of *Saxe-Gotha*.

† The Marriage was actually celebrated between them, in *July* 1733.

‖ The fourth married in 1734, to the King's Cousin, the Margrave of *Brandenburgh-Schwedt*.

Philip, Brother to the late King, is the first in Rank at Court, next to the King's Children: She was born Princess of *Anhalt-Dessau*. Her Royal Highness was lately chose Abbess of *Herford*, a sovereign Abby in *Westphalia*, (in a Town belonging to the King of *Prussia*, as part of the Principality of *Ravensberg*;) whose Canonesses must be all Princesses, or Countesses of the Empire. This Princess, tho' she is past her Bloom, is still the Ornament of the Court; and no Person can be more civil than she is to Foreigners; so that 'tis as much a Pleasure as a Duty to pay one's Court to her. When the King is at *Berlin*, and the Queen has no Drawing-Room, the whole Court repairs to the Margravine's House, where her Royal Highness daily keeps an elegant Table; to which she admits the Quality of both Sexes. She is the Mother of two Princes and a Princess; the Sons are the Margraves *Frederic* and *Henry*, and the Daughter is married to the hereditary Prince of *Wirtemberg*. The young Margrave *Frederic* resides at *Schwedt* upon the *Oder*, where he has a very fine House; but does not come to Court but when he can't avoid it. The young Margrave *Henry* resides commonly at *Berlin*. Both these Princes are handsome, lusty, and well shap'd.

The Margrave *Albert*, the King's Uncle[*], lives in his Majesty's Palace, tho' he is eight Months of the Year at *Frederichsfelde*, a Pleasure-House about a League from *Berlin*. He is the second Son of the Elector *Frederic-William*, and *Dorothy* of *Holstein Glucks-*

---

[*] This Prince died in 1731. His eldest Son, the Margrave *Charles*, succeeded him in the Grand Mastership of the Order of St. *John*; and had his Regiment of Foot in the Service of *Prussia*. Prince *Frederic*, his Royal Highness's second Son, had his Regiment in the Service of the States General of the *United Provinces*; and the Count *de Truchsses-Walbourgh*, a Major-General, had his Regiment of Horse. He was sent to compliment *Lewis* XV. upon his Coronation; and afterwards on the same Commission to the Emperor at *Prague*. His Wit and Politeness were applauded at both those Courts.

Glucksburg: He is well shap'd, has a noble Air, and has been in his time a very good Dancer: He is fond of Grandeur and Pleasures. At the beginning of the last War he distinguished himself very much at the Siege of *Keyserswaert*, and other Places, where he commanded the Troops of the King his Brother. His Royal Highness is Governor of *Pomerania*, Knight of the Black Eagle, and Colonel of a Regiment of Foot, and of another of Horse, in the King's Service: He has also a Regiment of Foot in the Service of the *United Provinces*; and is Grand Master of the six Commanderies of the Order of St. *John* of *Jerusalem*, who, at the Alteration of Religion in the time of *Luther*, withdrew from the Grand Master of *Malta*, and assum'd to themselves a Right of chusing a Grand Master under the Protection of the Elector of *Brandenburgh*. The Margrave marry'd a Princess of *Courland*, Heiress to the Freeholds of her Uncle Duke *Ferdinand*, the last of her Family. This Princess, tho' not reckon'd a Beauty of the first Rate, has a great Share of Charms and Good-nature, Modesty and Politeness. Their Royal Highnesses are perfectly civil to those who have Access to them; which is the reason, that notwithstanding the little Concern they have in Business, they have always a numerous Court. They have three Princes, and two Princesses. The eldest of the Sons is *Charles*, a Prince whose Person and Character are very amiable. The eldest of the Daughters is married to the Duke of *Saxe-Eysenach*.

The last Prince of the Royal Family, is the Margrave *Christian-Lewis*, third Son of the Elector *Frederic-William* by the second Marriage. This Prince is Governour of the City and County of *Halberstadt*; he has a Regiment of Foot, is Knight of the Order of the Black Eagle, and Commander of that of St. *John*. He studied at *Leyden*; after which, he serv'd serv'd with distinction in *Italy*. He now lives retir'd from Court at *Malchau*, a House about a Mile from *Berlin*, which the late King bought of the Heirs of M. *de Fuchs*, his Minister of State. There the Margrave, who has a Relish for the Pleasures of private Life, passes his Time in Hunting, Reading, and every innocent Pleasure that an agreeable Country is capable of furnishing. This Prince has been a handsome well-made Man; he has a grand Air, and there's something heroic in his Physiognomy: In the very Flower of his Youth he was a constant Admirer of Virtue, and might ever be quoted for an Example of Sobriety. He is so exceeding fat, that it's fear'd he won't live to be a very old Man*.

All the Princes of the Royal Family wear the *Prussian* Order, *viz.* that of the Black Eagle; and receive it as soon as they are born. 'Tis an Orange Ribband, to which is appendant a Cross enamel'd with blue, resembling the Cross of *Malta*. A Star of Silver is embroider'd on the Coat; and in the middle of it is an Orange Escutcheon, over which is a black Eagle crown'd with Wings display'd, holding in one of its Talons a Crown of Laurel, and in the other a Thunder-bolt, with the Motto, SUUM CUIQUE, in Letters of Gold. This Order was instituted by *Frederic* I. the sixth of *January* 1701, O. S. on account of his Coronation at *Koningsberg*. He call'd it the Order of the Black Eagle, because a Black Eagle forms the Arms of *Prussia*; and he chose an Orange Ribband, in memory of the Electress his Mother, who was a Princess of *Orange*; in Right of whom he pretends to be next Heir to *William* III. King of *England*, and Prince of *Orange*.

The

---

* He died suddenly in *August* 1734, at *Malchau*, aged 57, being born the 4th of *May* 1677, O. S. He was not married.

The Princes of the Royal Family are not exempt from passing thro' the Degrees of military Service; and 'tis not here as in other places, where they have Regiments and Governments as soon as they are born. The King will have them to know how to obey, before they come to command; and 'tis an Encouragement to the Officers to find themselves so far honour'd, as to be on a Par in the Service, with those who are born to be their Sovereigns. The Prince Royal has a Regiment of Horse *. M. *de Lopel* †, a Major-General, commanded that Regiment formerly, but the King preferring him to the Government of *Cuſtrin*, this Regiment has for Colonel M. *de Wreech*, a Person of a good Family in the new Marquisate. His Father, who was one of the King's Lieutenant-Generals, had serv'd the late Elector *Frederic-William*, the late King, and his present Majesty. M. *de Wreech*, whom I am speaking of, was, at his return from his Travels, appointed by the late King a Gentleman of his Bed-chamber: After that Prince's Death, his present Majesty enter'd him into his Service, and gave him a Troop of Horse. This Gentleman distinguished himself greatly in 1708, at the Battle of *Audenarde*; where he was *Aid de Camp* to the Marshal *de Natzmer*, then General of the Cavalry: He had a Horse kill'd under him, and was taken Prisoner; but the Enemy in their Flight not watching him very strictly, he found means to get off when the Night came and put an end to the Battle. He lay hid in a Ditch till next day, in danger every moment of being knock'd on the head by our own Men; but when the Day broke, he rejoin'd his General, who had receiv'd a
slight

---

* The King thought fit some time ago, to confer this Regiment of Horse upon his second Son, Prince *Augustus-William*, and to give the Prince Royal a Regiment of Foot.

† M. *de Lopel* died the beginning of 1733, in his Government of *Cuſtrin*.

flight Wound in the Head. M. *de Wreech* is one of the richest Subjects the King has; but he is worthy of his Fortune, and uses it like a Man of Quality. He is certainly a valuable Gentleman, has a noble Soul, and Sense and Knowledge enough to capacitate him to serve his King and Country both in Peace and War.

Berlin is not a City where you ought to look for the most lively Diversions; the King, to whose Will every body conforms, not being fond of them himself. Yet when once a Man is known there, he will find Amusement enough; for the People are affable and civil, make plentiful Entertainments, and have very good Wine.

When the King is absent, the Queen has a Drawing-Room every Night, from seven o'clock till ten; when her Majesty sups with the Princes and Princesses of her Family, and other Persons of Distinction of both Sexes. But when the King is at *Berlin*, the Queen keeps no Drawing-Room, unless some Foreign Prince happen to be there. Then there are Assemblies in the City alternatively, among Persons of the first Rank, at which they sometimes dance; and the King and Prince Royal frequently honour these Assemblies with their Presence. When there is no grand Assembly, there are particular Societies, where they sup, and play at small Game.

The Ministers of most consequence at this Court are Messieurs *d'Ilgen*, *Grumkau*, and *Knipbausen**; these are they who treat of Foreign Affairs, and thro' whose hands pass the Secrets of State: but the King's Prime Minister is the King himself, who is inform'd of every thing, and is desirous to know every thing. He gives great Application to Business, but does it with extraordinary Ease; and nothing

---

* The first and the last have been dead some Years, and their Places supply'd by Messieurs *Bork* and *Poddewitz*, who have a just Title to the intire Possession of the King's Confidence.

thing escapes his Penetration, nor his Memory, which is a very happy one. No body knows better than he where his Government is strong, and where 'tis weak; and no Sovereign in the World is of more easy Access, his Subjects being actually permitted to write to him, without any other Formality than superscribing the Letter, *To the King.* By writing underneath, *To be deliver'd into his Majesty's own Hands,* one may be sure that the King receives and reads it, and that the next Post he will answer it, either with his own Hand or by his Secretary: these Answers are short, but peremptory, and they prevent a tedious painful Attendance. The King, who is an Enemy to vain Pomp and Pageantry, always goes abroad without any Guards, with only a small Retinue, and sometimes too walks on foot; he makes his Greatness to consist in solid Power, in the having his Troops well disciplin'd, his Places kept up in good Order, his Arsenals well provided, and his Treasury full enough to enable him to oppose his Enemy in case he be attack'd. He never aims so much as to disturb his Neighbours, much less to rob them: I heard him say one day, that *he had no Intention of attacking any body, nor of beginning a War; but if he was attack'd, he would defend himself the best he could:* a Conduct which he has religiously observed ever since he has been plac'd upon the Throne, even towards *Charles* XII. King of *Sweden,* notwithstanding what is said of him by a certain Author, who from sorry Memoirs has wrote that Prince's Life. But I will not deviate from my Subject.

There's no Town in all the King of *Prussia*'s Dominions, except *Neufchâtel,* where he has not been; no Province which he does not know full well; not a noble Family but he can tell their Revenues; nor a Court of Justice but he is well acquainted with their chief Members. His Behaviour is plain; he
knows

knows no Gallantry, and does not eafily pardon it in his Officers. He is fo true to his Confort the Queen, that he wifhes all Men would follow his Example, and that every Hufband would live only with the Woman whom God has allotted him. His Diverfion is Hunting; and for this reafon, he refides commonly at *Potzdam* or *Wufterhaufen*, which are Pleafure-Houfes four Miles from *Berlin*. Yet he generally goes on *Saturdays* into his Capital, where he holds a Council on *Sunday*, and returns on *Monday*. In the Winter he makes a longer ftay at *Berlin:* but let him be either here or there, he is on the Parade every Day at ten o' clock, when his Soldiers mount the Guard; after which he gives Audience to his Minifters, and holds a Council, or goes abroad for the Air. At Noon the King appears in a great Saloon, where are all the Generals and Officers, the Foreign Minifters, and all the Court in general: There he converfes a few Moments, and then goes into another Room, where he dines with the Queen, the Princes and Princeffes of his Family, and any other Perfons whom he has caufed to be invited. His Table is commonly fpread for eighteen Guefts. After he has fate about an Hour and half at Table, he retires to his Clofet till fix at Night, when he appears again in the Room where he held his Levee: There his Majefty gives Orders to the Marfhal *Wartenfleben* Governor of *Berlin*, and to the Marfhal *Natzmer* Commandant of the Gendarmery. After this, he talks a-while with thofe that are prefent, and then paffes into a Room at fome diftance from his Apartment, to which the Queen repairs fometimes with one or two Ladies in company. There are ten or a dozen Officers whom the King honours with his Confidence, who play here at *Picquet*, *Ombre*, and *Backgammon*. Here they alfo fmoak, and to this Place the King fends for fuch as he has a mind to talk with about special Affairs. I have been there twice upon such an account. Here there is no manner of Restraint, but every body sits down, the King dispensing with all the Respect that is due to him, and at eleven o' clock he dismisses the Company and retires.

The King hunts when he is at *Potzdam* and *Wusterhausen*; but in other respects he leads the same Life there as he does at *Berlin*. At *Potzdam* he hunts the Stag, having for that end caused a great Forest to be paled in, where he has made noble Roads.

The Castle at *Potzdam*, which is very convenient, was built by the Elector *Frederic-William*, who commonly resided at it; and after having run his glorious Race, died here the 29th of *April*, 1688. King *Frederic* I. made considerable Embelishments to it, particularly the great Gate opening into the main Court of the Castle, which is an admirable Piece of Architecture that was design'd by M. *Bot*, my Hero for Buildings. But all that the late King did, does not come up to the Works that have been added to it of late Years. The Town of *Potzdam* has been augmented two Thirds; the Streets are as strait as a Line, with Trees planted, and Canals cut in them after the manner of *Holland*; the Houses are uniform and built with Bricks. Besides a great Hospital, which the King has founded here for his Soldiers Orphans, here is a considerable Fabric for Armourers, who make all those Arms for the Forces and Arsenals, which were formerly made at *Liege*.

This Town is the Garrison for the first Battalion of those *Tall Grenadiers*, so much talk'd of in *Europe*. I protest to you that they exceed the common Report, being the compleatest, the finest, and best-disciplin'd Body that can be imagin'd. The Men are of all Nations, there being scarce a Prince in *Europe* but takes a pleasure in sending Recruits to it. Some of these Grenadiers have had 1500 Crowns Lift-Money; and several receive two Florins *per diem*: Some of them are very rich; others there are who trade, and have good Houses at *Potzdam*. The tallest and the best Man among them all was one call'd *Jonas*, (lately dead) who work'd heretofore in the Mines of *Norway*. The famous *Huguetan*, whom *Frederic* IV. King of *Denmark* created Count *de Guldenstein*, took him from the Mines, and presented him to the King. He then stoop'd in the Shoulders, and hobbled in walking; but by tricking him up, they gave him that good Air which he wanted.

'Tis certain, there are no Troops in the World where the Peasant sooner shakes off the clownish Air, and more easily assumes the military one. This gigantic Regiment has requir'd great Pains, and considerable Sums to establish it; and I am assured it has cost the King more than six other Regiments. But 'tis all his Majesty takes delight in; and surely this Prince cannot but be commended for giving into a Pleasure so noble, and so innocent.

Having given you some Account of *Potzdam*, I must also mention *Charlottenbourg* another Royal House, a Mile from *Berlin*. This Castle stands on the *Spree*, so that one may go to it by Water: but the common Way is thro' the Park which is at the end of the great Walk from the new Town.

In the late King's time, whenever he was at *Charlottenbourg*, all the Road from *Berlin* to this Palace was lighted by Lanthorns erected on both sides.

Charlottenbourg was formerly call'd *Lutzenbourg*. It was a small Village belonging to M. *Doberginsky*, Steward of the Houshold to the Queen, (the King's Mother.) He had built a trifling House there, and that Queen taking the Air there one day, lik'd the Situation of the Place so well, that she bought it, and set about building there; but she died before all the

Works she had undertaken were finished. However, her Husband King *Frederic* I. caused them to be carried on, and made considerable Additions to them; and in order to perpetuate the Queen's Name, which was *Sophia-Charlotte*, he caused *Lutzenbourg* to be called *Charlottenbourg*. This Castle is one of the most considerable Structures in *Germany*; the Apartments are grand and splendid, and the Furniture very rich. There's a Cabinet adorn'd with the choicest Porcellane, ranged in such order as is surprising: In another Cabinet there are Lustres, a Tea-Table with Dishes, a Coffee-Pot, and the whole Equipage in short of solid Gold. The Chapel is one of the most superb that can be; every side being adorn'd with Gold and Painting. The Orangery is one of the most magnificent in *Europe*; not only with regard to the Beauty and Number of its Trees, but the Greatness of the Building in which they are kept all the Winter.

I could tell you of several more Houses which the late King had in the Neighbourhood of *Berlin*; but as they were suffer'd to run to ruin after he died, I think I had better entertain you with the Characters of the prime Nobility at this Court.

The Count *de Wartensleben* is the oldest Marshal. He is by Birth a *Westphalian*, and pass'd his early days in the Service of *France*. He was Commander in chief of the Troops of the Duke of *Saxe-Gotha*, when King *Frederic* I. called him to his Service. The Count *de Wartemberg*, who was at that time the Chief Minister, wanted a Person to be at the head of the Troops, who should be intirely devoted to himself: This was an Obedience he did not expect to find in the Counts *de Lottum*, *Dhona*, and *Denhoff*, nor in the other Generals whose long Services and Birth might make them aspire to this military Dignity. He believed the fittest Person to be his Tool would be a Foreigner that should be oblig'd oblig'd to him for his Fortune: Therefore he caus'd the Marshal's Batoon to be given to the Count *de Wartensleben*, who answer'd to a tittle the Intention of the Minister his Benefactor. 'Tis true, that he never seconded his Revenge, but neither did he oppose it. He did the Business of his Office, and meddled not with the Intrigues of the Court. It may be said of him, that he never deviated from the Path of Equity, and in Justice to him it must be own'd that he always did good, when it was in his power. Since the Death of the late King, his Authority and Interest are very much lessened. Besides, he is too far advanc'd in years to concern himself with almost any Business at all.

The General whose Power is most rever'd, is the Prince *Leopold* of *Anhalt-Dessau*. In consideration of his high Birth, and the Rank of Sovereign which he holds in the Empire, I ought to have nam'd him first; only the Count *de Wartensleben* is the oldest Marshal.

The Prince of *Anhalt* is Marshal, Governour of the City of *Magdebourg*, Colonel of a Regiment of Foot, and Knight of the Order of the Black Eagle. This Prince, who is a Person of a good Stature and noble Presence, happy Features and a lively Aspect, was born with all the Qualifications of a General and a Soldier, being vigilant, laborious, indefatigable, equally patient of Heat and Cold, Want and Abundance; Brave even to Intrepidity, and possibly never equalled in this respect, unless we except *Charles* XII. King of *Sweden*: Being a Man of unexampled Rigour in Military Discipline, he will be obey'd; but then he rewards his Soldiers when they do their Duty, and sometimes makes himself familiar with them: A warm and constant Friend, but an implacable Enemy when he thinks himself not well us'd; haughty to his Equals, civil and courteous to his Inferiors. In his Youth, he was a Wine-Bibber, and a Deboshee;

but it has been observ'd, that neither Wine nor Women can detain him, when he is in the pursuit of Glory. He is a religious Observer of his Promises, and never makes any but after mature Reflection. He is an Enemy to the Pomp and Constraint of the Lives of Great Men; an Œconomist, perhaps more than becomes his Dignity; and is an absolute Master in his Family and his Government, having poor, but dutiful Subjects, and well-regulated Finances.

The Care of the Prince of *Anhalt*'s Education was committed to M. *de Chalisac*, a Native of *Guienne*. This Gentleman found an ungovernable Temper in the young Prince which he had much ado to manage. The Prince happen'd very early to have a liking for Madamoiselle *de Fohsen*, (whom he afterwards marry'd) which being not at all pleasing to his Mother, (who was born Princess of *Orange*) she thought the best way to cure him of his Fondness for her, woud be to send him abroad; and therefore appointed M. *de Chalisac* to travel with him to *Italy*, and accordingly they made that Tour.

Chalisac, who was my particular Friend, and whose Memory I honour, told me that this Prince's extraordinary Vivacity and Intemperance, had often made his Heart ake; but that whenever he happen'd to run astray, he was sure to reclaim him by setting the Motives of Honour and Ambition in his View. To this purpose he related what happen'd when they were at *Venice*, viz. that the Prince came home one Morning very much in Liquor, after having spent the whole Night in a Debauch; and M. *de Chalisac* reproving him, perhaps a little too sharply, as the young Prince thought, he ran and snatch'd up a Pistol, and returning with it to his Governour, said, *You Dog, I must kill you.* M. *de Chalisac*, without appearing

pearing surpriz'd, looking sternly at the Prince, made him answer; *Shoot me if you think fit; but think how worthy a Figure you'll make in History, when it shall be recorded that a Prince of* Anhalt, *a Prince of a Family that has given Emperors to* Germany, *murder'd his Tutor.* These Words spoke with an Air of Authority made such an Impression on the young Prince, that he laid down his Pistol saying, *You are indeed in the right; I should have committed a villainous Action.*

The Prince on his Return from *Italy* to *Dessau* shew'd that Time and Absence had not that Effect upon him as they generally have upon Lovers. He returned as much in love with Madamoiselle *de Fobsen* as he was at setting out. He married her in 1698, and soon after, *viz.* in 1701, she was by the Emperor acknowledged a Princess of the Empire. He has had five Sons and two Daughters by her, the eldest of whom is dead.

But the Embraces of a tender Spouse cou'd not keep him at home; a Warrior he was born, and a Warrior he would be. The War being then kindled between the Emperor and the *French*, the Prince went to serve in the Army on the *Rhine*, and was present at the taking of *Keiserswaert*. Soon after, King *Frederic* I. gave him the Command of 6000 Men, whom he sent to the Emperor's Assistance in *Italy*, where he signaliz'd himself in every Campaign, but especially at the raising of the Siege of *Turin*. The Duke of *Savoy*, afterwards King of *Sardinia*, with whom the Prince had not a very good Understanding, doing me the Honour to talk to me about him one day, said, *The Prince of* Anhalt *has too much Fire; but when he is ripen'd by Age, he will be a great General. He was born with the Genius of a Captain, and he has contributed to save my Crown.*

When a Neutrality was agreed on for *Italy* between the Emperor, his Allies, and *France*, the Prince of *Anhalt* was recall'd, and the King gave him the Command of his Troops in *Flanders*, where he maintain'd the Reputation which he had acquir'd in *Italy*, and was continued in his Command till the Peace of *Utrecht*.

The Obstinacy of *Charles* XII. King of *Sweden* in refusing to hearken to a Treaty for the Sequestration of *Stetin*, having oblig'd the King of *Prussia* to make war upon him, the Prince of *Anhalt* serving under the King, who then commanded his Army in Person, had the Honour to defend the Isle of *Rugen*, against the King of *Sweden*, who came in the Night and attack'd it with Fury; but the *Swedes* were repulsed, after having lost a number of considerable Officers in the Action. Since the Treaty with *Sweden*, this Prince has had no occasion to signalize his Valour. He resides commonly at *Dessau*, or at *Magdebourg*; and does not come to Court but when Affairs call him. He has three Sons in the King's Service, of whom the two eldest have Regiments of their own, and the third commands his Father's.

The King, who has a great Affection for the Prince of *Anhalt*, makes no considerable Regulation with regard to his Troops, or in any thing relating to the War-Office, without his Advice. His Majesty has given him considerable Tracts of Land in *Prussia*, where 'tis said the Prince is building not only Villages, but entire Towns.

M. *d'Arnheim* is the third Marshal. This old Gentleman, who is past fourscore, learnt the Art of War under two Great Masters, the Elector *Frederic-William* of *Brandenbourg*, and *Montecuculi* the Rival of *Turenne*.

The Marshal *de Natzmer* is an old Soldier also, who has serv'd under several Commanders with very great Distinction;

Diftinction; particularly the Prince of *Waldeck*, General of the *Dutch* Forces, the Prince of *Orange* afterwards King of *England*, and laftly under the Duke of *Marlborough* and Prince *Eugene* of *Savoy*; who had all an Efteem for his Valour and Military Experience; this Marfhal having been in all the Battles which thofe Generals fought in the *Netherlands*, and having been always wounded or had a Horfe fhot under him.

After having mentioned the chief Commanders of the King's Forces to you, I thing it incumbent on me to give you an Account of thofe Perfons whofe Credit or Employments have the greateft Influence upon the Government; in which you will pleafe to excufe me, if I do not follow that Order I have hitherto obferv'd in my Narrative.

The Baron *d'Ilgen* Firft Minifter of State, was born of an obfcure Family in *Weftphalia*. After he had finifhed his Studies, he commenc'd Secretary to M. *de Meinders*, Minifter of State to the Elector *Frederic-William*, and to King *Frederic* I. His Difcretion and his Induftry foon procur'd him the Favour of his Mafter, who put him Governour over his Nephew the Baron *de Heidekam*. M. *d'Ilgen* travell'd with the young Baron to *Holland*, *England*, and *France*, in which Tour they fpent two Years. At his Return to *Berlin*, M. *de Meinders* enter'd him in Bufinefs, and the Elector *Frederic-William* dying not long after, he procur'd him the Office of Secretary to the new Elector. In this Employment he behav'd with fuch Circumfpection that he is ftill continued in it, notwithftanding the many Changes that have happen'd in the Miniftry. The Baron *de Fuchs* one of the moft able Minifters that ever *Germany* produc'd, being charm'd with his Genius, gave him fuch a Recommendation to the late King, that he preferr'd him to a Seat in the Council, where *Ilgen* foon found out the way to make himfelf neceffary. The

Count

Count *de Wartemberg*, whose Abilities were not so great but he stood in need of a Second, being then at the Head of the Council, consulted in all matters with M. *d'Ilgen*, who, after the Count *de Wartemberg* retired, had the Province of Foreign Affairs committed to him solely, and has kept it ever since.

M. *d'Ilgen* has both Gaiety and Solidity in his Temper, a lively, fruitful Imagination, and a most pleasing Aspect. He is extremely sober, and an excellent Œconomist, being as great an Enemy to Pleasure, as he is a Friend to Riches. He is humble sometimes, even to excess; revengeful, crafty; a Master of his Temper, his Countenance, his Tongue, and his Eyes, which he accommodates altogether to the Situation of his Affairs. As by his Parts he raised himself, so by his Parts he supports himself. He is the sole Repositary of his own Secrets, having no Confident nor Favourite to share them. He is so indefatigable, that he composes and writes all himself, keeping his Secretaries only to copy. In short, he works like a Day-labourer, and makes the Ministry, as it were, a Handicraft. He speaks well, but writes better; he affects *double Entendres* in his Answers, and artfully has recourse, when he needs it, to an ambiguous Expression. He has so little scruple, in point of Oaths, that he takes and breaks them with equal Indifference. He never made himself a Creature, but always removed and humbled those that ever gave him any Umbrage. That which heightens his Character, and proves his Genius, is, that he has supported himself a long time, without Kindred, Friends, or Creatures, and perhaps without being too much honoured by the Favour of his Master*.

M.

---

* Since the writing of this, he is dead, and succeeded in the Management of Foreign Affairs by M. *de Borck*, Lieutenant-General

M. *de Grumkau* Minister of State, Lieutenant-General of the King's Forces, Colonel of a Regiment of Foot, and Knight of the Orders of St. *Andrew* of *Muscovy*, and of the White-Eagle of *Poland*, is descended of an illustrious Family in *Pomerania*. His Father was Grand-Marshal of the Elector *Frederic-William*, and died in that Post, at the beginning of the late King's Reign. M. *de Grumkau* being left a Minor, was sent very young to *France*, to learn his Exercises, where he acquitted himself with Diligence, and the Approbation of his Superiors. At his return to *Berlin*, *Frederic* I. appointed him Gentleman of his Bed-chamber, and gave him a Company of Foot. Soon after which, he married Madamoiselle *de la Chevallerie*, who was Maid of Honour to the Queen *Sophia-Charlotte*. It was not long before he was advanced; and during the last War he served as a Brigadier in the Army in the *Netherlands*. At the same time he had the Care of the King's Affairs with my Lord Duke of *Marlborough*, and Prince *Eugene* of *Savoy*. His manner of Be-

neral of the King's Forces, Knight of the Black-Eagle and St. *John*, Governor of *Stetin*, and Colonel of a Regiment of Foot. This Gentleman is descended from a very good Family in *Pomerania*, and served with Distinction in the Army in *Flanders*. Since the Peace of *Utrecht*, he has been twice charged with the King's Affairs at the Emperor's Court, where he was highly esteemed, especially by Prince *Eugene* of *Savoy*. Those Foreign Ministers who have to do with him, and who knew M. *d'Ilgen*, observe a great Contrariety in the Characters of the two Ministers. The one was a Man of Intrigue, Craft, and Mystery, the other, of Candour, Sincerity, and a noble Frankness. M. *de Tublmeier*, Nephew to the late M. *d'Ilgen*, who is Secretary of State for Foreign Affairs, was, as it were, born to the Business; having been trusted from his Youth by his late Uncle. The Foreign Ministers speak well of him: he is very assiduous in his Office, and indeed suffers no Business to sleep in his hands.

The Person who has the Affairs Criminal in his Cognizance, is M. *de Vitban*, Minister of State, and Auditor-General of the Army. He succeeded M. *de Catsch*; is a Native of *Cologn*; and as he was at *Berlin* without Relations or Friends, his Advancement is only to be ascribed to his own Merit and Abilities.

Behaviour shew'd that he was fit to be employ'd in great Affairs: but the Count *Wartemberg*, the Favourite, and Prime-Minister, being jealous of his Genius, kept him as much as he could out of any Share in Authority, and chose rather to prefer him by War, than to employ him in the Ministry. The Favourites (Messieurs *de Camke*) who succeeded *Wartemberg*, perceiving M. *de Grumkau*'s superior Abilities, were not more favourable to him than the Count was. He was preferr'd to be a Major-General at one of the last Promotions that was made by the late King; and *Frederic-William*, on his Accession to the Throne, made him Lieutenant-General, and Minister of State.

M. *de Grumkau* is good-natur'd, civil, and affable. He has the Manners and Sentiments of a Man of Quality, as he really is; he is generous, liberal, loves Splendor and Pleasures, but is not so much addicted to them as to neglect the Affairs of the Ministry. He is laborious, has a clear and quick Apprehension; a pleasant, lively, and penetrating Fancy; and is no Enemy to Satyr, when it does not attack his Neighbour's Reputation. As he is of a beneficent Temper, he has Friends, and makes himself Creatures. Of all the Ministers, he speaks to the King with the greatest Freedom; and I believe one may safely venture to put him in the Rank of Favourites.

The Baron *de Knipbausen**, Minister of State, and Commander of the Order of St. *John*, is descended of an illustrious Family in *East-Friesland*. In the late King's time, his Father was President of the Chamber, which is properly, Superintendant of the Finances. No Minister has been employed in more Embassies. He was the King's Resident in *Spain*, with *Charles* III. the present Emperor; he was

---

* He fell into Disgrace, after this Account of him was written, and died at his Commandery.

was the same in *Denmark*, *Muscovy*, and *France*; and every where supported the Dignity of his Master, and the Honour of his Character. So many Embassies had very much disconcerted his Affairs; and talking to me one day at *Paris* about his Lady, who was the Daughter of M. *d'Ilgen*, 'I know, 'said he, that her Rank is not equal to mine, and 'that I may be reproach'd for having married her; 'but I can return the same Answer which they re-'port of the Count *de Lude* (Governor to *Gaston* 'of *France*, *Lewis* XIIIth's Brother) who, when 'he was ruin'd like me, married a Tradesman's 'Daughter; *Could I do better*, said he, *when I was* '*persecuted Day and Night by my Creditors, than to* '*take Refuge in a Shop, rather than be carried to an* '*Alms-House?*'

M. *de Kniphausen* has a wonderful natural Genius, and would have every Talent requisite for a Minister, if he was not quite so averse to Labour; but being as lazy as his Father-in-Law is laborious, Affairs suffer in his hands by delay. Not but that he knows how to dispatch them, if he will, for nobody is more lively nor more vigilant than he, when he sets his heart upon a thing; but he is naturally indolent, being fond of his Ease and good Cheer.

The Baron *de Gobren*, who is Director of the Chamber of Finances, and of the Post-Office, is a Man of a good Family in the Marquisate of *Brandenburg*. He has not been many years in the Ministry, but has the Reputation of an upright Man, and one not to be corrupted. He is very reserved, and a Person of few Words, which gives him an Air that those who are not conversant with him mistake for Haughtiness.

M. *de Creutz* has a happy Physiognomy, being a mixture of hard Features with mild ones, that carry an Air of Probity and Frankness, which of all external Appearances is undoubtedly the most
ad-

advantageous. He is polite, and magnificent; has an extraordinary Vivacity, an admirable Facility of expressing himself, and an easy, affable, and genteel Behaviour. He never promises but when he means to perform, and his Word may be safely depended on. I always found him very sincere, and I cannot help saying, I love him. *Frederic-William* called him to his Councils, he having been his Secretary when he was Prince-Royal. His Assiduity and Punctuality in performing the Duties of his Office, had procured him the King's Affection to such a degree that his Majesty continues to honour him with his Good-will, and gives heed to his Representations*.

M. *de Creutz* is one of the richest Subjects in the Country, having had a very great Estate by his Wife: She has also brought him a Daughter, an only Child, who is said to have a great deal of Wit; and being a rich Heiress into the bargain, she will not fail of Suitors.

M. *de Vierec* is a Man of Quality, and a Native of *Mecklemburg*; his Father was Counsellor of State to the late King, and his Envoy-Extraordinary in *Denmark*. The Son, of whom I am now writing, quitted the Service of Duke *Anthony-Ulric* of *Brunswic-Wolfembuttle*, to be a Gentleman of the late King's Bed-chamber. When he came to Court, he had no Relations there, but he was so happy as to raise himself Friends; for his modest Air, and his polite and submissive Deportment, gain'd him the Good-will of the Favourites; and as he lov'd Play, he soon made himself acquainted with the Court-

---

* M. *de Creutz* died the beginning of An. 1733. leaving only one Daughter, who is married to M. *de Hacke*, a Gentleman of a good Family, and his Majesty's Aid-de-Camp and Favourite. This Marriage was solemnized with a great deal of Pomp, and honoured with the Presence of their Majesties, the whole Royal Family, and the Duke of *Lorrain*.

Court-Ladies, who always gave him their good Word.

In 1711, when the Count *de Dohna* went as the King's Ambassador to *Francfort*, for the Election of an Emperor, he desir'd of the King that M. *de Vierec*, who was reckon'd the most sober young Man at Court, might be Marshal of the Embassy, which was perform'd at the King's Expence. M. *de Vierec* acquitted himself so well in that Employment, that he had the same Post at the Congress of *Utrecht*. He had afterwards, for a while, the Care of the King's Affairs at the Court of *France*, when the Duke of *Orleans* was Regent; and at his Return from thence, he was employed in the Regency of *Cleves*; from whence he was called home to better Preferment, by means of *Gerstorf*, whose Daughter he had married. For this General's only Son being killed in *Sicily*, his Majesty, in order to comfort the Father, whom he lov'd, and who he saw took it very much to heart, declared M. *de Vierec* his Son-in-Law, Minister of State. M. *de Gerstorf*'s Daughter dying afterwards, M. *de Vierec* thereby came possessed of a very great Estate, and married again to the Daughter of the Count *de Finck*, who was formerly the Prince-Royal's Governor.

M. *de Vierec* is perfectly polite, and altogether as modest now as he was before he was a Minister; but he is close and reserv'd, mysterious more than needs must, and jealous. His Circumspection, which extends to the minutest things, gave him the Air of a Minister, before he had a thought, perhaps, of ever being one. What with his Kindred, his Estate, and his Preferment, he is become powerful at Court.

These, Sir, are the Persons of the greatest Consequence at the Court of *Prussia*, with whom I had a particular Acquaintance. I am not so vain as to think I have painted them in their true Colours;

but

but such as they appear'd to be in my eyes, I have represented them to you. Men are not always the same; nor do they appear in the same light to all that see them; every Man having his own way of thinking, and few judging solidly.

I have now told you all the Particulars that I know of this Court. What remains for me is to mention some things to you, which are worth your seeing, if ever you live to come hither.

Such are the King's Cabinets of Medals and Antiquities; that of Natural Curiosities, in which are a great many things not to be seen elsewhere; the Chymical Laboratory, with its Furnaces and Instruments of a new Invention; the magnificent Theatre, which the King caused to be built for Anatomical Demonstrations, with all the Curiosities and Instruments which are there kept; the Royal Library, one of the most valuable and compleat in all *Germany*, where, besides scarce Books and Manuscripts, is a very curious *Chinese* Printing-Press.

All these things would be worth particularizing; but to do this, a Man must have a larger Acquaintance here than I pretend to: Besides, my Relation is already spun to such a length that I believe 'tis time to conclude it.

I will, however, just acquaint you of a Foundation by the present King, in favour of the young Gentlemen of his Dominions, which are the Academies of Cadets, in *Berlin*, *Magdebourg*, and other Towns. where they are taught the Rudiments of War; so that 'tis a Nursery from whence the King makes a Draught of good Officers. His Majesty has moreover ordered his Generals of Foot to take each a young Gentleman, whose Fortune does not happen to be equal to his Birth, to keep them as Pages, and to make them learn their Exercises, and every thing that an Officer ought to know.

know. An excellent Institution this, and a fine Resource for the poor Nobility!

I am preparing to set out forthwith for *Hamburgh*, *Hanover*, and the Court of *Brunswic*; and after I have made that Tour, you shall have a second Letter from me. Mean-time, I am, *&c.*

LETTER II.

SIR,   *Hamburgh, June* 20. 1729.

NOthing gives me greater pleasure, than the Approbation with which you are pleased to honour the Account I sent you of the Court of *Prussia*; which I esteem as an infinite Reward for the little trouble it cost me. You must not imagine that I can ever be weary of writing to you; I can never do any thing more agreeable to myself, than to contribute to your Amusement; and shall think myself exceeding happy, if I can succeed.

I set out from *Berlin* upon the 10th of *June*, and in less than four Hours came to ORANJEBOURG, a royal Seat, which King *Frederic* I. caused to be built, and to which he gave the Name of *Oranjebourg*, to perpetuate the Memory of his Mother, who was born Princess of *Orange*. This Prince, great in every Action, spar'd no Cost to render this House worthy of his magnificent Taste. The Situation of this Place is very charming, in the midst of fine large Meadows, with Canals cut in them after the manner of *Holland*. The Apartments of the Palace

lace are grand, tho' the rich Furniture it had formerly has been removed to *Berlin*. The present King not taking a fancy to it, all runs to ruin; the Gardens, which were the finest in *Germany*, are not kept in order; the great Vessels of Porcellane; which were not to be match'd in *Europe*, the late King having procur'd the choicest Rarities of that Ware, that were in the Magazines of *Holland*; all these fine things, I say, are pass'd into the hands of the King of *Poland*, at *Dresden*. The Gallery and the Salon of *Oranjebourg*, which were furnish'd with them, and which were reckoned among the Beauties of *Germany*, are of no account now but for the Richness of their Cielings.

From *Oranjebourg*, I went and lay at FERBELLIN, a Town which is only remarkable for a Victory gain'd here by the Elector *Frederic-William* over the *Swedes*. The latter enter'd his Dominions, while he was engag'd with his Army in defence of the Empire then attack'd by the *French* on the *Upper-Rhine*. The Elector being inform'd of the Invasion of his own Country by the *Swedes*, came away from the *Rhine* with his Troops, and by one of the bravest Marches that ever any General made, deliver'd it from the Enemy. He surprized them in *Ratenau*, a Town in the Marquisate of *Brandenbourg*, the Garrison of which he made Prisoners; and then continuing his March, he came up with the *Swedes* near *Ferbellin*, at a time when the latter thought him still upon the *Rhine*, and gain'd a compleat Victory. A venerable old Gentleman, who was very near the Elector's Person at this Battle, told me, that before the Engagement began, the Prince being at the head of his Army, took out his Pistols, fir'd them in the Air, and lifting up his Eyes to Heaven, said, *'Tis to thy Glory,* GREAT GOD, *that I discharge my Arms; defend my Cause, thou knowest it to be just; punish my Enemies.*

nemies. Then drawing his Sword, and turning about to his Soldiers, *My Comrades,* said he, *I desire no other Defence, nor no other Weapons, but the Protection of God, your Courage, and my Sword. Follow me therefore, my Friends, do as I do, and be assur'd of Victory.*

In this Battle, *Forbenius,* the Elector's Gentleman of the Horse, perceiving that a white Steed which his Master rode, made his Person a very plain Mark for his Enemy, so that they had singled him out to fire at, desir'd the Prince to change Horses with him. The Elector, who had a great Soul, above all Fear, refus'd at first to do so, but upon the repeated Instances of *Forbenius,* he consented to it; and the Moment that the Gentleman mounted the Horse which the Elector quitted, a Cannon-Shot kill'd him dead upon the Place, so quick, that he expir'd without the Comfort of knowing that he had thereby preserved the Life of his Master.

HAMBURGH, a Hanse-Town in the Circle of Lower *Saxony,* is, without dispute, one of the richest and most considerable Towns in all the Empire of *Germany.* It depends solely upon its Magistrates, who are chose by the Burgers themselves. Its Liberty has been often contested by the Kings of *Denmark,* who as Dukes of *Holstein,* pretend that *Hamburgh* is built upon their Territory, and that therefore they ought to be the Sovereigns of it. The Electors of *Brandenbourg,* and the Princes of the House of *Brunswic,* always opposed the Incroachments of the *Danes*; nor will they suffer any Power whatsoever to oppress the City of *Hamburgh,* because, if it were possible, they would be glad to annex it to their own Domains. The City being exposed to these Attacks, has taken all the Measures possible to be in a condition to defend its Liberty. 'Tis very well fortified, maintains a good

Garrison, and has an Arsenal provided with all Necessaries.

The Commerce of *Hamburgh* is considerable, tho' 'tis very much lessen'd since *Frederic* IV. King of *Denmark*, prohibited the Importation of Merchandize from *Hamburgh* to his Dominions *.

The manner of living in this City is different from that of all the Hanse Towns. Here is a tolerable Opera all the Year round †; charming Walks, choice Company, much Visiting and hearty Cheer. There are several good Houses of the Nobility, where Foreigners are well receiv'd. The Merchants are affable and civil; most of them in their youth travel to the most remarkable Countries of *Europe*, where they then pass for Gentlemen of *Holstein*. As they are rich, they can easily afford to make a good Appearance where-ever they come. There they learn that polite Air, and that Behaviour which one would wish to see in all Gentlemen of good Families. The only thing for which I find fault with them, is, that they treat their Wives too much like the *Levant* People, where the Women are only suffer'd to go to the Mosques; so here, the Women scarce go any where but to Church, or if they at any time take the Air, 'tis in company with their

---

* This Resolution was taken by his Majesty in 1725, on account of a Recoinage, which the *Hamburghers* thought necessary, partly in order to hinder their Silver from being carried out of their City to *Denmark*. This Dispute had considerable Consequences; so that the King of *Denmark* not being able to bring the *Hamburghers* to his Terms, push'd Matters so far as to fit out a couple of Frigats to cruise at the Mouth of the *Elbe*, which seized all Merchant Ships bound for that City. But in *March* 1736, the Affair was happily accommodated.

† It was set up, carried on, and directed by some of the Foreign Ministers residing at *Hamburgh*, who had each his particular Province: so that M. d'A——— presided at the Rehearsals, M. de W——— regulated the Dances, and M. S——— had the ordering of the Clothes, the Head-dresses, the Paint and the Patches of the Actresses.

their Husbands: and a Foreigner is so seldom admitted to their Assemblies, that when he is, those poor Women are as much astonish'd at the sight of him, as a Sultana would be to see a Capuchin enter the *Seraglio*.

There's a great many worthy People here. I have made an Acquaintance with M. *de Brocks*, one of the Magistrates, who has acquir'd a Reputation for his Skill in Poetry, by such Compositions as cannot but convince Foreigners, who understand the *High-Dutch*, that as good things may be said in that Language, as in any other*. This M. *de Brocks* is of an amiable Character, civil, and complaisant, and has acquir'd the Love and Esteem of all that know him.

Most of the *European* Princes have Residents here, for which reason here are several Chappels of the *Roman* Catholicks, who otherwise would be obliged to go to the Church at *Altena*, as the *Calvinists* are forc'd to do, the *Lutheran* being the Religion that is uppermost at *Hamburgh*; but the *Jews* have their Synagogues here. What an odd Establishment is this in a Christian Country! † how uncharitable, and even nonsensical! and how must it make the *Turks* laugh! We grant Synagogues to the *Jews*, the Enemies of JESUS CHRIST, who would crucify him again, if they had not done it already; and we refuse Churches and Temples

* This is what scarce any body has doubted of, but Pere *Bouhours*.

† The *Hamburghers* have nothing to fear from the *Jews*, with regard to their Republic, but they cannot so well trust the turbulent and enterprizing Temper of the *Roman* Catholic Clergy, who aim at their Churches. The popular Commotions which are but too frequent at *Hamburgh*, would soon furnish those Gentlemen with an Opportunity to re-assert Claims which are incompatible with the present Liberty of the City. But this Pretext, how plausible soever in favour of the Papists, is not at all conclusive against the *Calvinists* at *Hamburgh*, who surely might be as safely tolerated as the *Jews*.

to those that believe as we do in JESUS CHRIST! No, were you to call me Heretic a thousand times, I would say, HOLLAND FOR EVER! where 'tis a Maxim, to leave every Man to his Conscience; and where they think it would be a Contradiction to admit People to be their Fellow-Citizens, and to deny them the Liberty of worshipping God in their own way.

The Emperor's Minister, who has the Title of *His Imperial Majesty's Plenipotentiary* to the Circle of Lower *Saxony*, commonly resides at *Hamburgh*. The last Gentleman that had this Employment was the Count *de M..tsch**; and since his being made Vice-President of the Emperor's *Aulic* Council, it has not been fill'd up †.

The Populace of *Hamburgh*, just such another ungovernable Herd as the *Amsterdam* Mobs, having taken it into their heads some years ago, out of a mad sort of Zeal for Religion, to plunder the House and Chapel of the Emperor's Resident; the City in order to make Satisfaction for the Insult, was condemned to build a House which was to be the Residence of the Emperor's Minister always for the future. For this end, the City bought the Palace of the late Baron *de Gortz*, a Man of great Fame in the History of *Charles* XII. King of *Sweden*; and whose Fortune and Catastrophe are worthy your notice.

Henry Baron *de Gortz* was born of an independent Family in *Franconia*, which is a Province that abounds with Nobility of Distinction. He enter'd young into the Service of the Duke of *Holstein-Schlaswic*, and rose to be his Minister. He was a Man generous,

---

* His Post of Plenipotentiary of the Circle of Lower *Saxony*, was conferr'd in 1733 upon the Count *de Seckendorf*, one of the Emperor's Lieutenant-Generals; but the Functions of the Embassy are perform'd by the Baron *de Kurtzrok*, the Imperial President.

† In 1734, he was install'd Vice-Chancellor of the Empire, in the room of the Count *de Schonborn*, Bishop of *Bamberg*, who retir'd.

rous, noble, and magnificent, even to Profusion; vigilant, full of Projects and Stratagems; a Man whom nothing could surprize, nothing dissuade from a Design that he had once form'd; whose Ambition was boundless, and who always aim'd to do something to be talk'd of. In the *North* there was no Intrigue in which he had not a hand, and into which he did not likewise draw his Master, whom he push'd upon Enterprizes so far above his Power to execute, that he thereby lost his Dominions. The Baron *de Gortz* thought *Holstein* too narrow a Sphere for him to move in, and therefore he attach'd himself to *Charles* XII. King of *Sweden*, after that Prince return'd from his long Stay at *Bender*. *Charles* was just such a Master as the Baron wanted, and he just such a Minister as was necessary for the King of *Sweden*; nor was there ever in the World a greater Sympathy between two Men. *Gortz* was born to form great Designs, *Charles* to put them in execution; and the constant Design of both was only to throw *Europe* into a Ferment.

The Baron, besides other happy Gifts of Nature, had the Talent of insinuating and pleasing. He soon got an Ascendant over *Charles*, to such a degree that tho' this Prince was never to be advis'd by his Ministers, yet the Baron's Opinion was a Law to him. *Gortz* frighten'd *Europe*, and made *Sweden* tremble; being as much fear'd and dreaded there as the King himself. The *Swedes* were uneasy to see so great a Share of Authority vested in a Foreigner; and therefore form'd Parties and Cabals to strip him of it; but they durst not discover their Designs. The Minister knew all the while they envy'd him, but was in no manner of Concern about it; for being sure of the Favour of the King, he despised the Hatred,

both

both of the Populace and the Great Men *.

But after the Death of *Charles* XII. who was killed at the Siege of *Frederickshall*, in the Month of *December*, the *Swedes* did not fail to punish him; for the Baron, before he cou'd have Intelligence of the King's Death, was actually put under an Arrest; and upon that Occasion he said to the Officer, *Surely the King must be dead!* From that Moment he was never once heard to complain or murmur; for he was intrepid even to Death; the Sentence of which he received with a wonderful Constancy of Mind, chose to die like a Philosopher, and thought too freely of Religion to the very last. A Divine, who is now one of the King of *Denmark*'s Chaplains, turn'd his Heart, and brought him to acknowledge that 'twas the Hand of God which smote him. He was conducted to the Place of Execution in a mourning Coach, in which the Chaplain rode with him. He had a long Robe of black Velvet, ty'd with Ribbands over his Shoulders; and as he was mounting the Scaffold, which was hung with black Cloth, perceiving one *Duval*, a *Frenchman*, who was his Steward, he held out his Hand, saying, *Farewell* Duval, *I shall eat no more of thy Soups*. When he was on the Scaffold, an Officer of Justice read a Paper to him with a loud Voice; in which it was declared that he was degraded from the Rank of Nobility, and that the Queen had order'd him to be beheaded. *Alas!* said he, *I am born a free Baron of the Empire*. Sweden *cannot take from me what it never gave me; and if I had really deserv'd to be degraded, none has a Right to do it but the* Emperor. Having requir'd one of his Valets de Chambre

---

* The common People cou'd never forgive him for his manner of raising Taxes; by filling the King's Coffers with all the Silver of the Kingdom, and substituting instead of it a Copper Money, which will perpetuate his Memory; especially the Coins on which he caus'd the seven Planets to be engrav'd; which are sought after, and hoarded up as Monuments of his Administration.

ALTENA. 57

bre to undress him, he deliver'd the Ribband of the Order of the Black Eagle of *Prussia* to a Gentleman who stood near him, and enjoin'd him to carry it to one of his Kindred, that he might return it to the King of *Prussia*. Then he fell on his Knees, without shewing the least Sign of Fear; and receiv'd the Stroke of Death with a Constancy of which there are very few Examples. His Head being expos'd to the People, was a pleasing Victim to their Hatred and Revenge. The Baron's Corpse was interr'd, at the Place of Execution, from whence one of his Footmen took it away in the Night-time, put it into a Barrel, and carry'd it to *Hamburgh*; where it was laid upon a Bed of State, and bury'd with all the Formalities fitting the Rank which he had held in the World.

Within a Cannon-Shot of *Hamburgh*, stands the Town of ALTENA, which belongs to the King of *Denmark*. The *Swedish* General, *Steinbock*, reduc'd it to Ashes, the 9th of *January* 1712, by way of Reprisal, as he said, because the *Danes* had burnt *Staden*: but there was this Difference, that the *Danes* had besieg'd *Staden* in form, and destroy'd it by their Bombs; whereas *Steinbock* acted the part of an Incendiary. As soon as he appear'd before *Altena*, he sent in a Message to advise the Inhabitants to retire with what they could carry off, for that he was going to destroy their Town. The Magistrates came out in a Body, and falling at his Feet, begg'd for Mercy, and offer'd him a considerable Sum of Money. *Steinbock* insisting on more, they granted him his whole Demand, only they desir'd Time to go to *Hamburgh* for the Money. The merciless General would admit of no such Delay. The poor Inhabitants were oblig'd to turn out; the Mothers carry'd out their Infants; the young Fellows, the paralytick old Men; some groan'd under Loads of Furniture; all lamented their Fate,

and

and uter'd Cries that wou'd have almost pierc'd a Stone. The *Swedes* stood at the Barriers, with flaming Torches in their Hands, to see them pass; and before the poor Inhabitants were all gone out, they enter'd the Town, and set fire to all parts of it; not sparing even the Vaults of the Dead.

Never was a greater Desolation known; but what compleated the Ruin of the *Altenois*, was the Necessity of the Times, which was such as oblig'd the *Hamburghers* not to entertain them. Several prejudic'd Authors have said that the *Hamburghers*, insensible, if not overjoy'd at the Calamity of their Neighbours, kept their Gates shut, that they might see them perish. But the truth is, that the *Hamburghers* were oblig'd to be thus strict; because the Plague raging at that time in *Holstein*, the Elector of *Hanover* had forc'd them to stop all Commerce with that Country; threatning them, that if he heard they had the least Communication with *Altena*, he wou'd prohibit his Subjects from all manner of Correspondence with the City of *Hamburgh*. Besides, it wou'd not have been prudent in the *Hamburghers* to have open'd their Gates in the Night-time; for the *Swedish* Army being so near, they could not tell but the *Swedes* might come into the Town as well as the *Altenois*. To the Misfortune of the Times therefore must be ascribed the Distress of the Inhabitants of *Altena*, most of whom perished with Cold, Want, and Despair.

Frederic IV. King of *Denmark*, being touched with Compassion for the Misfortune of his Subjects of *Altena*, relieved them as far as the Necessity of the Times wou'd give him leave. He caus'd them to be supply'd with Materials for rebuilding their Houses; and now *Altena* has recovered her Losses: for the King of *Denmark* has not only granted it many new Privileges, but has caus'd a Harbour

ALTENA. 59

to be made there; and does all that is in his power to draw a Trade to it. This City being a privileg'd Place for Bankrupts, many of that Character come from *Hamburgh* to settle here; and there is a general Toleration for those of all Religions, who have their Churches and Temples here; which draws such numbers of People, that in time *Altena* will probably become *Hamburgh*, and *Hamburgh Altena*: For the *Hamburghers*, on the contrary, will tolerate no Christian Sects; tho' they grant the *Jews* the public Exercise of their Religion, as has been already observed. The Governour of *Danish Holstein* resides here, who is the Count *de Reventlau*, Brother to the * Queen of *Denmark*. I am, &c.

* Second Wife of King *Frederic* IV. who died in *October* 1730. Her being so much in favour with that Prince, was the cause of her Disgrace after the Death of that Monarch; and she retir'd to the Isle of *Fuhnen*, where she leads a very melancholy Life.

LET-

LETTER III.

SIR, *Hanover, July 5, 1729.*

THIS Letter is to acquaint you of some things that I remark'd in the Road from *Hamburgh*, and in this City itself; where I have now been these three Days.

I set out from *Hamburgh* the 22d of *June*, and went by Water to HARBOURG, having sent my Chaise thither the Day before. This Town is a Dependant on the Dutchy of *Lunenbourg*, and belongs to the Elector of *Brunswic-Lunenbourg*. It has nothing very remarkable but its Castle, which is a Pentagon, lin'd with a good Cover'd-Way. Madamoiselle *d'Olbreuse* [*], whom the Duke of *Zell* marry'd, had the Title of Madame *de Harbourg*, till she was recogniz'd by the Emperor a Princess of the Empire. For by the Laws of *Germany*, a Prince of a Sovereign Family can marry none but a Princess, or a Countess. If he weds a private Gentlewoman, he not only marries below himself, but his Wife does not go by his Name; and the Children of such Marriage cannot succeed, unless the Emperor declare the Mother a Princess; as he commonly does in favour of Princes of antient Families.

Between *Harbourg* and *Zell*, which is twelve Miles, there is scarce any thing but Heath. The Post-Stages, which are of four Miles, are very ill serv'd,

---

[*] She was called *Eleanor d'Emiers*, and was the Daughter of *Alexander d'Olbreuse*, a Gentleman of *Poictou*.

serv'd, and the Inns the worst in *Germany*; all which together render the Road extremely disagreeable.

ZELL is a little Town with great Suburbs. All its Buildings are of Timber, except the Churches, the Castle, and the House of Correction, which are of Brick. There is a Trade from hence to *Bremen*, by the River *Aller*.

After the Death of *George-William*, the last Duke of *Zell* *, this City, and its Dependency, the Dutchy of *Lunenbourg*, devolv'd to his Nephew *George*, Elector of *Brunswic-Hanover*, afterwards King of *Great Britain*. This Prince had a Regency at *Zell*, which judged all Causes, without any Appeal but to the Council of State at *Hanover*. The President of it at this time, is the Baron *de Friesberg*, a Person of a good Family in the Country of *Hildesheim*; who has been a long time the Elector's Envoy at the Diet of *Ratisbon*, where I knew him, and received a world of Civilities from him. He is esteem'd for the prudent Management of his Office, and his noble manner of living. There are a great many Persons of Quality settled at *Zell*, who for a trifling Expence enjoy the Pleasures of agreeable Society. They visit and regale one another very much, and are not wanting in Civilities to Foreigners. Monsieur *de Schulenbourgh* †, Lieutenant-General of the *Hanoverian* Horse, and Knight

---

* The House of *Brunswic* has for its Head *Ernest* of *Zell*, who by *Bernard* and *Albert* the Great, the Son of *Otho* the Infant, descended from the Familys of *Este* and *Witikind*. *George-William* Duke of *Zell*, was Grandson to *William*, the second Son of *Ernest*; from whom came the two Branches of *Lunenbourg-Zell*, and *Lunenbourg-Hanover*; both which were united in the single Family of *Hanover*, by the Death of the Duke of *Zell*, who left no Issue besides a Daughter married to his Cousin *George* I. King of *Great Britain*, as well as Elector of *Hanover*.

† Monsieur *de Schulenbourgh* died the beginning of the Year 1733.

Knight of the *Prussian* Order of the Black Eagle, is the Governour of this Town. He is a Gentleman of good Extraction, of Behaviour, Noble, Polite, and Easy; and though he is Father of a numerous Family, he affects to live grand, and keeps a very good Table. One of his Sons is in the Service of *Prussia*, the others are in that of the King of *England*. I mention them to you, because they are worthy Gentlemen; and whoever knows them, cannot but esteem them.

Here are a great many *French* People, *Catholick* as well as *Protestant*, of whom the former have a Chapel, and the latter a Church; but the Religion which is predominant, is the *Lutheran*. The last Dutchess of *Zell*, of the Family of *Olbreuse*, being a *French* Woman, fill'd her Husband's Court and Guards with her own Countrymen; who were even preferr'd before the Natives of *Zell*. I have been told that these *Frenchmen* really thought themselves so much at home, that there happen'd to be one day no less than a dozen of 'em at Dinner at the Duke's Table, who all except the Prince were *Frenchmen*; which one of them observing, said to the Duke, *My Lord, this is really very pleasant; there is no Foreigner here but you!*

In the Neighbourhood of this Town there's the Castle of *Ahlen*, where, (about nine Years ago,) the unfortunate Daughter of the last Duke of *Zell*, by Madamoiselle *d'Olbreuse*, ended her Days, after she had been retir'd thither about thirty six Years: She had been promised in Marriage to *Augustus-William*, the hereditary Prince of *Brunswic-Lunenbourg-Wolfembuttle*; but her Father the Duke, by the Intrigues of the Princess *Sophia*, Dutchess of *Hanover*, marry'd her against her Will, and against the Consent of her Mother, to the hereditary Prince *George-Lewis*, who was afterwards King of *Great Britain*, by Right of his Mother, and who died in the

the Year 1727, as he came to make the Tour of his hereditary Dominions. She was sixteen Years old at her Marriage with that Prince, who was then twenty-two.

Tho' there's a good deal of Heath between *Zell* and *Hanover*, yet the Country is very well cultivated; for the Inhabitants not only make Turfs of the Heath for Fewel, but it serves also for Pasturage, and for Manure. 'Tis about five *German* Miles from one Town to the other, and I travell'd it in less than five Hours.

HANOVER, the Capital of the Electorate of *Brunswic-Lunenbourg*, is bigger than *Zell*. The River *Leine* divides it into the old and new Towns, which are both encompass'd with Ramparts that scarce deserve the Name. There is nothing very extraordinary in the Palace or Castle, which is rather commodious than magnificent; and the Town of *Hanover*, generally speaking, is but ill built. The most remarkable Structure in it, is the *Roman Catholick* Church, which was granted to those of that Communion by *Ernest-Augustus* of *Brunswic-Lunenbourg-Hanover*; that being one of the Conditions which the Emperor *Leopold* demanded of him when he honour'd him with the Electoral Dignity. That Prince moreover engag'd to admit of an Apostolical Vicar in his Dominions, and to give him leave to reside at *Hanover*, as *Spiga*, who lately died at *Francfort**, did for many Years. Divine Service is perform'd in this Church as regularly as in a Cathedral; and they who officiate in it are Missionaries. The number of Catholicks is very considerable; but few Persons of Quality are

---

* Pope *Clement* XII. on his Accession to the Pontificate, appointed for his Successor *Schorror*, Bishop of *Helenopolis*, a Native of *Bonn*, in the Electorate of *Cologne*; a Prelate as amiable as venerable.

are of that Communion, the Nobility being all *Lutherans*.

When *George* I. King of *Great Britain* left his *German* Dominions to take poſſeſſion of his Kingdom, he was willing that all Affairs at *Hanover* ſhou'd continue on the ſame footing as they were before he was called to the Throne; and he left behind him Prince *Frederic* his Grandſon, now Prince of *Wales*; who not only had a Drawing-Room every Day, but the ſame Attendance as had the Elector before he was King.

His Majeſty King *George* II. has made no Alteration in the Eſtabliſhment of the King his Father. When he ſent for the Prince of *Wales* to *England*, he order'd the Courtiers to continue their Aſſemblies at the Caſtle; and that his Table ſhou'd always be ſerv'd in the ſame manner as if he himſelf was at *Hanover*. His Majeſty keeps up the ſame number of Gentlemen, Pages, Domeſtics, and Guards; and the ſame number of Horſes, Grooms, &c. in his Stables. There's a *French* Comedy acted three times a Week at the Palace, to which all People are admitted *gratis*; and there are frequently Concerts, Balls and Aſſemblies. The Gentlemen who do the Court-Honours at theſe Entertainments, and who invite Perſons to dine or ſup at the King's Table, are either M. *de Hardenberg*, the Grand Marſhal, or, in his abſence, the Baron *de Gortz* *, Chief Steward of the Houſhold; or elſe M. *de Rheden*, Captain of the Caſtle of *Hanover*.

In the King's abſence, the Government is compos'd of a Council of State, whereof M. *de Hardenberg* is Chief or Preſident; which meets every day in an Apartment of the Caſtle. To this all the Courts of Juſtice in the Dominions of *Hanover* are ſubject, and accountable. The Council of

---

* He retir'd ſome Years ſince from Court, to his Eſtate at *Schlitz*, in *Franconia*.

of State receives its Orders immediately from the King; and they are counter-signed either by the Count *de Bothmar*, or by M. *de Hattorf*, the two *German* Ministers that attend his Majesty's Person.

The Count *de Bothmar* * is an old Gentleman, who for a long time resided in quality of the Elector's Envoy at the Court of *England*, where, by his prudent Management for his Master, he cherished the most incontestable Right that a Prince can possibly have to a Crown; I mean, the Voice of the People.

M. *de Hattorf* is not only the Minister's Son, but has been his Co-adjutor, for they had both the War-Office in their Province; for which reason they were called *Louvois* and *Barbesieux*, a Comparison which does no Dishonour either to the one or to the other: for if the two *Hattorfs* have not made such a Blaze in the World, 'tis because they had not a *Lewis* XIV. for their Master, for they were not inferior to the *French* Ministers in Capacity, and Application to Business, and had not their Pride and Arrogance.

M. *de Munchausen* is one of those Ministers of State who bears the most Sway. He is of a Temper beneficent, mild, civil, very candid, sober, and religious. He lives with Dignity, and his House is as open to Foreigners as any in the City.

The Marshal Baron *de Bulau*, is Commander in chief of the Forces †. He has no manner of Dependance

---

* The Count *de Bothmar* died at *London* in the beginning of *An.* 1732, in a very advanc'd Age, and much lamented by all that knew him. The Baron *de Hattorf* succeeded him in the Ministry to the King as Elector.

† Since this was written, the continual Ailments and great Age of M. *de Bulau*, have obliged the King to make an Alteration in the Command of his Troops. M. *de Hardenberg*, a Knight of the *Teutonic* Order, is Commander in Chief of the Horse, and M. *Melvil*, who is descended of a noble Family in *Scotland*,

dance on the Council of State, and receives his Orders immediately from the King, by M. *de Hattorf* the Secretary at War. The Promotion which the King makes of Officers is by the Recommendation of M. *de Bulau*; and such as would enter into the Service must make their Application to him. He serv'd with Distinction in the *Netherlands*, under my Lord Duke of *Marlborough*. He has actually under his Command 18000 Men, which is the Complement of the King of *Great Britain*'s Forces, as Elector. His Majesty indeed, keeps in pay 12000 *Hessians*, * and 4000 Men of the Troops of *Wolfenbuttle*. 'Tis true, those Forces are paid by *England*, but to me it seems they are only to defend the King's Dominions in *Germany*.

Tho' the Sovereign is absent, yet here are not wanting Amusements; there being many good Families, and a number of amiable Persons.

The lovely Countess of *Delitz*, Niece to the Dutchess of *Kendal*, cou'd not fail of Adorers, even in the most barbarous Countries; for the Charms of her Mind are not inferior to the Beauty, Sweetness, and Gracefulness of her Person.

No Lady can have a better Temper or Behaviour than the Baroness *de Bulau*, Daughter-in-law to the Marshal, and Daughter to the late Countess of *Platen*: her Husband is a worthy Gentleman, and keeps a very good House.

The Count *de Platen*, hereditary Post-Master-General, is one of the richest Subjects in the Electorate, and one that spends the most Money. A Foreigner will always have cause to speak well of M. *de Rheden*, Captain of the Castle, and M. *de Wagenheim*, the great Cup-Bearer. Messieurs *d' Ilten*
live

Scotland, has the Command of the Foot. They are both Officers of Reputation, and signaliz'd their Valour during the late Wars.

* These auxiliary Forces have been of late years disbanded.

live splendidly; and both the Brothers, the eldest of whom is a Colonel of the Guards, are amiable and infinitely polite. If ever you come hither, you will certainly have reason to be fond of their Company.

The Situation of *Hanover* is very agreeable; and in its Neighbourhhood are several pretty Seats. Among these *Herenhausen* (the House of the *Lord*, or the *Master*) is a Castle which was built by Order of the Elector *Ernest-Augustus*, the King's Grand-Father. This House, to which a strait Walk leads, bears no proportion to the Magnificence of its Gardens, which are undeniably some of the finest in all *Europe*; being particularly adorn'd with Water-Works that throw the Water up much higher than the famous Fountain at *St. Cloud*, which was always look'd upon as the most considerable of the kind *.

Between *Hanover* and *Herenhausen*, there are two fine Seats; of which, one is call'd *Fantasie*, i. e. *the Whim*; and the other, *Monbrillant*, or, *Mount-Pleasant*. They were built by two Sisters-in-law, viz. Madame *de Kilmanseck*, (who after her Husband's Death, was by King *George* I. created Countess of *Arlington*) and the Countess of *Platen*. These two Houses are a Proof of the good Taste of those Ladies, who were really an Honour to *Germany*, for their Beauty, good Sense, Manners, and Genius. They both died in their Prime, a little time after one another; my Lady *Arlington* in *England*, and the Countess of *Platen* at *Hanover*, to which she was not only an Ornament, but a Lustre.

---

* These Works were set up by the Direction of Wm. Benson, Esq; who went over to *Hanover* for that purpose in 1716, was soon after made Surveyor-General of His Majesty's Works in *England*, and is now one of the Auditors of the Imprest.

The Dominions of *Hanover* are so considerable, that I have been assured the Revenues are no less than six Millions of Crowns *per An.* Whether this be true, I do not know; but I tell you what I was told myself.

Hamelen upon the *Weser* is the only Town that can be reckon'd a Place of Defence. *Hanover*, *Zell*, and *Lunenbourg*, have Ramparts; *Harbourg*, a Castle, or Citadel; but all so inconsiderable, that they are not worth mentioning.

There are few Sovereigns whose Finances are in so good a Condition as this Elector's; which has been the happy Produce of three succeeding Reigns; and the good Oeconomy wherewith they were managed by the three last Princes of the Electoral Family, has contributed infinitely to the Figure it makes at this time. Mean-while, notwithstanding these Regulations, the People were never oppress'd, and the Princes always lived with a Splendor suitable to their Grandeur. *Ernest-Augustus* obtained the Electoral Dignity, not without making great Presents to the Court of *Vienna*, at a time too when his Power was limited to the Dutchy of *Hanover*, and the Bishoprick of *Osnabrug*. Tho' this Prince had a numerous Family to provide for, he lived with Splendor, was fond of Magnificence and Pleasures, gallant, generous, and liberal; and when he died, he left no Debts to pay, and his Finances were in a good State.

George I. his Son and Successor kept up a considerable Body of Troops, and had a very splendid Court. As his Acquisitions were great, he distributed his Favours where-ever he was inform'd there was a Necessity; and when he came to the Throne, he made no Reform in this Court; so that their not seeing him was the only Token of his Absence. At his Death, he left immense Sums in his Treasury, fury, and so glorious a Character, that his Subjects still bless the Memory of his Reign.

GEORGE II. his Son, and the Heir of his Crown, his Dominions, and Virtues, behaves in the very same manner. While he lives and acts like a King, he neither gives, on the one hand, into the Extravagance of vain Pomp and Pageantry, nor on the other, into that sordid Thriftiness which debases Royal Majesty, and extinguishes the Love of Subjects. He accumulates Treasure without oppressing his People, who love him, and offer up their Prayers for him, as I do for your Preservation; and

Am, &c.

LETTER IV.

SIR, *Blanckenbourg, July* 30, 1729.

I WAS six Hours travelling from *Hanover* to BRUNSWIC, the Capital of the Dutchy of that Name, which is a very great City, with Houses for the most part of Timber. It was formerly a Free and Imperial City, and one of the *Hanse*-Towns; but falling under the Sovereignty of the Princes of the House of *Brunswic*, they reduced it to a level with the other Towns of their Dominions. It belongs to the Duke of *Brunswic-Lunenbourg Wolfembuttle*. The Duke *Anthony-Ulric* began to fortify it; and his Son *Augustus-William*, the present Duke*, perfected

* He died in *March*, 1731, without Issue by either of his three Wives; who were, 1. *Christina-Sophia* of *Brunswic*.

2.

fected what remained unfinished at his Father's Death, and made *Brunswic* a Place which cannot be besieged without a numerous Army: But then on the other hand, it would require such an Army to garison it as the Duke could not furnish without the help of his Neighbours, and which besides, wou'd not perhaps be extraordinary convenient for him to introduce. The said Duke has caused a new Palace to be built, which is large and magnificent, and the Furniture is rich, new, and excellently well chosen. Among the rest, there are very fine Pictures, and a Cabinet full of Curiosities.

The Duke of *Blanckenbourg*, Brother to the Duke of *Wolfembuttle*, has a particular Palace, where he resides in the Fair-time, but it did not appear to me to be a House of any consequence.

The Fairs of *Brunswic* contribute very much to make it a rich and famous City, there being two held every Year, and a considerable Trade carried on at both.

There is very good Diversion during these Fairs; for then all the Ducal Family is generally at *Brunswic*; to which foreign Princes come often, and there is always a great Concourse of the Nobility. The Duke sends every Morning to invite the Quality of both Sexes, who at Noon repair to the Palace. The Grand-Marshal, for avoiding all Disputes about Precedency, causes the Ladies to be match'd with the Gentlemen by the drawing of Tickets; and sometimes it happens that a Dutchess

is

---

2. *Sophia-Amelia* of *Holstein-Gottorp*, and 3. *Elizabeth-Sophia* of *Holstein-Norbourg*, whom he left a Widow, after two Years Marriage. His Brother *Lewis-Rodolph*, Duke of *Brunswic-Lunenbourg* and *Blanckenbourg*, succeeded him. He was born in 1671, and in 1690 married *Christiana-Louisa* of *Oetingen*, by whom he had three Daughters; the eldest of whom was married to the Emperor *Charles* VI. the second to the *Czarowitz*, Son of *Peter* the Great; and the third, to the Duke *Ferdinand-Albert* of *Brunswic-Lunenbourg* and *Bevern*.

is at the lower end of the Table, which is served with very great Magnificence and Elegance. When there are too many Guests to sit at one Table, the two Brothers keep each a separate Table at his own Palace. At Night, the Company repairs to the *German* Opera, which being ended, they pass into Rooms joining to the Theatre where they play, and sup, and then dance. The Ball is open'd by the Gentleman who happened to draw the first Number in the Morning, and continues till Day-break.

The Ducal Family of *Brunswic-Wolfembuttle* consists now but of two Brothers; the eldest of whom, the Duke * *Augustus-William*, has had three Wives, but no Issue. He is married to a Princess of *Holstein-Norbourg*.

These two Princes are so far advanced in Years, that the Duke *Ferdinand-Albert* of *Brunswic-Lunenbourg-Bevern*, Son-in-law to the Duke of *Blanckenbourg*†, is looked upon as their presumptive Heir. *Europe* produces few Princes of more distinguished Merit, who have equal Knowledge, more Learning, and Integrity, or more Valour and Experience in War. He has acquired a noble Reputation in *Hungary*; and he is not only a Brother-in-law to the Emperor, but one of his favourite Generals, and has a Regiment in his Service ‖.

---

* The Branch of *Brunswic-Bevern* is descended from *Henry de Danneberg*, eldest Son of Duke *Ernest*, Head of the *Brunswic* Family. *Henry* left two Sons; the youngest of whom, *Augustus* of *Wolfembuttle*, had three Sons who form'd three Branches, *Brunswic*, *Wolfembuttle*, and *Bevern*. The two first were united in *Anthony Ulric*. *Ferdinand-Albert* I. Chief of the Line of *Bevern*, left five Sons and a Daughter. Three of his Sons are dead; of whom the Eldest lost his life at the Battle of *Schellenburg*, in 1704; the Third died in 1706, when he was Provost of St. *Blaise* of *Brunswic*; as did the Fifth also, in 1706, at the Battle of *Turin*. There remain two Sons, *viz.* Duke *Ferdinand-Albert* II. and Duke *Ernest-Ferdinand*.

† See the foregoing Note.

‖ This Prince was Veit-Marshal-General of the Emperor's Forces,

BRUNSWIC.

His Family consists of four Sons and three Daughters* by his Wife *Antonietta-Amelia* of *Brunswic-Blanckenbourg*. These are very hopeful young Princes. The eldest, whose Name is *Charles*†, is of a lovely Make, and has Sense infinitely beyond his Years. The eldest Princess, *Elizabeth-Christina* ‖, at twelve Years of Age may pass for one that is compleatly grown; her Air is noble and modest; her Features regular; in a word, she is form'd to make that Prince happy who is one day to be her Husband.

The Court of *Wolfembuttle* is numerous, and when assembled does not want for Magnificence.

The Ministers of most Power are the Baron *Stein*‡, and the Count *de Debn* **. The former is

---

Forces, and in that Quality he commanded the Emperor's Army, in the War which *France* declared against his Imperial Majesty in 1733. He acquired great Reputation at the Head of a very weak Army, by hindering the *French* from doing any thing more than taking Fort *Kehl* in the first Campaign, when the Emperor was surpriz'd and unprovided. At the Opening of the Campaign in 1734, this Prince oppos'd the Designs of the Marshal *Berwick*, by Lines which he cast up at *Muhlberg*, and which were of good service to Prince *Eugene*, in facilitating his Retreat towards *Heilbron*, when he came to take upon him the Command of the Imperial Army. That great General own'd he never saw any thing look better, or that was stronger and better disposed than those Lines, which the Duke of *Brown* had guarded till then, with an Army of not 25000 Men. His most Serene Highness was in 1734, declared by the Dyet of the Empire, Velt-Marshal-General of the Armies of the Empire.

* He had fourteen Children, viz. seven Sons and seven Daughters, the last of whom was born in 1732.

† He married *Philippina-Charlotte*, the King of *Prussia*'s third Daughter, in 1733.

‖ This Princess was married to the Prince Royal of *Prussia*, in 1733.

‡ The Baron having quitted the Service of *Wolfembuttle*, is actually a Minister of State at *Hanover*.

** The Count *de Debn*, after being disgrac'd, went to *Denmark*, of which he already wore the Order of *Dannebroc*, and obtained the Title of one of the King's Counsellors of State.

From

is descended of an illustrious Family in *Swabia*: He was in the Service of the Landgrave of *Darmstadt*, and his Envoy at the Dyet of *Ratisbon*, and several Courts, where he made himself considerable by his Eloquence, the Justness of his Sentiments, by the Ease with which he expresses them, and by his Politeness.

The Count *de Dehn* is a Native of *Mecklemburg*, where he was born of a good Family, and enter'd very young a Page to Duke *Anthony-Ulric* of *Brunswic-Wolfembuttle*. He had the Happiness to please that Prince, but much more his Successor, the Duke *Augustus-William*, who of his Page, made him his Favourite and Minister, heaped Wealth and Honours upon him, and match'd him to the Daughter of his Chancellor, who was one of the richest Heiresses in all *Germany*.

The young Minister finding himself rich and powerful, quickly thought the Court of *Wolfembuttle* too narrow a Stage for Action. He had chose the Count *de Fleming*, Prime Minister of the King of *Poland*, for a Model. He saw that this Minister, under pretence of important Negotiations, went to the chief Courts of the Empire to make a Parade of his Riches; and young *Dehn* long'd with Impatience to imitate him. He procur'd himself to be nominated the Duke's Envoy Extraordinary to *Holland* and *France*, where he vy'd in every respect with the Ambassadors of the chief Crowns. In fine, after having staid about eighteen Months at *Paris*, he went away very much lamented by the Merchants and Workmen with whom he had dealings. He came to *Wolfembuttle* to receive the Applauses of his Master, and

From that time he stay'd at his Estate in the Country of *Wolfembuttle*, till the Year 1734, that the King of *Denmark* appointed him to go to *Petersburg*, to fill up the Post of his Envoy Extraordinary vacant by the Death of M. *Westphal*.

and to rest himself after the Fatigues he had undergone in his important Negotiations.

As Count *Fleming* was honoured with the Orders of *Denmark*, *Russia*, and *Poland*, his Rival too thought he could not do without one Ribbon at least; and thinking the Order of *Dannebrock* the most proper for him, because it was white, he demanded and obtained it of *Frederic* IV. the King of *Denmark*. When he saw himself thus adorn'd, he procured himself to be sent to *Vienna*. What business he had there, I know not; but he was scarce ever from the Emperor, and in order to be nearer to his Person, he lodged just by the Palace of the *Favorita*. He often relieved the Cares of the Ministry by making some Entertainment or Ball. He had an admirable Genius for Dancing, so that every body thought him the Inventor of Country-Dances. The Emperor gave him the Title of a Count, with which he returned to his own Court.

When Glory has once fir'd a noble Soul, nothing can keep it within Bounds. The Count *de Debn* had lost his first Wife, who left him the Heir of three great Estates; and he married again to an amiable Lady, who return'd him Love for Love. Tho' he was dear to his Master, yet he could not resolve to continue at *Wolfembuttle*, because he had a Taste for nothing but Treaties and Negotiations. He returned a second time, as Envoy Extraordinary to the *States-General*, but did not stay long at the *Hague*; for after having had his publick Audience, wherein he assured their High-Mightinesses of the sincere Affection of his Master for their Republic, and of his own personal Joy to find himself seated in an Arm-Chair in their Assembly, he went over to *England* to reside at the Court of his *Britannic* Majesty. He was admired for his Grandeur, as much in *England* as elsewhere; but the Air of that Country not agreeing with the Delicacy of his Constitution,

ſtitution, he return'd to *Germany*; and, after having made a tour to the chief Courts of the Empire, he is come back to *Wolfembuttle*, where he ſtays in expectation that ſome great Event or other will turn up, that he may be employ'd in ſome remarkable Embaſſy, whereby *Europe*, attentive to every thing that relates to him, may have freſh Proofs of his great Talents.

The Baron *de Hagen* is Commander in Chief of the Duke's Troops, which actually amount to above 4000 Men, and 'tis ſaid, that his Highneſs's Revenues exceed two Millions of Crowns. His Subjects are not the worſt uſed of any in *Germany*. 'Tis a good fruitful Country; the Peaſants, who are ſober and laborious, are as clowniſh and as ſtupid as thoſe that herd with the Hogs in *Weſtphalia*; but they are robuſt, ſtrong, and good Soldiers.

In *Brunſwic* there is a Catholick Church which is ſmall, but neat. The Duke *Anthony-Ulric* cauſ'd it to be built at the time he embraced the Catholick Religion; which he did, after full Conviction, not many Years before his Death.

Saltzdahl, a Pleaſure-Houſe belonging to the Duke, is a League from *Brunſwic*, and from *Wolfembuttle*. It was built by Duke *Anthony-Ulric*, one of the moſt magnificent Princes of his Time, and one who had the moſt elegant Taſte. This Houſe is worthy of nice Obſervation. It has a great Gallery with a Collection of Pictures in it by the chief Painters, which is not to be met with elſewhere. In one great Cabinet there is very fine Porcellane; and in another, a vaſt number of Veſſels and Urns painted by *Raphael*. In ſhort, the Curious can't want here for Entertainment.

The Road from *Brunſwic* to WOLFEMBUTTLE is as pleaſant as moſt Roads. We croſs a little Wood through which there are ſeveral Routes cut, and as we come near the Town, several pretty Seats appear in view.

The Town of *Wolfembuttle* is not half so big as *Brunswic*, nor is it better built, the Houses being of Timber. The Fortifications seem to me to be in good Repair. The Castle, or Ducal Palace, is ancient, and makes no great Appearance, but 'tis commodious, and has good Lodging-Rooms. That which most deserves the Attention of a Traveller, is the Library, which is one of the best chosen in *Europe*, and contains very scarce Books and Manuscripts.

As I had left the Court at *Brunswic* I did not stay many Hours at *Wolfembuttle*, but came to lie here at BLANCKENBOURG, where I have all that Heart can wish for.

The Duke is as affable and as civil a Prince as any in the World. In his Youth he visited the principal Courts of *Europe*, where he contracted a great Politeness, and a solid Taste of Elegancy. He loves the *Belles Lettres*, protects the Arts and Sciences, and looks out for Men of Ability to serve him. He is magnificent, generous, a good Prince, and a kind Master. He was at one and the same time, the Father of an Empress, and the Grand-Father of an Emperor. As a Father, he has a considerable Pension from the Emperor of *Germany*; and as a Grandfather, he has been honour'd with the Order of St. *Andrew* of *Muscovy*, founded by *Peter* the Great, which is a blue Ribbon, with St. *Andrew*'s Cross appendant to it enamell'd with blue. This Prince is also a Commander of *Suplenbourg*, a Commandery of the Order of St. *John*, annexed to the House of *Brunswic*. He has had three Daughters by his Wife *Elizabeth-Christina* of *Oetingen*.

The Dutchess, tho' advanc'd in Years, retains an Air of Grandeur and Majesty which strikes the Beholders, and her Features discover the Marks of that

that shining Beauty which she had in her Youth. But what renders this Princess more venerable than even her Birth, is her solid Piety, her just Discernment, her lively Imagination, her noble and easy manner of expressing herself, and her Principles of Humanity, accompany'd with a Generosity free from all Ostentation.

I had the honour to pay my Duty to her at *Brunswic*, some Years ago, when she receiv'd me with such Tokens of Goodness as rejoic'd my very Heart; and upon all Occasions since, she has been pleas'd to give me fresh Proofs of it. As I can be of no service to this Princess in any Case, nor so happy as to be able to contribute to her Glory, 'tis my Ambition to make every one, and you, Sir, in particular, sensible of the Respect and Attachment with which I am devoted to her, and of the grateful Sense I have of the Benevolence with which she has honour'd me.

The Courtiers of *Blanckenbourg* are, like their Master, very polite. M. *de Munchausen* is the chief of the Duke's Council, and was formerly in the Service of the Duke of *Wolfembuttle*. He is a Gentleman of great Learning, Labour, and Vigilance, and has a distinct and noble Manner of Delivery. He is heartily attach'd to his Master; and the Courtiers seem'd to me to have an Esteem and Affection for him. Men of solid Judgment, and who have been more conversant with this Minister than I, have assured me that he is one of the greatest Genius's at this present, in *Germany* [*].

M. *de Sporck* is the Grand-Marshal, which Employment he acquits himself in with very great Politeness and Care. He is come of a good Family, his
Father

---

[*] Since the Duke succeeded his Father, M. *de Munchausen* is become first Minister of State, and manages all the Branches of that Office with that Care and Justice which procure him universal Love and Esteem.

Father being Minister of State, and Director of the Dutchies of *Zell* and *Lunenbourg*. M. *de Polentz* * does the Honours of the Court under him, in quality of Great Cup-Bearer. As he had his Education at Court, he is vastly polite; and Foreigners cannot but be pleas'd with his good Behaviour.

The Duke and Dutchess delight to see Foreigners at their Court, whom they load with Civilities, and will have them always to dine and sup with their Highnesses. After Dinner, they take the Air, or make Visits; and in the Evening there's an Assembly in the Dutchess's Apartment, where they play, then sup, and afterwards every one retires. We have had a Comedy twice or thrice, which is acted by the young People of the Family, who perform their Parts very well; especially in the Tragedies of *Corneille* and *Racine*, translated into *High-Dutch*.

The Pleasures of the Carnival are more gay, at which time the Duke makes Entertainments: There's a Ball, a Masquerade, and Comedy at Court, every Day; and for the time there's so great a Concourse of Strangers here from the neighbouring Towns, that sometimes 'tis impossible to get a Lodging.

The Town of BLANCKENBOURG is small, and the Houses ill built, and inconvenient. The Duke has done all in his power to engage the Inhabitants to build; he has offer'd them Materials *gratis*, and has moreover endeavour'd to inspire them with a Taste for the Arts; but all without Success.

I never in my whole Life, saw People more indolent and clownish than those of *Blanckenbourg*, and the neighbouring Towns. They are so bigotted to old Customs, that they say, *My Father liv'd so, and so will I*; *My Father did not do this, nor will I*. I cannot conceive how People, so dull as they are, and so strongly attach'd to the Institutions of their

Fore-

---

* He is at present Marshal of the Court; M. *de Miltitz* is Great Cup-Bearer, and M. *de Rossing* Great-Huntsman.

Fore-Fathers, came to give into *Luther*'s Reformation *.

Blanckenbourg is a petty County, which Duke *Anthony-Ulric* yielded in his Life-time to his second Son, to make him some sort of Compensation for the Right of Primogeniture, which he had newly introduc'd into his Family, to that Son's prejudice: For the Princes of *Brunswic* had for a long time been us'd to a Partition of Lands in their Families. The *Hanover* Branch was the first that abolish'd that Custom, pernicious to great Families. Duke *Anthony-Ulric* was only restrain'd from it by Pr. *Lewis* his second Son, whom he lov'd more than his eldest; and not caring to leave him without Dominions, to the Discretion of a Brother, he gave him Possession of this State in his Life-time; because he was of Opinion, that after his Death, his Will wou'd have the Fate of not being executed by his Successor, according to the Custom introduc'd among Sovereigns. With them 'tis a Right of Regale, but for us to do so, is a Crime.

As the County of *Blanckenbourg* does not give Admittance into the College of Princes at the Dyet of the Empire, so it does not give the Rank of a Sovereign Prince to the Person in possession of it. The Duke, in order to procure himself both these Privileges, made a Treaty with the Elector of *Hanover*, whereby he got that Prince to yield him the Vote and Seat which he enjoy'd in the Dyet for his Dutchy of *Grubenhagen*: And the Duke, on his part, engag'd never to vote at the Dyet but in conformity to the Sentiments of the Elector. After his Decease, or if he happens to succeed his Brother, the

---

* The reason is, perhaps, because out of *their Attachment to old Customs*, they had the Curiosity to go a little higher back than their Fathers.

the Vote and Seſſion for *Grubenbagen* revert to the Elector *.

This, Sir, is all that I can ſay to you at preſent. Their Highneſſes being to ſet out in a few days for *Oetingen*, where they uſe to go every Summer, I propoſe to go forthwith to *Leipſic* and *Dreſden*: And at the latter Place I hope to hear from you.

I am, &c.

LETTER V.

SIR, *Dreſden, Auguſt* 30. 1729.

FROM *Blanckenbourg* we have till'd Lands, and fruitful Fields; with Woods of Oak interſpers'd all the way, till we come to MAGDEBOURG, the Capital of a Dutchy of that Name, formerly an Archbiſhoprick, but ſeculariſed at the Treaty of *Weſtphalia*, in favour of the Houſe of *Brandenbourg*, to whom that Dutchy was yielded in exchange for their reſigning Hither *Pomerania* to *Sweden*. This City has for theſe two Cen-

---

* The Duke of *Blanckenbourg* being become Duke of *Wolfembuttle*, by the Death of his Brother, has ſcarce made any Alteration in his Court. The Perſons who were heretofore his Creatures and Favourites continue in the ſame Employments. The Dutcheſs Dowager remains at *Brunſwic*, in the fine Houſe which the late Duke caus'd to be built; and of which the ſaid Prince made a Preſent to her, with all its rich Furniture. This Princeſs is immenſely rich, and lives with very great Dignity. Her Steward is M. *de Wederkopf*, who was formerly Privy Counſellor to the King of *Denmark*, and his Envoy Extraordinary at the Court of *France*.

Centuries past, suffer'd very much. It was besieg'd by the Emperor *Charles* V. who squeez'd considerable Sums from it. But it fared worse in that unhappy War which divided *Germany* during the space of 30 Years; for the Counts *de Tilly* and *Papenheim* commanding the Imperial Army in 1631, took it by Storm, put the Inhabitants to the Sword, and reduc'd the whole City almost to Ashes. Nevertheless, 'tis since pretty well recover'd, and has some fine Houses. The great Square before the King's Palace has few equal to it for its Extent, and for the fine Houses that encompass it, which are all uniform, three Stories high, and were all raised in this Reign. In this same Square there's an Arsenal, which really is not so magnificent as that of *Berlin*, but may be rank'd among the chief Arsenals in *Europe*. This is a populous Town, and has a more flourishing Trade than any other City in the King of *Prussia*'s Dominions.

The great Church, which was formerly the Metropolitan, is ancient, and one of the largest and most magnificent Buildings in *Germany*. It has still some Reliques to shew, particularly the Basin in which *Pilate* washed his Hands, after having pass'd Sentence of Death upon our Saviour; the Lanthorn * which *Judas* made use of when he went to apprehend him; a Thorn of the Crown that was planted on his Head: and things of the like kind.

The Chapter of *Magdebourg* is still, bating the change of Religion, on the same footing as before the Reformation. The Canons must all make Proof of their Nobility; tho' 'tis a *Punctilio* with which the King, who confers all the Prebends and Dignities of the Chapter, sometimes dispenses. The present

---

* The Treasury of St. *Dennis*, near *Paris*, boasts also of this Lanthorn; so that *Judas* must have had at least two Lanthorns.

sent Provoſt is the Duke of *Saxe-Barbi*, who succeeded his Father in that Dignity, which brings him in 12000 Crowns a-year. He lives in a fine Houſe on the great Square, fronting the Palace, built by the Order of King *Frederic* I. who alſo caus'd a Citadel to be erected here, on the other ſide of the *Elbe*, over which there is a Bridge. That King began likewiſe to fortify the Town; and King *Frederic-William*, who carried on, and finiſh'd the Fortifications, has now made *Magdebourg* one of the moſt important Places in *Europe*. M. *de Walrave*, Chief Engineer, had the Direction of thoſe Works, which are a Proof of his great Ability.

The Margrave *Albert* of *Brandenbourg* *, Brother to the late King *Frederic* I. is Governour of the Dutchy of *Magdebourg*; as is the Prince of *Anhalt-Deſſau* of the Town, where he has a numerous Garriſon under his command. The Arſenal, which is a fine Structure, and full of Cannon, and ſmall Arms, is worth ſeeing.

The King of *Pruſſia* having it much at heart to render *Magdebourg* a flouriſhing Town, has transferr'd the Regency of the Dutchy hither, which was heretofore at *Halle*; and for this reaſon there are ſeveral good Houſes in the Town. The Dutchy of *Magdebourg* is one of the beſt Provinces in the *Pruſſian* Dominions. It has a great Income from the *Elbe*, and the Salt-Works. The Catholicks are allowed a Toleration of their Religion in the Dutchy, and have Churches in the Town.

The Roads from *Magdebourg* to *Leipſic*, are ſo bad at this time, by reaſon of the Rains that have fallen for ſome Days paſt, that I have been three Days in getting from the one Town to the other. Indeed I went ſome Leagues out of my way, on purpoſe to ſee Barbi and Cohten. The firſt of theſe Towns belongs to a Prince of the Houſe of *Saxony*,

---

* He died in 1731, as is before obſerved.

Saxony, of the Branch of *Weissenfeld*; and has nothing considerable but the Prince's Palace, which makes a good appearance, and has commodious Apartments, elegantly furnished. There is a Salon, and a Closet, the Cielings of which are painted by *Peine*, and not the worst things he has done. The Palace has Gardens delightfully situate by the side of the *Elbe*. The Duke *de Barbi* is the only Prince of the House of *Saxony* who professes the *Calvinist* Religion, in which he was educated by his Father, who was at first a *Lutheran*. This Prince is a comely handsome young Man. He married N... *de Wirtemberg-Oels**, but has no Children. He has been in the Service of *Prussia*, and is Grand Provost of the Chapter of *Magdebourg*, and Knight of the Order of the White Eagle of *Poland*.

COHTEN, which is bigger than *Barbi* by one half, belongs to a Prince of *Anhalt* †; the only one of his Branch, tho' he has had two Wives. I desired leave to kiss his Hand; but he excus'd himself by pretending an Indisposition. I have observed that petty Princes are always more difficult of Access than great ones. The Town has no Fortifications; and I walk'd about a good while to see if there was any thing remarkable, but 'twas to no purpose; and I was oblig'd to confine myself to my Inn, which was one of the worst in *Europe*.

LEIPSIC stands in a fruitful Plain. This City, so famous for its Fairs, and for its University, may justly

---

* Her Name is *Augusta-Louisa*, she was born the 11th of *January* 1698, and is the Daughter of *Christian-Ulric*, Duke of *Wirtemberg-Oels* and *Bernstadt*, by his 3d Wife, *Sophia Wilhelmina*, of *East-Friesland*.

† This is *Augustus-Lewis*, who in 1728, succeeded his Brother *Leopold*. His second Wife *Emilia* of *Promnitz*, dying in 1732, he marry'd his Sister *Ann Frederica* of *Promnitz*; which Match, at that time, made a very great Noise. The Curious are referr'd to a Paper call'd *le Glaneur*, or the Gleaner, published in 1733, for what was said upon it. This Prince has had Children by his three Wives; and two Sons in particular by his second.

justly pass for the Jewel of the Electorate of *Saxony*; not only for the Beauty of its Structures, but for the considerable Revenue which it yields to its Sovereign, the King of *Poland*. 'Tis small, and fac'd with Ramparts, and a Ditch; but all these Fortifications are of little consequence. Its Castle, or rather Citadel, which joins to the Town, is a Place of greater Importance. There is always a good Garrison and Governour in it, who is at present General *Baumgarten*. As the Castle passes under the Denomination of the King's House, the *Roman* Catholicks have had a Chapel there ever since *Augustus* II. embraced their Religion.

The Suburbs of *Leipsic* are very large. The City has four Gates newly built of Free-Stone, which are magnificent, tho' not according to the Rules of Architecture.

At each Gate they have newly set up a Mile-Post, such as the *Romans* had formerly. There are the like Posts at the Gates of all the Towns, and even at the Villages in the Electorate of *Saxony*. From hence they count the Leagues, which are divided at the end of every Quarter of a Mile, by other Posts not so big, upon all the great Roads, shewing the Distances of the Places, and of the chief Towns; which is a mighty Convenience to Travellers, who were heretofore often impos'd upon by the Post-Masters, as to the Length of the Roads.

The Houses of *Leipsic* are large, very high, and substantially built of Free-Stone; and their being adorn'd with great fine Windows helps to set them off to the Eye. The Ground-Floors of most of the Houses are Warehouses, in which the foreign Merchants store the Goods they sell at the Fairs, which are three in number every Year, *viz.* at *New-year's-day*, *Easter*, and *Michaelmass*. The Concourse of Foreigners here at the Fair-Season, is so great that 'tis often a hard matter to get a

Lodg-

Lodging here for Love or Money. I myself saw in 1709, at the *New-year's* Fair, the late King of *Prussia*, the King and Queen of *Poland*, and 44 Princes or Princesses of Sovereign Families. The two Kings and the Queen lodged at the House of *Appel*, a Merchant; where the King of *Poland* always resides when he comes to *Leipsic*.

The University, formerly so famous, is very much decay'd: That of *Halle*, its Neighbour, and its Rival, in the King of *Prussia*'s Dominions, takes away a great many Students from it. They say that for some time past there have been more able Professors at *Halle*, where besides 'tis much cheaper living than at *Leipsic*; and where the Students are not such Spendthrifts, nor so much addicted to Expence and Gallantry.

The Gardens of Messieurs *Appel* and *Pose*, Merchants, in the Suburbs, are worth seeing. The first is large and magnificent: In the second are very uncommon Plants, cultivated with very great Care. The Gardeners of *Leipsic*, who are reckon'd the best in all *Germany*, value themselves upon forcing Nature; so that I have seen here, at *Easter* Fair, the Fruits, Flowers, and Pulse, of all the Seasons. The Asparagus here is delicious, and extraordinary large. Another Nicety at *Leipsic*, is its Larks, which are sent over all *Germany*; nay, to *Poland*, *Holland* and *Denmark*. I was assured, but I will not vouch for the Truth of it, that the very Custom-Duty paid for Larks at *Leipsic*, amounted to 12000 Crowns a-year; which Sum I thought the more considerable, because I think I have heard it said, that 60 Larks pay but a * Grosh the Duty; judge then how many there must be to make up the Sum of 12000 Crowns. But be it true or false, 'tis certain that there is not a Country in the World where these Birds are taken in such quantities; for,

* 'Tis the 24th part of a Dollar, or about 2 *d*. ¼ *Sterling*.

from *Michaelmass* to *Martinmass*, the Fields are cover'd with 'em.

Another Singularity is the multitude of Nightingales, in the Woods near *Leipsic*; whereof they take great numbers, and keep them in Cages: The Innkeeper's Daughter, where I lodged, had seven of them; and I have seen a great many at other Houses.

'Tis surprizing that so plentiful a Country as *Saxony* shou'd have no better Ordinarys. I don't mean *Leipsic* and *Dresden*, where, considering one is in *Germany*, we come off pretty well; tho' were it so in *Holland*, the *Netherlands*, or in *France*, we shou'd not think ourselves well us'd. I mean the little Towns and Villages in a Road so frequented as that from *Leipsic* to *Dresden*. There's Provision to be had at these Ordinarys, but then 'tis so ill dress'd, and the Houses so nasty, that 'tis enough to turn one's Stomach.

Setting out from *Leipsic*, at the opening of the Gates, I came betimes to WERMSTORF, or HUBERTSBOURG, (St. *Hubert*'s Palace,) a magnificent Hunting-Seat, which the Electoral Prince of *Saxony* is building at the Entrance of a Forest, where there are several Roads cut. This House is five Miles from *Leipsic*, and eight from *Dresden*; and when 'tis finish'd, will be large and magnificent: Men are hard at work upon it, and the main Body of it is already compleated. Their Royal Highnesses, the Prince and Princess, generally hunt here at Spring and Autumn. The Equipage for the Stag-hunting is very fine, the Liveries being Yellow, with Facings of blue Velvet, and Silver Lace at all the Seams.

After I had walk'd an Hour or two at *Hubertsbourg*, I proceeded on my Journey, and came to Dinner at MEISSEN, the Capital of *Misnia*. This City has nothing particular, besides its Manufacture

of

of Porcellane, which is so finely painted and enamell'd with Gold, that it is more beautiful than the Porcellane of *Japan*, and much dearer. The Invention of it is owing to an Alchymist, or one that pretended to be such; who had persuaded a great many People he cou'd make Gold. The King of *Poland* believ'd it as well as others, and to make sure of his Person, caus'd him to be committed to the Castle of *Konigstein*, three Miles from *Dresden*. There, instead of making Gold, that solid precious Metal, which puts Mankind on committing so many Follies, he invented Brittle Porcellane; by which, in one Sense, he made Gold, because the great Vent of that Ware brings a deal of Money into the Country.

After having pass'd the *Elbe*, over a wooden Bridge, going out of *Meissen*, I came in less than three Hours to DRESDEN, the Capital of the Electorate of *Saxony*. The City is pretty large, fortify'd with Art and Regularity; and very lightsome. Its Houses are high and substantial, the Streets broad, strait, well pav'd, neat, and in the Night-time well lighted. There are great Squares in it; and the whole City is so well laid out, that *Dresden* may be rank'd among the finest in the World.

The *Elbe* divides it into two Parts; which are distinguished by Old and New *Dresden*, and join'd together by a Bridge of Stone.

In order to give you a more perfect Idea of this City, I shall point out to you such things as I took most notice of. I shall begin with Old *Dresden*, which is the first that we come to from *Meissen*. At the Entrance of the Town, on the right hand, there is a great House, called the Palace of the *Indies*, or *Holland* House, which the King bought some Years ago of his Prime Minister, the Marshal Count *de Fleming*. All the Rooms of this Palace, which consists of three Stories, are so many Closets of *Japan* and *China* Wares. I don't believe that all the Warehouses in *Amsterdam* put together, are capable of furnishing such a quantity of uncommon old Porcellane, as is to be found here. The value of it is computed at a Million of Crowns. The very Houshold-Goods are *Indian*. There is one Set of Furniture, the like of which I never saw elsewhere: It consists of Feathers of various Colours, and all natural; inlaid with so much Art, that it might be taken for a fine flower'd Sattin.

This magnificent Palace has a Garden belonging to it, which looks towards the *Elbe*. It is adorn'd with Statues of white Marble, which the King caus'd to be purchas'd at *Rome*, of the Cardinals *Annibal* and *Alexander Albani*, Nephews to *Clement* XI. These Statues are much more priz'd here than they were at *Rome*.

Near the Palace of the *Indies* stands that of the Cadets; a magnificent Structure built by the States of *Saxony*, for maintaining two Companies of Cadets, all Gentlemen of the Country; who are there instructed in all the Sciences fitting for Persons of Quality.

Farther up in the same Street, there is an Amphitheatre, or Area, for the Battles of wild Beasts; of which a great number is kept for that purpose. Here are Lions, Tigers, Bears; in short, all the fiercest Animals from the four Quarters of the World.

The Bridge over the *Elbe*, which joins Old *Dresden* to the New, is scarce to be parallel'd, either for its Length or Substance. It has lately been made broader by forming Demy-Arches which support the Riders on each side. The Barriers are of Iron, well wrought. An Equestrian Statue of the King is going to be erected upon it.

The

The Palace or Castle joins to the Bridge, at the Entrance of New *Dresden*. This is an ancient Structure, which makes but a mean Appearance; and 'tis said, that the King intends it shall be pull'd down, and another built in its room; and that his Majesty has set apart eight Millions of Crowns for the Expence of it.

The inside of the Castle surpasses the outside. The State-Room is splendidly furnish'd. The Great Gallery contains several Curiosities, such as antique Busts, Vessels, and Pictures.

This Palace has two Chapels, one of which belongs to the *Roman* Catholicks, and the other to the *Lutherans*. The first was heretofore the Theatre for Operas, but the King turn'd it into a Chapel, upon account of the Marriage of his only Son with the Archdutchess, eldest Daughter to the Emperor *Joseph*; the second was always the Chapel of the Electors of *Saxony*. The King might, if he pleas'd, have order'd Mass to be celebrated in it, but he wou'd not give his Subjects that Handle for Complaint; besides, the late Queen, his Wife, having always stuck to the *Lutheran* Religion, in which she was born, he left her that Chapel for her use. The Treasure of it is extremely rich, and contains Vessels, Chasubles, and other things heretofore consecrated and given to this Chapel by the Piety of the Electors.

The Royal Treasury, commonly call'd the *Grune Gewölbe*, (the Green Vault,) is in the Palace. They are three arch'd Rooms, which contain immense Riches, and shine all over with Gold, Precious Stones, and Diamonds. 'Tis one of the finest Places in the World. There are several Sets of Brilliant Diamonds, Rubies, Emeralds, Pearls, Saphirs, and other Precious Stones. Every Set is compleat, and consists of Buttons for Clothes, Loops for Hats, Swords, Hangers, Canes, Sleeve-Buttons,

tons, Shoe-Buckles, Muffs, and Sword-Belts, Snuff-Boxes, Watches, Tweezer-Cases, Pocket-Books; in short, all the Jewels that can possibly be imagin'd, even to the Furniture of a Horse; so that were I to write down every Particular, I should furnish you a Volume. And they all look the better, for being ranged with wonderful Nicety in Cases of Crystal.

To the Castle belongs a Garden, call'd the *Zwinger Garten*, which is the *Tuilleries* of *Dresden*, but not extensive enough to deserve the Name of a Garden. 'Tis encompass'd with Buildings of Free-Stone, which are Green-Houses for Orange-Trees. The Structure consists but of one Floor, on which are rais'd six large Pavilions, *viz.* three in front at the Entrance, two on the sides, and one over the Portico at the Entrance; which have all a Communication with one another, by a Platform that has Balustrades adorn'd with Statues. It wou'd be hard to say what Order of Architecture prevails most in this Edifice, the Carv'd-Work with which it is decorated, being more of the *Gothic* than the modern Taste.

Near to this Building there's a Palace which makes a great Shew, but the Apartments are by much too small, and too low for the Ornaments employ'd about them. The King caus'd this House to be built for the Countess *de Cosel*, at the time when that Lady was in high Favour. No Cost was spar'd in it; but 'tis pity that a more skilful Architect had not been pitched upon to conduct it.

There are five or six other Houses, which are here call'd *Hotels*, but in *Italy* wou'd certainly pass for Palaces. The Hotel *de Fubl* in the Street of *Pirnitz* is one of this number. It was erected by the Great Marshal *de Fubl* who on his Death-bed left it to his Wife, of whom it was purchas'd by the Count *de Fleming*. That Minister sold it soon after

after to the King, who made confiderable Embelifhments in it, and furnifhed it richly. In this Condition his Majefty gave it in 1728, to the Marfhal *de Wackerbarth*, to make him amends when he had been burnt out of the Houfe he liv'd in, as Governour of *Drefden*. After this, the Governour's Houfe being rebuilt, the King bought the other Houfe again of the Count *de Wackerbarth*, and has made it a Depofitary of his Medals, Antiquities, and Curiofities.

To be fure you have heard that this Fire broke out at the Governour's Houfe in the Night-time, while the King of *Pruffia* was here. His Majefty actually lodg'd at the Governour's Houfe; and was in Bed when the Fire burft out with fuch fury that he had but juft time to make his Efcape in his Night-Gown, and to fave a little Box in which there were Papers of confequence; for the Floor of his Bed-Chamber fell in, the moment after the King was gone out of it. An Officer, his Wife, and her Maid-Servant perifh'd in the Flames. The Count *de Wackerbarth* only fav'd his Wardrobe and his Plate; for his fine Library, and a noble Collection which he had of Drawings, one of the compleateft and beft chofen Setts in *Europe*, were confum'd.

The Hotel of *Hoybm* is the moft confiderable Building in *Drefden*. In about fix Years time it had four different Owners. It was founded by the King's Favourite, the Count *de Fitztuhm**, his Great Chamberlain, and Minifter of State; who having been kill'd in a Duel at *Warfaw*, by the Count *de St.*

---

* He had been in the King's Service ever fince he was only Prince of *Saxony*, and always took care to keep in Favour; he being, of all the Favourites, the Perfon that had the greateft Share of the Prince's Confidence: Neverthelefs, he ow'd his Advancement, and his illuftrious Poft of Minifter of the Cabinet, to the Intereft of the Countefs *de Cofel*, who caus'd the Chancellor *Beichling*, who had always been the Favourite Minifter, to be turn'd out.

St. Gilles, a *Piedmontese* that came to *Poland* to seek his Fortune, his Widow sold it to Marshal *Fleming*, who dying at *Vienna* not long after he had purchased it, the House fell to his Son, a weakly Child, who did not long survive him. His Mother, who was a *Radzivil*, was his Heiress, and one of the greatest Matches in *Europe*. She was soon after married again to a *Polander* whom she follow'd into his own Country; and when she left *Dresden*, she sold her House to the Count *de Hoym*, who at present occupies it.

Not far from this House are the King's Stables, which are well worth seeing, there being a great number of wonderful fine Horses, and some of all sorts of the rarest Breeds. Over the Stables, are Rooms full of fine Equipage, consisting of sumptuous Saddles and Housings, Sleds and magnificent Harness. Many of these Equipages are of the *Turkish* Mode, and plated with massy Silver, adorn'd with precious Stones.

The Arsenal, which is much boasted of here, cannot be reckon'd a fine one by any but such as have not seen the Arsenal of *Berlin*, to which it is not to be compar'd. There are several Rooms in it full of Arms, Brass Cannon, Helmets, and Cuirasses, which are the Tapestry of Arsenals.

Thus, Sir, you have all that I observed in *Dresden*: it remains for me to give you some Account of its Suburbs, and of the Pleasure-Houses which the King has in the Neighbourhood of this City.

The Suburbs of *Dresden* are very extensive, but have no Building of consequence, except the Palace in the King's great Garden, built by his Majesty's Mother, and that call'd the *Turkish* Palace, because it is furnished entirely after the *Turkish* manner. The King gave an Entertainment at this Palace to the Princess his Daughter-in-law, on account of

her

her Arrival at *Dresden*, which was so particular that I think it deserves a Digression.

Upon the Feast-Day, the whole Court appeared at the *Turkish* Palace, in the Habits of *Turks*. The King came in the Dress of a *Sultan*, but without any Attendance. His Majesty was soon after follow'd by the Princess his Daughter-in-law, with her Ladies. Her Royal Highness, for whom the Entertainment was made, found a Body of Janizaries drawn up in the Court-Yard of the Palace. The King receiv'd her at the Entrance of his Apartment, and conducted her into a Hall spread with fine Tapestry, and laid with Cushions richly embroider'd.

The King and Princess being seated, were served by twenty-four Negroes in sumptuous Dresses, with Sherbet, Coffee, and Sweet-Meats, in great Vessels of massy Silver; nor were scented Waters, and perfumed Handkerchiefs forgot. After this Collation, they drew near the Windows to see the *Pillau* (which is the Rice of *Turky*) and the King's Bounty-Money distributed to the Janizaries. This was follow'd by a Comedy, with an Entertainment of *Turkish* Dances. Then came the Supper, the Guests sitting cross-legg'd upon the Cushions, and the Courses being served up after the fashion of *Turky*, by the Negroes and young *Turks*. While they were at Table, the Company was diverted by the various Leaps and Postures of certain Tumblers and Rope-Dancers. Supper being over, they went into the Garden, which was illuminated with several Thousands of Crystal Lamps. There was Tilting, and shooting at the Mark, and whenever the Mark was hit, a Sky-Rocket was sent up, which for the time seem'd to sprinkle Thousands of Stars among those in the Firmament. After this, the Company retir'd into the Palace, where the King and the Princess open'd the Ball, and there was dancing till five o'clock in the

the Morning, when the Ball was concluded with a sumptuous Breakfast that was serv'd at the several Tables, after the manner of our own Country; which, with the leave of the *Mussulmen*, is as good as theirs.

The finest Royal Houses, are *Pilnitz* and *Moritzbourg*. The King, who is certainly of all Sovereigns the most magnificent, keeps Men continually at work, in embellishing those Places. The Works are carried on by the Direction of Monsf. *Bot*, whom I think to be not inferior to *Bernini*, and I doubt not, such is my high Idea of him, that as he is supported by the Generosity of a Great King, he will accomplish such Works as are worthy of himself, and of his Master too.

I have now done with the Description of the Palaces and Royal Houses, in which, I own I have been defective, and would gladly have been excus'd from giving it; but you would have it, and I cou'd not help gratifying you. I pass now to something more important; and shall entertain you with the present State of the Royal Family, and the Characters of the most distinguish'd Persons at Court.

FREDERIC-AUGUSTUS II. King of *Poland*, and Elector of *Saxony*, is the Chief of this August Family. This Monarch, whom no Man surpasses in Strength and Dexterity, and whom few Princes equal in Generosity, is the second Son of *John George* III. Elector of *Saxony*. He succeeded his Brother *John George* IV. in the Electorate, and was chose King of *Poland* after the Death of the Great *Sobieski*, notwithstanding the Intrigues of the Emissaries of *France* who declared for the Prince of *Conti*.

When *Frederic-Augustus* ascended the Throne, he brought all the Virtues to it fitting for a Great King. The Agreeableness of his Person, his Majestic Air, his Heroic Strength, his Good-Nature, his Politeness, and his well-known Valour, were

the least of his Qualities. Never was any Prince more magnificent, nor did any one either give more, or with a better Grace. As a General and a Statesman, he was never too much lifted up by Prosperity, nor shock'd by Adversity; so that he was observed, when in the depth of his Misfortunes, to act and treat even with his Enemies, with that Air of Complaisance and Satisfaction, which Men inur'd to great Affairs know how to assume, in the midst of the cruellest Mortifications. This Prince, in his Youth, travelled to the chief Countries of *Europe*, and where-ever he came, was admir'd for his Strength, his Air, and Dexterity. Amongst other Adventures, a very odd one befel him in his Travels, at *Venice*. There happen'd to be in that City a famous Astrologer, who had the Reputation of being well read in the Book of Fate. The King, who was only Prince at that time, had a mind that he should calculate his Nativity, and for that purpose went to the Astrologer's House, accompanied by two Gentlemen. They were all three dress'd in plain Apparel, and the Prince, to disguise himself still the more, had conceal'd his brown Hair under a fair Peruke. He enter'd the last Man, into the Astrologer's House, and seem'd to be rather as an Attendant, than a Companion of the others. But to him the Astrologer first address'd himself, calling him by the Titles of *My Lord* and *Highness*. The Prince told him that his Rank in the World was much too mean for such high Compliments; but the Astrologer made answer, he knew very well whom he spoke to, and that it was in vain for him to think of concealing himself from such a Man as he. The Prince and his small Retinue were then conducted by him into a Closet, where he shewed him a Looking-Glass. *Cast your Eye on that Mirror*, said he to the Prince, *and there you will see the principal Events of your Life.* The Prince without
any

any scruple, look'd accordingly, and saw himself at first in the Habit of an Elector; afterwards, with a Crown on his Head, and a royal Mantle on his Shoulders; and at last, full of Wounds, and bath'd in his Blood.

This Story, which I should not give you for true, if I had not heard it from a great Nobleman who told me he had it from the King's own Mouth, is however, not without a Parallel; for it is pretended, that a Mason told Madam *de Maintenon*, when she was no more than Madam *Scarron*, what her Fortune and Rank would be in *France*. I could mention several other Instances to you of the same nature, which all surprize me, tho' they don't convince me. Be it as it will, two Articles of the Prediction made to the King of *Poland* are fully accomplished; as to the third, may Heaven confound the Astrologer *.

The King of *Poland* spends part of his time in his Kingdom, and part of it in his Electorate. 'Tis true, that he seems to take more delight in *Saxony* than in *Poland*; and 'tis in my Opinion very natural for him to do so; *Saxony* being his hereditary Country,

---

* This part of the Prophecy did not take place, for the King of *Poland* died in his Bed at *Warsaw* the 1st of *Feb.* 1733, N. S. This Monarch set out in the Month of *January*, from *Dresden*, to hold the Dyet of *Poland*, which was open'd at *Warsaw*, and every thing seem'd like to pass to the Satisfaction of the King and Kingdom, when these fine Hopes were demolished by the Death of this Prince, who in his last Sickness, preserved the Character of the Hero, betraying neither Fear nor Folly; all his Wish being that he might live to embrace his Son.

The King found himself in a declining State, several Years. During the last Dyet at *Grodno*, a Mortification seiz'd his Foot; for which reason, M. *de Petit*, a Surgeon of *Paris*, whom the King sent for on purpose, cut off two Toes, and set his Majesty upon his Legs again, but told him withall, he must observe such a Regimen as he prescribed to him, or else it would break out again. But the King finding himself better, neglected *Petit*'s Advice, and died of the Mortification, as the Surgeon had foretold.

Country, where he is so absolute that his Will is the Law of his Subjects, by whom he is rather ador'd than belov'd: besides, 'tis *Saxony* that furnishes him wherewithal to support his Dignity, and offers him every thing conducive to the Pleasures of a Great King; and it is there that he has a Court, the most brilliant in *Europe*, not only for its Splendor, but for Magnificence and Pleasures; whereas in *Poland*, he has only the vain Pageantry of Royalty; being under greater Limitations than any Sovereign in the World; so that the least Innovation, the least Act of Authority, makes the *Poles* clamorous, and they presently think they are excused from paying him that Obedience which they owe him. All the Gentlemen here are their own Masters; and the Noblemen behave so much like Sovereigns, that they never go to Court but to demand Favours, which if they obtain, they go away ungrateful, and if they are deny'd, they retire with the Intention of taking a Revenge on the first Opportunity: For the Climate being rough, the People are fierce; and the King, tho' adored in *Saxony*, is scarce beloved in *Poland*.

The Electoral Prince, this King's only Son, is lusty, proper, and well made, and like the King his Father is adroit in all bodily Exercises. He loves Pleasure, but 'tis with Moderation, and is heartily attach'd to the Religion which he has embrac'd. He is stiff and reserved, without being haughty, which is a Temper that he derives from the late Queen his Mother*, whom he very much resembles. To such as have the Honour of Access to him, and of being known to him, he is gracious, familiar and very civil. His Royal Highness has been admir'd for his good Qualities in a great

* *Eberhardine of Brandenbourg-Bareith* Queen of *Poland*, and Electoress of *Saxony*: she died at her Seat at *Pretch* near *Wittenberg*, some Years before the King.

part of *Europe*, particularly in *Germany*, *France*, and *Italy*, where he has spent several Years. No Son can have more respect to a Parent than he has for the King his Father, whose Will and Pleasure he never oppos'd in any one Instance; and whose Person he has always honour'd even in his Ministers. Of all Pleasures he seems to bestow most Time in Hunting; nevertheless he makes it only as an Amusement without being passionately fond of it. His Royal Highness's Confident is *Solckoffski* or *Sulkowski**, a *Polish* Gentleman who was once his Page; and by thus making him his Favourite, for which he cannot but be applauded, he shews that he is capable of distinguishing true Merit. I had frequently the Honour of making my Compliments to this Prince while he was at *Paris*, and this is now the second time that I have had the same favour at *Dresden*, where I find he is the same gracious Personage as ever. The last time that I had the Honour of being introduc'd to him he talk'd a great deal to me about *Paris*, and when he dismiss'd me, he said he was sorry to think that *Dresden* would not afford me so many Pleasures as *Paris*.

The same Day that I waited on the Prince, I was introduced to the Princess his Royal Highness's Consort, who is the late Emperor *Joseph*'s eldest Daughter. The Voice of the People is unanimous in the Character of this Princess. All Mankind agrees that she has not her superior for Good-nature, Piety, Charity, Modesty, and in a word for all, the Virtue of the Soul: To please her Husband, and to give her Children an Education suitable to their Birth, is her principal Endeavour. 'Tis rare to find a happier Couple than their Royal Highnesses; for Marriage, which generally cools the warmest Passions, seems on the contrary to have animated their reci-

---

* This Prince succeeding his Father in the Electorate, and afterwards in the Throne of *Poland*, rais'd M. *Solckofski* to the Dignity of a Count, and appointed him his Master of the Horse, and one of his Cabinet Ministers.

reciprocal Affection to such a degree that they are a Pattern for the Imitation of their Court.

Their Royal Highnesses Children are so young that I shall say but little of them *. Their eldest Son very much resembles the Pictures that I have seen of the Emperor *Joseph* when he was a Child. This young Prince seems to me to be of a very delicate Constitution, and has so great a Weakness in his Knees that he can scarce stand: The Physicians say it will go off as he grows up, but their Promises are no Gospel for me.

The two Princes of the Blood, who commonly reside at *Dresden*, are *John Adolphus* of *Saxe-Weissenfels* †, a Prince of uncommon Merit, whose Sentiments and Actions are no disparagement to his Birth; and *Maurice-William* of *Saxe-Zeits*, the last of his Branch. He was persuaded by his Uncle the late Cardinal *de Saxe-Zeits* to abjure the *Lutheran* Religion and to embrace the ecclesiastical State: He is Bishop of *Konigsgratz* in *Bohemia*, Provost of *Alten Ottingen* in *Bavaria*, and a Canon of *Cologne, Liege*, and *Aichstedt*, and is descended from such a Family that it may be presum'd, he will some day or other, be advanc'd to the Purple ‖.

N. B. *What follows, is a more particular Account of the Electoral Family of* Saxony, *translated from the Baron's State of it; which is prefix'd to the second Edition of these* Memoirs.

Augustus III. King of *Poland* Great Duke of *Lithuania* and Elector of *Saxony*, was born the seventh of *October* 1696. He is the only Son of *Augustus* II. the last King of *Poland* and of *Eberhardina* of *Brandenbourg-Bareith*. His Grandmother, *Anne*

Princess

---

* The Electoral Prince (now Elector of *Saxony* and King of *Poland*) has eight Children, *viz.* three Princes and five Princesses; so that the Electoral Branch is not like to be extinct very soon.

† The Velt-Marshal the Count de *Wackerbarth* being dead, the Elector nam'd this Prince Generalissimo of the Troops of the Electorate in 1734.

‖ This Prince has for some time past resided at *Konigsgratz*.

Princess Royal of *Denmark*, Widow of *John George* the third Elector of *Saxony*, took care of him in his Infancy, and impress'd him with those Sentiments of Piety, Humanity, and Justice, which render him at this day the Darling of his People, and the Pattern of Kings.

At a proper Age, the King his Father took him out of the hands of the Women, and committed him to the Care of Monsieur *de Miltitz*, a Gentleman of a good Family; whom Learning, good Behaviour and solid Virtue render'd worthy of such an Employment.

The Prince, who always found Charms in Virtue, was sensible of the Merit of his Governor: He lov'd him, was inseparable from him, and receiv'd his Advice with a Docility, which, at his tender Age, was a presage he wou'd be possess'd of that Fund of Wisdom which now renders him worthy of his Throne.

While the young Prince was under the Conduct of the Women, God was pleas'd to touch the Heart of the late King his Father: That Monarch, who happen'd to be born a *Lutheran*, was converted to the *Roman* Catholick Religion, and not long after elected King of *Poland*; and his Majesty being convinc'd of the Purity of the Religion which he had embrac'd, was inclin'd to make a Convert also of the Prince his Son. Nevertheless, such was the Respect the King had for her Royal Highness his Mother, that he was loth that august Princess shou'd be an Eye-witness of the young Prince's renouncing a Religion which she had taught him, and to which she was strenuously attach'd: He resolv'd therefore to remove him, and sent him to *Francfort* to be present at the Coronation of the Emperor *Charles* VI. His Companion in this Journey, was M. *de Miltitz*; but as this Gentleman's Attachment to *Luther*'s Doctrine made the King apprehensive that he wou'd thwart his Views, he recall'd recall'd him, and appointed the Count *de Cofta,* and the Baron *de Hagen,* to be his Son's Governors.

The Count who was a *Polander* and Palatine of *Livonia,* was not only of noble Birth, but a Gentleman of folid Piety, profound Learning, great Probity, and as much refpected for his Principles as belov'd for his good Behaviour and Politenefs.

The Baron *de Hagen* was of a Family of some Diftinction in the Electorate of *Triers*: He was Ambaffador from the King at the Emperor's Election, and at his Coronation at *Francfort* : His Behaviour was more grave than the Count *de Cofta*'s, but he was not inferior to the Count for Learning, Integrity, and good Senfe.

Under the Conduct of thefe two Gentlemen, the Prince set out to vifit a part of *Germany* and *Italy,* where he embrac'd the *Roman* Catholick Religion; his Profeffion of which, was however for a long time as private as it is now exemplary; for he did not declare his alteration of Religion 'till after the Death of her moft Serene Highnefs his Grandmother, who died the firft of *July* 1717. During this the Prince made the Tour of *France,* where, tho' he travell'd under the Name of the Count *de Mifnia, Lewis* XIV. caus'd all the Honours to be paid to him which were due to the Son of a great King.

The Court of *France* was charm'd with that Politenefs, that noble Modefty, and that Fund of Wifdom which accompany'd this Prince's Actions and Converfation: They admir'd him and were forry for his Departure. He travell'd a fecond time to *Italy,* where he acquir'd that fine Tafte of Men and Things and that Knowledge of Architecture, Painting, and other curious Arts, which is fo ufeful for great Princes. *Germany,* upon the return of this Prince, blefs'd itfelf for having given him birth, and offer'd up Prayers that all its Princes might be like him. His Royal Highnefs ftay'd a confiderable while at *Vienna,* where

where he maintain'd the Reputation he had acquir'd in the several Countries he had seen. He returned at length to *Saxony*, where there was an universal Joy for his Arrival. The *Saxons* were charm'd to see the Prince that was design'd by Heaven to be their Sovereign, so worthy of that Command. One day or other, they said, we shall lose the most righteous of Kings, and the best of Masters, but we shall find restor'd in his Son, his heroic Stature, his majestic Air, his Magnanimity, the same Temper for Goodness, Equity and Generosity; the Spirit of the great *Augustus* will be always present with us; and all our Loss will be that of his Personal Appearance.

Not long after the Prince's Return to *Dresden*, *Augustus Christopher* Count *de Wackerbarth** treated at *Vienna* for the Marriage of his Royal Highness to the most serene Archdutchess *Maria Josepha*, eldest Daughter of the late Emperor *Joseph*. The Count *de Flemming*, Prime Minister and Velt-Marshal of *Saxony*, solemnly demanded the most serene Archdutchess in Marriage; and the Prince repair'd to *Vienna* to espouse her. The Ceremony was perform'd in the Chapel of *la Favorita*, with all the Pomp suitable to so great a Match. Some Days after this, their Royal Highnesses set out for *Dresden*, where they were receiv'd with an unparallell'd Magnificence. *Augustus* II. the most splendid of Kings, and a Prince who had the best Fancy for ordering of Entertainments, outdid himself; he thought nothing too good for celebrating the Nuptials of his so worthy a Son, with a Princess whose Ancestors were all Emperors.

The Rejoicings having lasted forty Days, the King set out for his Kingdom, leaving the Prince Regent, as he always did whenever he went from his Electorate. In

---

* Who died, *August* 13, 1734, a Minister of the Cabinet, Velt-Marshal and Governour of *Dresden*.

In 1726, the Prince himself took a Journey to *Poland*, to which Country he had once before accompanied the King his Father in 1711, but then made no long stay. There he won the Hearts of the chief Nobility, who from that moment thought him worthy of succeeding one day to their Governor, the Great *Augustus*. They were pleased to see, that he honour'd their Countryman, the Count *Sulkowski*, with his Confidence, and they thought it a happy Omen for their Nation, blessing their Stars, that the Prince distinguished Virtue in one born among themselves.

His Royal Highness being convinced that of all the Sums laid out by Princes, there are none less liable to censure than what they expend in Buildings, undertook that of *Wermsdorf*, which he afterwards call'd *Hubertsbourg*; and he finish'd that great Work in a little time, by the assistance of the King his Father: For, in short, it would have been impossible for his Royal Highness to have defray'd all the Expence of it himself. It was already very wonderful to see with what Prudence he directed his Finances. His Revenue being settled, his Expence was suitable to his Rank; he had a numerous Houshold, his Hunting-Equipage was sumptuous, yet he did good to all that made their Necessity known to him; his Charities were truly Royal, every body was paid; the Noblemen and the Tradesmen receiv'd their Pensions and Salaries punctually; and his Accounts were so regularly kept and discharged by the Count *Sulkowski*, that the Prince was never in debt.

The Prince commonly spent the Season for hunting the Stag at *Hubertsbourg*, and employ'd the remainder of his time at *Dresden*, in all manner of Exercises, being admired in every Action, for the Grace, Strength, and Dexterity with which he perform'd it, as well as for the Sobriety and Regularity of his Manners; for he kept as regular Hours then, as he does now.

Augustus III. never knew what it was to be idle or vicious. Such is his Chastity and Fidelity to his august Spouse, that he never gave her the least Reason so much as to suspect his Honour. He games only for amusement, and never plays so high that the loss of the Stake can put those out of temper who have the Honour to be of his Party. But of all the Virtues of *Augustus* III. there is none, most certainly, which has made him more the Favourite of Heaven, than the inviolable Respect he always manifested for the King his Father, who tenderly lov'd him; and never was a Son, Heir to so powerful a Dominion, more affected for the loss of a Father, than he was when he heard of the death of his. His Affliction was impress'd deeply in his Countenance, when he receiv'd the homage of his capital City, at his first appearance in publick; and to this very day, he is ready to melt in tears at the sight of any Object that calls him to mind; for which reason the People of *Dresden*, rather than renew his Sorrow, forbear the mention of a King whom *Europe* has plac'd in the Rank of its greatest Men.

Prince FREDERIC-AUGUSTUS, when he became Elector, did not alter his Manners, but retain'd the same Piety, the same Regularity. He kept most of the Servants of the late King his Father, and settled Pensions on those whom he thought fit to dismiss. His first Care, when he came to the Electorate, was to provide himself with Ministers, whose Candor and Sincerity were above Envy it self. For this purpose, he call'd to his Cabinet Council, the Count *de Gabaleon-Wackerbarth-Salmour*, M. *de Baudissin*, the Count *Sulkowski*, and M. *de Bruhl*; to the two last of whom he committed the Direction of Affairs.

All *Saxony* applauded this Choice, and doubted not of being very happy under the Reign of a Prince, who was capable of forming so true a Judgment of Persons for his Ministers. But what the *Saxons* saw with extraordinary Satisfaction, was the sure Proof the King gave of his Gratitude and Esteem for Virtue, in recalling M. *de Miltitz*, heretofore his Governor, who for some Years past was retired to his Estate. This Gentleman wou'd fain have been excus'd from returning to Court, alledging his great Age, and his being a Stranger to Business; when his Majesty sent him word, that he requir'd no more at his hands than what his Health wou'd permit; that he knew his Probity, his Love for his Country, and his Attachment to himself; that therefore he was willing he shou'd be near his Person, and assist him with his Advice, which he knew wou'd be solid, by what he gave him when he had the charge of his Education. In this manner FREDERIC AUGUSTUS, by the display of his Gratitude, an uncommon Virtue (especially among Princes) encourag'd his Courtiers to do what might also give them a Title to it.

These great Qualities procur'd him the Suffrages of the most judicious Part of the Republic of *Poland* which chose him for King. His Majesty having sent the Count *de Gabaleon-Wackerbarth-Salmour*, and M. *Baudissin* to *Warsaw*, with the Character of Plenipotentiaries, to take care of his Interests, these Ministers found the *Polish* Lords very much divided: Foreign Gold, with the Intrigues, Cabals, and ensnaring Promises of a Minister who was lavish of it; all these had corrupted a great number of them, and others were oppress'd, and must undoubtedly have submitted to Violence, if they had not had a very great share of Courage and Love to their Country. God, who never abandons the Virtuous, was their Support and their

Pro-

Protector, as well as the Shield of the Plenipotentiaries, whose sacred Character could not guard them from all manner of Outrage. And tho' the Blood of the *Jagellons*, which flows in this Prince's Veins, tho' his being the Son of one of the greatest Kings that *Poland* ever had, as well as his own Dignity of a Sovereign, ought to have procured him the Respect of all the *Poles*, yet every Person and Thing belonging to him at *Warsaw*, was maltreated. Such was, at that time, the unhappy Fate of *Poland*; Oppression and Tyranny having succeeded the glorious, mild, and peaceful Reign of *Augustus* II.

Mean time, those generous Noblemen who had so bravely stood up in the defence of the Liberties and Honour of their Country, after having tried all their Efforts to reclaim their wandering Brethren, found they could not succeed, and therefore broke up; after which, they met in the very same Place where *Henry de Valois* had been elected, and there they chose and proclaim'd AUGUSTUS Elector of *Saxony*, King of *Poland*. They then sent a Deputation to his Majesty, to intreat him to come immediately, with the Queen his Consort, to take possession of the Throne. The King comply'd with their Intreaty, and set out from *Dresden*, after having return'd solemn Thanks to God, the sovereign Disposer of Crowns, and of the Fortune of Kings.

In a few days the Queen followed the King, and overtook him at *Tarnovitz*, where their Majesties received the grand Deputation from *Poland*; and after giving them Audience, proceeded in their Journey towards *Cracow*. There the King made his Royal Entry on the 14th of *January* 1734, and on the 17th of that Month, their Majesties were consecrated and crowned by *Lipsky* the Bishop of that See.

Some time after this august Ceremony, which, in *Poland*, is absolutely necessary and essential for a King Elect, the Queen return'd to *Saxony*; but the King staid at *Cracow*, where he held a Diet, in which he made several Regulations for restoring the Tranquillity of the Kingdom. When the Diet was ended, his Majesty march'd towards *Dantzic*, which the *Russians*, his Allies, had invested, in order to drive out the Primate and his Adherents, who were retir'd thither.

But after a March of several Days, which the Severity of the Weather render'd very painful, his Majesty yielded to the Instances that were made to him from *Saxony*, to assist in Person at the opening of the Assembly of States which he was under a necessity of calling; and he returned to *Dresden*, where his Arrival caus'd an inexpressible Joy. Mean time the Army, under the Command of the Prince of *Saxe-Weissenfels* continued its March towards *Dantzic*.

The King was accompanied by a great number of *Polish* Noblemen, who finding themselves unable to oppose the Rage of the Primate's Party in their several Countries, came to seek shelter in *Saxony*, where his Majesty receiv'd them, and still entertains them, in a manner which cannot but convince them of his Gratitude, and give them greater Hopes of what Favours they may expect, when the Tranquillity of *Poland* is restor'd.

The King, after his Return from *Cracow*, summon'd the States of his Electorate, and open'd the Assembly with the usual Ceremonies. He was seated on his Throne, accompanied by the chief Lords of his Court, as well the *Polish* as *Saxons*. M. *de Miltitz*, his Privy Counsellor, sat on the Right-hand of the Throne; and, in the King's Name, made a Speech to the States, wherein he declared to them that his Majesty intended to make no Innovation

vation in the Affairs of Religion, but to let his Proteſtant Subjects enjoy their Privileges, as they had been granted and confirm'd to them by the late King. Then they told him the Motives which had engag'd the King to call them together, and demanded the neceſſary Subſidies for defraying the extraordinary Expences which his Majeſty had been neceſſarily involved in thro' the Calamities of the Time. M. *de Heſler*, Adminiſtrator of the Office of hereditary Marſhal of *Saxony*, return'd an Anſwer in the Name of the States, and ſpoke with a Dignity, and all the Decorum due to ſo auguſt an Aſſembly. He aſſur'd the King of the reſpectful and inviolable Fidelity and Attachment of his Subjects to his ſacred Perſon. And in truth, 'tis impoſſible for a People to be better affected to their Sovereign, and more diſpoſed to contribute to every thing that is capable of augmenting his Glory.

The King's voluntary Declaration to his States that he would make no Innovation in the Affairs of Religion, won the Hearts of his Subjects to ſuch a degree, that there is not a *Saxon* who would make any ſcruple to ſacrifice his Life and Fortune for his Service. And the ſaid Declaration does equal Honour to the Juſtice of the Monarch, and the Wiſdom of his Miniſters.

While the King was employ'd with his States in ſecuring the Happineſs and Tranquility of *Saxony*, his Majeſty received Advice, that his Army, after having join'd the *Ruſſians*, had obliged the *Dantzickers* to ſurrender, and that the *Poliſh* Lords of the contrary Party petition'd for leave to remove to ſome Place where they might pay him their homage. The King, in imitation of the great Emperor whoſe Name he bears, after having made a Conqueſt, thought, like him, of nothing more than to make thoſe happy whom the Fortune of War had ſubmitted to his Arms. His Majeſty did not take

any

any advantage of his Victory, but forgetting past Offences, repair'd to the Abbey of *Oliva*, near *Dantzic*, where he receiv'd the Submission of the *Dantzickers*, and the Allegiance of the Lords that were the Primate's Adherents. By his Modesty and Goodness, he charm'd the Vanquished, and convinc'd them of their Obligation to pay him that Esteem which before perhaps they did not think was their Duty to grant to him. The Greatness of his Soul, which inclines him to sympathize with the Misfortunes of the Unhappy, hinder'd him from entering *Dantzic*, the desolate State of that City being so afflicting a Scene to him, that he cou'd not bear to see it. The *Dantzickers*, by their submission, were become his Subjects; their present Misfortunes, and their past Mistakes, affected him to such a degree, that he was fearful of being put in mind of them, and refus'd to appear among them, crown'd with those Laurels which he had reap'd by their defeat. So much Modesty, worthy of the most glorious Triumph, gain'd him the Prayers of the People, in which his Majesty saw more Charms, than he wou'd have found in Trophies, and the most stately Triumphal Arches.

The King having provided for the pressing Necessities of his Kingdom, return'd to his Electorate, where the States continued their Deliberations ever since his Absence. Now that his Majesty is return'd, the Care of the State is almost his constant Employment. His Recreations are either taking the Air on horseback, Hunting, the *Italian* Opera, or else going to Concerts, which the Queen, who is a great Lover of Music, causes to be perform'd in her own Apartment. Their Majesties generally dine together, and admit the Nobility of both Sexes to their Table.

There,

There, the King observes that Temperance which so much becomes sovereign Princes. All his Hours, as has been already observ'd, are regulated; and all his Actions accompanied with Devotion, good Order, and Equity. Never did King better discharge that sacred Character; being always firm and tranquil, Danger cou'd never affright him. He accepted the Crown, tho' he saw he cou'd never fix it on his Head without infinite Pains, Peril, and Cares. The Advantage he had gain'd over his Enemies did not seem to have flush'd him; he was sorry he had not been able to reclaim them by gentle Methods, and ascribes the happy Success of his Arms solely to Providence.

Thus have I given you a very imperfect Account of the Virtues and Actions of a King, which plainly denote that the perfect honest Man (a Title not unworthy even of the sacred Majesty of Kings) forms his Character. As for his Stature, 'tis such as, one wou'd think, those ought to have who are born to command. He has a robust and vigorous Constitution, a sound Judgment, a happy Memory, a generous and beneficent Soul, the necessary Constituents of the Hero and the Christian. His Conduct is regulated by a great Attachment to the Principles of Religion. His Aim and his Application are to render his Subjects happy; and he only longs for Peace that they may taste the Fruits of it.

As to her MAJESTY the QUEEN, the Name of that august Princess, whom Heaven has endowed with all manner of Virtues, to be the worthy Wife of a King, is MARIA JOSEPHA, who was born the 8th of *December* 1699, and is the eldest Daughter of *Joseph* Emperor of the *Romans*, and of *Wilhelmina-Amelia* of *Brunswic-Lunenbourg-Hanover*. Her Marriage to the King, then the Prince Royal, was celebrated at *Vienna*, the 20th of *August* 1719,

betwixt

betwixt 8 and 9 a Clock at Night, in the Chapel of the Palace of the *Favorita*, by the Pope's Nuncio, who next day perform'd the solemn Mass. In a few days after, this Princess set out with her Husband for *Saxony*. It has already been observed with what Pomp she was received by the King her Father-in-law; and the Veneration paid her by the Subjects, was equal to the Magnificence of her Reception by the King. The Returns that the Princess made on her part, manifested a Goodness which nothing cou'd resist; so that she had the Homage and the Hearts both of the Courtiers and the common People. Being the Daughter of a Princess, whom the World respects even more for her Virtues than for the Splendour of that extraordinary Grandeur with which she is inviron'd, her Royal Highness's sole Concern was to walk in the Steps of that august Mother, the Pattern of Princesses, and the Honour of Religion. She conceiv'd a Respect for the King her Father-in-law, and the Queen her Mother-in-law, from which she never departed; and now that she is a Sovereign, she has no other Cares than to render a Nation happy which is worthy of being so for its Affection and Fidelity to its Electors. She is inviolably attach'd to her Duties, full of Tenderness and Respect for her Husband, and always wisely employ'd in what may procure him solid Comfort. She continually gives him Examples of Piety and Charity; she is beneficent to all that make their Necessities known to her, and seems to think every unfortunate Subject merits her Protection. The Care she takes of her Children is not only the Care of a tender Mother, but of a Queen, who, in love to the State, is desirous to form their Minds, so as to render them worthy of being its Sovereigns, and to procure them the advantage of being more respected, if possible, for their Virtues than their Birth.

The Queen, who went with the King to *Cracow*, and there receiv'd the Crown, return'd after her Coronation to *Saxony*, where she is belov'd and reverenc'd by People of all Ranks. This august Princess seems to have an Air of Gravity, as have all the Princes of the most serene House of *Austria*; but as she is serious, so she is discreet, modest, and good-natur'd. She was educated, as are all the Archdutchesses, in the knowledge of Things useful for those who are born to govern States; she speaks several Languages very readily, and particularly the *Latin*, in such a manner as both charms and surprizes the *Poles*. She is Mistress of History and Geography, and has a solid Taste of Musick, Painting, and all the Sciences in general: Yet never did Queen take less Pride in her Talents; for, by kindly condescending to accommodate her self to the Capacities of those with whom she converses, she conceals all her Superiority. Her high Rank serves only to render her affable; she is the Mother of the People, and particularly of the Poor. And to sum up the Character of this great Princess, it may be said in short, that she is a virtuous Wife, a faithful Companion, a tender Mother, and a compassionate Sovereign.

His Royal Highness the PRINCE ROYAL and ELECTORAL was born at *Dresden*, the 5th of *September* 1722, and baptized in the *Roman* Catholick Church, by the Name of *Frederic-Christian*: He is handsome, and has a Countenance full of Good-nature, and indeed his Goodness charms all that pay their court to him. His Knowledge and Learning are beyond one of his tender Years; he talks several Languages justly, and with ease; and his strong Inclination to follow the wise Counsels of his Governor, the Count *Gabaleon-Wackerbarth-Salmour*, is a sure Presage that when he comes to the Age of Maturity, he will walk in the glorious Steps of the King his Father.

As to their Royal Highnesses the other Princes, the eldest of them, Prince AUGUSTUS-ALBERT-CHRISTIAN-XAVIER was born the 25th of *August* 1730. He is handsome, full of Life and Spirit, and already discovers a great Inclination to every thing military. He is infinitely better pleased to see the Officers of his Regiment about him than the Women his Attendants. The Noise of Drums and Trumpets is the most agreeable Music to him, and according to all appearance, 'tis what he will always prefer to the Flute. When he went with their Majesties to *Cracow*, and heard talk of the Ravages committed by the Palatine of *Kiow*, he said, he had a mind to go and fight him, and cut off his Head. In fine, all the Actions of this young Prince give hopes that he will add one to the Number of Heroes descended from the august Blood of *Saxony*.

CHARLES-CHRISTIAN-JOSEPH came into the World *July* 13. 1733, so that his Royal Highness is too young as yet for any Character in History; and I shall proceed next to their Royal Highnesses the Princesses.

Her Royal Highness MARY-AMELIA, their Majesties eldest Daughter, was born at *Dresden*, the 24th of *September* 1724. She is fair, very well shap'd, and has the Air of her Mother. Her Features are regular, and 'tis heartily to be wish'd that the Small-Pox may spare them. The Care the Queen takes of her Education is so well bestow'd on her, that she is much better form'd than Princesses of her Age generally are.

MARY-ANNE-SOPHIA was born the 24th of *August* 1728. She is brown, and likely to be much admir'd for her Beauty. There is something in her Physiognomy so subtle and witty, that she has already secur'd the Suffrages of the Courtiers.

The Princess MARY-JOSEPHA was born the 4th of *November* 1731. Heaven has been pleas'd to grant her a share of Beauty with all the Princes and Princesses her Brothers and Sisters.

I should make some mention of all the PRINCES and PRINCESSES of the BLOOD, *viz.* all the most serene Dukes, Princes and Princesses of the Family of *Saxony*, particularly those who are deriv'd from the *Albertine* Branch, as descending with the King from the Elector *John-George* I. who form'd the four Branches, *viz.* the Electoral Branch, and those of *Weissenfels*, *Mersbourg*, and *Zeits*. But as this is only an Epitome of *Augustus* III's Court, I shall only take notice of those Princes who reside there; *viz.* JOHN-ADOLPHUS Duke of SAXE-WEISSENFELS, and the Princess CHRISTINA of SAXE-WEISSENFELS.

The Duke, who was born *September* 4, 1685, is of a good Stature. His Air, Behaviour, and way of thinking, denote his Birth; and never was Prince more worthy of being so. He is beneficent, generous; and all the Qualities which attract Love and Esteem are united in his Person. After having spent his early Days in the Service of *Hesse-Cassel*, he enter'd into that of the late King; and in the several Campaigns which he made in *Germany*, *Italy*, *Flanders*, and *Poland*, he always signaliz'd his Valour; and particularly not long ago, when he supported the Reputation of the King's Arms before *Dantzic* in a conspicuous manner. His Goodness, his Modesty, and his Care to distinguish true Merit, gain him the Love and Veneration both of the Officers and Soldiers. This Prince is actually a Lieutenant-General in the Emperor's Army, General of the *Saxon* Horse and Foot, Colonel of the Life-Guards, and of a Regiment of Foot, and Knight of the Order of the *White-Eagle*. He
is

is the Widower of *Caroline* Princess of *Saxe-Eyse-nach*, and professes the *Lutheran* Religion.

The Princess CHRISTINA of SAXE-WEISSEN-FELS, who was born the 27th of *July* 1690, adheres to the *Roman* Catholic Doctrine, Prince *Albert* her Father being a Convert to that Communion. She is of a good Stature, has a grand Majestic Air, and her Behaviour is graceful and polite. Her most serene Highness receives all that draw near to her with Respect and Kindness, and demonstrates her high Birth only by discharging the Obligations of it. She is so firmly attach'd to the Queen by the Bands of Love and Virtue that she is caress'd and distinguish'd by her; and all the Court honours and respects her more out of Inclination than Duty.

You will not perhaps be sorry to know the Names, &c. of the late King's legitimated Natural Issue, who are rank'd immediately after the Princes of the Blood. They are four Sons and three Daughters, of whom I shall now give you an Account, and who were their Mothers.

1. Count *Maurice* of *Saxony* is the eldest of the late King's Natural Children, by *Aurora* Countess of *Koningsmark*, the most worthy of her Sex in *Europe* to be the Mistress of a great King; and of all the King's Favourite Ladies, she kept longest in his Favour, so that after her Retirement she acquitted her self so well that she continued in the possession of his Majesty's Esteem and Regard. She is still living, and after having been a Prioress of the Imperial *Lutheran* Abbey of *Quedlinbourg* she rose to be the Abbess. The Count is a Lieutenant-General, and Colonel of a Regiment of Foot in *France*.

2. The next is the Count *Rotofski* or *Rutowski*, Lieutenant-General, and Colonel of the Crown-Guards, who owes his Birth to the King's tender Passion for *Fatima* a *Turkish* Lady who was taken Prisoner ve-

ry young, and fell to the share of M. *Schoning*, a Lieutenant-General in the Service of the Elector of *Brandenbourg*, who carried her to *Berlin*, and had her baptiz'd without altering her Name, tho' she afterwards went by that of Madame *de Spiegel*. Madamoiselle *de Flemming*, known by the Name of *Brebentau*, having married the Palatine of that Name, took a fancy to her, obtain'd her of M. *de Schoning*, and carried her with her into *Poland*, where from a Slave she became the King's Mistress, tho' Madame *Brebentau* did not perceive it till *Fatima*'s Waist betray'd her. She had as much Wit as Beauty, and every body said she deserv'd her Fortune. Nevertheless, she did not enjoy it long; for Madame *de Lubomirski*, who was Wife to the Great Chamberlain of the Crown, stole away the King's Heart from her. The Count *Rutowski* is a Major-General of the King's Forces, Colonel of the Life-Guards, and of a Regiment of Foot, and Knight of the Order of the *White-Eagle*. This Nobleman very much resembles the late King his Father, having his Strength, Dexterity, Valour and Politeness. He had his Education in *France*, and from thence went into the Service of *Victor Amadeus* the late King of *Sardinia*. Then he enter'd for a little while into the Service of the King of *Prussia*, and at length fix'd himself in that of *Saxony*, when he signaliz'd his Valour at the Siege of *Dantzic*, and afterwards made the Campaign as a Voluntier in the Imperial Army on the *Rhine*. As for his Religion, he professes the *Roman* Catholic.

3. The third of the late King's Natural Sons is *George* Prince *de Teschen*, otherwise call'd the *Chevalier de Saxony*, whom he had by Madame *de Lubomirski* above mentioned, who was Niece to the famous Cardinal *Radjowski* Archbishop of *Gnesna*, and Primate of *Poland*. After this Lady had indulg'd the King's Passion she got a Divorce from

Prince

Prince *Lubomirski*, and took the Title of the Princess *de Teschen*, which was granted to her by the Emperor. This Son of her's was brought up in the *Roman* Catholic Religion. He is a Colonel in the King's Service, and Knight of the Order of the *White-Eagle*. He is a well-set Man, has a noble Air, and supports his Title by a great share of Valour and good Sense. He is perfect Master of military Architecture, and has great Talents for War, which he cultivates to such a degree that his very Amusements are the Study of what a great Captain ought to know. This Desire of his to be qualify'd some day or other for the Command of an Army engag'd him, at his return from the Siege of *Dantzic*, to repair to the Army of Prince *Eugene* of *Savoy* to improve himself in the Art of War under that Great Master.

4. The fourth and youngest of the Natural Sons of the late King of *Poland* is the Count *de Cosel*, Knight of the Order of the *White-Eagle*, whose Mother was the Countess *de Cosel*; which Lady is also Mother to the Countesses of *Friesland* * and *Moschinski* †. The Count is a tall handsome Youth, modest and reserv'd, and more prudent than might be expected from his Years. This Nobleman, who does not disparage his Birth, is now making the Campaign upon the *Rhine* in the Imperial Army. He is of the *Lutheran* Communion.

Madame *de Cosel* is of the Family of *Bruchstorf*, and a Native of *Holstein*. She was Maid of Honour to the Dutchess of *Wolfembuttle*, when the Count *de Hoym* Minister of State to the King of *Poland* married her: The Count soon after the Marriage carried her to *Dresden*, where the King fell in love

---

* She died at *Dresden* soon after this was written.

† Count *Moschinski*, the Husband of this Lady, was Great Treasurer of the Court in *Poland*, and is Great Faulconer in *Saxony*.

love with her, and no sooner made it known to her but gain'd her compliance. M. *de Hoym* enrag'd at this, demanded a Divorce from her, which his Wife readily came into; so that the Consistory of *Dresden* declared their Marriage null and void. M. *de Hoym* married again, and Madame took the Title of the Countess *de Cosel*; but this Lady at once lost the King's Favour and her Liberty into the bargain, and is kept close Prisoner in a Castle, where she has nothing to do but to indulge her melancholy Reflections upon the Revolutions of her Fortune *.

The NATURAL DAUGHTERS of the late King are, 1. The Countess of *Bilinski*, (Sister of the Count *Rutowski*) who was born in *Poland* as well as her Brother, and educated in the *Roman* Catholic Religion. *Augustus* II. gave her in Marriage to the Count *Bilinski*. The Countess's frequent Ailments obliged her to go to *Paris* for her Health; so that not being of this Court, 'twill not be expected I should give her Character.

2. The

---

* Madame *de Cosel* may thank no body but herself for her Disgrace; for when she was in Royal Keeping, she had the assurance to threaten the King more than once that if ever he abandon'd her she wou'd pistol him. The King, who knew her to be a Woman that always kept her word, thought it his best way to be beforehand with her, tho' it was not till some time after that he caus'd her to be arrested. Madame *de Cosel*, who was retir'd to *Berlin*, did not dissemble her Chagrin; and 'tis said she declar'd in publick that the King should pay dear for being so false to her: Threats which his Majesty wou'd perhaps have despis'd, if Madame *de Cosel* had not refused to give him back a Promise which he had made to her of marrying her in case the Queen shou'd die. Mean-time the King desir'd of the King of *Prussia* to give orders for arresting her, which was done accordingly; and Madame *de Cosel* was carried under a Guard to *Saxony*, where she remain'd a Prisoner till the death of the King. But we have been told by the publick News-Papers that she obtain'd her Liberty in 1734.

2. The Countess of *Orselska*, who was born at *Warsaw*, of one *Renard* a *French* Woman, and bred up in the *Roman* Catholic Faith: She is of a good Stature, and very charming. Of all the late King's legitimated Children his Majesty seem'd to be fondest of this. She was at first very much neglected, and it did not appear that the King ever intended to own her. But Count *Rotofski* seeing her at *Warsaw* in a Plight too mean for her Birth took the freedom to mention her to the King her Father, and told him that she merited some Kindness from him. The King thereupon desir'd to see her, and she came into his Presence in the *Amazonian* Habit, which was her favourite Dress. The King thought she resembled him very much, and not being able to resist the tender Impressions of Nature he embrac'd her, and call'd her his Daughter. At the same time he order'd the whole Court to acknowledge her in that Quality, gave her a magnificent Palace, with Diamonds without number, and settled great Pensions on her. 'Tis certain, in short, that never was Daughter more like her Father; she had the same Features, Temper and Genius. It was impossible for her to be handsomer with a more grand Air. She is fond of Magnificence, Expence, and Pleasures. One of her Diversions is to dress in Mens Apparel. It was in this Habit that I saw her the first time, when she was on horseback, in a purple Habit embroider'd with Silver, and wore the blue Ribband of *Poland*. Being all alone, I could not learn who she was, but really took her to be some young Foreign Nobleman whom I had not yet seen. I never beheld any body sit better than she did on horseback, or have a more amiable Air; insomuch, that many Ladies would have been glad of a Lover so handsome. The same evening I saw her at the Ball, where she was still dress'd like a Man, only her Habit was more rich than it was in the morn-

ing, and her dishevell'd Locks of Hair hung down in fine Curls about her Shoulders; so that *Cupid* himself was not more tempting when he appear'd before *Psyche*. Her good Mien, and the graceful Air with which I saw her dance a Minuet, made me inquire who this pretty Youth was? Count *Rotofski*, who overheard me, made answer, *The young Man whom you admire wou'd do you no great harm if you were a Woman, but may possibly hurt you as the Case stands; but come along with me,* continued he, taking me by the Hand, *I will make him known to you, then leave you to come off with him as well as you can.* I guess'd by these Words that the Person he was going to usher me to was the Countess *Orselska*; and I was confirmed in my Suspicion when I heard Count *Rotofski* say to her, *Sister, here is a Gentleman who has all due Respects for you, and who, I'll engage will be ready to serve you in whatever you shall require of him.* Madamoiselle *Orselska* smiling at this Discourse, I saluted her with all the Respect which I ow'd to her Rank, and she receiv'd me in the most obliging manner possible. I saw her next day in Womens Apparel, and thought her still more amiable. I visit her every day, and now whenever I go to her I generally find with her *Charles Lewis*, a younger Prince of the Family of *Holstein-Beck*, who 'tis said is the happy Man for whom she is design'd in Marriage [*].

3. The Countess *Moschinski*, Daughter of the Countess of *Cosel*, was born at *Dresden*, and match'd by the late King to the Count *de Moschinski*, a *Polish* Nobleman. Her sober and courteous Deportment,

---

[*] This Marriage was actually consummated at *Dresden*. But since the King's death, the Prince of *Holstein* has abandon'd his Wife, whom he only married with a view of obtaining some considerable Employment from the King. The present Elector has eas'd her of most of that Wealth which the late King had heap'd on her.

ment, and the Goodness of her Temper, have procured her both Love and Reverence.

Having now treated of the Princes of the Royal Family, I proceed to give you an account of the chief Noblemen of the Court; and in the first place, of the MINISTERS of the CABINET.———These are, 1. *Waldemar* Baron *de Lowendahl* Grand Marshal, Knight of the *Saxon* Order of the *White-Eagle*, and of the *Danish* Order of the *Elephant*, who by his Post of Grand Marshal holds the first Rank at the Court of *Saxony*, because the Elector is Arch Grand-Marshal of the Empire. He is a *Dane* by birth, and is descended from a Count of *Guldenlowe*, a natural Son of the Blood-Royal of *Denmark*. He spent his youthful Days in the Service of the *States-General*, and was made a Captain in the Blue Guards; which he afterwards quitted, and went into the Service of the Emperor *Leopold*, and distinguish'd himself in quality of a Lieutenant-Colonel in 1683, at the raising of the Siege of *Vienna*; after which he return'd to *Denmark*, where he serv'd with Honour. But leaving that Court upon some Disgust, he came into *Saxony*, where *Augustus* II. declared him President of the Chamber, which Office he held when the King of *Denmark* recall'd him home. It was with the Approbation of his Master the King of *Poland* that he return'd to *Copenhagen*, where his *Danish* Majesty gave him the Command of his Army in *Norway* against the *Swedes*; which Commission he discharged with so much Honour, that he was dignify'd with the Order of the *Elephant*, as he had already been by that of *Dannebroc*. He might, had he pleased, have enjoy'd the greatest Offices in *Denmark*; but he had promised *Augustus* II. not to forsake him, so that he refus'd all the Advantages which *Frederic* IV. offer'd him, and return'd into *Saxony*. After the death of the Count *de Phlug*, the late King appointed him Grand Marshal, which Office he still executes

executes with Honour. Tho' he is now advanced in years he has a sound Constitution, and the Air, Behaviour, and Way of Thinking of a Man of his Quality. Being affable and polite, he does the Honours of the Court in a Gentleman-like manner, for which the Courtiers reverence him, and the King professes an esteem for him. His Majesty is the sixth King whom this Minister has serv'd. He has married to his second Wife a Lady of the Family of *Rantzau*, in the Country of *Holstein*, who bears a valuable Character, and is as polite as can be desired, speaking *French* as well as if she was born at *Versailles*. The Grand Marshal has two Sons by his first Marriage with a Lady of *Revenclau:* his youngest, *viz. Woldemar* Baron *de Lowendahl* is Major-General of the King's Armies, Inspector General of the *Saxon* Infantry, and Colonel of a Regiment of Foot. He was fourteen years old when the Grand Marshal sent him to *Denmark*; where he made a Campaign at Sea under Admiral *Tordenschild*. At his return to *Dresden* he carried a Musket, and afterwards pass'd through all the subaltern Degrees. When he was but a Lieutenant he accompany'd General *Seckendorf* to *Vienna*, where the Marshal Count *Guido de Staremberg* gave him a Company in his Regiment, and he distinguish'd himself in a particular manner at the Sieges of *Temiswaer* and *Belgrade*, and in *Sicily*. Since that, he enter'd into the Service of *Augustus* II. who gave him a Regiment. Afterwards he made two Campaigns as a Voluntier with the Imperialists in *Corsica*; and upon all occasions manifested that Valour, Skill, and Prudence, as he did lately in the Defence of *Cracow*; where, with a weak and sickly Garrison, he not only made a vigorous stand against the Attacks of the Primate's *Polish* Adherents, but also obliged them to retire. This General is so fond of signalizing his Bravery, that he was scarce return'd from *Poland*,

but

but he went to make the Campaign as a Voluntier, with the Imperial Army on the *Rhine*. He lives magnificently, keeps a good Table, and is very civil to Foreigners.

2. *Anthony* Count de *Lutzelbourg*, who is by birth a *Lorrainer*, and an exemplary Professor of the *Roman* Catholic Religion, is Lieutenant-General of the Forces, Knight of the Order of the White Eagle, and General of the Horse. He is pretty tall, and has a chearful Countenance, with a noble easy Behaviour, which shews the Man of Quality. His Merit procured him the Honour of being the King's Governour after the Decease of the Count *de Cosia*, which Post he held 'till his Majesty came of age, when he was appointed Steward of his Houshold, and was as much esteem'd by their Royal Highnesses as he is valued by the Courtiers, and belov'd by the Domestics of the Prince who are under his command: but his frequent Ailments oblig'd him to quit that Office: Nevertheless he was last year at *Vienna*, where he receiv'd for the King his Master the Investiture of the Feudatory States of the Empire, and concluded the Treaty of Alliance still subsisting between the two Courts.

3. *Henry-Frederic* Count of *Friesland*, is Great Chamberlain, General of the Infantry, Lieutenant-General of the King's Forces, and Knight of the Order of the *White-Eagle*. He is descended from a Family which has for a long time been of illustrious Rank in *Saxony*. He spent part of his Youth in the Service of *Peter* the Great, Czar of *Muscovy*, and signaliz'd his Valour very much at the Battle of *Pultowa*; where *Charles* XII. King of *Sweden* in a few Hours lost all the fruit of nine years Toil, and of an infinite number of Victories. Soon after this great Battle he shew'd his Wisdom to be equal to his Bravery at the Battle of *Pruth*; which though it did not turn out so much to the Czar's Honour, was

was altogether as fortunate to him, since it extricated that Prince out of the worst scrape that perhaps ever King was reduced to. He enter'd afterwards into the Service of the late King; who being sensible of his Merit, raised him to the greatest Dignities of his Court, and married him to one of the Daughters that he had by the Countess of *Cosel.* The Great Chamberlain, who has the Looks and Behaviour of a Man of Quality, thinks and acts too like a Nobleman. Few Persons surpass him in Politeness and Learning: He is perfect Master of several Languages, and of every thing that forms the Minister and the General. He loves Literature and the Arts, and was always their Supporter. He lives handsomely, and has such a Presence as commands the Veneration of all that have to do with him.

4. *Joseph* Count *de Gabaleon-Wackerbarth Salmour,* the adopted Son of the Velt-Marshal *Augustus Christopher* Count *de Wackerbarth* who succeeded Marshal *de Flemming* in the chief command of the Troops in *Saxony,* and was not only Marshal, but a Minister of State, Grand Master of the Artillery, Governour of *Dresden,* and Knight of the Order of the *White-Eagle.* The Father was born of a good Family in *Mecklembourg;* but from his very youth he attach'd himself to the Elector of *Saxony;* and by his own Merit, and the Friendship of his Predecessor Count *Flemming,* he was raised to the chief Posts in the Army and the Court. In 1709 he had the Command of the *Saxon* Troops before *Tournay,* as he had in 1715 before *Strahlsund,* when 'twas besieg'd by the Kings of *Denmark* and *Prussia,* and defended by *Charles* XII. King of *Sweden.* M. *de Wackerbarth* was made Count of the Empire by the King his Master, while that Prince was Vicar of the Empire, after the death of the Emperor *Joseph.* After being grac'd with this Dignity,

nity, the Count *de Wackerbarth* was employ'd in sundry important Negotiations, especially at *Vienna*; where he married a *Piedmontese* Lady, the Dowager of *Charles* Margrave of *Brandenbourg*, Brother to *Frederic* I. King of *Prussia*, who when he was but very young at the University of *Turin*, married her by the Left-hand, as you know is the Fashion among our Princes when they marry below themselves. However the Lady went by the Name of Madame *de Brandenbourg* to the very day that the Count *de Wackerbarth* married her, being so proud of the Title that she was resolv'd never to part with it 'till she was married again: Notwithstanding the advantageous Offers made to her from the King of *Prussia* to engage her to renounce it, her refusal of which was the more generous because it was at a time too when she was in narrow Circumstances; yet her constant Answer was, that nothing in the Universe should tempt her to debase herself; and that she had rather be poor, and pass for the Wife of the Margrave of *Brandenbourg*, than be rich, and pass for his Mistress. Before she became Madame *de Brandenbourg* she was the Widow of a certain Count *de Salmour*, by whom she had a Son whom she engaged the Count *de Wackerbarth*, when she married him, to adopt for his own. I confess I never saw this Lady; for at the time of my former Voyage hither she was at *Vienna*; and now she is dead. They talk of her still as one of the acutest Women of her time. But to return to the Marshal; he is very civil, lives with great Splendor, and his House is open to all Foreigners. He is mighty intimate with the Count *de Flemming*, Prime Minister and Favourite of the King; so that they fully contradicted the Proverb, *That Fire and Water can't agree*; for Count *Flemming* was lively almost to the Degree of a Fury, whereas the Count *de Wackerbarth*, on the contrary,

abounded

abounds with Phlegm *. We go back now to his adopted Son *Joseph* above-mention'd, a *Piedmontese*, at present one of the Ministers of the Cabinet †.

He is also Knight of the Order of the *White-Eagle*, and Governour of his Royal Highness the Prince Royal and Electoral. He bears the Name and Arms of *Wackerbarth*, by reason of his being adopted as above by the Velt-Marshal his Father-in-law; upon whose death, he succeeded to his Estate. He took to arms betimes; but having received a Wound in the Foot, which he feels to this day, he was oblig'd to quit a Profession in which he distinguish'd himself, and apply'd afterwards to Affairs of State. The late King sent him to the Courts of *Bavaria* and *Vienna*, where he supported the Prerogatives of his Character with Dignity, and gain'd the extraordinary Esteem of their Imperial Majesties and the Ministers. *Augustus* II. recall'd him from *Vienna*, and sent him to *Rome*, to the new Pope *Clement* XII. The *Romans*, those Masters in the Art of Politics, were soon convinced that this Minister knew more than they could teach him: They admired the Prudence and Resolution with which he behav'd when the *Sbirri* presum'd to invade the Franchise of his Quarter; and all own'd that the most experienced Minister could not have better supported the Honour of his Master. At his Return from *Rome*, the late King, to the Satisfaction of all Men, appointed him Governour to Prince *Frederic*, the present Prince Royal and Electoral; the Count having all the necessary Qualifications to fill that Post with Honour: For besides a

good

---

* He died in *August*, 1734; and was succeeded in his Employments by the Prince of *Saxe-Weissenfels*, and the Count of *Friesland*.

† The Count *de Wackerbarth Salmour* distinguish'd himself, in the year 1733, when the new Elector sent him Commissary Plenipotentiary to *Poland*; where he manag'd the Interests of his Master so well, that he was chose King.

good Share of Religion, he is a Gentleman of known Candour, great Experience in Bufinefs, and abundance of Good-nature, Politenefs, and Modefty: And he is not only deeply learn'd, but always ftudious how to anfwer the great Truft repos'd in him by their Majefties; and as the Method he takes to inftruct the Prince has won him his Royal Highnefs's Efteem and Friendfhip, fo it cannot fail of procuring him one day the Praife and Gratitude of thofe who are concern'd for the Glory of the Royal Family.

When *Auguftus* III. came to the Government he fent the Count, with M. *de Baudiffin*, in Quality of his Plenipotentiaries, to the Republic of *Poland*; in which Poft he anfwer'd the Expectation which the King had of his Capacity. His Wifdom got the better of all Oppofition; and he had the advantage of triumphing over the Intrigues and Cabals of the Primate. After the King had been proclaim'd the Count fwore, in his Majefty's Name, in the Church at *Warfaw*, to the Obfervation of the *Pacta Conventa* drawn up by the Members of the Republic; and then accompanied the Grand Deputation of the *Polifh* Nobility at *Tarnowitz*. 'Twas he that made anfwer, in the Name of their Majefties, to the Harangues of the Bifhop of *Cracow* declaring the Republic's Acknowledgement of his Title, and their Obedience. And the Anfwer he return'd was in the two Languages in which the Prelate addrefs'd him: He fpoke in *Latin* for the King, and in *French* for the Queen.

The Count being return'd to *Drefden* fince their Majefties Coronation, is wholly taken up in the Education of the Prince Royal; and his care of him has been crown'd with fuch Succefs, that we may prophefy his Royal Highnefs will one day draw down that Bleffing of God upon himfelf, which is upon the Head of the Juft.

5. *Wolff*-

5. *Wolff-Henry de Baudiffin*, General of the Horse, Colonel of a Regiment of Carabiniers, and Knight of the Order of the *White-Eagle*, and that of *Dannebroc*, has all the Qualities requisite for a well-born Gentleman, *viz.* an agreeable Aspect, a good Stature, a noble Air, easy and engaging Behaviour, approv'd Valour, a Generosity free of all Ostentation; and finally what is superior to all these Qualities, he has a Fund of Probity and Candour which nothing can corrupt. He is a Native of *Holstein*, and spent his early Years in the Service of *Sweden*, and afterwards in that of the Duke his Sovereign, who gave him a Regiment, with which he serv'd all the last War in the *Netherlands*, in the Post of Major-General. *Augustus* II. calling him to his Service, made him Lieutenant-General of his Forces, and then General of the Cavalry. When *Augustus* III. came to the Government he summon'd him to his Cabinet-Council, and sent him as his Plenipotentiary to *Poland*, where he had a hand in every Transaction for the Advantage and Honour of the King. He afterwards commanded the Army which his Majesty was obliged to carry into his Kingdom for the Defence of his oppressed Subjects; and there he fell so dangerously ill that he was obliged to return to *Germany*, to make use of the Waters of *Pyrmont*, by which he found benefit; and he is now at *Dresden*, where his Seniority gives him the Command in chief of the Forces.

6. *Alexander-Joseph* Count *de Sulkowski*, Starost of *Sokolnick*, Chief Huntsman of *Lithuania*, Master of the Horse, Great Master of the Wardrobe, Major-General of the King's Forces, Colonel of the Crown-Guards and of a Regiment of Foot, and Knight of the Order of the *White-Eagle*, is a *Polander*. Being taken into Service very young as Page to the King, then Prince Royal and Electoral, he accompanied him in his Travels, and there
acquir'd

acquir'd a good Fund of Knowledge. His great Sobriety, his Affiduity, his Application to the difcharge of his Duties, his Senfe, and his fincere Attachment to Religion, won his Mafter's Heart, of which he keeps poffeffion even to this day; with a Diftinction that does him the more Honour, becaufe he derives it from the King's thorough conviction of his Merit.

The Count is of a good Stature, has a noble and modeft Air, and a Candour in his Converfation and his Action, which is very engaging. He is civil, and makes no other Ufe of his Favour but to do as much Good as he can, without prejudicing the Interefts of the King whom he ferves with Gratitude, Affection, and Zeal. He is a generous Minifter, and his Houfe is open to all Perfons of Diftinction.

After he had ferv'd as a Page, he was by the late King made a Gentleman of the Bed-Chamber; and not long after that, his prefent Majefty, who was then ftill Prince Royal, declar'd him Director of his Hunting Equipage, and trufted him with the Management of his Domeftic Affairs. The late King alfo appointed him one of his Chamberlains.

At the famous Camp at *Zeithaim*, the Count commanded an Independent Company. He difcover'd fo great Application, and fuch a happy Genius for the Art of War, that the late King, whofe Penetration nothing cou'd efcape, took it for a good Omen, and gave him a Regiment of Foot. Thus did the Count make his way towards the fplendid Fortune which he now enjoys. M. *de Bruhl* refigning his Poft of Great Mafter of the Wardrobe, foon after the King's Acceffion to the Government, his Majefty gave that Poft to his Favourite. He afterwards call'd him to his Cabinet Council; and at his Coronation, he made him Knight of the Order of the White Eagle. After the Court's Return

turn from *Cracow*, the Count went to the Army before *Dantzic*; where he gave demonstration of his being as good a Soldier as he is an able Statesman. It being not compatible with his Ministry to be long absent, and *Dantzic* being on the point of capitulating, he went to give the King an account of the Success of its Siege, and the Prosperity of his Arms. He accompanied his Majesty to the Abbey of *Oliva*, and by his Prudence contributed very much to put such *Polish* Lords in mind of their Obedience, who had thought of being exempted from it. And his only View being more and more to deserve that Favour with which the King honours him, and being desirous of having it in his power to serve him, as well in his Armies, as in his Cabinet, he went last of all to the Imperial Army, in order to qualify himself for a Command under Prince *Eugene* of *Savoy*.

To complete the good Fortune of this Count, he married a Lady, who, besides her Birth and personal Charms, has a Character which gains her the Applause and Veneration of all that know her. She is hereditary Baroness of *Stein*; and when he marry'd her, she was Lady of Honour to the Queen. They are both Members of the *Roman* Catholic Church.

7. *Henry de Brubl*, Knight of the Orders of *Poland* and *Prussia*, a Member of the Privy-Council, President of the Chamber of Finances, Director General of the Excise, and Vice-President of the Taxes, is the Son of *John de Brubl*, who was of the Privy-Council to *Augustus* II. and Grand Marshal and Director of the Privy-Council to the Duke Regent of *Saxe-Weissenfels*. He is by Birth a *Saxon*, and has a Brother who is Knight of the Teutonick Order. He made great progress at *Leipsic* in the *Belles Lettres*, and in the Exercises suitable to a Person of his Extraction. His Recreations

ations there, were Music, and Conversation with Persons of his own Taste. He sometimes made Verses, which were esteem'd for the bright Thoughts in them, and the Harmony of the Versification. When he quitted *Leipsic*, he was enter'd Page to the late King: In this Post he behaved with so much Sobriety and Assiduity, that his Majesty soon distinguish'd him from the Croud, admitted him to Familiarity with him; and finding he had a sound Judgment, a quick Apprehension, a Penetration beyond what might be expected from one of his Age, and that he was a Person of Discretion, and inviolable Secrecy, join'd with a noble Freedom, and such a happy way of expressing himself as to render the most difficult Subjects easy and pleasant; he readily judg'd that such a one was fit to be employ'd in great Affairs. He had a mind to instruct him; and having nominated him one of the Gentlemen of his Bed-Chamber, he had him under his Eye. M. *de Bruhl* improv'd so well from the Lessons of this great Master, so thoroughly study'd his Humour, and so exact'y suited himself to his Genius, that he made himself necessary. His Application, his Love to Business, and the Ease with which he dispatch'd it, won him the intire Confidence of *Augustus* II. who declar'd him Great Master of the Wardrobe, and a Privy Counsellor; and to him he moreover committed the Direction and Regulation of Affairs, Foreign and Domestic. Never had the King shewn more Affection or Esteem for any of his Favourites; yet this Nobleman took ne'er the more State upon him for it, but living always humble, polite, and ready to do Services, he made himself Friends, and secur'd himself by that means against all the Hatred and Envy with which Courtiers are very ready to treat those who are in Power.

When the King of *Prussia* went to the Camp at *Zeithaim*, he conferr'd his Order of the Black Eagle upon M. *de Bruhl*: The late King also honour'd him with that of the White Eagle; but this was at a time when this Minister had no Relish for Honours, and wou'd have been glad to have renounc'd them for ever, if he cou'd thereby have prolong'd the Days of a Master so worthy of Immortality.

It was in those last Moments, when the Professions of Friendship cannot be so much as suspected, that *Augustus* II. gave his Favourite his Order, as a certain Token that he retain'd a value for him even to Death. This great King having finish'd his glorious Career, M. *de Bruhl*, without suffering himself to be too much cast down, knowing that an Ocean of Tears was too little to shed for the Loss he had sustain'd, thought of nothing more than paying the due Devoirs to the deceas'd Sovereign, and to the Prince, his Son and Successor. Having therefore caus'd the Corpse of the former to be embalm'd, and put a Seal upon all the Effects which belong'd to him, besides securing the Jewels and Papers of Consequence; he came to *Dresden* to join the Elector, now King of *Poland*, who received him with such Marks of Kindness, as were enough to have put the deceas'd Monarch out of the Minister's Thoughts, if his Gratitude had not dictated to him, that such a King and such a Master ought never to be forgot.

The King confirm'd him in all the Employments and Honours which he had held by the Favour of *Augustus* II. and moreover appointed him one of the Ministers of his Cabinet. Some time after this, his Majesty declar'd him President of the Chamber of Finances; consequently, this great, this true King, by distinguishing Merit, did farther Honour to the Memory of his august Father, since

he

he did what that magnanimous Prince wou'd have undoubtedly done for his Favourite.

At this time the Minister resign'd to the King his Office of Great Master of the Wardrobe, which his various Occupations did not permit him to manage with that Care he thought was necessary. After the Return of the Court from *Cracow*, whither this Gentleman had accompany'd the King, he marry'd the Countess *de Collowrat*, one of the Queen's Ladies of Honour, whose high Birth was supported with such personal Qualities as can never be enough commended. The Bride being a *Roman* Catholic, the Ceremony of the Marriage was performed at *Moritzbourg*, in presence of their Majesties, by the Bishop of *Cracow*. Never was a Couple better match'd; the Lady's Person being a Collection of Charms, and M. *de Bruhl* a Man of as noble Presence as one wou'd wish to see; which he generally sets off with a rich Dress of a good Fancy. No body at Court surpasses him in a generous way of living; for he keeps a noble Table, and at his House Persons of Distinction have their Assemblies. This Minister has something so attracting in his Looks and Behaviour that he easily wins the Hearts of People who are the most indifferent to him. He is so polite, affable, and engaging, that he listens attentively to those who lay their Wants before him, returns them courteous and distinct Answers; and whenever he is constrain'd to give a Denial, he does it in such a manner as plainly demonstrates his Concern that 'tis not in his power to oblige. And 'tis owing to this Good-nature of his, and to the Kindness with which he treats his Inferiors, that he can boast of possessing the Love and Veneration of the Public.

In short, the Count *de Solkouski* who has the first place in the Cabinet, and this Gentleman who has the second, are the Ministers who decide all Affairs with the King's good Pleasure. They are Gentlemen who know nothing of Jealousy nor Envy; and, as they act from one and the same Principle, so they have both the same View, which is to increase, if possible, the Glory of the King, and the Happiness of the Government.

The Office of all the abovemention'd, as Ministers of the Cabinet, is so eminent at this Court that it gives those who are invested with it the Precedence of all the Generals, both of Horse and Foot.

Besides these, there are three other Ministers of the Cabinet, who, tho' retir'd from Court, enjoy the Rank and Pensions annex'd to the Ministry. They are the Count *de Manteuffel*, the Count *de Promnitz*, and the Marquiss *de Fleuri*.

Ernest Count *de Manteuffel*, Knight of the Order of the White Eagle, is descended of a Family which has been for a long time of distinguish'd Rank in *Prussian Pomerania*. He was Gentleman of the Bed-Chamber to *Frederic* I. King of *Prussia*. Certain Ballads being handed about at Court, which were insulting Lampoons upon the Count *de Wartemberg*, the King's Prime Minister and Favourite, M. *de Manteuffel* was charged with being the Author of 'em; who knowing that the Favourite wou'd not put up with the Affront, retir'd to *Saxony*, where the Count *de Flemming*, who then bore the greatest sway at the King of *Poland*'s Court, receiv'd him as his Countryman, and employ'd him in foreign Affairs; which he managed with the Approbation both of his Majesty and the foreign Ministers he had to treat with. M. *de Manteuffel* kept in with the Favourite without giving into the Flattery which that Minister expected from his Creatures; and while the King was Vicar of the Empire, he made M. *de Manteuffel* a Count of the Empire. His Majesty had some time before honour'd him with the Order of the White Eagle, and preferr'd him to his Cabinet Council; and after Marshal *Flemming*'s Death,

Death, M. *de Manteuffel* * had the principal Direction of the foreign Affairs. But this able Minister, and one of the chief Ornaments and Confidents of the late King's Court, retir'd from it in 1730, to his Estate in *Pomerania*, and now resides at *Berlin*; where he still enjoys a Pension of 24000 Crowns, or 12000 Rixdollars, which was secur'd to him by the present Elector. It adds to his Character, that after he was retired, the Want of him was lamented.

He is pretty tall, well set, has a grand Air, and is one of the handsomest Men that I have seen. His Behaviour is noble and easy, he has a good Fund of Learning, an extraordinary Memory, and such a Happiness of expressing himself that when he talks he never fails to give Pleasure. He lives nobly, and when he was at *Dresden* his House was open to all Persons of Distinction and Merit. He married a Baroness of *Pludouska*, who is, as well as himself, of the *Lutheran* Religion.

Erdmann, Count *de Promnitz*, is more at his Estate than at Court; he is also Knight of the Order of the White Eagle. He married a Princess of *Saxe-Weiſſenfels*. He always distinguish'd himself by his Zeal, and his Attachment to the Royal Family; of which he gave Proofs by raising an Independent Company at his own Expence, for the Service of the late King, which he sent to reinforce his Majesty's Troops in the Camp before *Zeithaim*: And for the same Use he has since rais'd a Regiment of Horse.

Francis Vicardel, Marquiss *de Fleuri* and *de Beaufort*, is a *Savoyard*. He was the King of *Sardinia*'s Minister, and his Envoy to the Court of *Vienna*, when the late King of *Poland* invited him into his Service, admitted him to his Cabinet Council,

---

* He was created a Count of the Empire (not by the King of *Poland*, but) by the Emperor. As he is a Lover of the Belles Lettres, in the late War he wrote and publish'd several solid Pieces, which were well penn'd.

cil, and made him a Knight of his Order. This Minister is endow'd with all the Talents that can be desir'd in a Man who has an Employment. He has an agreeable Aspect, engaging Manners, a just Discernment, a quick Apprehension, and a very even Temper. But his frequent Ailments disabling him from the Exercise of his Talents, he desir'd, and obtain'd leave to retire to his Estate in *Savoy*; and the late King, who had always a great and noble Soul, being desirous that he shou'd be a Witness of his Goodness and Royal Magnificence, secur'd the Enjoyment of his Pensions to him; which the present King has also been pleased to confirm.

Another of the Cabinet Ministers, who was also formerly Prime Minister to the late King of *Poland*, was the Count *de Hoym*, descended from one of the principal Families in *Saxony*, and Brother to the Gentleman that married Madame *de Cosel*. I knew him intimately before he was advanc'd to the Ministry, at *Paris*, and at *Vienna*, as well as here at *Dresden*. You must have seen him in *Silesia*, where he has a very fine Estate. There is not a Minister at this Court more civil, more learned, or a better Friend to learned Men. During his long Residence at *Paris* as Ambassador from the King of *Poland*, his House was open to all Men of Learning as it is now at *Dresden*; and he had the splendid Title given him of the *Mecænas of Saxony* *.

They

---

* He was disgrac'd in 1731, upon which he retir'd to his Estate. The Catastrophe of this Gentleman is so tragical an Incident, that it will be proper to give a short but true History of it, as it is related in the following Circular Letter, wrote by the King of *Poland*'s Order, to his Ministers abroad, for the Information of all the Foreign Courts. The Letter was dated at *Warsaw*, the 12th of *May*, O. S. 1736, as follows.

SIR,

They who are actually PRIVY COUNSELLORS, or MINISTERS OF STATE here, are eight in number. They are descended from some of the best Families in *Saxony*, and profess the Protestant Religion. The Detail of their Characters, their Experience, and their Merit, wou'd oblige me to transgress the Limits of this Work, were I only to treat of those who are bound by their Employments to attend the King's Person, and who compose his Majesty's Houshold. But for the Reputation of the Privy Council, 'tis proper just to observe that all its Members are Subjects who do Honour to the King's Choice; that they are vigilant for promoting

SIR,

'THE tragical Death of the Count *de Hoym* having been variously reported both in printed Papers and written Letters, and with Circumstances not strictly true; the King has order'd me to give you an exact Information of this Affair.

'You will remember what the late King, of glorious Memory, signified to his Ministers abroad, concerning the Reasons and Circumstances that preceded, accompanied, and followed the Disgrace of the Count *de Hoym*.

'This Count having been a second time arrested for other Crimes, after the Death of the late King, was committed in 1733, to *Sonnenstein*, from whence the present King was so merciful as to release him some Weeks after; contenting himself to bind him again by Oaths stronger than the former; whereby the Count obliged himself to continue quiet at his Estate, without concerning himself with any but his own private Affairs.

'Yet towards the close of the Year 1734, and at the time when the King was in *Poland*, the Count, notwithstanding his Engagements, took the Opportunity of his Majesty's Absence, to set on foot other Intrigues, in defiance of his Oaths and his Promises; whereof the King being timely inform'd, order'd him to be arrested and committed Prisoner to *Konigstein*; which was the reason of his attempting his Life by a Pistol, whereof I acquainted you by my Circular Letter of the 15th of *January*, 1735.

'An Information was afterwards preparing for the Trial of him and his Accomplices; but not many days after the first Examination, the said Count being stung by the Remorse of

ting the Good of the Public, and that in their Deliberations they manifest their Zeal for the King, and their Affection to their Country.

The President of this Council, is *Alexander de Miltitz de Scharffenberg*, who is a Native of *Saxony*, the same that was the King's Governour; of whom so much has been already said, that I avoid to make any more particular mention of him here.

Two of the Privy Counsellors are Counsellors of the Conferences, which are held in presence of his Majesty, *viz. Gotlob-Frederic* Baron *de Gersdorff*, and *Bernard* Baron *de Zech*. The former comes from an ancient Family of Distinction, which has

'his Conscience, and vexed to see all his Pranks laid open, chose to shorten the Course of Justice by putting an end to his own Life, notwithstanding the undeniable Proofs he had before experienc'd of his Majesty's Clemency. For this purpose he first pretended to be sick, and having order'd his Domestics not to disturb him, he hang'd himself the 21st of *April* last, at Night, with a Handkerchief ty'd to a Hook that supported his Looking-glass. The Letter he wrote to his Domestics with a Pencil, and which was found upon the Floor, is an indisputable Mark of the deliberate Purpose and cold Blood with which he executed this Design. Moreover, in searching his Pockets a Razor was found on him, with a Penknife, Scissars, and the like Instruments.

'The Family of the Deceas'd having petition'd the King not to proceed against the Corpse with the Severity of the Law, his Majesty has been so good as to order the Body of the Self-murderer to be privately interr'd, just without the Church-Yard of the Garrison at the Fort of *Konigstein*.'

I am, &c.

The Night before the Count dispatch'd himself, he left a Note upon his Table for his two Servants, as follows:

'BE prudent, make no Noise or Alarm, untie me immediately, put me to Bed, and then shut the Door after you, by bolting it when you are out, which you may do by the help of this Pack-thread; and by this means no body will know you have been in my Chamber. The World will doubtless believe I died of an Apoplexy; if you perform my Orders discreetly and faithfully, my Family will pay you 1000 Ducats, on sight of this Note.

has given several great Men to this State. The latter has acquitted himself with Success in the several Negociations wherein he has been employ'd. They are both laborious, vigilant, upright Men, and of great Experience in Business.

The King's GREAT OFFICERS are,

I. The GRAND MARSHAL; which Office is now held by *Waldemar*, Baron *de Lowendahl*, who has under him

The Gentlemen of the Bed-Chamber,
The Pages,
The Huntsmen,
The Musicians of the Chapel and the Chamber,
The Dancers,
The Comedians,
The Trumpeters,
The Footmen,
The *Turks*,
The *Heydukes*,
The Messengers,
The *Negroes*;

and in short, a considerable number of other Officers and Domestics of the King's Houshold. His Jurisdiction extends not only over those that I have mention'd, but also over all Foreigners of Quality who happen to be at *Dresden*; and there is a Tribunal or Court for this purpose, of which the Great Chamberlain, the Great Master of the Kitchens, the Great Cup-Bearer and the Marshal of the Court are Members.

II. The GREAT CHAMBERLAIN; who is at present *Henry-Frederic* Count of *Friesland*. 'Tis he that receives the Ambassadors and other foreign Ministers, and introduces them to an Audience of the King. He has under him the several Chamberlains.

III. The MASTER of the HORSE, *Alexander-Joseph* Count *de Sulkowski*, is in possession of this Office, which is one of the best and noblest Employments

ployments at Court, the Person who is invested with it being serv'd by the King's Equipages and Livery, and having the disposal of all the inferior Offices appertaining to the Stables. He has under him the Equerries, the Prickers, and all the Workmen employ'd for the Service of the Stables, and the making of the Equipages.

He that is the only chief Equerry is *Adolphus de Brubl*, one of the King's Chamberlains. He officiates in the absence of the Master of the Horse, is Brother to *Henry de Brubl* Minister of the Cabinet, and resembles him in Candour and Integrity. His Honesty, which is imprinted on his very Countenance, reflects a Lustre on all his Actions. He is so sensible of the Charms of Friendship that he fulfils all the Obligations of it; and besides those Qualities of the Mind, he makes an agreeable Appearance, is dextrous in his Exercises, has a solid Relish of the Arts and Sciences, is perfect Master of Music, and plays on several Instruments.

He was heretofore in the Service of the Duke Regent of *Weissenfels*, and next in that of the Duke of *Saxe-Weimar*, who had such an Esteem for his Merit that to him he referred the Direction of his Court. Nevertheless he left this Prince, and enter'd into the Service of the late King, who conferred those Employments on him which he now enjoys. Since he came to Court, he married a young Lady of Quality of the Family of *Opelen*, whose Fortune and Charms into the bargain made her such a considerable Match that she did not want Suitors.

IV. The GREAT HUNTSMAN. The Gentleman who at present possesses this Office, one of the most lucrative at Court, is *Charles de Leubnitz*. It gives him the Superintendance over all the Officers of the Venery, in which Number are included the Rangers, the Verdurers, the Gentlemen and Pages, and

and above a hundred Huntsmen or other Persons depending on them. The Great Huntsman is a Protestant, as well as his Lady, who is of the Family of *Schaurot*.

V. The GREAT MASTER of the KITCHENS is *Adolphus* Baron *de Seyffertitz*, of a Family which has been for a long time distinguish'd in this Electorate. His first Step at Court was in the Employment of Gentleman of the Bed-Chamber. *Augustus* II. at the request of the late Czar *Peter the Great*, plac'd him Governor to the Czarowitz when that young Prince came into *Germany*. He continued in this Post till after the Marriage of the Czarowitz to the Princess of *Brunswic-Wolfembuttle-Blanckenbourg*. After his return to *Saxony* he accompanied the late King to *Berlin*, when his Majesty together with *Frederic* IV. King of *Denmark*, went thither to make a visit to *Frederic* I. King of *Prussia*. In 1711, M. *de Seyffertitz* was appointed Marshal of the Embassy which *Augustus* II. sent to *Francfort*, for the Election of an Emperor. His Imperial Majesty *Charles* VI. at the Ceremony of his Coronation, made him a Knight of the Empire, and at length the late King made him one of his Chamberlains, and then Great Master of the Kitchens, which Office he manages with Dignity and Politeness. He married a Lady of the Family of *Haxthausen*, Widow of the Count *de Beichling* the Great Faulconer. They are both of the *Lutheran* Communion.

In the absence of the Grand Marshal, the Great Master of the Kitchens officiates, and at the grand Ceremonies wears like him a Staff tipp'd with Silver gilt. Under his Province are the Comptrollers of the Kitchen and of the Houshold, the Clerks of the Kitchen, the Purveyors, the Cooks and Turnspits, the Pastry-Cooks, the Pursers, Fishmongers, &c.

VI.

VI. The GREAT CUPBEARER is *John Adolphus de Haugwitz*, a Gentleman of good Extraction. His Father was Grand Marshal to the late King. He is a handsome Man, has a noble Mien, performs all sorts of Exercises with a Grace and with Dexterity, and does the Honours of the Court in a becoming manner. He is of the Protestant Religion, and married to a Lady of the Family of *Beist*. His Employment sets him above all the Officers of the King's Buttery, Cellar, and Pantry. In the absence of the Grand Marshal and the Master of the Kitchens, he officiates for them, and at great Ceremonies he carries like them a Staff of Silver gilt.

VII. The GREAT FAULCONER is an Office held by *Anthony* Count *de Moschinski*, a *Polish* Nobleman, and a *Roman* Catholic. He was formerly Page to the King, and attended his Majesty in his Tours to *France* and *Italy*, where he acquir'd great Politeness, and a very engaging Deportment. At his return to *Dresden*, he was made one of the Gentlemen of the Bed-Chamber to the King, who was then the Prince Royal. Afterwards the late King appointed him one of his Chamberlains; and when the Count *de Fitztuhm* unhappily lost his life at *Warsaw*, his Majesty who had given his Office of Great Chamberlain to the Count *de Friesland*, bestow'd that of *Great Faulconer*, which was held by that Nobleman, upon the Count *de Moschinski*, who was grac'd almost at the same time with the Order of the *White-Eagle*, and the Post of Treasurer to the Court of *Poland*. His Majesty also granted him in Marriage one of his natural Children, the Daughter of the Countess *de Cosel*. Never was a Person more deserving of Honours than the Great Faulconer, who is truly magnificent, and makes such an Appearance, that he does an Honour to his Character. By his Behaviour he engages the Friendship and Regard of all that have to do with him. He has

under

under his command the Officers of the Faulconry or Mews where the Hawks are kept, the Faulconers, and in general all those Persons that have any relation to the Faulconry.

VIII. The GREAT MASTER of the WARDROBE is *Alexander-Joseph* Count *de Sulkowski*. He has under his Jurisdiction the *Catholic* Clergy, the *Physicians* of the *Body*, the *Footmen*, the *Secretaries, Writers* and *Clerks* of the *Chamber*, the *Inspectors* of the *Chamber* of *Curiosities*, the *Ushers* of the *Chamber* and of the *King's Closet*, his *Peruke-makers, Surgeons* and *Taylors*, the *Negroes, Dwarfs*, and *Pages* of the *Back-Stairs*, the *Architects, Engineers* and *Designers*.

IX. The POSTMASTER-GENERAL is *Maurice-Charles* Count *de Linar*, who is also one of the Chamberlains, and a Knight of the Order of St. *John*. He is descended from a Family which has been of Eminence for a long time in this Electorate. His good Mien is answerable to his Birth, and by his Politeness, his Manners, and his Expences, he does an honour to the Prince that employs him. The King, after his Coronation, sent him to *Muscovy* to notify the Accomplishment of that Ceremony to the Empress of the *Russians*, and he still continues at that Princess's Court, to take care of his Master's Interests, which he does in a way that cannot but turn to his own Advantage, and the Honour of the King. * This Gentleman was also employ'd by the late King at the Court of *Prussia*, and at the *British* Court when at *Hanover*, and always discharg'd his Commissions with such Success as was crown'd with his Majesty's Approbation.

X. The MARSHAL of the COURT is *John-George d'Einsiedel*, who is also a Privy-Counsellor, and a Gentleman of a good Family, his Ancestors having pos-

* In *October* 1736, he return'd to *Dresden*.

possessed the chief Offices of the State. He has visited the principal Courts of *Europe*, where he contracted that polite Turn which is seen in his Behaviour. He is a handsome Man, has a noble Air, and his Demeanour is answerable. He knows a great deal, and performs all the academical Exercises very well. He married the Daughter of the General Count *de Flemming* Governor of *Leipsic*, who was a rich Heiress, and to be valued for the Qualities of her Mind. The Marshal of the Court and his Lady are both of the *Lutheran* Communion. His Office joins him in Commission with the Grand Marshal, the Great Master of the Kitchens, and the Great Cup-Bearer; and like those Officers he carries the short Staff of Silver gilt at the grand Ceremonies. 'Tis commonly he that makes the Court-Entertainments.

Curt d'Einsiedel Marshal of the Court, and one of the Chamberlains, is remarked for his genteel Mien and Extraction. His good Qualities and Deportment render him worthy of all Employments. He is of the establish'd Religion of *Saxony*, and lately married Madamoiselle *de Schoneberg de Maxen*, whose Personal Charms are an Ornament to the Court.

Ernest-Ferdinand d'Ermandsdorff, Marshal of the King's Houshold, and one of the Chamberlains, has procur'd himself Esteem by his Merit as well as his good Birth and Breeding. Besides his Knowledge of various kinds which qualifies him for Business, he is Master of several Languages, particularly the *French*. He married a Lady of the Family of *Hesler*, and they are both of the *Lutheran* Religion.

XI. The CHAMBERLAINS. Of these there are too many to be all mention'd here, so that I shall only take notice of the twelve Pensioners who are in waiting about their Majesties, and without regarding the Seniority of their Admittance. They com-

commonly attend the King and Queen, each a whole Week in their turn, and have the Rank of Major-Generals. The finest Prerogative of their Employment, is the Honour of eating with their Majesties when they are in Waiting, and of being the Depositaries of the Petitions which are presented to the King in his Passage.

1. *Henry Rodolph de Schonfeld*, Lord of *Lowenitz*, is the King's first Chamberlain. He has a fine Presence and Behaviour, and a sweet and amiable Temper. He keeps a handsome Table and Equipage, suitable to his Fortune. He attended the King, by his Majesty's Order, to *Cracow*; and lastly to *Oliva*.

2. *Helmuth de Plesk* is of a Family in the Dutchy of *Holstein*, of some Note for their great Estate there, and for the Rank they bear at the Court of *Denmark*, where several Lords of *Plesk* are in the Ministry. The Gentleman here mention'd is actually the King's Envoy Extraordinary to the Court of *Denmark*.

3. *Augustus-Henry Gottlob*, Count *de Callenberg*, is of this Electorate, where his Family has for a long time enjoy'd a considerable Rank, and a fine Estate. He has been the King's Envoy Extraordinary to the Courts of *France*, *Brussels*, *Cologn*, *Triers*, and the Elector *Palatine*, to notify the Death of the late King, and the Accession of their present Majesties to the Electorate. He married the Countess of *Bose*, lives nobly, and adorns the Court by his Politeness. He is of the Protestant Communion.

4. *John-George de Carlowitz* is of the same Religion. He is a *Saxon*, and married to Madamoiselle *de Neitsch*. He has a peculiar Talent of gaining the Love of all Mankind; which he owes to his Travels, and his natural Genius.

5. *Frederic-Augustus de Brandstein*, after having finish'd his Studies at *Wittenberg*, travell'd to good

purpose to the principal Countries of *Europe*. At his return the late King declar'd him a Gentleman of his Bed-Chamber, and some time after one of his Chamberlains. He is well descended, and what is convenient for a Courtier, he adheres to the Religion which is upermost in the State.

6. *Detler-Henry d'Einsiedel*, Brother to the Marshal of the Court, honours his Name by his personal Qualities. He is a handsome tall Gentleman, has a grand Presence, and few Gentlemen surpass him in Good-Manners, Address, and polite Literature. He study'd at *Wittenberg*, and afterwards made a Visit to the principal Courts of *Europe*: The last he made was to that of *Sweden*, whither he was sent by the King to notify the Death of his late Majesty, and the Accession of his present Majesty to the Electorate.

7. *Sigismond d'Arnim*, is not only one of the King's Chamberlains, but Colonel of a Regiment of Horse. He is of an ancient Family which has Lands in *Lusatia*. His Employments are owing both to his Birth and personal Merit. He is of the Religion of the Country.

8. *Maximilian*, Count *d'Herzan*, is of *Bohemia*. The late Countess his Mother was the Queen's first Lady of Honour, and attended her Majesty hither from *Vienna*. He is able to cut a Figure at Court, but is absent above half of his time; and is a *Roman* Catholic.

9. *Charles-Christian de Minckwitz*, is a Gentleman of a fine Mien. As he has been a great Traveller, he has acquir'd a great share of Knowledge and Politeness. He was born a *Saxon*, but has embrac'd the *Roman* Catholic Faith; tho' he has defeated himself by it of the Reversion of a considerable Inheritance.

10. *Henry-Augustus de Breitenbauch*, is a Gentleman of fine Sense and Manners suitable to his Extraction.

traction. Such is his good Taste and Skill in Music, that he has been singled out for the Direction of the King's Pleasures. He is of the Communion of the Country, and marry'd to a Lady of the Family of *Schonberg*.

11. *Nicholas-Schwizinski* is a Native of *Poland*; he has valuable Qualities, and a great Attachment to the *Roman* Catholic Religion.

12. *N. N. de Sebgutt-Stanislawski* is of a Family which was formerly possess'd of a great Estate in *Silesia*, with the Title of the Counts *de Sebgutt*, till the Conquest of the Country by the *Teutonic* Knights, when his Ancestors remov'd to *Prussia*; and spreading afterwards in *Poland*, they assum'd the Name of *Stanislawski*, as what was more agreeable to the *Poles*. This Chamberlain is a Person of strict Honour and Integrity, without any manner of Guile. He spent his Youth at the Academy of *Berlin* which was erected by King *Frederic* I. and afterwards enter'd as Gentleman of the Bed-Chamber to *Augustus* II. who not many Years after made him a Chamberlain of *Poland*, and put him upon the Establishment of *Saxony*; and when the present King came to the Government, he continued him in his Employment. His Majesty also made choice of him to attend him to *Cracow*, and lastly to *Oliva*.

XII. Of the STEWARD of the QUEEN's HOUSHOLD. Since the Queen's Arrival at *Dresden*, there have been four Stewards of her Majesty's Houshold. The Count *de Diedrichstein* was the first that had this Place, which he resign'd for the Grand Priory of *Bohemia*. His Successor was the Count *de Konigsegg* who actually commands the Emperor's Army in *Lombardy*. This General being recall'd to *Vienna*, was replac'd by the Count *de Wratislau*, and he by the Count *de Waldstein* who lately quitted that Post to go and take possession of the Office of *Landshauptmann*, or Intendant of *Silesia*, which was conferr'd on him by the Emperor. The Count *de Wratislaw*, who has the care of his Imperial Majesty's Affairs at this Court, officiates there again as Steward. This is the Officer who leads the Queen, and gives Orders to all her Officers and Domestics, and who must be apply'd to by those that solicite for an Audience of her Majesty.

XIII. The *Queen's first Lady of Honour*, is *Theresa* Baroness of *Stein*, and Countess Dowager of *Collowrat*; who honours her Station by her Virtues, and by the Dignity with which she fills it. The late Count *de Collowrat* her Husband was Great Chamberlain of *Bohemia*, and one of the chief Noblemen of that Kingdom. This Lady, his Relict, is a *Roman* Catholic, and is such in an exemplary manner. Those Ladies who want to kiss the Queen's Hand, or to pay their Duty to her, must apply to this Lady, who introduces and presents them. She has the Precedence before all other Ladies, and only yields it to the Princesses of the Blood.

XIV. Of the *Governess of the Ladies of Honour, and of the Ladies of Honour themselves*. In the absence of the first Lady of Honour, the Governess of the Ladies officiates. The Baroness Dowager of *Robr* worthily fills this Station, and has under her six Ladies, two of whom, *viz.* the Countesses of *Waldstein* and *Kokersowitz*, are Ladies of the Bed-Chamber; a Title which procures them Admittance to the Queen's Closet. All the Ladies of Honour must always appear in the Court-Dress. Their manner of Living is such that it obliges Calumny itself to respect them.

XV. Of the *Lords and Ladies that are attach'd to the Court by their Offices, or by the Favours of the King.*
Tho'

Tho' the *Polish* Lords cannot be put upon the Eſtabliſhment of the Court of *Saxony*, that there may be nothing in common between the two States, yet it may be thought inexcuſable not to mention in this place *John-Alexander Lipſki*, Biſhop of *Cracow*, Duke of *Servia*, and Great Chancellor of *Poland*; not only becauſe this Prelate, who is deſcended from one of the beſt Families in the Kingdom, was appointed Biſhop of *Cracow* by the late King, but becauſe he has given ſignal Proofs of his Gratitude and Attachment to the auguſt Family of his Benefactor. The Virtues of this Gentleman intitle him to Reſpect: He is pious without Hypocriſy, generous without Oſtentation, magnificent without Pageantry, officious meerly for the Pleaſure of obliging, a Courtier without Servility, a Man ſtrictly attach'd to his King and his Country, learned without being poſitive, a great Orator, a good Biſhop, and a wiſe Miniſter, always ready to embrace a good Propoſal, and firm to ſupport it, laborious, vigilant, acting only out of Principle, and by conſequence ſuſceptible of Friendſhip, and ſcorning Revenge. The late King, out of his Eſteem for the Qualities of this Prelate, made him Biſhop of *Cracow*, Great Chancellor of *Poland*, and honour'd him with his Order of the White Eagle. By this means he ſo rivetted him to his Intereſt, and to that of the Prince his Son, that after his Majeſty's Deceaſe, his moſt Reverend Highneſs directed Affairs in ſuch a manner that the Republic choſe his Son for their King. *Auguſtus* II. being proclaim'd accordingly, the Prince and Biſhop was appointed Head of the Embaſſy which the States of the Kingdom ſent to the new Monarch at *Tarnowitz*, to carry him the Diploma of his Election. He ſpoke upon this occaſion with a noble Eloquence, rendering to their Majeſties all due Reſpects, and yet maintaining the Dignity of the moſt Serene

Republic. Having difcharg'd this Commiffion, he went before the King to *Cracow*, made his Entry there, and took poffeffion of the Bifhoprick. Some days after this, he confecrated and crown'd their Majefties in his Metropolis. When the King return'd to *Saxony*, the Prelate followed him, and attended him to *Oliva*; and 'twas he that receiv'd the Allegiance and Homage of the *Dantzickers* to his Majefty. He is fince come hither to rejoin the Court, is belov'd, reverenc'd, and every one does Juftice to his Virtues.

Charles-Lewis, Prince of *Holftein-Beck*, Colonel in the Service of the King, and Knight of the Order of the White Eagle, is the fecond Son of the late *Lewis-Frederic* Veldt-Marfhal of *Pruffia*, Governour of *Koningsberg*, and Knight of the Order of the Elephant. This Prince married *Anne* Countefs of *Orfelfka*, the legitimated Daughter of the late King.

George-Ignatius, Prince *de Lubomirfki*, Sword-Bearer of the Crown, Lieutenant-General of the King's Forces, Colonel of the Life-Guards, and Knight of the Order of the White Eagle, is defcended from a Family of very great Diftinction in *Poland*. After he return'd from his Travels, being attach'd to the Court of *Auguftus* II. he married the Daughter of the Count *de Fitztuhm*, who was Great Chamberlain; a Lady of fuch Beauty, fuch perfonal Charms, and fuch fine Senfe, that fhe engages the Veneration of all that know her. Prince *Lubomirfki* is a jolly handfome Man, very polite, thinks and acts agreeable to his Birth, has a good fhare of Literature, and is perfect Mafter of Mufic. He lives in a handfome manner very fuitable to his Rank.

The *Princefs* of *Tefchen* is a *Polifh* Lady, and ally'd to the greateft Families in the Kingdom. Her Uncle was the famous Cardinal *Radjowfki*,

Archbishop of *Gnesna*, and Primate of the Kingdom. She was formerly marry'd to Prince *Lubomirski*, Great Chamberlain of the Crown; but the Marriage was dissoved, so that she quitted the Name of *Lubomirski* for that of *Teschen*, which she still bears, tho' she afterwards marry'd Prince *Lewis* of *Wirtemberg*. This Princess supports her Rank with Dignity, has a grand Air, is respected for a noble distinguish'd and engaging Behaviour, and lives in so handsome a manner, that she is one of the most shining Ornaments of this Court.

Josepha Countess *de Lagnasco* is the Daughter of the Count *de Wallenstein*, who was Great Chamberlain to the Emperor *Joseph*, and one of the most worthy Noblemen of the Imperial Court, by *Eleonora* Countess of *Losenstein*; a Lady whose Memory is with Justice rever'd by all *Vienna*. The Countess *de Lagnasco* was the Widow of Count *Thaun*, when she marry'd the late Count *de Lagnasco*, Minister of the Cabinet to *Augustus* II. General of the *Saxon* Cavalry, Captain of the Horse-Guards, and Knight of the Order of the White Eagle. Since that Nobleman's Decease, which was in *April* 1732, his Widow has always liv'd at *Dresden*; where she enjoys the Esteem of their Majesties, and the Veneration of the Courtiers. This Countess is Mistress of several Languages to Perfection, thoroughly understands Music, and sings with Grace and Method. Her noble generous way of living, and her graceful and distinguish'd Behaviour cannot be express'd, nor indeed equall'd to any thing but the Goodness of her Temper. The late Count *de Lagnasco* is of a good Stature, and his Behaviour polite and civil. I think you know that he was of a Family in *Piedmont* of some Distinction. How, or when he first enter'd into the Service of the King of *Poland*, I cannot tell you; but I know that he presently insinuated himself

self into his Master's Favour, by his very great Assiduity, agreeable Temper, and by a vast Complaisance to enter into his Pleasures. He establish'd himself so firmly in the King's Favour that the Count *de Flemming* look'd upon him as the only Rival he had to fear, and therefore he never much lik'd him. The Count *de Lagnasco* was employ'd in several Embassies; and when he had finish'd that at *Rome*, which was his last, there was a Talk that he was to go Ambassador to *Vienna*, and that the young Count *de Wackerbart* was to go to *Rome*. I must further acquaint you that M. *de Lagnasco* was happy in all respects, even in Marriage, not only with his first, but his second Wife, who, when he married her, was a young, rich, brisk Widow. His first Wife was the Daughter of the Count *de Noyelles*, Lieutenant-General in *Holland*, a Lady of great Virtue, esteemed by all the People at the *Hague*, and possess'd of a considerable Estate, of which, dying young, and without Issue, she made her Husband sole Heir.

Francis, Count *de Montmorency*, is a Name too well known to speak of his Extraction. He was a Colonel in *France* when he went into the Service of *Augustus* II. who receiv'd him with that Demonstration of Esteem which that King was so ready to grant to Persons of Merit. His Majesty first appointed him Major-General of his Forces, and some time after he declar'd him a Lieutenant-General, and Captain of his Horse-Guards. At that time the Count married Madame *Potschin*, Widow of the Great General of *Lithuania*; a Lady whose Birth, Qualities, and Fortune, recommended her for a very considerable Match. The Countess *de Montmorency*, in the time of her former Husband, went to *Paris* for the Recovery of her Health, and receiv'd extraordinary Honours at the *French* Court, where she was admir'd for her Politeness, *the Court of* SAXONY.   153

the Delicacy of her Sentiments, and the Ease with which she express'd them in the Language of *France*; from whence they conceiv'd an advantagious Idea of the Court of *Augustus* II. not imagining how 'twas possible for the Manners of a Foreign Lady so much to resemble their own. She is also as much rever'd at *Dresden* as at *Paris*; and all that know her, agree she is highly to be valued for her Sentiments.

Antoinetta of *Lichtenstein*, Countess of *Wallenstein*, is Wife to *Leopold* Count *de Wallenstein*, heretofore Great Master of the Queen's Houshold; a Lady both belov'd and honour'd at this place, for her Virtues and civil Deportment; and as she is preparing to follow her Husband into *Silesia*, she will carry with her the Esteem of their Majesties, and leave the Court sorry for her Absence.

XVI. *Of the Foreign Ministers who reside at this Court.*

Francis-Charles Count *de Wratislaw*, one of the Emperor's Privy Council, and Knight of the Orders of *Russia* and *Poland*, resides at this Court in quality of Ambassador from his Imperial and Catholic Majesty. He is descended from one of the greatest Families in the Kingdom of *Bohemia*, and a Family which has given wise Ministers to the august House of *Austria*. This Gentleman has been for a long time in the Management of the most important Affairs: He was Ambassador for the Kingdom of *Bohemia* to the Dyet of the Empire at *Ratisbon*: From thence he went in the same Character to *Poland*, where he was present at the Dyet of *Grodno*. The Emperor afterwards nam'd him Great Master of the Houshold to the Princess Royal and Electoral, now Queen of *Poland*. The Count having worthily acquitted himself of that Office, was for several Years Ambassador

bassador at *Russia*, where he concluded that happy Alliance subsisting between the two Empires, and acquired the Esteem of the Empress, who honou'd him with her Order of St. *Andrew*; *Augustus* II. having before given him that of the White Eagle.

This Minister, since his Return from *Muscovy*, has moreover been charg'd by the Emperor with important Commissions to the Courts of *Prussia*, *Brunswic*, and *Holstein*. At length he is come back again to this Court, as Ambassador from his Imperial and Catholic Majesty; and officiates also as Great Master of the Queen's Houshold. This Nobleman is of a middling Stature, of a happy Physiognomy, is civil, beneficent, and loves Grandeur and Pleasures, but does not abandon himself to them so far as to neglect the Interests of his Master, whose Affairs he negociates with a noble Candour which has render'd him as much esteem'd at the Courts where he has resided, as he is beloved for his Affability and Politeness. His Wife is the Countess of *Kinski*, whose Father was Great Chancellor of *Bohemia*, under the Emperor *Leopold*, and whose Brother is now in that Office under the most August *Charles* VI.

Hermann-Charles Keyserling, Plenipotentiary Minister from the Empress of the *Russians*, is of a Family of Note in *Courland*. He study'd at *Koningsberg* in *Prussia*. After he had visited the principal Courts of *Germany*, and return'd to his own Country, he was made Gentleman of the Bed-Chamber to the Dutchess of *Courland*, *Anne* of *Muscovy*, the present Empress, who employ'd him in several Commissions to the Courts of *Prussia* and *Poland*. Nevertheless he quitted her Service for one of the judicial Offices in that Country.

When *Anne* came to the Throne, the States of *Courland* deputed M. *Keyserling* to that Princess, who

who offer'd him an Employment at her Court, and appointed him Vice-President of the Chamber of Justice of the *Russian* Empire. Some time after, she made him President of the Academy of Sciences at *Petersbourg*, and sent him to this Court, where he discharges his Ministerial Office with universal Approbation. The Wife of this Minister is the Daughter of the Starost *Forchs*, who, for opposing the Pretensions of a certain Power which challeng'd more Respect, was assassinated at *Mittaw*. Both he and his Lady are of the *Lutheran* Communion.

John-Hartwig-Ernest, Baron of *Bernsdorff*, Gentleman of the Bed-Chamber to the King of *Denmark*, and his Majesty's Envoy at this Court, is of a Family which is possess'd of a fine Estate in *Mecklembourg*, and has given an able Minister to the House of *Hanover*. The Envoy, of whom mention is here made, does honour to his Character, and behaves with a Prudence not inferior to Ministers of the greatest Experience.

By the Detail I have now given you, Sir, you must have observ'd that the chief Employments of the Court are in the hands of Foreigners, and that *Saxons* have little to do in Affairs of State, for which they are oblig'd indeed to the Count *de Flemming*. This vain, haughty, and imperious Minister expected every one shou'd truckle to him. He found that Foreigners were much more submissive than the *Saxons*, who are by nature stately, and Enemies to Slavery in any shape. Count *Flemming* being dead, it's probable that the *Saxons* will be more employ'd than they have been; and indeed they have Capacities equal to any Nation in the World. They are well made, robust, agile, laborious, good Soldiers, cunning Courtiers. They have naturally more Spirit than the *French* allow to the *Germans*; they improve in the Sciences, and
in

in bodily Exercises, and they have good Writers among them upon all sorts of Subjects; witness the Works of M. *Leibnitz*, the famous Philosopher, and of *Thomasius*, one of the most able Civilians of his time. The *Saxons* are addicted indeed to all Pleasures in general, but to none so much as the Bottle and Gaming. They love Pomp and Expence, and are naturally not very engaging, being exceeding ceremonious, and affecting more than all the *Germans* to ape the *French*, with whom they sympathise very much, particularly in their Fondness for new Fashions, their Forwardness to make new Acquaintance and Friendships, and perhaps too in their Readiness to fall out with them upon very trivial Occasion.

Since I have spoke so much of the Men, I must also give you some account of the *Saxon* Women. They are all of a fair Complexion, and there are among them the finest Faces in the World. They are generally well shap'd too, which is what they are chiefly taken notice of for: They are tall and slender; they dance well, and have a surprising genteel Air, which they take great care to improve by rich Dress. One Fault I find with them is, that they are very affected, and that they have too much Action when they talk. As to their Tempers, they are reckon'd to be good-natur'd; but then they are subtile and crafty. They love Dress and Ornament more than all Women that I ever saw. They are lively and gay, and passionately fond of Dancing and Merriment. When they are told that they are handsome, they are so far from being surpriz'd that they look upon it as a Compliment due to them. When once they love, they love with Tenderness; and there are among them such Examples of Constancy as would eclipse even a *Cleopatra*, or a *Clelia*. These heroic Sentiments of Love they learn from Romances, which they are

vastly

vastly fond of: But this must be said to their Honour, that Gallantry does not take up so much of their Time and Thoughts as to make them neglect their Business; for they are laborious, dextrous, and amuse themselves with all sorts of Work. They do every thing too with a good Grace; and in a word it may be added to their Praise, that a *Saxon* Woman wants nothing more to make her amiable, but an Inclination to acquire that Character.

Pleasures and Recreations commonly attend the Ladies so closely, that in treating of the one I can't but remember the other; and the Inhabitants of *Dresden* are so much devoted to Pleasures, that I think I ought to put them into a separate Article. When the King is at *Dresden* there are Pleasures in abundance, such as Plays, Masquerades, Balls, Feasts, Running at the Ring, and Races on Sleds, Turnaments, Hunting-Matches; but when the King is in *Poland* there's a very great *Vacuum*. The Electoral Prince and Princess are often at *Wermstorff*, alias *Hubertsbourg*; and even when their Royal Highnesses are in Town, they are pretty retir'd: They see Company while they are at Dinner, but for the rest of the day none come near them besides the few that have the honour of their Confidence. The rest are scatter'd up and down the Town to the great Disappointment of Foreigners that happen then to be here; for there's no body keeps open House, they being all select Societies to which 'tis very difficult to gain admittance. If one is invited to dine with some Lord of the Court, one has a good Dinner 'tis true, but after Dinner is over a Man knows not how to bestow himself. One is sure of finding Company no where except at the Houses of Madame *de Brebentau* the Widow of the great Treasurer of *Poland*, and of the Countess *de Lagnasco*; nor are their Houses always open, for Madame *de Brebentau* is often

often sick, and Madame *de Lagnasco* often abroad, or engag'd in Parties with the Electoral Princess, and then one knows not where to go; for there's no Play to be seen, and as for the young People, they amuse themselves with the common Pleasures of that Stage of Life; they drink, they game, and do something more.

When the King is at *Dresden*, the People partake in most of the Pleasures of the Court, the generality of the Entertainments which the King gives being public. Plays and Masquerades are free for any People of Fashion; there's nothing to pay, and all divert themselves as they like best. The Citizens Wives are more tractable here than in any Town in *Germany:* They love to imitate the Ladies of Quality, and 'tis sometimes as good as a Comedy to see what Airs they give themselves.

They are extremely fond of Dressing, which Luxurious Taste extends even to Wives of the Mechanics, and of the Livery; so that were a Stranger to come hither on a Sunday or a Holiday, when every body is dress'd, he wou'd be tempted to think that *Plutus* had scatter'd all his Wealth among these People; and a very great Nobleman, who 'tis like was not acquainted with the God *Plutus*, returning home once from *Dresden*, told his Wife that he was come from a City to which the Devil had carry'd all the Money.

The Parsons here do indeed cry aloud against these Abuses, but the worst on't is, that like the Clergy in many other Places, they preach what they don't practise; and while they are declaiming against Luxury and new Fashions, they suffer their Wives and Daughters to be the first to set off their Charms with the gayest and the newest Patterns.

While I am speaking of the Pastors, I must be a little more particular. These Gentlemen stand very high in the Opinion of the Laity, and are

ready

ready to think themselves Bishops. Having such Notions as these in their Heads, they anathematise all that are not *Lutherans*: The *Catholics* and the *Reform'd*, or, to speak as they do, the *Papists* and *Calvinists*, all Christians in short who are of a contrary Opinion to those charitable Ecclesiastics are damn'd without Mercy. Yet by the Appearance of these severe Judges, one would think they preach'd only Peace and Paradise; and they have such a meek, humble, modest, and timorous Air, that you wou'd be apt to take them for Saints.

A few days ago I had an Adventure with one of those Clergymen, which I will acquaint you of, because I think it may give you an Idea of their Character; for he that sees one of them, sees all.

I happen'd to be making a Visit to a *Lutheran* Lady, who passes for a very devout one: There was already a pretty deal of Company, and who should come in to add to it but a Minister that was a Doctor, and by consequence a Man of Importance; as such too he was receiv'd by the Mistress of the House, who said to me as soon as she saw his Face, *You will now see a holy Man*. The good Man, or Saint, as he wou'd be reckon'd, enter'd the Room with his Eyes cast downward, making profound Reverences, and prostrating himself in such a manner as if he had said *Domine non sum dignus*. At last, after a great many Compliments, he sat down, was silent for a few Moments, and then he spoke. His Words were all sacred, and his Sentences such as if the wise Man himself had spoke with his Lips: *God be prais'd* was in every Phrase, and he was hearken'd to with as much Attention as an Oracle. I listen'd to him first like the rest, but at length I thought I might as well talk to a pretty young Lady that sat just by me. The Doctor offended to see the little Regard I paid to what he said, enquir'd of the Mistress of the House who I was.

She

She told him my Name, and withal that I was once a *Calvinist*, but that I was turn'd *Papist*. What a Thunder-stroke was this to the Doctor! He threw himself to the back of his Chair, lifted up his Eyes to Heaven, sigh'd, and cry'd out, *Das Gott erbarme*, i. e. *God help us.* Then transported by a Fit of Zeal, he turn'd about to me and ask'd me what had induc'd me to embrace a Religion which he treated as Idolatry? I told him that I did not think he need to give himself any Trouble about my Conversion, since according to his System I was damn'd when a *Calvinist* as well as when a *Catholic*. *The Case is not quite the same*, said the Minister; but to turn *Papist*! cry'd he, to *adore Baal*! *to become a Disciple of Antichrist! alas! it were better to be a damn'd Calvinist!* I own that I had much a-do to help laughing outright at the Minister's impertinent Zeal: yet I had the Discretion to contain myself, for I had a mind to see to what length he wou'd carry his sanctify'd Rant. He said indeed a great deal, and because I made no Answer, he thought he had convinc'd me, if not touch'd me to the quick. He was actually applauding himself for the good Work he had wrought upon my Soul, when I told him that he ought not to conclude from my Silence that he had convinc'd me; that it neither consisted with my Character nor my Temper to dispute about Religion, that I left every Man to his own Opinion, and that I knew which to adhere to. *What Blindness is here!* cry'd the Doctor again, *What a mad Papist are you? If you will not be of our Communion, return to the Religion which you have abandon'd, in which there are some Hopes at least that God will pardon you.*

The fanatical Doctor concluded his Exclamations by a Prayer, in which he begg'd God to preserve every good *Lutheran* Soul from the Errors of Popery;

Popery; and then he went away, leaving the Company more scandaliz'd than edify'd by his Zeal.

Formerly the Preachers had the pleasure of venting their Choler in the Pulpit, but the King by a wise Decree, which indeed ought to be followed in all Countries, has confin'd them to the Preaching of the Gospel, and to treat of Controversial Matters no farther than is merely necessary for the People's Instruction. For the rest, the Parsons need not fear being soon supplanted, for the *Saxons* are hearty *Lutherans*; and if they tolerate the Catholics, 'tis because they cant help it. They have excluded them from Offices in the Courts of Judicature, and from the Privilege of enjoying Lands; but they have not been able to keep them out of Places in the Ministry, or at Court, nor from Employments in the Army, which are three very engaging Articles to make Proselytes among the Gentry.

Thus, Sir, you have all that I can say to you relating to *Dresden* and *Saxony*. 'Tis now high time to put an end to my Legend. I kiss your hand, and am, &c.

LETTER VI.

Weimar, Sept. 5. 1729.

SIR,

BEFORE I write you an account of what became of me when I left *Dresden*, I shall endeavour to give you the Intelligence you desire concerning the late Count *de Flemming*, Prime Minister and Velt-Marshal of *Saxony*. That Nobleman was of a good Extraction, being descended of a Family which pretends to derive its Origin from that of *Flemming*, which has been of considerable Rank for a long time in *Scotland*, *Sweden*, *Germany*, and *Poland*. My Lord *Wigtoun* is the Chief of that Family in *Scotland*.

James-Henry Count *de Flemming*, whose Pourtraiture and Character you desire of me, was born the 8th of *March* 1667. His Father was President of the Regency of *Stargard*, the Capital of *Prussian Pomerania*, who had three Sons, of whom this Count was the second. He had an Education suitable to his Birth. He study'd first at *Francfort* upon the *Oder*, and afterwards at *Utrecht* under the celebrated *Grævius*, where he learnt *Latin* to such a degree that he always spoke it with very great Eloquence. After he had finish'd his Studies he enter'd into the Service of *Brandenbourg*, where the Baron *de Span*, his Uncle by the Mother's side, was Velt-Marshal. His first Preferment was to a Pair of Colours; but in a little time he had a Company given him, which he commanded at the Battle of *Orbassan* in *Piedmont*. In 1694, he enter'd as a

Lieutenant-Colonel into the Service of *John-George* IV. Elector of *Saxony*; upon whose Death, and the Succession of *Frederic-Augustus*, *Flemming* obtain'd a Regiment, and accompany'd the new Elector into *Hungary*, where he commanded the Emperor's Army against the Infidels during the Campaigns of 1695, and 1696. There it was that *Flemming* kill'd in a Duel the Baron *de Lovel*, who was Lieutenant-Colonel in the Service of *Saxony*. In 1697, he was sent into *Poland*, where, by the Interest of his Cousin-german, the Daughter of Velt-Marshal *Span* of *Berlin*, Wife of M. *Brebentau* Palatine of *Marienbourg*, who died Great Treasurer of *Poland*, and by the Credit of *Benedict Sapieha* he had the Happiness of getting his Master chose King of *Poland*. This Negotiation obtain'd him the Post of Major-General, and laid the Foundation of his Fortune. In 1700, he was made a Lieutenant-General, and in that Quality laid siege to *Riga*, which the King of *Sweden* oblig'd him to raise. In 1702, he marry'd *Sapieha*, a Daughter of one of the chief Noblemen of *Lithuania*. He was wounded the same Year at the Battle of *Clischhoff*, at which time the King of *Sweden* being every where victorious, demanded that the King of *Poland* shou'd deliver up *Flemming* to him. But upon this he retir'd to *Brandenbourg*, till King *Stanislaus* had made *Charles* XII. easy. *Flemming* being return'd to *Saxony*, fought a Duel with M. *de Schulembourg*, who giving him a Fall, insisted that he should beg his Life; but *Flemming* got out of this ugly Scrape by a scurvy Joke, and *Schulembourg* gave him his Life. The latter was a younger Lieutenant-General than *Flemming*, but in every respect his Rival, and wou'd have been a Marshal if his Fortune had been as good as his Valour. At the Battle of *Frauenstad* in 1705, where he was defeated by the *Swedes*, *Schulembourg* quitted the Service of *Saxony* and went into that of *Venice*. By this means *Flemming*, who had now no Rival left, was made a Marshal, and happen'd to be at *Dresden* when the King of *Sweden* made that strange Visit to the King of *Poland*; at which time, if *Augustus* had been as ungenerous as *Flemming*, *Charles* wou'd have been detain'd. Many People accuse *Flemming* of having perſuaded the King his Maſter to deliver up *Patkul*: This I can't pretend to affirm, but that there was a mortal Antipathy betwixt him and the Miniſter of *Ruſſia* is certain; for the latter having preſented a Memorial to the King of *Poland*, ſetting forth the wretched condition of the *Muſcovite* Troops in the Pay of *Saxony*, concluded it with theſe *Latin* Words,

DIXI, ET SALVAVI ANIMAM.

Which Memorial, when *Flemming* had read, and found himſelf not very well uſed in it, he took a Pen and underwrote theſe Words,

MALEDIXISTI, ET DAMNABERIS.

After the Diſaſter which *Charles* XII. met with near *Pultowa*, *Flemming* contributed very much to the Re-eſtabliſhment of King *Auguſtus* in *Poland*. He confirm'd the Alliance betwixt his Maſter and the Czar, made Peace with the Confederates, and concluded another Alliance with *Denmark*. The Czar and the King of *Denmark* honour'd him with their Orders of Knighthood, and he had that of *Poland* before. He went Ambaſſador to the unſucceſsful Congreſs at *Brunſwic*, and was afterwards at *Hanover* to attend *George* I. King of *Great Britain*. When the King of *Sweden* return'd to *Pomerania*, *Flemming* left no Stone unturn'd to draw the King of *Pruſſia* into his Maſter's Alliance. He had ſome Years before procur'd him the Sequeſtration of the Town of *Stetin*, and 'twas lucky enough

for

for him that the Pride and Obstinacy of the King of *Sweden* obliged the King of *Prussia* to declare himself his Enemy. At that time *Flemming* was rather a Courier between *Dresden*, *Berlin*, and *Warsaw*, than an Ambassador and Prime Minister, which Dignity he enjoy'd after the Death of the Prince *de Furstemberg* his Predecessor. When the Peace of the North was settled, *Flemming* went Ambassador to *Vienna*, where he concluded the Marriage of the Electoral Prince of *Saxony* with the Archduchess, eldest Daughter to the Emperor *Joseph*, tho' the Contract had been settled before by the Count de *Wackerbarth*, who it may be said had the Pains to negotiate it, and *Flemming* the Glory of finishing it.

At this time Count *Flemming* had resign'd all the Salaries of his Employments in *Saxony*, and only reserv'd to himself the private Perquisites and the Franchise of the Post-Offices; and his Journeys, which were very frequent, were all at the Expence of the King. It was about this time that he caus'd his Marriage with *Sapieha* to be dissolv'd, and marry'd one *Radzevil*, by whom he had a Son, who was but a Year and a half old when the Count died at *Vienna*, to which place he was return'd with the Character of Ambassador. He left all his Estate to this Child, without making any Intail on his Family; so that when this Son died, who did not long survive him, his Estate went to Madame *de Flemming*, who by marrying again carry'd the Bulk of it into another Family. They say that his Inheritance was worth sixteen Millions of Crowns, exclusive of what he had expended during the Splendor of his Fortune, which lasted thirty Years, or thereabouts. Whether *Richelieu* and *Mazarine* got greater Estates, I cannot say; but in *Germany* there is not an Instance of one sooner acquir'd, more resplendent, and better supported than his was. He was Prime Minister, Velt-Marshal of

Saxony, and Master of the Horse of *Lithuania*; by which Offices he gain'd immense Sums. He made considerable Purchases in *Silesia* and *Poland*, but very little in *Saxony*. Whether he left any thing to the King is not said; tho' he ought really to have made him some Restitution, and he might naturally have given up with a good Grace what he cou'd not but foresee wou'd be taken by force from his Heir. As it was just that his Succession shou'd pass thro' the Purgatory of a *Chambre Ardente*, the King establish'd one, which 'tis said has adjudg'd eight Millions to his Majesty, and the same to his Widow; which is a very fair Dividend.

Count *Flemming* was taller than ordinary, but a handsome Man; he had very regular Features, a lively Eye, a disdainful Sneer, a haughty Air, and he was really proud, and beyond measure ambitious. He was generous to a degree of Ostentation, and always aim'd to do something to be talk'd of. He was vigilant, laborious, indefatigable, allow'd himself little Sleep; and whenever he took a Debauch, a Nap of two Hours set him to rights again. It was no more for him to go from a Debauch to Business, than from Business to a Debauch; and he never fatigu'd himself, but dispatch'd the greatest Affairs with so much Ease as if they were only a Diversion. He lov'd to banter, but did not always make use of the Terms suitable to his Character; and Persons who did not dare to answer him again, were commonly the Butts of his Raillery. He was polite when he had a mind to it, but in the general Course of his Behaviour he carry'd an Air fitter for a Captain of Dragoons than for a Marshal and a Prime Minister. He never did a thing for any body without some View; he scrupl'd neither Cunning nor even Perjury, and provided he could gain his Ends, all ways were alike fair to him. All his Life-time he took care to do his own Business first,

first, and then his Master's the King's; and I question whether I do him any Injustice if I say that he was the King of *Prussia*'s Minister, much more than the King of *Poland*'s.

This, Sir, is all that I have to say to you concerning Count *Flemming*. I have told you very nakedly what I always thought of him, and I don't believe that I have mistaken his Character. Be this as it will, my Decision is of too little weight to do either Good or Harm; the Publick will always judge of him according to their best Information. I proceed now with the Narrative of my Travels.

After I had set out from *Dresden* I went to *Altenbourg* in hopes of finding the Court of *Gotha* there, which I had been told, intended to spend the Remainder of the fine Season there; but it was set out the Night before for *Gotha*, where I hope to see it to-morrow.

The City of ALTENBOURG is the Capital of a County of that Name, of which the Duke of *Saxe-Gotha* is the Sovereign. This Prince has a Palace there which makes a handsome appearance, but I shall say nothing more of it because I neglected to go and see it. The Peasants of the County of *Altenbourg* are the richest in *Germany*, and may almost vye with those of *Holland*. I have been assur'd that some of them have given 20 or 30000 Crowns in Marriage with their Daughters; and like the *Dutch* Peasants, they take care to match them to none but the Sons of substantial Farmers.

As I left *Altenbourg* I came upon a fine Causey with a Row of Trees on each side, which brought me to the Frontiers of the County. I afterwards fell into very bad Roads all the way to *Leipsic*, where I stay'd but a very few Hours, and proceeded the same day to MERSEBOURG. This City was much more considerable formerly than now. It was the

See of a Bishop, but was seculariz'd by the Treaty of *Passaw* in favour of the House of *Saxony*. Its Situation is charming, with Gardens and Meadows all round it, and its Walls are wash'd by the River *Sala*. The great Church which was formerly a Cathedral is a *Gothic* Building, where there is a stately Tomb of the Emperor *Rodolph* of *Schwartzbourg*, who died after he had lost one Hand in a Battle he fought with the Emperor *Henry* IV. with whom he was Competitor. This Prince a few Moments before he expir'd, took up his Hand that was cut off, and holding it up to those who were about him, said to them, *Behold this Hand; 'tis the same that I lifted up when I promis'd Faith and Allegiance to my Emperor and Lord; but by your Advice and Instigation I have not kept my Promise to him, for which you will one day give an account to God.* Some time after this unfortunate Prince's Death, the Emperor *Henry* IV. coming to *Mersebourg* and taking a view of *Rodolphus*'s Tomb, of which he admir'd the Magnificence, certain Flatterers told him that the Tomb ought to be destroy'd as too pompous for a Rebel; but the Emperor scorning such a pitiful Revenge, made answer, *Wou'd to God that all my Enemies were thus pompously interr'd.*

The City of *Mersebourg* is the Residence of a Duke of the House of *Saxony*, who is Sovereign of all the Country that formerly constituted the Bishoprick, which enables him to keep a splendid Court*. The next day after my Arrival I had the Honour to pay him my Compliments, and had a very satisfactory Reception. The Prince conducted me into a Hall which was hung with Bass-Viols from the Bottom to the Top, in the same manner as an Arsenal is with Helmets and Breast-Plates. In the middle of the Hall there was a Viol which was di-

---

* The Duke of *Mersebourg* died in 1731, and was succeeded by his Uncle, the Duke *de Springberg*.

distinguish'd from the rest. It reach'd up to the very Cieling, and there was a Ladder set, which such as had the Curiosity to take a particular View of it were oblig'd to ascend, for surely it was the most stately Instrument of the kind that ever was made. The Duke made me take particular notice of it, and was pleas'd with the Admiration which I express'd of it. He regal'd me also with some Airs upon another Bass-Viol which he call'd his *Favorite*, and which was but one fourth part as big as the other.

After this Concert I din'd with the Duke and Duchess. This Princess is the Daughter of the late Prince of *Nassau-Idstein*, than whom there cannot be a more amiable Lady. She has an Air of Mildness, Goodness and Prudence diffused over all her Features; and her Wit is of the same Stamp as her Beauty, amiable without Parade and Ostentation. Some of her Courtiers assur'd me, that her Mind is as charming as her Person. If that be true, which I am loth to doubt of, this Princess deserves a more splendid Fortune than what she enjoys.

After Dinner, I was one at a Match of Quadrille with the Duchess, and at night there was dancing, and I never saw any body dance with a better Grace than this Princess. The Ball held till the Night was far advanced, when there was a grand Supper, which was no sooner over than I took leave of the Duke and Duchess and retir'd to my Quarters, with a design to set out in a few Hours and proceed in my Journey. At my Lodging I found a Gentleman from the Duke, who said to me, ' That as he
' was passing by he saw my Men packing up my
' things, and that therefore he came in purely to
' wish me a good Journey. He assured me that
' he had a secret Kindness for me; that I might
' safely take his Word; that he was Sincerity it
' self; and that he wish'd 500000 Devils might
' twist his Neck if he was not heartily my Friend:
' And

'And to give you proofs of it, *said he*, I will treat
'you with some Trifle, such as a Dram of An-
'niseed, Orange-Water, or Ratafia. Upon my
'word my Apothecary has what is choice good;
'he lives but at the end of the Street; Come, I
'will shew you the way to his House.'

While he harangu'd me in this manner he reel'd, being so drunk that he cou'd not stand. I thank'd him therefore for his Love, and told him that I did not drink Drams, but that if he had a mind to any Liquor of that sort, I would send for some for him; and I bid my Landlord fetch it. The Apothecary, as ill luck would have it, was not yet got up.
'Soho, here, *said my new Friend*, there is nothing
'to drink but Aquavitæ; here, Landlord, a Glass
'of Brandy, Pipes and Tobacco. You must have
'something, *said he*, to be doing.' Every thing he call'd for being brought, my Gentleman drank two or three Glasses of Brandy, and smoak'd as many Pipes of Tobacco. I hoped to see him tumble down, and by consequence to get rid of him, when he took it into his head to call for some Dishes of Tea that I had order'd to be made for my self, and which made him so sober that he recover'd his Reason. I laid hold of this happy Interval (for I heard him calling out for Brandy, which I apprehended would occasion a Relapse) and talk'd to him about his Master's Bass-Viols; upon which, without much Intreaty, he said to me, 'You know, Sir, that every Man al-
'most has his particular Whim, Princes as well as
'private Persons. One is an Admirer of Magnifi-
'cence, another of Troops, and a third of Mistresses.
'As for my august Master, his Fancy runs only
'on Bass-Viols, and whoever sollicits him for an
'Employment or any other Favour, can't do better
'than to accommodate his Arsenal with one of these
'Instruments. That very large one, *said he*, which
'you saw in the Room where all his Viols are, was

'pre-

' presented to him by one who wanted to be a
' Privy-Counsellor; his Petition was granted, and
' had he ask'd for any thing else he might have
' had it.' This officious Gentleman told me a great
many other Particulars which let me into the very
Chronicle of the Court of *Merseburg*; but I don't
trouble you with it, because the Truth is not to be
told at all times.

My Equipage being ready, I set out for NAUM-
BOURG, where I arrived at Noon. This City was
formerly the See of a Bishop. Its ancient Cathedral
is still standing, and tho' *Lutheran*, has a Chapter
and Canons who must prove their Nobility both by
the Father's side and Mother's side, by sixteen Descents. When this Bishoprick was seculariz'd it
was said that no Catholic Prince could ever be
possess'd of this State. Therefore when the last
Duke of *Saxe-Zeits*, Administrator of *Naumbourg*,
turn'd Catholic, the King of *Poland* as eldest of
the *Saxon* Family and Executor of the *Pacta* or
Conventions made between the Princes of that Family, took possession of *Naumbourg*. The Duke's
being reconciled to the *Lutheran* Communion was
to no purpose, the King did not restore his Dominions to him, but still possesses them, tho' he is more
a Catholic than the Duke of *Zeits* perhaps ever
was. You know that this Prince has left a Nephew who would have been his Heir, if he had not
been a Catholic and a Priest. This is the Prince
who, I acquainted you from *Dresden*, was Bishop
of *Konigsgratz* in *Bohemia*. He was born a *Lutheran*,
as are all those of his Family. His Uncle the Cardinal of *Saxe*, Brother to the Duke of *Zeits*, made
him embrace the Roman Catholic Religion when
he was very young, and afterwards persuaded him
to enter into Ecclesiastical Orders, by which step
he deprived his Nephew of the glorious Prerogative of being a Sovereign Prince, and transferred his
Rights

Rights to the King of *Poland* his diftant Coufin.

Naumbourg is famous for its Fairs, which next to thofe of *Leipfic*, are the moft confiderable in *Saxony*. The Suburbs of this City are almoft all Vineyards; but why, I know not, for the Wine is fo deteftably bad, that they give it away in a manner for nothing.

Finding nothing at *Naumbourg* which was worth my while to ftay there for, I only chang'd Horfes and came hither. As one approaches this Place, we meet with Corn-Fields and Hop-Grounds inftead of Vines, and the Country rifes into Hills, fo that one does not fee the Town of WEIMAR till we are juft upon it. This City, which is not more confiderable than *Naumbourg*, is the Refidence of the Duke of *Saxe-Weimar*, who has a Palace here which does not want for Magnificence, and tho' unfinifh'd, has an air of Grandeur. The Connoiffeurs in Architecture highly extol the grand Stair-Cafe there, which two Perfons may afcend and defcend at the fame time without meeting one another, and yet always keeping each other in view. It confifts of two Flights of Stairs upon one Spindle, laid one over the other in the fame Well of a fquare Form. The Curious who have obferv'd it, admire it, becaufe there are few fuch to be feen.

The great Hall which is an oval, is beautiful, but not lightfome enough. There are the Pictures of all the Dukes of *Saxe-Weimar* at full length, from the firft Duke that ever was down to the Father of the prefent. They are all drawn on Horfeback, and done by no mean Hand.

In the fame Palace is the Duke's Library, which tho' not very large, confifts of fundry fcarce Books. 'Tis open twice a week, when the Curious are not only permitted to perufe them, but even to borrow them, upon leaving a Note with the Librarian.

The Duke of *Weimar* spends very little Time in his Capital, but commonly resides at a Seat which he has caus'd to be built about a League out of Town. He has given it the Name of *Belle-Vue*, because of the fine Prospect which it commands from the Apartments of the first Story. The House is small and not very commodious, so that the chief Beauty of it is its Situation, which is very charming. The Gardens which are begun upon very good Plans will be beautiful when finish'd, as well as the Pheasant-Walk and Menagerie where there are Turkeys and all sorts of Fowl.

The Duke of *Weimar*'s Name is *Ernest-Augustus*: He is the eldest of the *Ernestine* Branch which lost the Electorate when *Charles* V. was Emperor. He marry'd a Princess of *Anhalt-Cothen*, who I have been told, was a Lady of distinguish'd Merit. She died and left him a Son and three Daughters.

The young Prince is about ten Years of age *. He can neither hear nor pronounce well, and is withal of a very tender Constitution. The Physicians say it signifies nothing, and that as he grows up he will acquire a Freedom of Speech. But I question it, and am apt to think rather that those Disciples of *Æsculapius* will send him into the other World. The only Hopes of any Male Issue of *Weimar* are founded upon this Child. The Duke of *Saxe-Eysenach* who is the next a-kin has no Children; so that the Dominions of *Weimar* and *Eysenach* too are ready to devolve to the Family of *Saxe-Gotha*. The Duke of *Weimar*'s Subjects teaze him very much to marry, but the Prince does not seem to be in a Humour to satisfy them; for I have often heard him say that he can't bear the mention of Marriage.

No

---

* This Prince died in 1732.

No body presumes to go to *Belle-Vue* without being sent for, except only on *Mondays* when poor People are permitted to go thither with their Petitions which they deliver to the Secretary, and he gives them to the Duke. Persons of Quality, whether Foreigners or others, that have a mind to speak with the Duke, apply for it to the Marshal of the Court, but are seldom admitted to an Audience.

The Duke has rarely any other Company at *Belle-Vue* but two young Ladies whom he calls his Maids of Honour, and three young Women, Citizens Daughters, who go by the Name of his Chamber-Maids; a Major of his Troops, and the Officer of his Guard, who is a Lieutenant or an Ensign. I had forgot to mention the Baron *de Brubl*, who is the Duke's Favourite and his Master of the Horse.

'Tis with these Persons that the Prince passes his Time. He wakes early in the Morning, but makes it late before he rises; for he takes his Tea in Bed, and sometimes plays on the Violin. At other times he sends for his Architects and Gardeners, with whom he amuses himself in drawing of Plans. His Ministers also come to him while he is in Bed to talk upon Business. About Noon he gets up, and as soon as he is dress'd, sees his Guard mount, which consists of 33 Men, commanded by a Lieutenant or an Ensign. He exercises his Soldiers himself, and corrects them too when they commit any Fault. This done he takes the Air, and at two or three o'clock sits down to Table, where the two Maids of Honour, the Master of the Horse, the Major, the Officer of the Guard, and even Foreigners if any happen to be there, are of the Company. The Dinner holds a long while, and 'tis sometimes three, four, and five Hours before they rise from Table. The Glass never stands still hardly, and the Duke talks a great deal, but the Conversation is commonly on Subjects that are not very agreeable. When Dinner is over they drink
Coffee,

Coffee, after which the Duke retires for a few Minutes, and then plays at Quadrille with his two young Ladies and the Major; but sometimes he does nothing but smoak Tobacco, and he often retires to his Chamber where he amuses himself with Drawing or else playing on the Violin till he goes to Bed.

There scarce a Week passes but the Duke gives an Invitation at least once or twice to all the Persons of Quality of the Court, and all the Officers of his Troops, at which time there are two great Tables spread, where they dine, play, sup, and afterwards dance till next Day.

The Duke's Troops consist of a Battalion of 700 Men, a Squadron of 180 Troopers, and a Company of Cadets on horseback. His Infantry consists of pick'd Men. Since the famous *Bernard de Weimar* who was Pensioner to *Lewis* XIII. King of *France*, no Duke of *Weimar* had so many Troops, and really they must be chargeable to the Duke whose Revenues 'tis said don't exceed 400000 Crowns. This Prince has made a Treaty with the King of *Poland*, whereby he engages to assist the King with his Battalion whenever his Majesty thinks it necessary for his Service; in which Case the King promises to give that Battalion the same Pay as he does his own Troops. Mean time the Duke is obliged to clothe them all according to the Pattern which is sent to him from *Dresden*; and indeed their Clothes are very rich, especially those of the Officers and Cadets, which are so bedaub'd with Gold and Silver Lace, that a Foreigner who comes to *Weimar* cannot but admire it.

The Duke's Family is very numerous, for besides the Prince his Son and the three Princesses his Daughters, he has a Sister, and a Mother-in-law, who is a Princess of *Hesse-Hombourg:* Mean time he
has

has a numerous Court, and may boast that some of them are Persons of very great Merit.

The Gentleman who is at the Head of Affairs is the Baron *de Reinbabe*, who has the Title of President of the Council of State. He is a Person of a good Family, in *Silesia*, has very great Abilities, and withal so much Good-nature and Modesty as are seldom to be met with. When he was young he travell'd very much abroad, where he learnt what was valuable in every Country that he came to. He speaks several Languages well, is a great Historian, a learned Civilian, and a good Poet. Notwithstanding the Business that goes thro' his Hands, and his Care of a numerous Family, he is always almost at his Studies, and never better pleas'd than when he is in his Library; yet he is no Enemy to Pleasures, but enjoys them without abandoning himself to them, and takes them as they fall in his way without pursuing 'em. To finish his Character I will add what was said of him by a Prince who knew him intimately: *If Probity was intirely lost in the rest of Mankind*, said he to me, *I think I shou'd be sure to find it again in the Baron* de Reinbabe.

The Baron *de Schmiedel* is Marshal of the Court and Director of the military Chest. He is a Person of great Piety, whose Aspect is not indeed the most engaging, yet a very good Man to have to do with. He is a sincere Friend, loves to do a kind Thing, is exact in the Duties of his Offices, an Enemy to Vice, and very much attach'd to the Interests of his Master, tho' he does not always please him because he has not the Talent of Dissimulation so necessary at Courts.

The Baron *de Studenitz* a *Silesian* is a Privy-Counsellor, and President of the Chamber. He was formerly in the Service of the Duke of *Saxe-Barbi*, and afterwards he enter'd into that of the Duke of *Saxe-Hilburgshausen*, whose Finances he directed

directed for several Years, in which he acquired a Reputation, and came to *Weimar* where he was continued in the same Employment. He is a Gentleman of very great Learning and Integrity, and having travell'd a long time in his Youth, very well knows how to carry himself.

M. *de Hering* is of a noble Family in the Country of *Anhalt-Cothen.* He is the Duke's Aulic Counsellor, a Gentleman of Worth, and both Learned and Polite. He is on the point of leaving this Court, which will be a Loss to the Duke that he will not easily repair.

M. *de Bruhl* the Duke's Master of the Horse and Favourite, is a *Saxon.* His Birth, good Qualities, and especially his sweet Temper render him very worthy of a Sovereign's Favour. Yet I doubt whether, notwithstanding so much Merit, he has a firm Footing in the Duke's Friendship; he has too much Candor, too much Sincerity, and is too zealous to do Services; and perhaps also too much attach'd to the Interests and Honour of his Master: for tho' these Qualities have the Appearance of Virtues, yet they are sometimes Errors in the Eyes of Princes.

Thus, Sir, have I given you the Names of the most distinguish'd Persons at the Court of *Weimar.* I set out to-morrow for *Gotha.* I hope for a Line from you at *Wurtzbourg,* and don't propose to write again to you till I know whether you are living or dead.

I am, &c.

LETTER VII.

SIR, *Gotha, Sept.* 9, 1732.

I Set out from *Weimar* at 5 o'clock in the Morning, and by eight was at *Erfurt*, where I walk'd about an Hour, and came at Noon to *Gotha*.

'Tis all a flat Country abounding with Corn. In time of Rain the Roads are so bad that sometimes it takes up a whole Day to come from *Erfurt* to *Gotha*. ERFURT is a City belonging to the Elector of *Mentz*, is the Capital of *Thuringia*, and may be rank'd among those of the second Class in *Germany*. Its Inhabitants are almost all *Lutherans*, yet the principal Churches belong to the Catholics. *Erfurt* is fortified with good Ramparts, and by a Castle on a Hill which absolutely commands the Town. There is always a good Garison in the Place, which consists of the Emperor's Soldiers and those of *Mentz*; and the Elector has a Governor here with the Title of *Stadtholder*, who presides in the Regency.

GOTHA, which is not near so big as *Erfurt*, is a City situate in the middle of a fine fruitful Plain, so that which way soever one approaches it, one always perceives the Castle or Palace of the Duke, which stands on an Eminence by itself, and has a Prospect of a vast Extent of Country. This Castle, which is one of the biggest in *Germany*, was built by *Ernest* Duke of *Gotha*, surnamed the *Pious*; who
caused

GOTHA.

caused both that and the Town to be encompassed with Ditches and Ramparts. To the Glory of this Prince, he undertook and finished these Great Works, at a time when *Germany* was so impoverished by intestine Wars that few of its Princes were able to erect Palaces*.

As of all the *Saxon* Princes of the *Ernestine* Branch, the Duke of *Gotha* is the most powerful, so his Court is of all the *Saxon* Courts next to that of *Dresden*, the most Numerous and the most Magnificent.

* The chief Trade of this Town is in *Woad*, of which they have three sorts. The first they sow about *Christmas*, the next in the *Spring*, *Summer*, and *Harvest*, of which they have three Crops, and the third grows wild. This Herb is such a sovereign Balsamic, that it cures Wounds almost with a touch, if taken in time. It resembles Plantain, but has a longer Leaf. The Roots fatten and improve barren Ground exceedingly, and being brought over to *England*, with *Clover*, *Cinque-Foil*, &c. grows with good Success in *Northamptonshire*, and other Places. In the Duke's Palace there is a Chamber of valuable Rarities, and a noble Library, of which the late Duke caus'd a Catalogue to be publish'd of the MSS. that the Learned might know where to have recourse to them. The Person he imployed to form it, was Dr. *Cyprianus* Ecclesiastical Counsellor and Assessor in the Consistory of *Gotha*. They are for the most part the MSS. of Ecclesiastical Authors, Ancient and Modern, especially the latter. There is a great Number of Papers and Letters in the *Latin* and *German* Languages, concerning *Luther's* Reformation, and several MSS. of the vulgar Translation of the Bible. There is a correcter Copy than that at *Leipsic*, of the Works of *Lactantius*; another of St. *Austin's* Treatise of the *City of God*, which belonged to *Willigise* Archbishop of *Mentz*, about the year 1000; another of the ancient Capitularies of the Kings of *France*, with the Salic Laws, and the Laws of the *Lombards*, *Almains*, &c. There are thirty one MS. Volumes containing the Abridgments of the Lives of the Emperors of the *West*, and of the *East*, their Pictures and Medals, and those of their Families, the whole collected in 1550, by *James de Strada* of *Mantua*. The Medals are very well design'd, and *Occo* the famous Antiquary affirms in a Letter quoted by M. *Patin*, that every Figure on them cost a Crown the engraving. There is a particular MS. which contains a Collection of Tracts by certain *Greek* Chymists concerning the desirable *Art of making Gold*. For the rest the Curious are referred to the Catalogue it self.

Nevertheless the Subjects of the Duke of *Gotha* †, are the least burthen'd with Taxes of any in *Germany*. To this Prince's wise Management of his Finances is owing not only his own Happiness, but that of his People too, by whom he is ador'd; and really he treats them more like a Father, than a Sovereign; and never makes them sensible of his Power, but when he is to do them Justice. He is a kind good Master, easy of Access, temperate in his way of Living, gives very great Application to the Affairs of his Government, loves Reading, understands Books, and knows every thing which a Prince ought to be acquainted with. As to his Person, he is handsome and comely; is civil in his Deportment, but reserv'd; and therefore seldom speaks to Strangers, if he can help it; but endeavours first of all to know those he has Business with, and when he has found out their Character, talks with them upon such Subjects as he thinks they are best acquainted with. He keeps regular Hours, rises at seven o'clock, first spends an Hour in Prayer, and the reading of some pious Treatise; and then gets himself dress'd, and gives Audience to his Ministers, or to other Persons that desire it. At Noon he dines with the Duchess his Wife, the Princes his Children, and other Persons of Distinction; stays about an Hour and a half at Table, and then takes a Walk in the Gardens of the Palace, or if the Weather does not permit, he employs himself in his Closet, or spends the Time in reading till five o'clock. Then he goes to the House of some Person of Distinction at his Court where all the Nobility have an Assembly, and plays at Ombre, after which he returns to his Palace, sups in the manner that he din'd, and at nine o'clock retires.

There is a Drawing-Room at Court three times a Week when the Company meets in a great Hall, where

† This Prince, who was *Frederic* II. died in 1732, *March* 12.

where they make Parties at Ombre and Piquet. At seven o'clock a large Table is spread, which is free for all the Company. Then a Carver cuts up the Victuals, which are handed to that, and to all the Gaming-Tables that are cover'd with Napkins. Those who don't play may sit down at what Table they like best. The Duke, the Duchess, or the Princes, generally do Foreigners the Honour to admit them to their Table. During the Supper there is a Concert of Music, and at nine o'Clock all the Company retires.

The Duke by his Marriage with *Magdalen-Augusta* of *Anhalt-Zerbst*, has seven Sons and two Daughters*: The eldest is the Hereditary Prince, who has been twice in *Paris*, and once in *Italy*, *England*, *Holland*, *Denmark*, *Sweden*, and at all the Courts of *Germany*, in which Travels he has acquir'd a great deal of Politeness and valuable Knowledge. I had the Honour of making my Compliments to him both at *Paris*, and the *Hague*, and found him of such a Temper as induces me to think that the Subjects of *Gotha* will be as happy hereafter under his Government, as they are under that of the Duke his Father. He was lately married to his Cousin-German *Louisa-Dorothea* of *Saxe-Meinungen*, a very lovely young Princess, who, with all her Graces and Charms, has abundance of Good-nature and Modesty †.

The Duke has all the Great Officers common to other Sovereigns. The Count *de Ronaw* is Great Marshal, and the chief Man at Court. They give him here the Character of Favourite; whether he is such I know not, but this I know, that he is not

---

* He had ten Sons and six Daughters by her. The Hereditary Prince who succeeds him is *Frederic* III. born *April* 4, 1699. He has a Brother named *William* born *March* 12, 1701. and some time an Officer in the *Dutch* Service.

† She was born *August* 10, 1710.

unworthy of it. I was very well acquainted with him at *Ratisbon* in 1720; he was not then in any Place, and expressed a Friendship for me; and now that I see him here in a Post, I find him the same Man as at *Ratisbon*, always a Friend to his Friends; which for a Favourite is a very great Character.

The Duke's Revenues are computed at a Million of Crowns a year, with which he maintains near 3000 Men of regular Troops. His Family is large and his Livery fine; his Guards are very well cloath'd; his Table is serv'd with more Delicacy than Profusion; his Palace is well furnish'd; every body punctually paid; and no body dissatisfied.

I don't mention the Library to you, nor the Chamber of Rarities, because I am not yet well enough inform'd of such Things there as are worth observing. I propose to take another Round before I go hence, and shall not fail to transmit to you what Observations I shall make there. Mean time, I am, &c.*

---

* Since these Letters were written the Face of the Court of *Gotha* is very much altered. The Duke therein mentioned is dead. The Hereditary Prince *Frederic* has succeeded him, and his Mother the Duchess Dowager retired to *Altenbourg*, with the Princesses her Daughters, who are *Frederica* born *July* 6, 1715, O. S. and *Augusta* born *Nov.* 18, 1719. and married *April* 27, 1736. to his Royal Highness *Frederic* Prince of *Wales*. The Duke's Brothers, who are *William, John-Augustus, Christian-William, Lewis-Ernest, Maurice* and *John-Adolphus*, are gone into the Service of the Emperor, the King of *Poland*, and the Prince of *Hesse-Cassel*. As to the Government, the Duke treads in the very Steps of his late Father. M. *Backover* is his Chancellor, and the First Man in his Council. M. *de Hering*, formerly in the service of the Duke of *Saxe-Weimar*, is Vice-Chancellor. The Count *de Renaw* is now Envoy at the Dyet of *Ratisbon*, M. *de Damnitz*, heretofore in the Service of the Prince *de Rudelstad*, is Grand-Marshal; and seems to have a Share in the new Duke's Confidence. This Gentleman is also a Major-General, and the Camp seems to be a fitter Element for him

LETTER VIII.

SIR, *Wurtzbourg, Sept. 22, 1729.*

WHEN I came hither I had the very great Pleasure to find your Letters, and to hear that you enjoy perfect Health. Continue, I beseech you, to write to me; that being the only Means by which you can persuade me what I wish to be convinced of more than any thing in the World, that my Letters are acceptable to you.

I have been in one of the most disagreeable Roads in all *Germany*; and tho' the Country abounds with Provisions of all sorts, I had like to have been famished in the Public Houses.

From *Gotha*, I went to EYSENACH, thinking to pass a few Days at that Court, but I found the* Duke sick, and the Hereditary Prince and Princess † absent, so that I had only my Labour for my Pains.

him than the Court.——— The Office of Master of the Horse is not yet fill'd up. M. *de Wurm*, a Person of Quality and Merit, was in possession of that Office in the late Duke's time, but he lately resigned it of his own accord. M. *de Stotterheim*, is to be appointed Great Cup-Bearer, who is as yet, I think, in the Service of some Foreign Prince.

* *John William* Duke of *Saxe-Eysenach*, died at sixty-one Years of Age, soon after having married to his fourth Wife *Mary Christina Felicite* Countess of *Linange*, the Widow of *Christian* Margrave of *Baden-Dourlach*.

† *Ann Sophia Charlotte* of *Prussia* Daughter of the late Margrave *Albert*, and Wife to *William Henry* the present Duke of *Saxe-Eysenach*.

As the Town of *Eysenach* offers nothing at all to View which is worth a Traveller's Attention, I set out the same Day for FULDE, where I arrived the next. You know, that this City is the Capital of the Principality of *Fulde*, the Sovereign of which is an Abbot, a Prince of the Empire, and Chancellor to the Empress. The present Sovereign is *Adolphus* Baron of *Bablberg*, who was chose by the Chapter of the Abbey Church in 1726, in the room of *Constantine* Baron of *Buthler*, who died suddenly, and not without suspicion of Poison. *Fulde* is a dirty little Town open on all sides, and has nothing remarkable but the Abbey Church, and the Prince's Palace, which are two Freestone Buildings that make a very grand Appearance. The Apartments of the Palace are very richly furnish'd. The last Abbot being a Man of good Understanding and great Views, caused this Palace to be so adorn'd as to demonstrate the Wealth of the Abbey.

The Prince Abbot has a Grand Marshal, a Master of the Horse, a Marshal of the Court, several Privy and Aulic Counsellors, a Number of Gentlemen, a Company of Horse-Guards well cloathed and well mounted, a Regiment of Foot Guards, eight Pages, a Number of Footmen, and several Sets of Horses. He gives a rich Livery, and in a word, his Houshold is spruce and magnificent. There are very few Sovereigns in *Germany* whose Table is better served; for there is plenty of every thing, particularly delicious Wines, of which they tipple to such Excess that in a very little time they are not capable of distinguishing their Liquor. There are, I believe, the hardest Drinkers here in *Europe*; and I being on the other hand but a Milksop, thought that *Fulde* was not a Country for me to pitch my Tent in. I dined with the Prince, went home drunk to my Quarters, slept sound, and next day set

set out for *Wurtzbourg*, where I am happily arriv'd after having gone through such horrible bad Ways, and met with such dismal Lodging, that I wish my Enemies were but condemned to travel this Road four times a Year.

Here I make myself amends for the Mortification which I met with coming hither. WURTZBOURG is a considerable City though not very large. The *Main* divides it into two Parts. It is the Residence of the Prince Bishop of *Wurtzbourg* Duke of *Franconia*. The Person who now enjoys that great Dignity is *Christopher Francis de Houtten*[*]. He was elected by the Chapter to succeed *John Philip Francis* Count de *Schonborn*, who was one of the greatest and most magnificent Prelates that perhaps ever fill'd the Episcopal See of *Wurtzbourg*. This Prince, in the five Years time that he has been Bishop, has done more things for the Embellishment of *Wurtzbourg* than ten of his Predecessors put together. He has furnished one Part of the Town with new Fortifications, and has laid the Basis of a stately Palace, which will be one of the greatest, the compleatest and most regular Fabrics that we have in *Germany*; he having for that end consulted the most skilful Architects, and sent for the most celebrated Sculptors from *Italy*. As he was a passionate Admirer of the Arts and Sciences, and perfectly understood them, especially Architecture; he chose the best Parts of all the Designs that were presented to him, and from them he compos'd the Plan of the Work, which was executed with such diligence that in four Years time two thirds of the Building were rooft. His unexpected Death put a stop for a while to this Great Work. The present

---

[*] His Successor was *Frederic Charles* Count *de Schonborn* Bishop of *Bamberg* and Vice-Chancellor of the Empire, who was before his Competitor. In 1734, he resigned the Post of Vice-Chancellor, and retired to his Bishoprick.

present Bishop took it in hand again, but after having made considerable Alterations in those great and magnificent Projects, the Work advances so slowly that when it will be finished no body knows.

The deceased Bishop *Schonborn* has also caused a Chapel to be built near the Metropolitan Church, which he has lined with very uncommon Marble brought for the purpose from *Italy* at a very great Expence. Brass, Gilding, and every thing that can render a Chapel superb, has been employed in it in a very curious manner. This stately Edifice is as yet imperfect, and will require great Sums to finish it. As it was designed for the Burial-Place of the Bishop and his Family, it is to be presum'd that the House of *Schonborn*, now so rich and so powerful, will not suffer a Monument to lie unfinish'd which is to perpetuate the remembrance of its Grandeur.

The Great Hospital founded by a Bishop whose Name was *Julius*, is worth seeing. 'Tis a stately Building, which looks more like the Palace of a Prince than a Hospital. Four hundred Persons of both Sexes are maintained in it. There are two fine Halls which are particularly made use of upon *Holy Thursday*. In the one, the Bishop performs the Ceremony of washing the Feet of the Poor, who are afterwards sumptuously feasted in it; and in the other, he regales his Chapter, and all his Family.

The Castle stands upon an Eminence on the other side of the River which we pass over a Stone Bridge, adorn'd like that of St. *Angelo* at *Rome*, with twelve fine Statues representing so many Saints. This Castle is a strong Place, and entirely commands the Town. The Form of it is quite irregular, it consisting of several Buildings erected by several Bishops. Those Prelates always liv'd in it, till the last, who, while he was building a new Palace in the Town, lodged in a neighbouring Gentleman's House,

House, from whence he could see how the Work went on. The Apartments of the old Castle are spacious and noble. I found in them all that Furniture with which they were adorn'd for the Reception of the Archduchess *Mary-Elizabeth*, when that Princess came to *Wurtzbourg* in her way to the Government of the *Netherlands*. I have not seen richer Furniture at the Palace of any Prince of the Empire.

In this Castle there are two things that are well worth seeing; the Arsenal and the Vault; the one full of all the Stores invented by *Mars* and *Bellona*, for the Destruction of Mankind, and the other furnish'd with every thing to satiate the Thirst of an Army of Drunkards. If ever you come hither and should have the Curiosity to visit these Magazines of *Mars* and *Bacchus*, I advise you to begin with the Arsenal, especially if you can get some Courtier to go with you; for these Gentlemen, tho' very civil, think, that the least thing which a Foreigner ought to do for them is to forfeit his Reason to them in this Vault. I am sure, I speak by dear Experience. Three days ago I told the Bishop that I had a mind to see the Castle. This Prince was so complaisant as to order one of his Gentlemen to go with me. My honest Companion fearing, 'tis like, that a Conversation *tete-a-tete* would be too melancholy, chose two Topers to bear us Company, whom *Silenus* would not have disown'd for his Children. Being a stranger to the Virtues for which those Gentlemen were eminent, I put my self entirely under their Direction without the least Apprehension of my Misfortune. When they had shewed me the Apartments, the Arsenal, Fortifications, and every thing, they carried me at last into the Vault, which I found illuminated like a Chapel wherein I was to lie in State; and indeed, my Funeral Obsequies were perform'd in Pomp, for the Glasses served instead

instead of Bells, and Torrents of Wine gush'd out instead of Tears: At length, after the Service was over, two of the Prince's *Heydukes* carry'd me to a Coach, and from thence to Bed; that was my Tomb. Yesterday I rose again, but scarce know at this Moment whether I am quite come to myself. 'Tis true that this does not give me much Concern, for ever since I have been here, I have followed the laudable Custom of getting drunk twice a-day. You perceive that I am improv'd by my Travels, and that I am apt enough to learn the pretty Manners of the Countries where I make any Stay. I fancy that you will find me very much alter'd for the better. There is nothing that accomplishes a Man so much as travelling; judge you of this by the Life which I lead here.

I rise at ten o'clock, my Lungs very much inflam'd with the Wine I drank the Night before: I take a large Dose of Tea, dress myself, and then go to make my Compliments to the Bishop. The Baron *de Pechtelsheim* the Marshal of the Court invites me to dine with the Prince: He promises, nay, and sometimes swears too that I shall not drink. At Noon we sit down to Table. The Bishop does me the honour to drink two or three Healths to me. The Baron *de Zobel*, Master of the Horse, and the Baron *de Pechtelsheim*, toast the same number to me, and I am under a necessity of drinking to no less than fourteen Persons at the Table; so that I am drown'd in Liquor before I have din'd. When the Company rises, I wait on the Prince to his Chamber-Door, where he retires, and I think to do the same, but I find an Embargo put upon me in the Antichamber by the Master of the Horse, and the Marshal of the Court, who with great Bumpers in their Hands drink the Prince's Health to me, and *Prosperity for ever to the most laudable Chapter of* Wurtzbourg. I protest to them that I am the

Bishop's

Bishop's most humble Servant, and that I have a very great Veneration for the most laudable Chapter, but that to drink their Healths wou'd destroy mine, and therefore I beg they wou'd excuse my pledging them; but I may as well talk to the Wind; these two Healths must be drank, or I shall be reckon'd no Friend to the Prince and his Chapter. If this were all my Task I shou'd be well off; but then comes M. *de Zobel*, one of the most intrepid Carousers of the Age, who squeezes me by the Hand, and with an Air and Tone of perfect Cordiality, says to me, *You love our Prince so well that you can't refuse drinking to the Prosperity of the illustrious Family of* Houtten. And when he has made this moving Speech, he takes off a great Glass to witness his Zeal for the Life of his Master; after which an officious *Heyduke* brings me a Glass, and being infected with the Goust that prevails at this Court, assures me that this Wine cannot possibly do me Harm, because 'tis the very same that the Prince drinks. By a Persuasion, founded on so just an Inference, I have the Courage to venture on t'other Glass, which is no sooner drank but I reel, and can drink no more; when in order to finish me M. *de Pechtelsheim*, one of the honestest Gentlemen living, but the stauncheft Wine-bibber that I know, accosts me with a Smile and says, *Come*, dear Baron, *one Glass more to better Acquaintance.* I conjure him to give me Quarter, but he embraces me, kisses me, and calls me *Herr Bruder*, (his dear Brother.) How can a Man withstand such tender Compliments! At last I put myself in a fit Posture to run away; I sneak off, steal down the Steps as well as I can, and squeeze myself into a Sedan which carries me home; where my People drag me out like a dead Corpse, and fling me on a Bed, as if the next thing was to lay me out. I sleep three or four hours, awake in a perfect Maze, put myself to rights again, and prepare to make Visits, or to receive them; but whichsoever I do, I presently find my self in such a pickle again, that I cannot walk alone. There's no such thing as Conversation here betwixt one Friend and another without the Bottle; so that I am tempted to think the Inhabitants of this City are descended from *Silenus*, and that the old Sot left them the Faculty of hard drinking for a Legacy, as St. *Hubert* bequeath'd to his Family the power of curing a Frenzy.

I din'd yesterday with the Reverend the *Scots Benedictine* Fryars, who gave me a hearty Welcome, and an excellent sort of Liquor call'd *Stein Wein*, or Stone-Wine, probably because it grows on a Rock; which is the only time that I have departed from the Regimen I keep to here, I mean that I was not drunk. The House of these *Benedictines* is one of the five Houses which form a sort of a Republic in their Order, and which, without depending on their General, chuse a President out of their number who has the direction of all their Affairs. These five Houses are in five different Towns, *viz.* at *Vienna* in *Austria*, at *Ratisbon*, *Wurtzbourg*, at *Doway* in *Flanders*, and at *Dieulegarde*, near *Pont-a-Mousson* in *Lorrain*.

These *Benedictines* put me in mind of the Reverend Fathers the *Jesuits*, who have a very fine House in this City: These are they who are Directors of the University, and instruct the Youth with a Zeal which cannot but confound their Enemies.

The Prince and Bishop lives in very great Splendor, and is one of the most powerful of our Spiritual Sovereigns. His Dominion includes seventy Bailywics, and his Country is the finest and fruitfullest in *Germany*. The only thing that is scarce here is Money, and this is owing to their want of Trade, and to the great number of Monks and
Priests

Priests who ingross all to themselves. The Bishop has 50000 Crowns a-year for his Privy-Purse. The Chamber is oblig'd to maintain him in every thing. It furnishes his Wardrobe, his Table, and pays his Houshold and his Troops, which actually consist of 3500 Men, who are commanded by General *Eib*, the Governour of *Wurtzbourg*. In time of War the Bishop has no less than 10000.

The Court is numerous, and I can assure you that upon Festival-Days 'tis very magnificent. On St. *Quilian*'s Day, who is the Patron of *Wurtzbourg* and *Franconia*, the Bishop repairs with a great Train to the Metropolitan Church. Six of the Bishops Coaches, drawn each by six Horses, begin the March, attended by twenty four Footmen and sixteen Pages; and above fourscore Gentlemen richly dress'd walk before the Bishop's Coach, guarded by two Files of Halbardiers. The Master of the Horse and the Marshal of the Court walk by the sides of the Coach, the latter bearing the Sword of the Duke of *Franconia* with the Point uppermost; and the Coach is surrounded by *Heydukes*, and followed by a company of Life-Guards.

The Bishop of *Wurtzbourg* has one Prerogative which the other Bishops have not; for while he officiates, his Great Marshal bears the Sword of the Duke of *Franconia* naked and upright till the Consecration of the Elements, and then he puts it up in the Scabbard, and carries it before the Prince with the Point downwards; which is a Distinction I take to be altogether as extraordinary as that of the Abbot and Count *de Gemblours*, the first Nobleman of the States of *Brabant*, who has the Privilege of celebrating Mass with his Boots and Spurs on.

The Bishop's ordinary Expence is perfectly suitable to the Dignity of a great Prince; and his Table,

Table, which is commonly spread for eighteen Guests, is serv'd with a Magnificence to the degree of Profusion; not that this Prince affects Pomp, but because he is oblig'd to conform to the antient establish'd Customs of his Court. This Prelate gives very great Application to the Affairs of his Government, for which purpose he rises early in the Morning: When he is dress'd he spends some time in Prayer, and then confers with his Ministers, or with the Chiefs of the several Tribunals. At ten o'clock he hears Mass, and afterwards goes to Council: At Noon he dines, and after having sate an Hour and an half at Table, he retires, and spends the Evening with his Family, which is numerous, and compos'd of Persons of Worth. In Carnival-time he makes great Entertainments twice or thrice a-week for all the Nobility of *Wurtzbourg*, and there is sometimes a Ball and even Masquerades at Court. In the Winter-time Persons of Rank have Assemblies for Gaming; and during the Carnival there's a Ball three times a-week in a House kept by the Undertaker, at which they bespeak Places beforehand, and where Foreigners are admitted *gratis*. All this wou'd be pretty enough if the Company was not sometimes disturb'd by People in Liquor, tho' 'tis true that such are not very chagrining to the Natives, who are us'd to such Sights; and the very Ladies, who elsewhere fly such Company, do not seem to have a staunch Aversion to them. Foreigners have reason to applaud the Civilities both of the Prince and his Courtiers. As for my own part I am infinitely oblig'd for the Respect they have been pleas'd to shew to me. The Prince heaps his Favours on me, and the Nobility their Courtesies. If it were not that one is forc'd to drink hard, I shou'd like the Town very well. Two Days hence I shall set out for *Anspach*, and
from

from thence I shall go by the way of *Nuremberg* and *Bareith* to *Prague*. I shall write to you by the very first Opportunity: Mean time I am, *&c.*

LETTER IX.

SIR, *Anspach, Sept.* 29, 1729.

I CAME in one day from *Wurtzbourg* to ANSPACH, which is twelve Miles, and pass'd thro' two or three little Towns not worth naming. *Anspach* is the Capital of the Margraviate so call'd, and the Residence of the Margrave of *Brandenbourg*, Chief of the second Branch of that Family settled in *Franconia*. 'Tis a small but pretty Town, and very well built. It has no Fortifications, and is only shut in by Walls surrounded with Walks which form a Bulwark. The Prince has a large Castle or Palace building here, which when finish'd will be magnificent. The late Margrave, Father of the present, had begun to build it according to the Models of an *Italian* Architect; but as he did nothing to answer the Opinion conceiv'd by the *Germans* that the *Italians* are the best Architects in the World, perhaps because he was oblig'd to patch up old Walls for the sake of some Rooms: Madame the Margravine Regent, Mother of the young Margrave, continued what her Husband began, but chang'd the Architect, and makes use of the Baron *de Zochau* to carry on those Works; who, tho' oblig'd to conform to what was done by the *Italian*, has succeeded much better than that Foreigner. Madame the Margravine Regent has like-wife caus'd some noble Gardens to be laid out; and this Princess spares no Cost for embellishing the Town of *Anspach*.

The Margravine Regent * is of the Family of *Wurtenberg*, and may be compar'd for Beauty with the finest Princesses in the World. Being left a Widow at twenty nine Years of Age, she renounc'd all Pleasures, and thought of nothing but the Education of her Son, and the Affairs of her Regency; both of which Duties this Princess discharges in such a manner that her Subjects bless her Government, and the young Margrave cannot but have very great Obligations to her.

Madame the Margravine, besides a charming Person, has a sparkling Wit and a solid Judgment, which she has taken care to cultivate by great reading, and maintains by a Piety and Charity truly Christian. There is in all her Actions such Politeness, and so much Good-nature, as gain her the hearts of all Persons. In fine, without flattering this Princess, I can assure you that her Life is a Pattern of Virtue. She is wean'd from all the Vanities of the Age; she wears neither Gold nor Lace, and has given her Diamonds, which were of very great value, to her Son. She keeps so retir'd to her Apartment, that she is never seen but at Church, at Table, or when she gives Audience; which she never refuses to any body unless when she is tir'd. She is incessantly employ'd, and takes delight in it. She is her own Minister, and her Counsellors are only the Executioners of her Orders.

'Tis pity that *Germany* is so soon like to lose a Princess who does her Country so much Honour: The Margravine is in so declining a Condition that

---

* *Christina-Charlotta de Wurtenberg*, Margravine Dowager of *Brandenbourg-Anspach*, who was Regent for her Son, died at *Anspach* in 1730, soon after she had resign'd the Regency to this young Margrave, and match'd him to *Frederica-Louisa*, second Daughter of the King of *Prussia*.

that there's no hopes of her Recovery. The Physicians have actually told her so; but the Princess, far from being terrify'd at the sad Tidings, receiv'd it like a Christian Heroine: *God gave me my Life,* said she to her Physicians, *he will take it from me when he pleases, his Will be done.* She continues to live in the way she always did; and the Approach of Death, which she sees advancing to her with slow Pace, gives her no Trouble nor Tremor; but submitting to the Decrees of Providence, she waits with Resignation for that awful Moment which often makes the stoutest Hearts tremble.

The young Margrave is actually at *Paris,* so that I cou'd have given you no manner of Account of this Prince, if I had not had the Honour to see him two Years ago. He was born the 12th of *May,* 1712. He is a handsome, comely, lively Man, has an extraordinary Memory, and if Age matures his Understanding, bids fair to be one day a Prince of a sublime Genius. His Governour was M. *de Bremer,* a Gentleman of *Livonia*; and his Præceptor M. *Neukirch* *, celebrated for several Essays in Poetry.

Notwithstanding the Reform which Madame the Margravine made in her Court when she came to the Regency, 'tis still very numerous. The Count *de Castel* is the first Man at this Court, and has the Title of Lord Steward. His Lady commonly attends Madame the Margravine, and does the Offices of Lady of Honour without affecting the Title. M. *de Bremer,* the Baron *de Seckendorf,* and the Baron *de Zocbau,* are Privy Counsellors; and the Baron *de Kinsberg* is Marshal of the Court. As to the Troops the Margravine Regent only keeps up such

---

* This was *Benjamin Neukirch.* He put *Telemachus* into Verse, and was the Author of a great many other Works, which shew that the *German* Language is capable of conveying as fire Sentiments as those which are more us'd by Authors. He died lately at *Anspach.*

such a number as is necessary to furnish her Quota to the Empire, and to guard her Person.

The Margraviate of *Anspach* is very much interspersed with Woods, which makes it a fine Country for Hunting. 'Tis said that it brings in 500000 Crowns every Year to its Sovereign. The Principal Towns are *Anspach* and *Schwabach*, in which Manufactures are erected that do great Prejudice to the City of *Nuremberg*.

I think I ought not to omit acquainting you with two things which are fondly believ'd by the common People, and which the Landlord of the House where I quarter'd affirm'd to me to be Facts. The one is, that there are no Rats in all the Country of *Anspach*, since one of the Family of the Rat-killing St. *Hubert* pass'd that way. The other is of the same Tenor, and admitted for a certain Truth by every Subject in the Dominions of the House of *Brandenbourg*, viz. When any one of this Family dies, whether Prince or Princess, a Woman in White always appears just before in the Palace. I know not whether you ever heard any thing concerning this Prophetess of Ill Luck. Be that as it will, the Story which is told of her is this:

Joachim II. Elector of *Brandenbourg*, having a mind to enlarge his Palace at *Berlin*, wanted to buy in several Houses; but an old Woman, the Owner of one of those Houses, resolv'd not to sell it to him upon any Terms. The Elector finding her so obstinate sent her the Purchase-Money and turn'd her out of it; upon which the old Woman swore in a Rage that she wou'd be an eternal Plague to *Joachim* and his Posterity. They pretend that the good Lady keeps her Word, and that she haunts all the Palaces of the *Brandenbourg* Family. Yet I never heard any body at *Berlin* say they had ever seen her there, tho' that is the Place where she ought naturally to have taken up her head Quarters.

My

My Landlord added to these fine Stories that the Margravine would not die yet a while, because the Woman in White had not yet appear'd to any body at Court.

I am, &c.

LETTER X.

SIR, *Carlsbad, October* 10, 1729.

WHEN I took leave of the Court of *Anspach*, I was honour'd with a precious mark of the Margravine's Goodness, *viz.* a weighty Gold Medal; and now I am again upon my Journey. I was not many hours in travelling from *Anspach* to *Nuremberg*, thro' a Country extremely sandy, but very well cultivated, and interspers'd with considerable Villages which in our Country wou'd be reckon'd Towns.

So much has already been said by others of the City of NUREMBERG, that I have very little to add to it. I assure you this Town is the most disagreeable Place in *Europe* to live in. The Patricians are the People of the first Rank there, and lord it like the petty Nobles of *Venice*. The Government here too has very great Resemblance with the *Venetian*, and they have a sort of Doge. In short they are very much like the Frog in the Fable that strove to swell it self to the Size of the Ox. Of these Patricians some are very rich, but they are so rude that no body visits them, and they scarce visit one another. Perhaps you will ask me what I mean by the Term *Patricians?* 'Tis this; they are Gentlemen:

men: There are Patrician Families old enough to dispute Antiquity with any of the Nobility whatsoever, and who were formerly admitted into all the Chapters. But now the case is otherwise; for the Nobility not only exclude them out of the Chapters, but dispute their being Gentlemen; pretending that they derogate from the Title by their Magistratical Offices. Such is, you know, our *Germanic* Vanity; the things which are honourable in other Countries, are with us diminutive: The Court, the Sword, and the Church, are the only Professions that a Gentleman can follow: If he has not the Talents proper for one or other of these, or if Fortune frown upon him, he had better be out of the World than take any Offices of the Magistracy upon him, or enter into Trade: He had better beg Alms nobly than marry beneath himself. But I shall not here set up for a Censor of the *Germanic* Customs. Let us talk of *Nuremberg*. This City has 6 Gates, 12 Conduits, and 118 Wells. Of the Churches St. *Laurence*'s is the biggest: There's a great many Reliques in it, particularly a part of the Manger in which our Saviour was laid, a piece of his Garment, and three Links of the Chains which bound St. *Peter*, St. *Paul*, and St. *John*. As the *Lutherans* make no great account of those Reliques, they wou'd do well to give them to some poor Catholic Convent, which would thereby soon be enrich'd.

You know that the Government here is altogether Evangelical, *i. e. Lutheran*. The Catholics have a small Church in the House of the Teutonic Order: The *Calvinists* go to the Church in the Territory of *Anspach*; but the *Jews* are not tolerated because 'tis said they formerly poisoned the Wells. They live in a Place not far from *Nuremberg*, but come to Town every Morning, paying something for their Entrance, have an old Woman set over them,

them, who is commonly both their Guard and their Guide, and are permitted to trade and trick wherever they can till Night, when they are obliged to retire.

In the Church of the Hospital is kept *Charlemain*'s Crown, said to weigh fourteen Pounds, the Sceptre and the Globe, in short all the Ornaments of Empire except *Charlemain*'s Sword said to have been brought from Heaven by an Angel, the same very likely that carry'd the holy Vial and the Oriflamb to *France*. That Sword is kept at *Aix la Chapelle*.

The Trade of *Nuremberg* is very much fallen off; for besides that the Toys and Knick-knacks which where formerly made in this City are much out of fashion, especially in *Germany*, the Manufactures which the Margraves of *Bareith* and *Anspach* have settled in their Dominions do considerable Prejudice to *Nuremberg*.

The Inhabitants of this City may be, (at least I think 'em so) the honestest People in the World, but they are the most horrible Complimenters that I know. I cou'd not set my Foot in a Shop, but the Master, the Mistress, the Children and the Apprentices waited on me into the very Street, thanking me for the Honour I had done them. My Landlord too, who saw me go in and out twenty times a day, receiv'd me always with great Ceremony, and ask'd me how I did. And when I went out he pray'd me not to leave his House long in Contempt, without honouring it with my Presence.

Nuremberg is the richest and most potent Imperial City next to *Hambourg*. The Domain of *Nuremberg* is even much larger than that of *Hambourg*, but the latter bears the Bell for Wealth. 'Tis said that *Nuremberg* has seven other Towns in its Territory, with 480 Villages and Parishes. Yet for all this 'tis not a rich City; for the Patricians pocket all the Money, and the Citizens are poor.

Next Day after my Arrival at *Nuremberg* I set out for *Christian*-ERLANGEN, a Town in the Margraviate of *Brandenbourg-Bareith*, which owes its flourishing State to a Colony of *French* People who fled out of *France* on account of their Religion.

Forty Years ago *Erlangen* was but a little Village in the middle of a Forest of Fir-Trees. The Margrave *Christian* giving shelter to the *French* who left their Country after the Revocation of the Edict of *Nantz*, assign'd them *Erlangen* to settle in. When they cut down the Woods they built the Town, to which they gave the Name of *Christian-Erlangen*, in Memory of *Christian* their Benefactor. All the Streets are in a strait Line. The *French* have set up all sorts of Manufactures here, and have made it one of the prettiest Towns of *Germany*. Madame * *Elizabeth-Sophia* of *Brandenbourg*, second Daughter of the Elector *Frederic-William*, and third Wife of the Margrave *Christian* Founder of *Erlangen*, caus'd a very handsome Palace to be built in the great Square of this City, to which there are noble Gardens. 'Tis at present occupy'd by *Sophia* of *Saxe-Weissenfels*, Widow of the last Margrave of *Bareith*. This Princess was to have dwelt at *Neustadt*, which was settled on her for her Dowry; but as 'tis a lonesome, melancholy, scoundrel Place, the Margrave Regent was willing she should live at *Erlangen*. The Margravine Dowager was one of the most beautiful Princesses in the World, of which she still preserves the fair Remains, and none can have an Air more grand. She lives at

---

* This Princess was the Dowager of the Duke of *Courland*, when she marry'd the Margrave *Christian* who was very old. After his Death she marry'd the Duke of *Saxe-Meinungen* whom she has surviv'd. She resides at *Coburg* in *Franconia*. She never had but one Son, and that was he who marry'd the present *Czarina*, but died soon after his Marriage.

at *Erlangen* with all the Dignity becoming her Rank. Foreigners are very well received at her Court, and particularly by the Princess herself, who for Politeness has few Equals.

From *Christian-Erlangen* I went in less than a Day to *Bamberg*, tho' I stay'd two or three Hours at FORCHEIM a Place in the Bishoprick of *Bamberg*, whose Buildings appear'd to me to be old and out of repair.

The Bishoprick of BAMBERG is the first Bishoprick of the Empire. The Bishop is Suffragan to no Archbishop. He depends only as to Spirituals upon the Holy See, and receives the Pall as an Archbishop. He has moreover this Distinction, that the Electors are his great Officers as they are those of the Empire, and he has the Privilege of summoning them to come and do the Duties of their Offices on the Day of his Installation. I have not heard that any Bishop ever made use of this mighty Prerogative, for the Retinue which those great Officers would bring along with them might be a Charge to him. The great Privileges which this Prelate enjoys are counter-balanc'd by one Mortification; for if the Electors happen to chuse an Emperor who has no Dominions, the Bishop of *Bamberg* would be oblig'd to yield him his Episcopal City and Palace. 'Tis said that the Emperor has the same Right to *Rome*, and that if he should chuse that ancient City of the World for his Residence, the Pope wou'd be oblig'd to yield him the Palace of the Vatican and to retire to that of St. *John de Lateran*. But I really think that the Holy Father and the Bishop of *Bamberg* will not be so soon turn'd out.

The late Elector of *Mentz*, *Lotharius Francis de Schonborn*, who was also Bishop of *Bamberg*, embellish'd the City with a new Episcopal Palace, a great and stately Building that stands on an Eminence,

nence, from whence there is an extensive Prospect of various Beauties.

The City of *Bamberg* is very well built, and has beautiful Churches. Herein is to be seen the Tomb of the Emperor *Henry* II. and his Wife the Empress *Cunegonda*. This Princess lies at the right hand of her Husband, because she kept her Virginity to her Death. Was not this abusing the Sacrament of Marriage?

The Bishop who fills the Episcopal See of *Bamberg* is *Frederic-Charles*, Count de *Schonborn*, Vice-Chancellor of the Empire. This Prelate being Minister of State to the Emperor commonly resides at *Vienna*, and is now there, so that I have nothing to say to you of his Court; but I reckon I shall be able to give you some Account of him after I have paid my Respects to him at *Vienna*.

The Neighbourhood of *Bamberg* is very agreeable, but as one comes to it from *Nuremberg* thro' a certain Forest of Fir-Trees, it strikes a Man with Horror to find an Avenue to it a quarter of a League in length form'd by Wheels and Gibbets. This, at first sight gives a Stranger no very great Idea of the Honesty of the People; but he is of another Opinion when he comes to know that these expos'd Malefactors are for the most part Foreigners. The Bishoprick of *Bamberg* is contiguous to seven or eight different States, and the Town it self lies in the greatest Road of all *Germany*, which is the Reason that 'tis so infested by Rogues from all Quarters. In the time of the Elector of *Mentz*, *Bamberg* was their *Ne plus ultra*, for that Prince gave them no Quarter: Being an Enemy to Wickedness, and one of the greatest Justiciaries that we have had in *Germany*, he sent all to the Gallows that deserv'd Hanging.

About a League out of the Town the Bishop has a charming Pleasure-House; but there is nothing in

all

all *Germany* more magnificent than the Castle of POMMERSFELDEN belonging to the Count *de Schonborn*, which is three Leagues from *Bamberg*. *Francis Lotharius de Schonborn* Elector of *Mentz* caus'd this stately Fabric to be built, the whole of which forms a great Body of Building flank'd by two Pavilions with two advanc'd Wings. The whole is regularly built, and decorated with well-fancy'd Architecture. The Entry is supported by several Colonnades, where the first thing that presents it self is the grand Stair-Case, which is extraordinary magnificent, and perhaps one of the best contriv'd in *Europe*. This Entry leads into a Salon which serves as a Passage to the Garden; 'tis in form of a Grotto adorn'd with several Fountains, Columns, and Statues of Marble: The Cieling is painted as well as the Sky-Light of the Stair-Case, and the Arches of the principal Apartments. They are all painted by Hands that the Elector sent for on purpose from *Italy*. I don't give you the Particulars of the great Salon, nor of the Apartments, because it would take up a Volume. The whole are laid out with Art, and furnish'd with great Choice, Judgment and Splendor.

 The Stables answer exactly to the Castle which they front. They are built in form of a Half-Moon with a Pavilion in the middle, which is an oval Salon, from both Sides of which you see all the Horses. The Mangers are of Marble in form of Shells, and the Racks of Iron neatly wrought in form of a Basket or Scuttle.

 The Salon in the middle of the two Stables is painted in Fresco, and looks one way to the Court, and the other to the Riding-House, where the Elector us'd to see the Horses manag'd belonging to the Studs of his Bishoprick near *Bamberg*, one of the best in *Germany*.

 The Gardens of *Pommersfelden* are very answerable to the Magnificence of the Buildings: In a word,

word, every Thing belonging to this fine House is worthy of it. The Builder of it had sublime Ideas: He spared no Cost to leave Monuments of his Grandeur and Wealth to Posterity, and has made a House of *Pommersfelden* which really surpasses some Royal Palaces. But 'tis time to take you out of this fine Place and to carry you back to *Bamberg*.

There is a good Number of the Nobility settled in this Town. The Chapter consists of Persons of Quality: It has the Right of chusing the Bishop; and 'tis he who governs in the Absence of the Prince. Such a Resort as here is of the Nobility makes the Time pass away agreeably; but they drink as hard here as at *Fulde* and *Wurtzbourg*, so that it looks as if Drinking was an inseparable Function of the Ecclesiastical Courts. Having some Relations in this Town I stay'd there three Days, during which I had the Pleasure of Drinking every Day with one of my Cousins out of a great Goblet of solid Gold which weigh'd to the Value of a thousand Ducats. You can't imagine how well the Wine went down out of a Cup of that Value. I heartily wish'd that my Cousin wou'd have dealt by me as *Joseph* did by *Benjamin*, and that he had put up his Cup in my Portmanteau, provided he wou'd not have sent to fetch me back again, as the Governour of *Egypt* did his Brother; but this was what my dear Cousin did not think fit to do. He made me drink my Skinfull of Wine, and only wish'd me my Pockets full of Gold.

From *Bamberg* I went to BAREITH the Residence of the Margrave of *Brandenbourg*. The elder of the two Branches of that Family settled in *Franconia*. *John George* Elector of *Brandenbourg* divided his Dominions between his three Sons: He left the Electorate with its Appendages to his eldest Son, and gave the Margraviate of *Culmbach* to *Christian* his second Son, and that of *Anspach* to his third Son.

Christian

BAREITH. 205

Christian form'd two Branches, that of *Bareith* and that of *Culmbach*. The Branch of *Bareith* became extinct in 1726, by the Death of *George-William*, whose Widow lives at *Erlangen*. *George-Frederic-Charles* Margrave of *Culmbach* his Cousin, succeeded him. This Prince has five Children, *viz.* * two Princes and three † Princesses. He marry'd *Dorothy* of *Holstein-Beck* at *Berlin* in 1709. I had then the Honour to see him: He was a Prince of a noble Aspect, very civil, good-natur'd, and temperate, and a Lover of Books and Men of Learning. He did an Act of Generosity that perhaps is not to be parallel'd, and which I relate to you as the most authentic Testimony that can be of his Good-nature and Integrity.

His Predecessor had left an empty Exchequer and a great many Debts; and the Margrave at his Accession to the Regency was oblig'd to pay the King of *Prussia* 460000 Florins, upon condition that his Majesty wou'd renounce any Pretensions he might have to the Margraviate, by virtue of the Resignation of all Rights to the Succession which had been made by the Margrave of *Culmbach* his Father, in favour of *Frederic* I. King of *Prussia*. To raise this Sum on People already overburden'd by the common Taxes, was to seek their Ruin. The Margrave in pity of their miserable Condition, chose rather to borrow this Money of the States of the Circle of *Franconia* at great Interest. When he found himself in peaceable possession of his Dominions by the Payment made to the King of *Prussia*, he undertook to pay off not only his own, but the Debts of his Predecessor. To enable himself to do this,

---

* The Hereditary Prince who is the eldest, marry'd the Princess Royal of *Prussia* in 1731.

† The eldest of the Princesses, *Sophia-Christiana-Louisa* was marry'd in 1731 to the Prince *Alexander de la Tour* and *Taxis*. She lately embrac'd the *Romish* Religion.

this, he began by turning off his Court, kept but a small Number of Counsellors and Gentlemen, and disbanded 3000 Men of the Troops which the late Margrave kept in pay to no purpose. He reduc'd his Table to the greatest Frugality; his Clothes were plain, and he avoided Magnificence and Gaming. Some time after this, he made another Reform in his House, and kept up but a very small Number of Domestics. He establish'd a Council of Regency, and to save the Expence which his Rank as a Sovereign would have engag'd him in whether he wou'd or not, he left his Dominions, and went to live incognito with the Hereditary Prince his Son at *Geneva*. I believe that both of them are actually at *Montpellier* *. He is resolv'd not to return to his Dominions till all his Debts are paid off. Mean time his Subjects wish for his Return with Impatience, for he has such a Kindness for them, and governs them with such mildness that they look on him as their Father and Benefactor. This Retirement of the Margrave from the Splendors of Sovereignty is the more to be commended because 'tis absolutely voluntary: He was not at all oblig'd to pay the Debts of his Predecessor; for they were of such a Nature as not to be rank'd among the Debts of the Government. Nevertheless it was his Pleasure to do it, and he chose rather to abridge himself of the Charms of Sovereignty than that People, whose Faith in the Government had made them part with their Money, shou'd lose their Debts. Such a glorious Action as this, is in my Judgment equal to the Laurels of twenty Victories: This was owing to his Virtue, whereas Victory is generally the Consequent of Chance and Fortune.

You will easily imagine that while the Sovereign is absent this City is not very gay. It appear'd

---

* The Margrave and the Prince are now return'd to *Bareith*, where they live with all the Splendor of Sovereignty.

pear'd to me the more melancholy becaufe I had feen it in the time of the late Margrave, at whofe Court there was continual Feafting and Jollitry.

The City of *Bareith* is inferior to *Erlangen*. The Margrave's Palace is a great old Pile, but not very commodious, and meanly furnifh'd. This Prince has a very pretty Houfe, a League from *Bareith*, call'd the *Hermitage*, which was built by Order of the late Margrave.

It ftands in the middle of a thick Wood, in which there are a great many Pavilions built, without any Symmetry indeed, but very ingenioufly contriv'd within for the Ufe to which they ferve. When the late Margrave came to the Hermitage, he and his whole Court were in the Drefs of Hermits. There were certain Hours in which the Hermit Brothers went to pay a Vifit to the Hermit Sifters, who liv'd in the Pavilions. The Brothers and Sifters who gave each other Collations, were fubject to certain Rules from which they could not be difpenfed but by the Remiffion of the Superior of either Sex, who were then the Margrave, and his Lady the Margravine. In the Evening they met again in the Hall of the Caftle, where they fupp'd; and that every thing might be done according to the Rules, at the beginning of the Supper certain Verfes were read, or fome little Story compos'd by one or other of the Hermit Brothers; then Silence was broke, and every one gave his Opinion upon what had been read, upon which there enfued a general Converfation. The Supper held till pretty late, and was commonly followed with a Ball. No body could be admitted into the Order without the general Confent of the Chapter. And the Superior himfelf had no Right but to propofe fuch as were Candidates for Admiffion. To give you all the Statutes of this Society, would be too tedious; befides I fhould be afraid of adding or diminifhing minishing to them, because I only have them from Tradition.

The Margrave has a Mother still alive, *viz.* *Sophia-Christina* Countess of *Wolffenstein*, who lives at *Copenhagen* with her Daughter the Princess Royal* of *Denmark*. The King of *Denmark* grants her the Title of Royal Highness, and causes the same Honours to be paid to her as to the Princesses of his Family.

The Margrave has also three Brothers and two Sisters. The eldest of the Brothers is a Major-General and Colonel of Foot in the Service of the Emperor, and the two others are in the Service of *Denmark*. The two Princesses are marry'd, one to the Prince Royal of *Denmark*, the other to *George-Albert* Prince of *East-Friesland*. So that the intire Family of *Brandenbourg-Culmbach* consists of Princes and Princesses to the number of twelve.

The Revenues of this Margrave are pretty near the same as those of the Margrave of *Anspach*. His Fortress is the Castle of *Plassenberg*.

From *Bareith* I came in two Days to CARLSBAD, a Place of Fame for its hot Waters, of which there are two Sorts differing from one another both in Strength and Heat. They derive their Source from the middle of a River form'd by Torrents from the neighbouring Mountains, whose Waters are extremely cold; yet they make not the least Alteration in the heat of the Mineral Waters. They are said to be very wholesome for all sorts of Maladies, particularly for the Gravel, and for the Barrenness of Women. M. *Hofman*, a celebrated Professor of Physic at *Hall*, has published a Treatise, wherein he examines the nature of those Waters, and prescribes how they ought to be used. The Manner is very disagreeable; you are obliged to be shut up in a Room, and be the Weather ever so hot,

---
* She is the present Queen.

hot, the Stove must be heated, you must be tormented by taking off two or three Pots of Water, which are almost equal to thirty Chocolate Cups; besides walking about very much, and sweating great Drops.

To make amends for the Fatigue of the Morning, there is good Company to be seen here all Day long; for Abundance of Strangers come to *Carlsbad*, particularly the Nobility of *Bohemia* and *Austria*. There are publick Walks and a great Room adjacent, where they play, dance and walk till the Evening. They who love to live by Rule retire without Supper.

Whoever would be well accommodated at *Carlsbad* must carry three things thither with him, his own Bed, Wine, and Cook; tho' a Foot-boy may serve for the Cook, because one is generally invited by the *Bohemian* or *Austrian* Noblemen, who always keep a great Table, and love Company to dine with 'em.

The Inhabitants of *Carlsbad* are generally Armourers, who work very neat and vastly cheap. At the Season for using the Waters, Merchants flock hither from all Parts, and *Carlsbad* is superior to many great Towns. I had a great deal of Amusement during the two different Seasons that I pass'd there, and I contracted a World of good Acquaintance, who, I hope, will be of Service to me at *Prague*, for which Place I propose to set out to-morrow. I am, *&c.*

LETTER XI.

Prague, November 15, 1729.

SIR,

I HAVE now been a Month in this City, yet it seems but as a Day; for I find infinite Amusements here, and a thousand things that I like, only I want your Company. The City of PRAGUE is ancient, and has been time out of mind, the Seat of the Kings of *Bohemia*. 'Tis without dispute one of the Biggest Towns in *Europe*. 'Tis encompass'd with Ramparts, and as well fortified as a Place of that Extent can be, and commanded by several Hills, which 'tis impossible to level. This City is divided by the River *Molde* or *Muldaw*, into two Parts, *viz*. *Old Prague* and *Little Prague*; and during the Course of the last Century, it suffer'd the greatest Cruelties that a City can possibly undergo in a time of War. The Archduke *Leopold* Bishop of *Passau* surpriz'd and plunder'd the lesser Part, and would have done the same by the old Town, if the Emperor *Matthias* King of *Hungary* had not come in time to relieve it. Nine Years after this, *Prague* was again plunder'd by those who were most concerned to preserve it; I mean the Imperialists, who, after the Battle at *Weissenberg*, near *Prague*, wherein they defeated *Frederic* Elector Palatine whom a Party had chose King of *Bohemia*, enter'd the City, and carried off inestimable Booty. *Prague* was used no better in 1631, by the Elector of *Saxony*, after that Prince made himself Master of *Bohemia*. The Great *Walstein* of so much Note for

his

his Glorious Actions, and his Tragical Exit, recover'd *Bohemia* from the *Saxon* in 1632, and took *Prague* by Storm. Some time after this the *Swedes* attack'd it, and took the lesser *Prague*; but could not force the old Town, it was so courageously defended by the Students and Burghers. The *Swedes* thereupon retired, and carry'd off immense Wealth. At length the Peace of *Westphalia* restored Tranquillity to *Bohemia* and the City of *Prague*, which has been subject ever since to the House of *Austria*; and the Kingdom which before was Elective, had the Mortification to become Hereditary.

The Situation of *Prague* is pleasant in the midst of Gardens and fine Fields, and 'tis adorn'd with noble Buildings, of which the Houses of the Counts *Tschernin* and *Sternberg* are as fine as any. The Furniture of the former is extremely rich; there is a Gallery adorned with excellent Pictures, a Cabinet of choice Porcellane with entire Services of the finest *Indian Lacca*; and another Room full of fine Arms and other Curiosities. Count *Sternberg*'s House is not so large, yet better contriv'd; and in *Rome* it self would pass for a fine Palace. But there is one built by the late Count *de Gallasch*, who died Viceroy at *Naples*, that bears the Bell above all. You know that Nobleman was prodigiously rich and magnificent. He spared no Cost in his Buildings. 'Tis pity the House is not well situate, but it certainly would be so, if the young Count *de Gallasch* was of the same Way of Thinking with his Father, who intended to have had five or six old Hovels belonging to it pull'd down to the ground, by which means he would have had a fine Square.

The Convents of both Sexes are another Ornament of this Great City. The House of the Reverend Fathers the Jesuits is one of the most magnificent. They have lately caused a Church to be built, which is one of the best adorned that I have seen out of *Italy*. If you were but here, we would go together and see all those Buildings. I would carry you first of all to the Cathedral, which is in lesser *Prague*, on the Top of the Hill call'd *Ratschin*, and from thence we would go and take a View of the Castle which is upon the same Hill.

The Metropolitan Church is a very antient Structure, which was burnt down by the *Swedes*, and is only rebuilt in part. Its Magnificence and Beauty consist in the thickness of its Walls and Arches; and the Architecture of this Church is such, that I fancy it would appear *Gothic* to the very *Goths* themselves. 'Tis in this Cathedral that the Kings and Queens of *Bohemia* are consecrated. The Archbishop of *Prague*'s Office is to perform the Unction upon both; but the Abbess of St. *George*, whose Abbey is also upon the Hill of *Ratschin*, is to place the Crown upon the Head of the Queen, and in this Function she is assisted by the Wives of the Great Officers of the Crown.

In this Metropolitan Church are preserved with great Veneration the Bodies of a couple of Saints extremely dear to the *Bohemians*. The one is St. *Wenceslaus* King of *Bohemia*, the other St. *John Nepomucene*. The latter was very lately canonized by Pope *Benedict* XIII. at the Request of the States of this Kingdom, who were at the whole Expence of the Ceremony, which was performed in the Church of St. *John de Lateran* at *Rome* with extraordinary Pomp.

The Story of this Saint is very singular: He was Confessor to the Wife of that cruel Emperor *Wenceslaus*, who was deposed by the Electors. That Prince being jealous of his Queen enjoined St. *John Nepomucene* to reveal that Princess's Confessions to him. He employed Presents, Prayers and Threats, to persuade the Saint to make this Discovery, but all to no purpose; upon which he caused him to be cast

cast headlong from the Bridge into the River of *Molde*. The Body was seen floating at some distance from the Place, attended with five Stars swimming on the Water; then he was added to the Number of the Saints and Martyrs, and his Corpse was taken out of the River, and carried with Pomp to *Prague*, where it was interr'd in the Church of *Dain* in the old Town, of which he was a Canon. His Corpse being found some Years ago, his Tongue appearing to be as fresh as ever, was taken out of his Mouth and put into a Silver Gilt Box; the Body was enclosed in a stately Coffin, and the whole carried with great Ceremony to the Cathedral. An Altar being erected in the middle of the right Wing of the Choir, there the Saint was interr'd in a Tomb of Silver Gilt; and the Tongue put into a sort of Tabernacle where it has wrought and does still work great Miracles. There is a great Concourse of People hither from all Parts to invoke this Saint, whose Tomb is loaded with precious Gifts, and adorned by the Empress with a rich Canopy. But no body has given more illustrious Proofs of Devotion to St. *Nepomucene* than the Prince *de Schwartzenberg* *, Master of the Horse to the Emperor, and the Count *de Martinitz* Marshal of the Imperial Court; who both ascribe the Conception of their Wives, and the Birth of their Sons, to the Protection of that Saint, tho' I should have thought all this feasible enough without a Miracle. The Princess *de Schwartzenberg* had not been married many Years before she had a Daughter †; her Husband had not seen her for fourteen Years after this, during which she had no Children. This is no more than common; after they came together again Madam is brought to Bed of a Son, in which tho' there is nothing but what is very

---

* He had the Misfortune to be killed as he was hunting in *Bohemia*, by the Emperor himself in 1732.
† She is now Margravine of *Baden-Baden*.

natural,

natural, yet 'tis cry'd up for a Miracle; the Birth is ascribed to the Devotion which the Princess paid to the Tomb of St. *Nepomucene* for nine Days together, and to make the Saint some amends, his Tomb and his Altar are adorn'd by a great many Vessels of Silver and Silver gilt.

As to Count *Martinitz* there seems indeed to be better colour for a Miracle in his favour. He had been married fourteen or fifteen Years, and his Lady never given the least Sign of Teemingness. She was in good plight of body, her Husband liv'd with her, and they went together several times to the Baths of *Carlsbad*, but all had signified nothing. The Count longing passionately for a Son had perform'd more than nine days Devotion successively, for he went the last Holy Year to *Loretto* and to *Rome*. But Heaven deaf to his Cries granted him no Heir; at last knowing not what Saint to pray to, his Lady propos'd, that they should go and worship nine days together at the Tomb of St. *Nepomucene*. They set out, they arrive at *Prague*, they prostrate themselves before the sacred Tomb. Soon after, Madame *de Martinitz* proves with Child, and at nine Months end is delivered of a Son. You may say whatever you please, but such a Favour sure was worth some Lamps of solid Silver before the Saint's Tomb; and the Count *de Martinitz* full of Zeal and Gratitude has given some that are very magnificent.

The *Bohemians* have so great confidence in St. *John de Nepomucene*, that they have almost forgot St. *Wenceslaus* their old Patron. There is no Church where St. *John* has not a Chapel, no Bridge without his Effigy; every body Gentle and Simple, Men and Women, wear his Picture as if it were the Badge of an Order, hanging to a straw-colour'd Ribbon, and you would swear that all the *Bohemians* were Knights of St. *Louis*. In short, St. *Nepomucene* is

the

the only Saint in vogue; and Presents are heap'd upon him to such a degree that if it continues much longer, he will be as rich as our Lady of *Loretto.*

The Palace or Castle which joins to the Cathedral is a great Building composed of several Main Bodies without Symmetry or Architecture. The Apartments are but low and plain, but here is one of the most beautiful Prospects in the World. The great Hall in which the Royal Feast is kept on the Day of the Coronation of the Kings is the largest of the kind, next to the spacious Hall of *Westminster.* The Palace-Gardens are large, but have nothing to recommend them besides their Situation. The Tribunals of the Regency meet in the Palace: The first of these consists of Stadtholders who are of the Emperor's Privy Council. They are to the Number of twelve, and represent the Sovereign. Most of them are the great Officers of the Crown. There must be always two of them private Gentlemen to take care of the Interests of the Gentry against the Nobility; for you must know that the Princes, Counts, and Barons, who compose the Nobility, form a separate Body here, and would think it a Disparagement to be call'd *Gentlemen*; tho' *Henry* IV. King of *France* counted it an honour to be the first Gentleman in his Kingdom, and King *Francis* I. whenever he affirmed a thing, said, *Upon the Word of a Gentleman.*

The Chief of the Council of the Stadtholders is call'd the *Great Burgrave,* whose Dignity is the highest in the Kingdom. He represents the Person of the Emperor, and is inferior to none but the Chancery of *Bohemia* which always attends the Emperor.

The Bridge over the *Muldaw* which joins little *Prague* to the old Town, is one of the longest and most substantial Bridges in *Europe.* It has on both sides

sides the Statues of several Saints, which if they had been done by a better hand, would have prov'd an Ornament. There is a Crucifix also which is pretended to be of Gold, and to have been erected formerly at the Expence of the *Jews*, pursuant to an Order of the Government, as a Punishment for their having crucified a Christian Infant upon *Easter-Day*, to insult the Memory of our Saviour's Death.

The *Jews* are the only Sectaries that are tolerated in *Bohemia*. There are some *Hussites* still subsisting, but they keep so close, that the Government does not seem to know that there are any at all. I was assur'd that in *Prague* alone there were no less than 80,000 *Jews*; whether there are quite so many, I know not; but 'tis certain they are very numerous. Their Quarter in the old City forms a little separate Town. They have all the Trade in their own hands, follow all sorts of Callings, and by their receiving all old-fashion'd things in Payment, they quite ruin the Christian Handicraftsmen. As these People multiply like Rabbets, 'tis said the Emperor is going to issue an Ordinance prohibiting any but their eldest Sons to marry; the Report of which is so alarming to the *Jews*, that they would advance great Sums to prevent its taking effect.

If we except *Rome*, *Paris*, and *London*, there is no City where there are more Gentry, or a Gentry that is more wealthy: Every body here lives grand; and in no Part of the World do the Nobility keep greater State, or take more Pride in their Substance. They are polite and civil to Strangers, whom they know to be Persons of Quality. For my own part, I like them prodigiously, and I can safely say it, I have hardly met with a Foreigner who has not the same Notion of *Prague* that I have.

There

There is not a Gentleman in this Country but has seen at least *Holland*, *France*, and *Italy*, and indeed they are under some necessity of travelling, for the Education they have at home is none of the best. But they don't travel as People of their Birth and Fortunes ought to do. They are commonly attended by a sort of Governors, who make it their Profession to ramble abroad with young Gentlemen, and are for the most part *Walloons*, *Luxemburghers*, *Lorrainers*, or *Liegeois*, Soldiers of Fortune, without Education, and without Manners; who think 'tis enough for their Pupils to see Houses and Churches, and having not the Courage or the Capacity to put themselves forward, or even to shew their Heads, don't care that their Gentlemen should keep Company. They tell *young Master*, that my Lord his Father, who put him under their Care, recommended Œconomy to them; that they might game at Assemblies, but that 'tis not well to play while they are travelling: Therefore the Spark is oblig'd to keep in his Quarters, or if he is perhaps permitted to go to the public Shews, even this Pleasure, because it is not to be had without Money, must be taken in Moderation; the Governor's Aim is only to crib all he can, and sink his Pupil's Money into his own Purse. This is so true that I have known some who never eat Suppers, yet always brought them to Accompt; many of 'em get a Profit by every thing they buy, and they make such hard Bargains that 'tis ten to one if they don't chouse the Merchant as well as their Pupil. If the Governor does not like the Place they come to, he must be gone, tho' it were the most proper Town in the World to form the young Gentleman; for the Govenor only writes to the Father or Mother that the Air did not agree with their Son, and that therefore he had remov'd him. The Generality of these wretched Guides maintain that six Weeks or three

three Months Stay at most is sufficient to know *Paris*; a Fortnight to be thoroughly acquainted with the Genius of the *English*; a Month to know *Rome*; a Week to see *Naples*; and so of the rest: And when they have shewn their Gentleman at *Paris*, the Anatomical Wax-work and the Observatory; at *London*, the Lions in the Tower; at *Rome*, the Catacombs; and at *Naples*, the Liquefaction of St. *Januarius*'s Blood, and Mount *Vesuvius*; they think they have done great matters, and away they go without having made an Acquaintance with one Soul at any of the Courts. They have seen the King of *France* touch for the Evil; The King of *England* go to the Parliament-House; and the Pope sitting in his Elbow-Chair, distributing his Benedictions. With a Mind thus adorn'd, the young Man, after eighteen Months or two Years Absence abroad, returns home. The Governor has two or three thousand Florins, and sometimes more as a Gratuity, besides his Stipend. Again, the worthy *Mentor* makes a Bubble of the Father who trusts his Son with him, and behold now, he is ready for another Tour. One would think that, instead of travelling in this manner, it were better to send abroad for the Plans of all the Towns, I am sure 'twould be cheaper; the Parents would have the comfort to see their Sons at home, and they would also have wherewithal to furnish a little Box in the Country.

There are no People of Quality in the World more addicted to an expensive way of Living than those of *Prague*, which is the Reason that for all their immense Revenues they are sometimes over Head and Ears in Debt; but by good Luck they have a Settlement which prevents them from total Ruin: For most of their Lands are intail'd for ever on the eldest Son of the Family, so that he can neither alienate nor incumber them without the Consent

sent of the whole Family, and of the King himself, which is a Thing very hard to be obtain'd. When an eldest Son of a Family has squander'd his Freehold, and runs himself more and more in debt, the Creditors, and sometimes the Parents themselves, present a Petition to the King and desire a Sequestration. The King after being inform'd of the List of the Debts, and of the *Majorat* (which is the Name they give here to the Lands that are intail'd) names Trustees for the Administration of the Estates of the Spendthrift, who is allow'd a Pension till all the Debts are paid. There's another very good Establishment here for securing the Sale of Landed Estates and Mortgages. Every Nobleman gives in a Particular of his Estate to a Tribunal which is call'd the *Landtaffel*, where the same is register'd. When a Person wants to borrow Money or to make a Sale, the Lender or the Purchaser has recourse to the *Landtaffel's* Office, where he sees whether the Lands are incumber'd; and if the Borrower's Debts don't exceed two Thirds of the Price at which they are rated by the *Landtaffel*, he may lend his Money very safely.

Tho' the *Bohemians* are brave and good Soldiers, yet they don't love the Service, I mean the Gentry: Most of them prefer the Civil to Military Employments, and a private Life to Posts in the Army or at Court. They are so us'd to be absolute Masters at their Estates where the Peasants are their Slaves, and to be homag'd like Petty Sovereigns by the Burghers at *Prague*, that they don't care to reside at *Vienna*, and to be oblig'd like other Subjects to pay their Court to the Sovereign and the Ministers. As soon as a Gentleman of *Bohemia* comes of Age, he is oblig'd to take an Oath of Fidelity to the Emperor as his King; which is a Law as much binding on the Nobility as the Gentry; and none of 'em dare to go out of the Kingdom without express

press Leave from the Emperor, on the Penalty of forfeiting his Estate. When the Noblemen are return'd from their Travels to *France* and *Italy*, they put in to be Chamberlains, not so much for the sake of engaging themselves to Attendance at Court as to procure a Precedency for their Wives, it being a Custom with most of 'em to marry as soon as they come of Age. Afterwards they aim to be Counsellors of State, and Stadtholders, and this is the *Ne plus ultra* of their Perferments. The Counsellors of State challenge the Title of *Excellency*: But this is what those who are not of that Denomination, and of as good Families as themselves, scruple to allow them, so that generally speaking they have it only given them by their Domestics and Dependants. So that one may say of their Excellencies what the Duchess of *Elbœuf* of the *Lorrain* Family said in *France* concerning the Princes of *Bouillon*, that they were *Domestic Highnesses*, because none but their own Servants give them the Title of *Highness*.

Of all the great and wealthy Families, those of *Lobkowitz*, *Kinski*, *Schlick*, *Collobradt*, and *Martinitz* are the only ones that make a Figure at the Imperial Court. 'Tis true there are several other Noblemen at *Vienna* who have Lands in *Bohemia*, but then their Families are not originally descended from that Kingdom.

The *Kinski*'s Family is actually the most splendid at Court. The are five Brothers of it in Employments. The eldest is the Great Chancellor of *Bohemia**. The second who is call'd Count *Stephen*, is Great Marshal of *Bohemia*, a Minister of State, and the Emperor's Ambassador at the Court of *France*†. The third, Count *Philip*, is the Emperor's

---

* His fickle State of Health oblig'd him to quit this Employment, in which he was succeeded by the Count *de Collobradt*, who in 1734 was made Vice-Chancellor.

† He is return'd to *Vienna* since 1732.

ror's Minister Plenipotentiary to *Great Britain*; and the two youngest are in the Army, where one of them is a Lieutenant-Colonel. Count *Philip* was sent Ambassador when but twenty nine Years old. He has demonstrated by his Conduct that Wisdom does not always stay for Age, and that he is the worthy Son of one of the greatest Ministers that * the Emperors *Leopold* and *Joseph* ever had. The City of *Prague* is a very great Loser by his Absence, for he liv'd there with Splendor, and his House was always open, particularly to Foreigners. For my own part I receiv'd such Civilities there as I shall never forget.

As I have told you that the Nobility of *Bohemia* are the richest in the Empire, I must also acquaint you that the Peasants there are miserable to the last degree; their Persons, and all they have, are at the Command of their Lord. The poor Wretches have often not a Bit of Bread to eat, in a Country which is one of the most plentiful in *Europe* for all sorts of Provisions. They dare not go from one Village to another to work, nor learn a Handicraft without their Lord's Consent. So much Subjection keeps the poor Creatures always trembling and humble, so that if you do but speak to 'em they are ready to lick the Dust off your Feet. The Severity with which these People are us'd is really terrible, but 'tis as true on the other hand, that gentle Usage has no Effect upon 'em; for they are excessively lazy and stubborn, and being moreover us'd to harsh Treatment from Generation to Generation, Blows scarce terrify them, tho' 'tis the only way to make 'em good for any thing.

The

---

* This Minister was Great Chancellor of *Bohemia* and a Knight of the *Golden Fleece*. Count *Joseph* was nominated Ambassador to *Great Britain* in 1736, in the room of his Brother *Philip*.

The *Bohemians* have a great many Talents for Music, so that there's no Village, be it ever so small, but the Mass is sung in Concert, and they are very happy at winding the Hunters Horn.

'Tis certain that this Kingdom is one of the best Countries in the Emperor's possession, and next to *Hungary*, brings him in most Money.

Bohemia is a Country of States, whom the Emperor as King of it, summons every Year to the City of *Prague*. They consist of the Clergy, Nobility, Gentry, and Towns. The Assembly is open'd by a Commissioner of the Emperor's Nomination, who lays before them his Imperial Majesty's Demands. The States, such is their Submission and Zeal, grant the full Demand which is commonly a very great Sum; yet for all this, the *Bohemians* wou'd not complain of Taxes if the Emperor resided among them, but they are sorry to see their Country exhausted to enrich the *Austrians* to whom they have a natural Aversion, and the *Austrians* as heartily hate the *Bohemians*.

I own to you I shall be sorry to leave *Prague*. I take the *Bohemians* to be the best People upon Earth, and *Prague* to be one of those Towns of the Empire where a Gentleman may have most choice of Company. The Ladies here are very amiable. Gaming, which may be call'd the universal Pleasure, is carry'd as high here as they please in Houses of the Quality, where Assemblies of both Sexes are held every Night, with good Cheer, particularly Pheasants and Ortolans in plenty; and upon Fish-Days, there are Trouts, Salmon, and Cray-Fish; and that there may be nothing wanting, *Bohemia* likewise furnishes good Wine. At the Estate of the young Count *Tschernin* at *Melneg*, there is a red sort not inferior to *Burgundy*. Of all these good Things many partake together, and for my part I own I am taken more with this

Pleasure

Pleasure than any other, because we make it last as long as we will, and then 'tis suited to all Ages.

There is a tolerable *Italian Opera* here. In Winter they have Races in stately Sledges: There is great Masquerading, and they dance till they are ready to drop to the ground: For this end there are public Balls which are extraordinary splendid, and might be compar'd, if any can be compar'd, with the Balls at the *Hay-Market* in *London*.

In the Summer-Time when there is not so much Company in Town, these Assemblies are thinner. The Gentry meet at Night in a Garden belonging to the Prince *de Schwartzenberg*, where they game, chat, and walk up and down, after which they always go to some House or other to sup. When one has a mind to go to the Country, we are sure of a good Reception, and the longer one stays the greater Pleasure one gives to the Master of the House. Here they pass the Time in Hunting of all sorts. Many of the Nobility keep Packs of Hounds, and others Hawks. The Generality keep Musicians in their Service, so that let the Weather be what it will, one may be always amused in this Country. Besides, one enjoys all the Freedom here that can be. After this, Sir, can you blame me for being sorry to leave *Bohemia?* But 'tis what I'm now preparing to do, and I purpose to go to *Vienna*. You will be so good as to let me have a Line from you there; for to be plain with you, to write three Letters for one is too hard. 'Tis true that your's are of inestimable Value, and that therefore you are in the right not to be lavish of them; but the same Reason justifies me in desiring them. Adieu, Sir: Love me always a little, and be assur'd that no Man is more than I, *&c.*

LETTER XII.

SIR,   *Vienna, Nov. 30. 1729.*

THE Court of Vienna consists of so many Princes and Noblemen, that it cannot be deny'd to be the greatest and most magnificent Court in *Europe.* Nevertheless Ceremonies, and the *Etiquette,* a Name by which they call ancient Usages, give it an Air of Constraint that is to be seen no where else. There's a universal Out-cry against the latter, and even the Emperor sometimes seems to be disturb'd at it, yet 'tis observ'd as strictly as if it was an Article of Religion, and nothing cou'd set it aside but an Oecumenical Council.

Notwithstanding this, a Foreigner of Quality (for such he must be here) finds Advantages at this Court which he does not meet with either at *Paris* or *London,* I mean Opportunities of making Acquaintance. After a Person has been to wait on their Imperial Majesties he need only be introduc'd into one single Family to be soon made known to all the rest, with this Advantage too, that go where you will, they speak the *German, French, Italian,* and *Spanish* Languages; whereas a Foreigner at *Paris* is under a Necessity of speaking *French,* and at *London English;* but a Man may shift very well at *Vienna* without the *High-Dutch* or *German* Language.

The Ministers and great Lords of the Court are Civil, Courteous, and of easy Access, especially to such as want no Favour of 'em, and come to *Vienna*
only

only for Curiosity or Business. The Way of these Gentlemen is to return no Visits: but they invite People to their Tables, which being always well fill'd, a Man soon gets a great deal of Acquaintance.

'Tis a very easy matter to be admitted to kiss the Hands of their Imperial Majesties, and even to obtain a private Audience of 'em; for there needs nothing more than to give in your Name to the Emperor's Great Chamberlain and the Empress's Great Master of the Houshold. When you kiss their Hands you bend one Knee to the Ground, and the Time for it is generally when their Majesties pass by to Dinner. But private Audiences are attended with more Ceremonies. The Great Chamberlain having appointed the Hour of meeting in his Antichamber, which is commonly five o'clock in the Evening, he repairs thither at that Time, and introduces to the Audience; and if he be absent, 'tis done by the Chamberlain in Waiting. The Ceremony observ'd is this: The Empreor stands up under a Canopy, leaning with his Back against a Table, and an Arm-Chair by his Side. A Screen of red Velvet with Gold Fringe is plac'd at the Entrance of the Room, so that the Emperor is not perceiv'd at the opening of the Door. Behind this Screen near the Door, stands the Great Chamberlain. As soon as the Person comes in sight of the Emperor he bends the Knee, which he repeats as he advances a little farther; and again when he comes near to his Imperial Majesty. To these Genuflexions the Emperor gives a Nod of the Head, hearkens very attentively to the Person who addresses him, and returns a succinct and gracious Answer. Then the Person kneeling with one Knee on the Ground kisses his Majesty's Hand, after which he retires, going backwards and making three Genuflexions as he did at Entrance. The same Ceremonies are observ'd at an Audience of the Empress,

Empress, who gives it standing juſt as the Emperor does, with this Difference only that the Emperor is all alone, and the Empreſs is attended with one of her Ladies of Honour, who neverthelefs ſtands off at ſuch a Diſtance that ſhe can't hear what is ſaid.

The Emperor commonly eats with the Empreſs and the Arch-Ducheſſes. But there are particular Days, ſuch as the Inſtallation of the Knights of the *Golden Fleece*, when the Empreſs herſelf is not allow'd to ſit down at Table with his Imperial Majeſty. The Dinner is commonly in the Emperor's Apartment, and the Supper at the Empreſs's. At Dinner two Chamberlains hold the Ewer for their Majeſties to waſh, and the Steward, or in his abſence the Great Chamberlain preſents them the Napkin, which is done after the manner of *Spain*, with one Knee on the Ground. The Number of Diſhes at the Emperor's Table is forty eight, and the ſame at the Empreſs's; but tho' their Majeſties eat together they are each ſerv'd by their own Officers and Cooks. They commonly drink both together at the firſt Time; and till they have drank, the Ambaſſadors, Courtiers, and Ladies all wait at Dinner. After the Emperor has drank, the Steward, the Maſter of the Horſe, the Great Chamberlain, and the Captain of the Guards receive his Orders: The Lady of Honour in Waiting and the Empreſs's Steward receive her Orders in like manner. None remain in the Room but the Officers neceſſary for the Service, and ſome curious People who are not us'd to ſee Sovereigns eat. On Sundays, Saints Days, and Days of *Gala*, which is the Name they give here to Days of Feſtival and Ceremony, the Dinner is attended with Muſic. I forgot to acquaint you that the Emperor is always cover'd at Table, and that when he puts his Hat on the Ambaſſadors put on theirs.

At Supper the Lady of Honour who is in waiting presents the Napkin, and the Ladies of the Bed-Chamber not only carve and hand the Victuals, but taste both the Meat and the Wine. The Pages carry the Dishes and Plates, and fetch the Wine from the Beaufet which they give to the Ladies, and they to their Majesties. During the Supper as well as at Dinner all the Gentlemen and Ladies stand up, so that here neither Princes nor Princesses have any Distinction shew'd them, but all Ranks are levell'd and confounded, and no body sits down in presence of the Sovereign.

On the Days of *Gala* the Court is extremely gay, and nothing is to be seen but Gold and Diamonds. The Days of this kind that are celebrated with most Splendor are those of St. *Charles* and St. *Elizabeth*, the Name Days of the Emperor and Empress. The Emperor, who commonly dresses very plain, is cover'd all over with Diamonds upon St. *Elizabeth*'s Day. And as for the Empress, her Apparel is commonly rich, and so loaded with Jewels upon St. *Charles*'s Day that she can scarce stand under it. Except on these Days of *Gala* the Court dresses very plain. 'Tis true that these Days are very frequent, and that consequently plain Clothes are not very much wore, for if it be a Holiday, or the Birth-Day of some Minister, or if some Lady of Distinction sends but for a Surgeon to bleed her, 'tis enough to put the whole City in *Gala*. These *Gala*'s may be divided into three Classes; the *Court Gala* which is universal both for the Nobles and Plebeians; the *Grand Gala* which is kept in the City is for the Festival of some Minister; and the third and last is the *Little Gala*, which is when the Ladies are let blood. A Husband makes a *Gala* here for his Wife, the Wife for her Husband, the Children for their Parents, and Brothers and Sisters for one another; so that to be sure two Thirds of *Vienna* are always in *Gala*; which made a *French* Jester say, 'twould take up a great deal of Brimstone to cure the *Austrians* of the *Gale* *. However, they take care not to appear in this domestic *Gala* before the Emperor and Empress, because it would be reckon'd a Disrespect to them.

On the great Festival-Days the Emperor goes with a grand Retinue to St. *Stephen*'s Cathedral: He takes up one whole Side of the Coach, and the Empress sits fronting him. Their Majesties are preceded by the Chamberlains and Knights of the *Golden Fleece* on horse-back: The Pages and Footmen walk bare-headed immediately after the Coach of the Master of the Horse, and their Imperial Majesties Coach is guarded on each side by a File of Archers, and attended by the Coaches of the Arch-Duchesses and the Ladies. Then the Horse-Guards appear with their Kettle-Drums and Trumpets, and the March is clos'd by the Pope's *Nuncio* and the Ambassadors with their Train, which consists of three magnificent Coaches and six Horses each.

On *Corpus Christi* Day the Emperor accompanies the Holy Sacrament, when the Streets thro' which the Procession passes are cover'd with Planks. Their Imperial Majesties repair in the Morning with great Attendance to St. *Stephen*'s Cathedral, and after assisting at Divine Service join in the Procession. The Emperor is immediately follow'd by the Empress, who is accompany'd by all the Ladies in rich Dresses, which renders this one of the most magnificent Processions in the World.

The same Honours and Respects are paid to the Empress Dowager as to the Empress Regent. She has her separate Houshold, and her own Guards. She has an Apartment in the Palace, but commonly lives in a Convent of her own founding in one of the Suburbs, and does not come to Town except on the great Festivals or for some extraordinary Function.

---

* This Word in *French* signifies a *Scab*.

tion. You know, without doubt, that the Empress Dowagers can never quit Mourning; their Apartments must be always hung with Black, and their Coaches and Liveries are of the same Colour: Nor can they be present at any Play, Ball, or Concert. In short by losing their Husbands they must renounce the Pleasures of this Life. These severe Obligations on a Widow are fully discharg'd by the Empress Dowager. Being retir'd to a Convent where she is almost continually prostrate before the Altars in Prayer and Supplication, she makes her Mansion a Place of Piety and Peace, and never appears in public but when Conveniency requires. This Princess was always an Example of the most uncommon Virtue. In the Life-time of her Husband the Emperor *Joseph*, she lov'd Pleasures and Grandeur; but when she became a Widow she renounc'd all, and only employ'd herself in Works of Piety, and in the Education of the two Arch-Duchesses her Daughters, whom she has now the Comfort of seeing marry'd to two powerful Princes of the Empire*. There's not a Person that draws near her Imperial Majesty but admires her eminent Qualities. I have not yet had the Honour this Journey of casting myself at her Feet, but the first Time I was here I had the Advantage of paying my Duty to her at *Schonborn*, where she then pass'd the Summer. I was receiv'd by her with such Proofs of her Kindness as charm'd me, and which I shall always remember with Pleasure and Respect. This Princess is the Daughter of *John-Frederic* Duke of *Brunswic-Hanover* and of *Henrietta-Benedictine* Princess Palatine. After the Death of the Duke her Father, who left no Son, she went with the Duchess of *Brunswic* to *France*, where this Princess was very glad to retire to her Sister the Princess of *Conde*. The Empress who was

then

* The Electresses of *Bavaria* and *Saxony*.

then the Princess *Amelia*, spent some Years in *France*, where she learned the Language and Politeness of that Nation to perfection, and in short acquir'd that Merit and Virtue for which she is now so much admir'd, and which perhaps have contributed equally with her illustrious Extraction to gain her possession of the first Throne in Christendom. The Marriage of her elder Sister to *Renaud d'Este* Duke of *Modena* obliging the Dutchess of *Brunswic* to leave *France*, and go and settle at *Modena*, the Princess *Amelia* follow'd her also into *Italy*. She had no reason to be sorry for her leaving *France*, and rejecting the Addresses of a *French* Nobleman who had presum'd to court her, for not long after her Arrival at *Modena* she was marry'd to the King of the *Romans*, afterwards the Emperor *Joseph*. This Empress is not only endow'd with the Christian but all the Moral Virtues, and there are few Princesses of a more generous Soul, of greater Courage, or of a Genius more sublime, more refin'd, or more adorn'd. There was a Time when she might be rank'd among the most beautiful Princesses of *Europe*: she still retains all the Marks of it; and therewith preserves such a majestic Air that whenever I behold her it revives the profound Veneration I have for her sacred Person.

The Emperor *Charles* VI. is of a middling Stature, and in good Plight of Body: He is of a swarthy hale Complection, has a brisk Eye, and thick Lips, for which last his Family in general have been remarkable. This Monarch is the second Son of the Emperor *Leopold* by *Eleonora* of *Newbourg*, and the fifteenth Emperor * of his Family. Being design'd when a Minor for Successor to *Charles* II. King of *Spain*, he had a grave Education suitable to the People whom he was one day to govern. This

made

---

* I conform to the Opinion of almost all the Historians, who do not place *Frederic* the Fair in the List of the Emperors.

made him contract an Air of Seriousness, which, to those who have not the Honour of Access to him, savours of Severity; yet he is affable and very humane.. He hears those with Attention that speak to him, and his Answers are full of Good-nature. When he attain'd to an Age hardly ripe enough for the Crown of *Spain*, he met with various Fortune in that Kingdom; but he supported himself in every Event with an heroic Magnanimity, being always submissive to the Will of that Providence which he knew was the Master of the Fortune of Kings. The Adversitys with which it pleas'd God to try his Patience by the Siege of *Barcelona* which he carry'd on in Person, and by the Loss of the Battle of *Villa Viciosa*, only serv'd to confirm his Constancy, and his natural Integrity, a Principle which renders him even more venerable than the Splendor of his Crowns and the vast Extent of his Power. Heaven, which always rewards Virtue, has granted this Monarch one of the best and most fortunate Reigns that any Emperor has had since *Germany* has been the Seat of Empire. He wants nothing to crown his Happiness but a Male Heir, which is so much the Desire of the People, as well as of the Emperor and the most virtuous Empress the World ever saw, that God grant he may have one.

This Princess is descended from the august House of *Brunswic*, to which *Europe* is at this Time oblig'd for two Empresses*, one King †, and a Queen ‖. She is the Daughter of *Lewis Rodolph* Duke of *Brunswic-Blankenbourg* ** by *Christiana-Louisa* Princess of *Oetingen*, of whom I gave you an

---

* The Empress Regent and the Empress Dowager.
† The King of *Great Britain*.
‖ The Queen of *Prussia*.
** The present Duke Regent of *Brunswic-Luxenbourg-Wolfembuttle*.

an Account in my Letter from *Blankenbourg*. The Character of this auguſt Princeſs for her Affability and Goodneſs is ſo well known in the World that 'tis needleſs to ſpeak of it here. You know likewiſe how beautiful and handſome ſhe was when ſhe was marry'd to the Emperor. And notwithſtanding the Pimples in her Face and her preſent Corpulency ſhe may ſtill be reckon'd in the number of the beautiful Princeſſes. Such an Air of Modeſty, Mildneſs, and Majeſty, accompanies every thing ſhe does, as inſpires thoſe that approach her with equal Courage and Reſpect. Her Duty is her Law, and her principal Care is to pleaſe the Emperor, whoſe Wiſdom ſhe knows to be ſufficient to govern his Dominions, and to him ſhe therefore leaves all Affairs. Indeed ſhe is very earneſt with him to get Favours for thoſe who petition her, which ſhe thinks a Happineſs to obtain, and ſhe beſtows them in ſuch manner as is very affecting to the Receivers. This Princeſs is charitable, generous, and magnificent. She maintains her Dignity without Conceit, and ſupports her ſolid Piety without Oſtentation. She was educated in the *Lutheran* Religion, but abjur'd it at *Bamberg* when ſhe came thither in her Way to be marry'd to the Emperor, then King of *Spain*, and is now a good Catholic, yet without any Hatred to the Proteſtants; being convinc'd that the Love of one's Neighbour is one of the Duties which God moſt ſtrictly enjoins upon Mankind, and that Charitableneſs and good Examples are the beſt Means to reconcile thoſe to the Church who are ſeparated from it.

In the ſame ſublime Sentiments of Virtue does the Empreſs educate the Archducheſſes her Daughters, and thoſe young Princeſſes are like to make worthy Proficients. The eldeſt Archducheſs *Mary Thereſa* is brought up in the agreeable Proſpect of being one day Miſtreſs of the vaſt Dominions poſ-

VIENNA. 233

fessed by the Emperor [*]. This young Princess has very much of the Air of the Empress her Mother; and if Heaven designs her for the Sovereignty of the Empire, God grant she may also resemble her in her Virtues!

The Emperor has three Sisters. The eldest is the Archduchess *Mary Elizabeth* Governess of the (*Austrian*) *Netherlands*; the second is *Mary Anne* Queen of *Portugal*; and the third is the Archduchess *Mary Magdalen*, who 'tis said is intended to be Governess of *Tirol*. The intire August House of *Austria* consists at present of the sacred Person of the Emperor and of eight Princesses [†], of whom three are married; and God grant it may be augmented by the Birth of a Prince; for without setting up here for a zealous Subject, I don't think that the Houses of *Austria* and *Bourbon* ought ever to be extinct, both of them having made the Fortunes of an infinite Number of Gentlemen.

The Emperor's ordinary Pastime (when he has a Desire to unbend his Mind from Affairs of State, to which he applies with all the Earnestness of a Monarch that loves his People) is Hunting, or Shooting at a Mark; and the Empress is generally a Sharer in his Diversions. His Imperial Majesty goes sometimes also to the Riding-House, where he exercises himself in Riding: At other times Music is his Amusement, which the Monarch not only performs by Book, but is also a Composer; and some Years ago an Opera was acted here of his composing. All the Actors as well as the Dancers and the Musicians of the Orchestre were Persons of Quality. The Emperor himself made one, and the two eldest Archduchesses his Daughters danced. The Spectators were the Empress Regent and the Empress Dowager, and every Actor had the Liberty

---

[*] Feb. 1. 1736. she was marry'd to the Duke of *Lorrain*.
[†] There are but seven Archduchesses since 1730; the Emperor's third Daughter being dead.

berty of carrying two of his Kindred or intimate Friends.

Tho' their Imperial Majesties are very fond of Music they have seldom more than two Operas in a Year, *viz.* on the Days of St. *Charles* and St. *Elizabeth*, and sometimes the same Operas are play'd again during the Carnival. At this time, which is devoted to Mirth, there is a Ball at Court, and on the Flesh-days there is commonly a great Masquerade representing a Country-Wedding. In the Palace there is a very magnificent Theatre, which indeed is almost the only thing there that is worth seeing, for the Imperial Palace is so wretched a Mansion that few Monarchs are lodged worse than the Emperor. The Furniture too is old-fashion'd and not very rich, which is somewhat unaccountable, because the Wardrobes are full of costly Pieces of Tapestry, stately Pictures, and other fine Goods which probably they are restrained from making use of by the *Etiquette*. The Emperor's Pleasure-Houses are no better than his Palace in the City. The Castle of the *Favorita* which is in one of the Suburbs, is a great Building full of Turnings and Windings like the Street which it looks into, and has more of the Appearance of a great Convent of *Capuchin* Fryars than of the Dwelling of a Prince who is the Head of so many Sovereigns. The Gardens are as mean as the House, and only considerable for their Extent. *Laxembourg* is still very much inferior to the *Favorita*; but the Court is there no more than a Month or six Weeks, during the Hunting of the Heron. The Ministers that are obliged to attend the Emperor thither have Houses there, which though not very grand, are commodious. When a Person goes to *Laxembourg* to pay a Visit to the Court he is under a Necessity of returning to *Vienna* for a Bed, which is a very great Inconveniency.

The Emperor *Joseph* had begun a very fine House at *Schonborn* about a League from *Vienna*, but did not live to finish it; and the Empress *Amelia* to whom the Emperor gave it, instead of carrying on the Works which her Husband had begun, lets it run to ruin; which is great pity, for if that Building had been finish'd the Emperor wou'd not have had a *Versailles*, but he wou'd at least have had a Mansion-House suitable to his Dignity. 'Tis said that a new Palace is going to be built for the Emperor; which, if true, 'twere to be wish'd that better Architects may be employ'd in it than those who have had the Direction of the new Stables and of St. *Charles*'s Church, which are Buildings lately erected with very great Expence, but without any Taste. The Stables are a Range of Buildings of a vast Length, divided into seven Pavilions which appear at first sight to be so many different Houses. The middlemost Pavilion which is design'd to lodge the Master of the Horse is much higher than the other six, which sink gradually on the two sides. Nor are the inner Rooms better contriv'd; for the Horses stand all in one Row, and the Stable is so narrow withal, that one is every Minute in danger from the Horses Heels; which is purely owing to the Indiscretion of the Architect, who having ground enough and to spare might for the same Expence have made something grand and noble.

Whether the same Architect that built the Stables had the Direction likewise of St. *Charles*'s Church, is what I know not; but if they are two different Men their Head-pieces are very much alike. This Church would perhaps have been admir'd in the Days of the *Goths*, but in so refined an Age as the present, one cannot look on it without being sorry for the Sums of Money laid out in it.

This bad Taste as to Buildings prevails too much at *Vienna*, not but that there are Hotels and even
Pa-

Palaces in which the Rules of Architecture are observ'd, but then the Builders are got into such a way of ornamenting and charging their Houses with Sculpture as is altogether contrary to the noble Simplicity of the ancient Arcitecture. The Palace of Prince *Eugene* of *Savoy* is stately, but situate in a narrow Street with a very little Court before it. The Stair-case is very well contriv'd were it not too much confin'd. The Apartments of the first Story are as well laid out as the Ground wou'd admit of. We enter first into a spacious Salon adorn'd with great Pictures representing the chief Victories of Prince *Eugene* over the *French* and the *Turks*. In the two Rooms next to this are very rich Hangings wherein the Maker *Devos* at *Brussels* has very correctly delineated the whole Military Science. The Bed-chamber beyond that has a Set of Furniture of green Velvet richly embroider'd with Gold and Silk. In the same Room there is a Lustre of Rock Crystal which is said to have cost 40,000 Florins. All the other Furniture is extraordinary magnificent, and wou'd be cry'd up at *Paris* it self, where it must be allow'd a Taste for fine Furniture prevails more than any where.

The Palace of *Lichtenstein* is bigger than that of *Savoy*, and not less magnificent. 'Tis worth seeing were it only for its Paintings. I pass over the Hotels of *Schwartzenberg*, *Daun*, *Diedrichstein*, *Harrach*, and several other noble Edifices, lest my Letter shou'd swell into a Volume.

The Palaces of the Suburbs are infinitely more grand than those of the City, and they have both Court-yards and Gardens. The most noble are the Palaces of *Trautsheim*, *Rofrano*, *Schwartzenberg*, *Altheim*, and *Eugene* of *Savoy*. This last especially is a superb Structure with magnificent Gardens, a fine Orangery, and a Menagery stor'd with the most uncommon Creatures that the four Parts of
the

the World can furnish. 'Tis in this fine great House that Prince *Eugene* passes the beautiful Season of the Year. There is not so fine a Sight as an Assembly at this Prince's House, for not only the outer Court, in which there's a fine Piece of Water, but the Gardens are illuminated by an infinite Number of Lanthorns made in form of a Bowl of extraordinary white Glass, which cast a very great Light and make a glorious appearance. The Assemblies at this Prince's House are always very numerous; for his Birth, Employments and Interest, draw a great Court to him.

Prince *Eugene* is of a middling Stature, and well made. His Air is extremely serious, and his Deportment grave and reserv'd; but notwithstanding that Reservedness he is a hearty Friend to his Adherents. He is a thorough Judge of Merit, and loves to distinguish it. He is perfectly genteel and civil, very polite to the Ladies, respectful and submissive to his Lord and Master, but without Flattery or Servility. He is generous and noble in every thing excepting his Apparel. He is an Enemy to Ostentation, Ceremonies, and Constraint. In his youthful Days he lov'd Pleasures, but he abandon'd them as soon as he was animated with a Thirst for Glory. He was born in *France*, but left that Kingdom in 1683, out of disgust that he was no more taken notice of, and came to *Vienna* just before the *Turks* laid siege to it. He made the Campaign as a Volunteer, and distinguish'd himself in such a manner that the Emperor *Leopold* gave him in *December* following that Regiment of Dragoons which still goes by his Name. When the Siege of *Vienna* was rais'd, he serv'd in *Hungary* under Duke *Charles* of *Lorrain*, and *Maximilian Emanuel* Elector of *Bavaria*. The first time that he obtain'd the Command of the Imperial Army was in 1697, when he began with the Victory at *Zenta* whereby 22,000 *Turks* lost their Lives; a Loss which they could not recover,

cover, and which put them upon suing for the Peace that was granted to them at *Carlowitz* in 1699. The Prince afterwards commanded in *Italy*, *Germany*, *Flanders*, and lastly in *Hungary*; and wherever he went Conquest attended him. To give you a Detail of his Atchievements would be to anticipate the History which is to immortalize them, and to which you will not take it ill if I refer you. As to the Dignities and great Employments of this Prince, he is Chief Counsellor of the Council of Conferences; President of the Aulic Council of War; Commander in Chief or Lieutenant-General of the Armies of the Emperor and Empire; his Imperial Majesty's Vicar-General in *Italy*; Colonel of a Regiment of Dragoons; and Knight of the Golden Fleece. All his Employments may be worth about 300,000 Florins a year to him. Besides this, he has a considerable Estate in *Hungary* and in the Neighbourhood of *Vienna*, which brings him in about 100,000 Florins *per Ann.* more. He holds those Lands by the Emperor's Bounty who gave them to him as a Reward for his important Services.*

The

---

* This great General who was born the 8th of *October* 1663, O.S. died on the 10th of *April* 1736, O.S. so suddenly, that when his Gentleman went that Morning, as usual, into his Chamber to awake him, he was found dead in his Bed. He had been the day before very gay with Company whom he entertain'd at Dinner, and made not the least Complaint of any Ailment, tho' he had for some time before been so indispos'd that he did not venture abroad. 'Tis supposed that he was choak'd by an immoderate Defluxion of Rheum with which he was now and then troubled. His sudden Death cast the City and Court of *Vienna* into such a Consternation as did prodigious Honour to his immortal Memory. On the 15th, after having lain three days in State, he was interr'd in the Tomb of his Nephew *Emanuel* Prince of *Savoy* (which the Princess of *Savoy* Countess of *Soissons* caus'd to be erected in the Metropolitan Church of St. *Stephen*) with all the Military Honours, and all the Magnificence due to his illustrious Birth, and to those important

The Marshal Count *Guido Staremberg* is one of those Gentlemen also who deserve particular respect for their Virtue. He is descended of a Family which has given great Generals and wise Ministers to the Emperors of the *Austrian* Family, and has supported the Glory of his Ancestors in a signal manner; *Hungary, Italy,* and *Spain,* have been Witnesses of Bravery and consummate Wisdom in the Art of commanding Armies, and have admir'd him the more because they saw him always gaining Victories with Armies ill paid, destitute of all Necessaries, and very much inferior to his Enemies. This General enter'd very young into the Service in quality of an Ensign, and advanc'd himself by degrees. He was made Lieutenant-Colonel a little before the *Turks* Undertaking against *Vienna,* and while it was besieg'd, serv'd as Adjutant to his Cousin *Ernest-Rudiger* Count *de Staremberg,* the Defender of *Vienna.* This Count *Guido,* after having been a few years in the Service, was preferr'd to the Regiment of Foot of which he is still Colonel. When

portant Services which he perform'd to the August House of *Austria* during the Reigns of three successive Emperors. A Will was found among his Papers, whereby he declar'd the late Prince *Eugene* of *Savoy* his Nephew who died the year before at *Manheim* his universal Heir. But after that time a Codicil was made, tho' never sign'd by Prince *Eugene,* declaring for his Heir his Niece *Louisa de Soissons* of *Carignan* (who was born *December* 16, 1686.) then at a *Nunnery* in *France.* The Prince left behind him a numerous and curious Library of Books, many of which he bought when at *London* of *Christopher Bateman* in *Pater-noster Row,* besides a fine Cabinet of Medals and other Curiosities. The Emperor has bought his Library of his Niece for 20000 Florins.

Since the Prince's Death the Count *de Konigseg* Vice-President of the Council of War, has the chief Direction of Military Affairs at this Court, and signs all Dispatches and Commissions which that Prince sign'd as first President of the said Council, for thirty-three years. His Regiment of Dragoons is given to Prince *Charles* of *Lorrain,* but the Honours he held as General in Chief of the Emperor's Forces, and his Imperial Majesty's Vicar-General in *Italy,* are like to continue vacant by reason of the Peace.

When he was very young he was made Great Commander of the *Teutonic* Order. I do not mention his Exploits to you, because they are so much celebrated by Fame that you cannot but know them. This General, tho' very much advanc'd in years, retains all his juvenile Ardor, and wou'd still be very capable of commanding.

Having mention'd two of the Emperor's greatest Generals you will not be sorry, I fancy, if I shou'd give you some Account also of his chief Ministers. They are five in Number, and are call'd *Counsellors of the Conferences*. Prince *Eugene* of *Savoy* is the first Counsellor, but without the Title of Prime Minister, that being a Dignity not known at the Imperial Court.

The Count *Lewis de Zinzendorf*, Chancellor of the Court, and Knight of the *Golden Fleece*, is the second Counsellor of the Conference. He is a Nobleman descended of a Family which has been for a long time eminent in *Austria*. His Mother was a Princess of *Holstein*, who married to her second Husband the Marshal Count *de Rabutin* Governor of *Transylvania*, but died a few years ago in a very advanc'd Age. I had the honour to know her the last time I was here; her House being the Rendezvous of all People of Rank. Count *Zinzendorf* was in the Ministry in the Reign of *Leopold*. He was that Emperor's Minister Plenipotentiary in *France*, while the Marshal *de Villars* was at *Vienna* with the same Character from *Lewis* XIV. At the Death of the Emperor *Joseph*, the Count *de Zinzendorf* was that Prince's Ambassador to the States-General, in which Character he was confirmed by the Empress *Eleonora* who was Regent during the Absence of King *Charles*. He repaired from the *Hague* to *Frankfort* to assist at the Coronation of *Charles* VI. and officiated at the Ceremony as Vicar to the Great Treasurer of the Empire, a Dignity which is Hereditary in his Family.

At the Congress of *Utrecht* which was open'd not long after, the Count *de Zinzendorf* assisted as the Emperor's first Ambassador. He afterwards went to the unsuccessful Congress of *Soissons*, and from thence to *Versailles*, where he succeeded so well with the Cardinal *de Fleury*, that he kept him tight in those pacific Sentiments which the Enemies of his Tranquillity, if not of his Glory, aim'd to make him give up. The Count is now return'd hither, and almost the only Man that acts in the Province of foreign Affairs. His Interest is very great, for besides the Esteem which the Emperor has for his Person and Services, he is related to all the most distinguished Persons at Court, and strictly attached to the Interest of Prince *Eugene* of *Savoy*, of whose Integrity and disinterested Zeal for the Emperor he is very sensible. The Count *de Zinzendorf* is pretty tall and has a happy engaging Aspect. His Deportment is noble. He is pretty reserv'd, but civil. He is very polite to Strangers, and his House is open to them. He keeps the noblest and most elegant Table at *Vienna*. He is magnificent in every thing he does, and all his Actions favour of the Man of Quality. He is Father of a numerous Family. The second of his Sons is a Cardinal and Bishop in *Hungary*[*]. Another is Knight of *Malta*, and Lieutenant-Colonel. As these are the two with whom I am best acquainted, so they are the only ones I shall mention. I know not whether 'tis possible for a Man to be more sprightly than they both are. The Chevalier has more Mettle and Life than a *Gascon*: He is very blunt in his witty Sallies, but the variety of them pleases, and their novelty and justness are surprizing.

The Count *Gundacker de Staremberg*, President of the Chamber of Finances, and Knight of the

[*] He is now Bishop of *Breslaw*, a Dignity which gives him a distinguish'd Rank in this Duchy.

Golden Fleece, is the third Counsellor of the Conferences. His Integrity is very much cry'd up, and he has manag'd the Finances in such a manner as to guard against the Public Hatred.

The Count *de Schonborn*, Bishop of *Bamberg* and *Wurtzbourg*, Vice-Chancellor of the Empire, is the fourth Counsellor of the Conferences *. You know, Sir, that the *Schonborn* Family has given us several worthy Gentlemen; but I may venture to say, with all due Regard to the Memory of those great Men, and without flattering the Vice-Chancellor, that of all the Family he has the greatest Capacity for Business, the most generous Temper, and the most engaging and most civil Behaviour. As this Prelate has not his Equal at *Vienna* for Grandeur and Riches, so he has not his Fellow for Magnificence. The Emperor has a singular Esteem for him. The Vice-Chancellor has the Chancery of the Empire under him, and no body above him but the Emperor, and the Elector of *Mentz*, who is the Great Chancellor of the Empire.

The Count *de Konigseck*, Vice-President of the Aulic Council of War, is the fifth Counsellor of the Conferences. This Nobleman, whose Extraction is from a Family of Distinction in the Empire, is one of the tallest and handsomest Men at Court: He is the Emperor's Ambassador Extraordinary at the Court of *Spain*. His Family has for a long time past been attach'd to the House of *Austria*. He studied at *Besançon*, and was design'd for the Church; but he quitted the Band, took to Arms, and

---

* The Count *de Metsch*, Vice-President of the Aulic-Council of the Empire, succeeded him in the Office of the Vice-Chancellor; and the Count *Aloysius-Thomas Raimond* of *Harrach Rohram*, heretofore Viceroy of *Naples*, hereditary Master of the Horse of Upper and Lower *Austria*, Marshal of the States of the Country, Knight of the Golden Fleece, is appointed Counsellor of the Conferences in the room of the Count *de Schonborn*.

and enter'd into the Service of the Emperor *Leopold*; in which he had not been many Years before he had a Regiment of Foot, and the Emperor *Joseph* made him his Chamberlain. He also gave him the Government of *Mantua*, from whence he was recall'd by *Charles* VI. and sent to take possession of the *Netherlands* in the Name of the Emperor, to whom they were evacuated for that purpose by the Maritime Powers. The Count *de Konigseck*, during his Administration of the *Netherlands*, concluded the Barrier Treaty with the States General. At *Brussels* he married Madamoiselle *de Lanoi la Motterie*, a young Lady of a good Family, and distinguish'd Merit. When he left the *Netherlands* he went Ambassador from the Emperor to the Court of *France*, where he gain'd great Esteem, especially from the Duke of *Orleans*, the Regent; a Prince who was an excellent Judge of Merit, and very sparing of his Applause. After three Years stay at *Paris*, the Count return'd to *Vienna*. He attended the Archduchess, Wife to the Electoral Prince of *Saxony*, in quality of Steward, to *Dresden*; and at his return went to the Government of *Transilvania*. But the Emperor recall'd him from this Post and sent him his Ambassador Extraordinary to *Spain*; where the Count is as much esteem'd as he was at *Paris*. 'Tis said that he is in entire Favour with their Catholic Majesties; nevertheless he makes such earnest Application to be recall'd, that 'tis said he will obtain his Request, and that his Nephew *, who is the Emperor's Minister Plenipotentiary to the States-General, is already nominated to relieve him †.

* The Count *de Konigseck Erps*. He actually went to *Spain*, with a design to relieve his Uncle; but as the Face of Affairs is alter'd at this Court, they are both return'd. The Count *de Konigseck-Erps* is at *Brussels* Counsellor of State of *Brabant*.

† The Count *de Konigseck* is return'd home from his Embassy to *Spain*. He actually officiates as Vice-President of the Aulic

In the Council of Conferences the moſt important Affairs of the Empire are taken into Conſideration, and the Emperor is always preſent.

Beſides the five Miniſters whom I have now mention'd to you, there are ſeveral others whoſe Intereſt is more circumſcrib'd. Every Kingdom ſubject to the Emperor has its Miniſter and particular Chancery.

Count *Badiani* directs the Affairs of *Hungary*, in quality of its Vice-Chancellor.

The Affairs of *Bohemia* are in the Province of Count *Kinſki*, the Chancellor of that Kingdom, who has a Vice-Chancellor under him, with a great many Aſſeſſors and Counſellors.

The Council of *Spain* conſiſts of a Preſident, Vice-Preſident, and Counſellors. Its Authority extends over all the Kingdoms that were formerly ſubject to *Spain*, but yielded to the Emperor by the Peace. The Count *de Monte-Santo*, a Grandee of *Spain*, Brother to the Count *de Cinfuentes*, Conſtable of *Caſtile*, is Preſident of this Council ‖; in which Office he ſucceeded the Archbiſhop of *Valentia*, who quitted his See to follow the Emperor whom he had acknowledg'd for his Sovereign in *Spain*.

Of all the Tribunals at *Vienna* the *Aulic Council* is the moſt venerable; becauſe 'tis the Parliament of the Empire. It is compos'd of a Preſident, *viz.* the

---

Aulic Council of War, and as Privy-Counſellor of the Conferences. He is Lieutenant-General of the Emperor's Armies, Colonel of a Regiment of Foot; and is lately created a Knight of the Golden Fleece. The Count *de Mercy* being kill'd at the Battle of *Parma*, the 29th of *June*, 1734. the Emperor ſent the Count *de Konigſeck* to *Italy*, and gave him the Command of his Army, which was in a very ſhatter'd Condition, and which the Count *de Konigſeck* ſet to rights again, in ſuch a manner as to command Reſpect even from his Enemies.

‖ His Name and Title is *Joſeph de Silva y Meneſes*, Marqueſs *de Villaſor*, Count *de Monte-Santo*.

the Count *de Wurmbrandt*; a Vice-Prefident, who is the Count *de Metfch*; and of eighteen Counfellors, among whom there muſt be ſix Proteſtants, and of theſe one muſt be a *Calviniſt*. This Tribunal judges of all Civil Cauſes between the Princes and private Men of the Empire. Its Authority terminates with the Emperor's Life; and 'tis on this account only that the ſupreme Tribunal of *Wetzlar*, which ſubſiſts even during the Vacancy of the Imperial Throne, challenges Precedence of the Aulic Council. 'Tis a Miſtake to think, as many Foreigners do, that the Aulic Council takes Cognizance of Affairs of State; for its ſole Buſineſs is to do Juſtice: It regiſters no Edict unleſs it be its own Sentences *; and is much more limited than the Parliaments of *France*, which have at leaſt the Privilege of loſing Time in Remonſtrances.

I perceive too that I am in a fair way to make you loſe a great deal, if I don't put an end to my Legend; which therefore I now do, and refer the reſt of the Remarks that I have to entertain you with to another Poſt.

I kiſs your Hand, and am, &c.

* They are barely *Opinions*, and do not paſs into Decrees till they are approved by the Emperor.

LETTER XIII.

SIR,   *Vienna, Decem.* 10. 1729.

THERE are some other Articles which I cannot but add to those I have already given you from *Vienna*. The Police of this City is administer'd by a Stadtholder. The Person that now fills that Post is the Count *de Kebvenbuller*; who is also a Minist r of State, and Knight of the Golden Fleece. His Functions are the same with those of the Lieutenant of the Police at *Paris*, and nothing makes the Difference but the Title; only it must be observ'd that the Stadtholder is always a Person of noble Extraction, and a Gentleman of the Army, whereas the Lieutenant of the Police at *Paris* is often of mean Extraction, but always a Gentleman of the long Robe.

The Governour of *Vienna* had seldom any other Title than *Colonel of the City*. The present Governour is the Marshal Count *de Daun*, the same that defended *Turin*, who was six Years Viceroy of *Naples*, six Months Governour of the *Netherlands*, and afterwards four Years Governour of *Milan* [*]. His Lieutenant-Colonel, who is the Count *Maximilian de Staremberg*, Lieutenant-General of the Emperor's Forces, and Colonel of a Regiment of Foot, commands in his absence, and has the Direction

---

[*] When he return'd to *Vienna*, after the *French* and *Savoyards* had taken *Milan* in 1733, several Articles of Complaint were exhibited against him; but he made so full a Defence against the Impeachment, that the Emperor has the same Confidence in him as before.

rection of the Fortifications, the Arsenal, and the Garison. This Garison consists of a Regiment of Foot, compos'd of veteran Soldiers, or the Burghers and Artificers of *Vienna,* from whence this Regiment never stirs. The Employments in this Corps are very lucrative; but as they don't lie in the Road to the Temple of Honour, they are not much solicited by Persons of any considerable Extraction. Yet this Regiment, as little esteem'd as it is, perform'd very good Services during the Siege of *Vienna* by *Kara Mustapha,* Grand Vizier to *Mahomet* IV. It acted then under *Ernest-Rudiger* Count *de Staremberg,* who was Commandant in the City; and both the General and his Garison acquir'd very great Glory by the Resistance which they made. But perhaps with all their Bravery they cou'd not have prevented the Place from being taken, had it not been for the Avarice of the Grand Vizier, who hoped to be Master himself of the vast Treasures that he knew were in the City, and was therefore against storming the Town, for fear lest if it were carry'd by that means, the Soldiers would have shar'd the Plunder.

The Siege of *Vienna* being foreign to my purpose, I shall say nothing of it. You know that it was raised by the Assistance that was brought to it by the brave *John Sobieski* King of *Poland*; who defeated the *Turks* on the 12th of *September,* 1683, and return'd home laden with Glory and Booty, having made himself Master of all the Grand Vizier's Equipage. Upon this occasion he said a pleasant thing in a Letter which he wrote to the Queen his Wife, who had not a very implicit Faith in the Maxims of *Seneca* on the Contempt of Riches; ' You
' shan't say when I come home, as the *Tartary*
' Women do to their Husbands when they return
' from the Army without Booty, *You are not a Man*
' *for me, because you come empty-handed;* for the
' Guard

'Grand Vizier has made me sole Heir of all he had.'

You need not be told that this was the second time the *Turks* were forc'd to raise the Siege of *Vienna*; for *Soliman* the Sultan besieg'd it in the Reign of *Charles* V. but with no better Success than *Kara Mustapha*. 'Tis true that the Disappointment he met with was not so fatal in its Consequence to the Sultan as the other was to the Vizier of *Mahomet* IV. who was strangled at *Belgrade* when *Mahomet* was there: And the Head of this Minister is still to be seen in the Arsenal at *Vienna*. The Translation of this *Turkish* Relique hither from *Belgrade* was pretty extraordinary. Some Years after *Kara Mustapha* had been strangled, when the *Germans* took *Belgrade*, the Soldiers being inform'd where the Grand Vizier was buried, open'd his Tomb in hopes of Treasure, but found nothing except the Body in its Shirt, on which there were several *Arabic* Characters, and an Alcoran. The Governour being told of it, remember'd that this very Grand Vizier, when he laid Siege to *Raab*, which he was oblig'd to raise, said, That if he took the Town he wou'd have the Head of its Bishop cut off, who was then the Count *Leopold de Collonitz*, and send it to the Sultan, to be reveng'd of that Prelate for taking Money out of the Convents, and encouraging the Garison therewith to make a vigorous Resistance. The Governour of *Belgrade* remembring, I say, the Menaces of the Grand Vizier, thought it wou'd be a very agreeable Present to the Count *de Collonitz*, now a Cardinal [*], to send him the Vizier's Head and Body too, together with the Shirt and Alcoran; and he put up the whole very neatly in a Crystal Shrine, adorn'd with Silver Plates, and sent it accordingly to his Eminence; who not thinking this odd Present a proper Relique to be deposited in his Chapel, gave it to the Arsenal here at *Vienna*,

---

[*] He was Uncle to the Cardinal *Collonitz* ABp. of *Vienna*.

Vienna, where I have both seen the Muſſulman and felt him. I wou'd fain have pluck'd ſome of the Hairs of his Muſtachio, but the Guardian of the precious Treaſure watch'd my Fingers too narrowly. They ſay that a piece of the Halter by which a Man hangs himſelf is lucky, and why mayn't there be the ſame Virtue in the Muſtachio of the Grand Vizier? Be it ſo or not, 'twill always deſerve an honourable Station in ſome Cabinet of Rarities.

Since the Siege of *Vienna* this City is much inlarg'd. Its Fortifications are ſo augmented too that if the *Turks* ſhould ever be prompted by their ill Fate to beſiege it again, they wou'd find a ſtouter Reſiſtance, and a greater number of their Muſtachios ſindged than they imagine.

The Emperor has lately given new Luſtre to his Capital, by prevailing with Pope *Benedict* XIII. to erect it into an Archbiſhopric. Several Biſhops, particularly the Archbiſhop of *Paſſaw*, have diſmember'd their Dioceſes to aggrandiſe its Juriſdiction. The Cardinal *de Collonitz* is the Perſon who at preſent enjoys this Dignity, which gives him the Character and Rank of a Prince.

The *Roman* Catholic is the only Religion exerciſ'd in *Vienna*, and in all *Auſtria*; but the Miniſters of the Proteſtant Crown'd Heads have the Liberty here, as well as elſewhere, of keeping a Chapel. When the holy Sacrament or the Viaticum is carried to any ſick Perſon, 'tis always attended by Guards who oblige all People that meet it to kneel. I have ſeen the Emperor, when the Viaticum was paſſing by, alight out of his Coach and accompany it to Church. This Prince, and indeed all thoſe of his Family, always paid a very great Devotion to the holy Sacrament of the Altar. Of this *Philip* IV. King of *Spain* gave a very edifying Proof; for this Monarch going the very day that the King his Father died, from the Palace of *Madrid* to the Monaſtery of St. *Jeronimo del Paſſo* in a cloſe Coach, that he might

be

be *incog.* alighted out of it to accompany the Viaticum which they were carrying to a sick Man; whereupon the Conde Duke *d'Olivarez* told him, That the King his Father was so lately dead that he ought not to have been seen in public. *My Lord,* said the King, *this Custom cannot excuse me from paying that Worship to God which I owe him.*

It may be said of the august House of *Austria,* That as few Princes equal them in Piety, so there are few that equal them in Birth. There may be Families that have been longer grac'd with the Diadem; but of these there are very few that have such great Alliances. There is no King, and not many Sovereign Princes but what are related to them; and there are very few Kingdoms to which the House of *Austria* has not given Queens. 'Tis now 300 Years that it has been Mistress of the Empire; and since *Albert* II. it has given thirteen Emperors to *Europe* successively. One of the Princesses of *Austria* had so many great Relations that I cannot help mentioning her. This was the Empress *Mary,* Wife to the Emperor *Maximilian,* Son to *Ferdinand* I. This Princess was Sister to *Philip* II. King of *Spain,* and the Daughter, the Wife, the Daughter-in-law, and the Mother of five Emperors; the Grand-daughter, the Daughter, the Sister, and the Aunt of four Kings of *Spain*; and the Mother-in-law of two Kings, *viz. Charles* IX. King of *France,* and *Philip* II. King of *Spain.* A modern Author says, that the Origin and Kindred of this Princess infinitely surpassed those of *Agrippina,* who, according to the Report of *Tacitus,* was the Daughter of *Germanicus,* the Sister of *Caligula,* the Wife of *Claudius,* and the Mother of *Nero.* But when I consider how perfect a Master you are, both of History and Genealogy, I ought to beg your pardon for my Impertinence in troubling you with these Instances.

What remains for me now, is to communicate some Remarks to you which I have made upon the *Austrians* in general. I shall begin with the Women, whom I shall paint to you, as *Burrbus* says, with the Freedom of a Soldier, who is not the best Limner.

The Women here, as in all other Countries, are either handsome or ugly. In general they are rather handsome than pretty, for they are dull Beauties. They are all tall and well shap'd; they walk well, but when they curt'sy, do it in such an aukward manner, that one would think their Backs were in danger of breaking. In their Dress they affect Finery rather than a good Fancy. Two or three excepted, there's none that lay on the Red, much less the White, and Patches are very little worn; in a word, they have nothing about them that denotes Coquettry. As to their Humour, they are reckon'd frank, tho' not easily made familiar; they are naturally vain, and like all our *German* Women, pretty reserv'd, and not so fond of Gallantry as they are of Gaming, Luxury, and Magnificence. Such is their Indolence that they concern themselves no more about their Houshold Affairs than if they were Strangers. They know no Books but their Prayer-Books, are extremely credulous, and give into all the Externals of Religion: This makes their Conversattion sometimes insipid; and unless now and then a Love-Story falls in, Rain and Fair-Weather are their general Topics. They have at least as great a Conceit of *Vienna* as the *Parisians* have of *Paris*; for out of *Vienna* they think there's no Salvation. But all these little Defects are repair'd by an uncommon Greatness of Soul, and Generosity. They are hearty Friends, and warm Protectors of those whose Interests they espouse. When they are in love, their Passion is sincere; and instead of ruining their Lovers, there are some who have

made

made the Fortunes of those to whom they have taken a Fancy. Upon this Head I have been told, that in the Reign of the Emperor *Joseph*, when Gallantry was more in vogue than 'tis now, there was a Lady, who being in love with a Gentleman, and having a mind to make his Fortune without the Censure of the Public, thought fit in an Assembly where her Spark cut at Basset, to punt against him. She set a Bett, without telling a Soul how much she stak'd. Her Husband coming into the Room where they were at play, she rose up, took the Marks that were against her, threw them on the Ground, and said to the Banker, loud enough to be heard by her Husband, *I owe you*, Sir, 40000 *Florins*. The Husband in a very great Surprize ask'd what was the matter? *I have been such a Fool*, said she, pointing to the Banker, *as to lose* 40000 *Florins to* Monsieur N..... *You have reason to chide me; but however my Debt must be paid*. The Husband indeed grumbled very much, and said he wou'd not pay. *What!* reply'd the Wife, *won't you pay the Gentleman? It shall fare the worse with you if you don't, for I am resolv'd to pay him in some Coin or other*. The Husband perceiving his Wife so resolute, and that if he did not deposite the Money it wou'd subject him to the Loss of what was more precious, chose rather to part with the Cash; and indeed he had no reason to repent of it, for the Lady's Heart was so won by it, that she renounc'd the Sight of her Lover from that Moment, and made a very sober Wife.

This, Sir, is all I have to give you concerning the Temper of the Women. Let me tell you also how they spend their Time. They rise late. As soon almost as their Eyes are open, they call for Chocolate, and send to their Husbands to know who they have invited to Dinner, and whether there is room for any more Guests. If the Lady does

not

not like the Company, she sends notice to some Lady of her Acquaintance that she intends to dine with her; but if there be room at home, as a polite Husband always takes care to leave some at the Disposal of his Wife, she sends an Invitation to whom she pleases. After this she dresses and goes to Mass; for here the Ladies are all so devout that there's none but what hears at least one Mass in a day. There they read in five or six different Prayer-Books, kiss all the Pictures that are at the head of the Prayers, and very devoutly toss their Beads. After the Office is over, they commonly chat a quarter of an Hour in the Church. Then they go abroad and make some friendly Visits, or else go home to receive them. At these Visits, they hear all the News in *Vienna*. During this they have all a little Box of *Indian* Lack upon their Knees, in which they thread Gold till Dinner-time. When that's over, they drink Coffee or play at *Quinze* till Night, when they go to Court. From the Empress's Apartment they adjourn to the Assembly, where they divert themselves at *Piquet*, or at *Quadrille*; and then retire, undress themselves, go to Supper, and thence to Bed, well pleased to think with what Indolence and Idleness they have spent the Day.

The Women of the second Class, in which I include the Gentlewomen that have no Titles of Honour, *viz.* the Wives of the Assessors, Referendaries and Agents of the Court, discover such an Air of Plenty and Prosperity as is remarkably surprizing. Their Houses are richly furnished, and their Tables well served. If a Referendary has a mind to a nice bit, no body must offer to take it; and the best of every thing is what they are sure to lay hands on. Belly-Cheer is one of those things which the *Austrians* generally think of most: They require a great many Dishes, and those well-cramm'd.

They

They are so very much accustom'd to this Profusion of Eatables that I have known some young People in *Austria* affirm they don't know what good Eating is in *France*, because they don't serve up a couple of Loins of Veal in one Dish. Different sorts of Wines are what they are also very much us'd to, which certainly is very expensive because foreign Wines pay considerable Duties; yet nothing less will serve them than eight or ten sorts of Wine, and I have been at Houses where there have been no less than eighteen. They place a Note upon every Plate expressing the several sorts of Wine at the Beaufet.

The Burghers and common sort of People mimick the Nobility as far as their Purses will afford; and it may be said that no Nation in the World is so extravagant as this.

The *Austrians* are naturally proud and haughty, and expect all Mankind should stoop to them. As their Sovereign is in the first Rank among the Christian Princes, so they think theirs to be the chief Nation in the World. Nothing is more vain nor more insupportable than a young *Austrian*, whose Father is in any Rank at Court. They are intoxicated with Pride and Presumption; and as they know themselves to be rich, and their Fathers to be great Lords, they think they may despise all the World, and lay aside that courteous and polite Behaviour which would so well become their Birth. Yet what I here observe to you concerning the young People is not so universally true as not to admit of great Exceptions, which is the Case of every thing asserted in the general.

The Court is not without Ladies who are much to be valued. The Empress Regent honours with her Confidence Madame the Countess *de Fuchs*, whose Husband was Minister of State to the Emperor, and his Plenipotentiary at *Hambourg*, where he died. This Countess is Sister to the Count *de Molard*,

Molard, Steward of the Emperor's Kitchens. She is a very polite Lady, and is so far from being envy'd for being a Favourite that all Persons of Distinction agree she deserves it, because she supports it with Modesty, and makes no other Use of it but to do good.

Madamoiselle *de Klenck* has a very great share in the Favour of the Empress Dowager, which I take to be a Reward due to her long Services, and to her Merit. She is chief Maid of Honour to that Princess, and has been engag'd to her ever since she has been at *Vienna*. If the Character of a thorough Gentlewoman may be attributed to any of the Sex, Madamoiselle *de Klenck* deserves it more than any other, it being impossible for a Person to have more Integrity, and more Generosity.

The Countess Dowager of *Altheim*, of the *Pignatelli* Family, in regard to whose Rank I ought to have mention'd her first, if I observ'd a very strict Order in my Writings, is a Native of *Spain*. The Count *d'Altheim* married her at *Barcelona*. Her Beauty was the more admir'd in *Spain* because she was fair. This Lady has a noble Air, and has a Genius capable for Affairs of the greatest Consequence. Their Imperial Majesties pay her great Distinction, and all the Courtiers honour and respect her, so that now in her Widowhood she continues in good Credit, and almost as much Authority as she had when that great Favourite her Husband was living.

The Gentry of *Austria*, and of all the Emperor's Hereditary Dominions, are so fond of the Title of Count, that the Gentlemen buy and sollicit it as eagerly as if it was a great Estate. 'Tis well for them that the Dispatch of their Patents does not cost much; for the greatest Privilege which this brings them is all a Chimæra. These Counts may be said to hold the same Rank among the ancient Counts

of

of the Empire as the King's Secretaries in *France* do among the Gentlemen of good Families.

As for Gentlemen, they are so common here that there are scarce any others to be seen. All the Agents of the Court, and all the Referendaries procure themselves a Title, tho' I know not why; for neither they nor their Wives dare to rank themselves among the Prime Nobility. This Madness of theirs to be enobled is so common, and so easy to be gratified, that I have known a Man, who was formerly Messenger to the Emperor *Joseph*, purchase the Title of Baron; and his Children begin to mix with the *Grand Monde*.

These, Sir, were all the Remarks that I made upon the *Austrians*. I must give you a few Particulars concerning the Emperor's Person. I have already said something to you of his Character: What follows is to shew you how grateful he is, and how friendly, Virtues which are the more to be esteem'd in him because they are not the most familiar to great Men.

The Emperor shows all possible Marks of Gratitude to those *Spaniards* who adher'd to him while he was at *Barcelona*. He has loaded them with Wealth and Honours; and if it's possible for one's native Country to be forgot, he has put them in a Situation to forget theirs. This particular Goodness of the Emperor extends to all that followed his Fortunes in *Spain*; whom he distinguishes upon all Occasions, and does them good preferably to his other Subjects. As to Friendship, no Monarch ever had more for any Favourite than *Charles* had for the late Count *d'Altheim*, his Master of the Horse. This Nobleman was the Emperor's Page, when he was only Arch-Duke; and he attended that Prince to *Spain*, where his Care, his Services, his Assiduity, and above all his Honesty and his Integrity, won him the intire Confidence of the young

Mo-

Monarch. When this Prince became Emperor he rewarded the Count with Honours, Wealth, and Dignities. He lov'd him as long as he liv'd, and his Memory is still dear to him. As soon as he died, the Emperor declar'd himself Guardian to his Children, gave Orders in what manner they fhou'd be brought up, and now treats them much more like his own Children than his Subjects. But what wou'd you fay of the Emperor's tender Love for the Emprefs? Some time ago this Princefs being dangeroufly ill, the Emperor not only fent for his Phyficians, and conjur'd them to employ all their Art to fave her Life, but promis'd them Rewards fuitable to that Service, and actually watched with her feveral Nights to fee her take the Remedies they prefcrib'd. Does not a Conjugal-Love fo perfect, deferve to be rewarded by the Birth of an Archduke? Adieu, Sir. If I were Emperor, you fhou'd be my Count *d'Altheim*; but in the Condition I am in, you are the Perfon whom I honour moft of all Mankind; and am, &c.

LETTER XIV.

SIR,   *Munich, Jan.* 5, 1730.

AS I came hither from *Vienna*, I stay'd two Days at LINTZ, the Capital of *Upper Austria*. This City lies on the *Danube*, over which there is a wooden Bridge. 'Tis a little Town, but well built, and has fine Churches. Its Inhabitants are thriving, and they drive a great Trade in Linnen Cloth. 'Tis the Residence of a great many Persons of Quality, and of the Regency of the Province, of which the Count *de Thirheim* is the Chief. This Nobleman lodges in the Imperial Palace, which stands upon an Eminence, and commands the City. The Building is commodious enough, but not so magnificent. The Emperor *Leopold* stay'd here during the Siege of *Vienna*; till not thinking himself safe in it he retir'd to *Passaw*. The Neighbourhood of *Lintz* is very agreeable. All the way hither from *Vienna* the *Danube* is lin'd on both sides with Vineyards; but from *Lintz* to this Place, instead of Vines, there are Plantations of Hops.

MUNICH, in the *German* Tongue *Munchen*, stands in the middle of a large Plain, and in the Center of *Bavaria*, of which it is the Capital City. The Walls of it are washed by the River *Iser*; 'tis a small Town, but better built than fortified, for within these few Years several fine Houses have been rais'd rais'd in it. The Elector's Palace is one of the biggest Piles of Building in *Europe*, but it wants a great deal of being so handsome a Structure as *Misson* and several other Authors have represented it; for its Magnificence consists principally in its Bulk. The chief Front, which looks towards a very narrow Street, has the Resemblance of a fair Convent; to which the Image of the Virgin *Mary* over the great Gate contributes not a little. That for which 'tis held in most Esteem is the great Apartment which is call'd the *Emperor's* Apartment. The Connoisseurs in Painting admire the Pictures in the great Hall, which represent both Sacred and Prophane History, and are performed by the Hand of *Candi*. The Chimney-piece in the same Room is very much esteem'd: Among other fine Figures with which it is adorn'd, there's a Statue of Porphyry that represents *Virtue* holding a Spear in the Right Hand, and in the Left a gilt Palm-Branch. In 1632, when *Gustavus Adolphus* King of *Sweden* made himself Master of *Munich*, he thought this so beautiful a Room that he was sorry he could not get it transported to *Stockholm*. In the Reign of *Ferdinand Mary*, Grandfather to the present Elector, great part of the Palace of *Munich* was reduc'd to Ashes, which Accident was, 'tis said, the Occasion of that Prince's Death; for being at *Straubingen* when he received the sad News of the Fire, he took Horse immediately and rode with such Fury to *Munich* that he receiv'd a Fall which in a little time prov'd his Death.

The present Elector *Charles-Albert-Cajetan* has embellish'd the Palace with a new Apartment, which, tho' not so big as the Emperor's, exceeds it in Magnificence. 'Tis adorn'd with noble Pictures, antique Busts, and Vases plac'd upon * Tables of very great

---

* In the Beginning of the Year 1730, this Apartment was burnt down by a Fire which broke out in the Night-time; so that the Elector and Electress had like to have been burnt in their Beds, and scarce any of the fine Furniture was sav'd.

great Value; and among other Things there's the Picture of the Virgin done by St. *Luke*.

There's a secret Passage from the Palace thro' little Galleries to all the Churches and Convents in the Town. The nearest Church is that of the *Theatins*, which together with their Monastery was built by *Maria-Adelaide* of *Savoy* Wife to *Ferdinand-Mary*. The Fryars of this Convent must be twenty seven in number, and all Men of Quality. They subsist by charitable Donations; but dare not ask Alms, and must wait for such Provisions as Providence shall please to send them. When they have suffer'd extreme Want at any Time for three Days together, they are permitted to ring a Bell as a Token of their Distress; but it has been observ'd that this never happen'd above twice since their first Establishment, because the Electors are too charitable to let them want. The Tomb of the Princes of *Bavaria* is in the Church of these honest Fryars.

The Church of our Lady is the parochial Church of *Munich*. In it is the stately Tomb of the Emperor *Lewis* of *Bavaria* who died of Poison. 'Tis adorn'd with a great many fine Figures of Brass and Marble. In this Church the Elector on the 24th of *April* last instituted the Order of St. *George*, by Authority of Pope *Benedict* XIII. The Ceremony was perform'd with a vast deal of Pomp, and the Elector of *Cologn* officiated at the High Mass. The Promotion consisted of three Grand Priors, six Grand Crosses, a Commander, and six Knights. Some time after this first Promotion the Elector made a second, in which he appointed one Grand Cross, and nine Knights. 'Tis said there will speedily be a third Promotion of eight more Knights, the whole Number being to consist of forty *.

The

---

* The Order consists at present of a Grand Master who is the Elector, and two Grand Priors, who are the Electoral Prince and Duke *Ferdinand*, six Grand Crosses, nine Commanders, and several Knights.

The Elector intends to annex Commanderies to his Order. They who are admitted into it must give Proofs of their Extraction from sixteen Descents; and this is so strictly observ'd that his most Serene Electoral Highness, as Grand Master of the Order, has renounc'd all Power of granting any Dispensation from it. According to the Statutes of this Order all the Knights are oblig'd to be Catholics, to defend the Faith and the Church, to protect Widows and Orphans, and to practise all the Christian Virtues. The Badge of the Order is a large Sky-blue Ribbon border'd about the breadth of an Inch with a black and white Stripe; and at the end of the Ribbon hangs a Cross enamell'd with blue, in the middle of which there is a St. *George*.

The Church and Convent of the Reverend Fathers the Jesuits are two very magnificent Structures. The Roof of the Church which is one single Nave is a Work of Skill and Ingenuity, wherein the Apertures are contriv'd with very great Art; for which reason, the Curious look upon this Fabric as a Master-piece of Architecture.

The Church of the Reverend Fathers of St. *Austin*, tho' but of a moderate Size, contains Beauties that are not always to be met with in greater Fabrics. The Pictures with which it is adorn'd are highly esteem'd, and good Judges agree there are few that can parallel them.

Tho' the Houses of *Munich* are all very well built, there are few that can be call'd Hotels or Palaces. The Count *Piosas* a *Piedmontese* has caus'd one to be built of late Years which is a considerable Structure with regard to the true Proportions of its Outside, and to the ingenious Distribution of the Apartments, which have fine Decorations and good Furniture.

The Court of *Bavaria* observes most of the Customs of the Court of *Vienna* in matters of Ceremony,

mony, but as for the rest, their Way of living is different; here being more Freedom, and more Diversion.

The Elector *Charles-Albert* delights in Pleasures and bodily Exercise, and acquits himself therein with a Grace. He is a comely Personage, and has a grave, noble, and majestic Air, so that he is taken for a proud Man; yet few Princes are more gracious and more civil to Strangers, and to his Subjects also he is easy of Access. He was full of Life and Spirit when he was a Prince, and now that he is a Sovereign is become sedate and moderate. He is genteel, talks *French*, *Italian*, and *Latin* well, is Master of History, and perfectly acquainted with the Interest of Princes in general, and that of his own Family in particular. He sticks to Business, and above all seems to be very earnest in redressing his Finances which he found in great Disorder when he acceded to the Electorate. The Elector was born the 6th of *August*, 1697. He is Son of *Maximilian-Emanuel* famous for his Victories and for his Disgrace, and of *Theresa-Cunegunda-Sobieski*, Daughter of *John Sobieski* King of *Poland*. When *Charles* came into the World he had a Brother living who was born of the Arch-Duchess *Mary-Maximilian*, *Emanuel*'s first Wife. This young Prince who all *Europe* expected wou'd be the Successor of *Charles* II. King of *Spain*, dying at *Brussels* the 6th of *February*, 1699, *Charles* thereby became the Electoral Prince: He was bred up at *Munich* with four of his Brothers, but both he and his Brothers surrender'd Prisoners to the Emperor *Joseph* after the Battle of *Hochstet*, which subjected all *Bavaria* to his Imperial Majesty. That Monarch had the young Princes remov'd to *Gratz*, where he caus'd them to be treated in a manner not so suitable to their high Birth as to their decay'd Fortune. When *Joseph* died, his Successor *Charles* VI. used the Princes

ces with less Severity, caus'd them to be honourably attended, and sent them Masters to instruct them; and upon the Peace of *Rastadt* which reinstated the Elector *Maximilian-Emanuel* in his Dominions, the Princes his Children were restor'd to him. They finish'd their Studies at *Munich*, after which the Elector sent the four eldest to *Rome*, where the second, whose Name was Duke *Philip*, died not long after he had been chose Bishop of *Munster* and *Paderborn*. *Charles* returning from *Italy* went to *Vienna*, made the Campaign of *Belgrade*, and some Years after that, he marry'd *Mary-Amelia-Anne* of *Austria*, the late Emperor *Joseph*'s second Daughter. In 1725, *Charles* and his three Brothers were at *Fontainbleau*, at the Marriage of *Lewis* XV. and next Year he succeeded his Father who died at *Munich* lamented as he was ador'd by his Courtiers.

The Electoress who is a little Woman, very much resembles the Empress her Mother, and has more Vivacity than is common to the Princes of the House of *Austria*. She prefers Hunting to all other Pleasures, and there are few Days but she partakes of that Diversion with the Elector, who, as well as the Princes his Brothers, is fond of it.

The Elector has by his Marriage two * Princes and two Princesses. The eldest of the Sons who has the Title of the Electoral Prince is call'd *Maximilian-Joseph*, and was born the 28th of *March*, 1727. His most serene Electoral Highness's three Brothers are Duke *Ferdinand*, the Elector of *Cologn*, and the Bishop of *Freisingen* and *Ratisbon*. Of these Princes Duke *Ferdinand* is the only one who resides at *Munich*. His most serene Highness is a Lieutenant-General, and has a Regiment of Cuirassiers in the Emperor's Service. He is also a Knight of the *Golden Fleece*, and Grand Prior of the Order of St. *George*. He marry'd *Mary-Ann-Caroline* of

New-

---

* The second is dead.

Newbourg, by whom he has two Sons and one Daughter. I have already told you that he was educated with the Elector his Brother, with whom he made the Campaign of *Belgrade*, travell'd several times to *Italy*, and last of all to *France*, where those Princes were admir'd for their Splendor, their Politeness, their good Taste, and their fine Understanding. One shan't find a Man more affable than Duke *Ferdinand* who is even ador'd at *Munich*, and is dearly belov'd by the Elector his Brother. The Duchess his Wife who is the best-natur'd Princess in the World makes grand Entertainments, and is particularly civil to Strangers.

The Bishop of *Freisingen* and *Ratisbon* spends more of his Time at *Munich* than in his Diocese. He is a Prince of great Penetration, Spirit and Vivacity, is generous, liberal, and charitable, extremely civil, and 'tis impossible to be acquainted with him without adding Love to that Respect and Veneration which are due to his Birth and Character. He enter'd very young into Orders, and was consecrated Bishop by his Brother the Elector of *Cologn*. 'Twas thought at first that he wou'd have made but an indifferent Ecclesiastic, but he has demonstrated that he knows how to reconcile the Gravity of a Prelate with the Magnanimity of a Temporal Prince.

The Court of *Bavaria* is without dispute the most gallant, and the politest in *Germany*. We have a *French* Comedy here together with Balls and Gaming every Day, and a Concert of Music three Times a Week, at which all the Company is mask'd; and after the Concert there's Gaming and Dancing. These public Assemblies, at which the Elector and the whole Court are present, bring in a great Revenue to the Elector's *Valets de Chambre*; for besides the Money which every one pays at Entrance, they are also paid for the Cards, and are
con-

concern'd in almost all the Banks; so that those Domestics have almost all the Cash of the Nobility, with whom they don't scruple neither to rank themselves. Besides these noisy Pleasures we have others that are more tranquil, I mean those of civil Society. Of this kind there's more here than in the other Towns of *Germany*; but more still among the Foreigners that are in the Elector's Service than among the *Bavarians*; for these are generally proud, tho' 'tis certainly more owing to their Opinion that it gives them a good Air to be so than to their Temper; and they actually become more sociable when they are made sensible that their grand Airs are not astonishing.

The Title of Count is as common here as at *Vienna*, and the *Bavarian* Counts have no greater Privileges than those of *Austria*, for they are as much Subjects as the meanest Gentlemen. I find that those in Places, and who bear any Rank at Court are much more polite than others. The Counts *de Thirheim*, *Torring*, and *Preising* who have the chief Employments are so civil that I believe there's few Foreigners but will give them their Encomium.

The Elector has a very large Houshold, and a number of great Officers. I'll mention some of them to you.

The Count *Maximilian de Torring-Seefeldt* is Steward of the Elector's Houshold, a Minister of State, and Knight of the *Golden Fleece*. This Nobleman who is advanc'd in Years, is good-natur'd and civil, speaks little, is naturally grave, not fond of Pomp, and lives retir'd in the middle of a Court, but when he makes any Entertainment does it with Grandeur. He never once abandon'd the Elector *Maximilian Emanuel* his former Master, but follow'd him in his Fortunes both good and bad.

The Count *Sigifmond de Thirheim* is Great Chamberlain, a Minifter of State, and Grand Croix of the Order of St. *George*. He is very tall, and tho' his Air is not the moft affable, he is courteous and civil. He lives very nobly, and does the Honours of the Court very handfomely; confequently he is generally beloved and efteem'd. He was Governor of the Elector, who, contrary to moft Princes that are not apt to retain an Efteem for thofe who once had the Care of their Education, gives great Proofs of his Regard for the Count *de Thirheim*.

The Count *Maximilian de Fugger* is Grand Marfhal*. As he does not live at *Munich*, I have nothing particular to tell you of him.

The Count *Maximilian de Preyfing* Mafter of the Horfe, Prefident of the Chamber of Finances, a Minifter of State, and Grand Croix of the Order of St. *George*, is a very polite Nobleman, but ferious and grave to the laft degree. 'Tis difficult for any Man to be more attach'd to his Religion, to have more Candor, and to be more upright than this Minifter. His Probity has brought Envy upon him, but it has procur'd him the Elector's intire Confidence, of which however the Count makes no farther Advantage than is requifite for his Mafter's Bufinefs. He is accus'd of being clofe-fifted, and of diffuading the Elector from giving Gratuities; but 'tis agreed that he is very charitable to the Poor. 'Tis a hard matter for a Minifter who has the Direction of the Finances to pleafe every body, and he is commonly the Butt of public Cenfure.

The Count *de Rechberg* Great Huntfman †, Minifter of State, Prefident of the Council of War, Lieutenant General, and Grand Croix of the Order of St. *George*, is Commander in Chief of the Elector's

---

* The prefent Grand Marfhal is the Count *Gaudentz de Rechberg*, a Grand Croix of the Order of St. *George*.
† The Baron *de Freyfing* is at prefent Great Huntfman.

lector's Forces: He accompany'd the late Elector to *France* where he acquir'd the Reputation of an experienc'd skilful General.

Ignatius-Joseph Count *de Torring* is a Minister of State, Grand Master of the Artillery, and a Grand Croix of St. *George*. He follow'd the late Elector into *France*, and after that Prince was restor'd he went as Minister Plenipotentiary to the Imperial Court, where he negotiated the Marriage of the present Elector with the Archduchess, youngest Daughter to the late Emperor *Joseph*.

I cou'd tell you of many other Persons of Distinction at the Court of *Bavaria*, only I fear that being too particular wou'd tire your Patience. The Ministers who bear the greatest Sway are the Counts *Maximilian de Preysing* and *de Torring*, and M. *d'Unertel*. The first is Director of the Finances; the second has the Province of Foreign Affairs; and the third takes care of Affairs Domestic and Military. These three Ministers are the Arbiters of *Bavaria*, and to them the Tribunals of the several Provinces must apply.

Bavaria is divided into four Cantons or Provinces, *viz.* the Cantons of *Munich, Burghausen, Landstrut* and *Straubingen*. Each of these Provinces has a Regency or Parliament; and an Appeal lies from Sentences therein pass'd to the Elector's Council of State.

'Tis certain that *Bavaria* is one of the best States in the Empire. 'Tis said that it brings in seven Millions of Florins, and I have been assured by Persons who have Opportunities of being inform'd of the State of the Finances, that there was a time when the late Elector received eleven Millions *per Ann.* The Riches of *Bavaria* are owing to the Exportation of Salt and Corn, and to the Consumption of the Beer brew'd in the Country, which is as good as any in the World. *Tirol*, and the Country of *Saltzbourg*, have almoſt all the Corn which they ſpend from *Bavaria*, and the Elector has a Florin for every Sack that is exported. Another thing which is a Treaſure to *Bavaria* is the Fir-Trees, a Wood that ſerves for every Uſe that can be imagin'd, whether for Building, or for Houſhold-Stuff. There is not a Province in the Empire where Proviſions are cheaper, and in the mean time there's a vaſt Home-Conſumption; for beſides that the *Bavarians* love good Eating and Drinking, the Country is very populous; and 'tis computed that the Inhabitants of *Munich* alone are above 40,000.

Of all the Sovereigns in *Europe*, next to the King of *France*, the Elector of *Bavaria* has the fineſt Pleaſure-Houſes, for which he may thank the Elector his Father who had a wonderful good Fancy and Judgment.

NYMPHENBOURG a ſhort League from *Munich* is a charming Place. The Caſtle is to be ſeen a great way off by reaſon of its Situation in the middle of a great Plain, ſo that from the Apartments of the ſecond Story one diſcovers a vaſt Tract of Country, and an infinite number of Rural Beauties that are in the Neighbourhood of *Munich*. *Mary-Adelaide de Savoy* (Mother to *Maximilian-Emanuel*) who was extremely fond of the Arts and Sciences, and knew them perfectly well, was the Perſon who laid the Foundations of that Caſtle. The Man that ſhe employ'd to build it was an *Italian* Architect whom ſhe ſent for out of *Italy* for the purpoſe. But all this Palace conſiſted only of one great Pavilion. *Maximilian-Emanuel* thinking the Caſtle too ſmall, cauſed ſeveral Manſions to be added to it, together with fine Stables and grand Gardens; in ſhort, he put the whole into that magnificent Condition we ſee it in at this day. His moſt ſerene Electoral Highneſs lets the Pavilion ſtand in pure reſpect to the Memory of his Mother who built it, but 'tis pity he does; for 'tis much higher than the rest of the Edifice, and is no good Ornament to the main Building. In order to give you a more perfect Idea of this House, I will tell you that it looks towards a great and magnificent Canal terminated at each end by a spacious Basin adorn'd with Waterworks and double Rows of Trees on each side which form the Avenues. We enter into the Castle by an Ascent of Marble Steps: The first Room we come to is a very great high Salon adorn'd with Architecture of Plaister of *Paris* very well executed. From each side of this Salon there is a Passage into several Apartments of which I shall not stop to give you the Detail, because I don't think it in my power to convey a suitable Idea to you of the Richness of the Furniture, and all the fine things that are in it. Imagine only that the late Elector who had an exquisite Taste, and a noble Soul, spar'd no Cost to adorn these Apartments. I pass to the Gardens which one enters from the Great Hall by a Descent of Marble Steps. The first thing that strikes the Eye is a Parterre of a vast Extent, at the Entrance of which there is a great Bason ornamented with a Group of Figures of mill'd Lead gilt with Water-Gold representing *Flora* receiving Flowers from *Nymphs* and *Cupids*. At the end of the Parterre there is one of the most agreeable Woods in the World, which is cut by three Walks in form of a Goose's Foot. The middlemost fronts the great Pavilion of the Castle, and has a large Canal in the middle of it of which one can't see the end: 'Tis terminated by a fine Cascade form'd by several Blocks of Marble, and adorn'd with fine Statues. The second Walk on the right hand leads one to the Mall which forms a Semi-Circle, and is one of the finest and longest I ever saw. At the Entrance of this Mall there is a Pavilion call'd *Pagodebourg* (the *Castle of the Pagode*;) 'tis two Stories high,

high, and built in form of the *Pagodes* Temples. I believe there never was any thing prettier. All the Furniture of this little Palace is *Indian*, of a charming Contrivance and Elegancy; and the whole is so well laid out that notwithstanding the smallness of the House, the Elector has every Convenience in it that can be desir'd. Over-against *Pagodebourg* on the other side of the Canal in the third Walk is *Badenbourg* (the *Castle of Baths*) which is a more considerable Building, and has all the Beauty of the Modern Bagnios. The Baths are spacious and lin'd with Marble. There is an Apartment consisting of several Pieces adorned with Stucco, and Pictures representing *Venus* in the Bath, *Diana* in the Water with her Nymphs, and the other Subjects of the Fable. The whole Apartment glitters with Gold, and the Furniture of it is rich, and of a charming Fancy. This beautiful House is surrounded with fine Pieces of Water adorned with Cascades and Statues. These Baths wou'd most certainly deserve a particular Description, and I am angry with myself for not being able to give it.

'Tis certain that next to the Gardens of *Versailles*, there is none so magnificent as those of *Nymphenbourg*; which is a Place that Art and Nature seem to have joined their Forces in order to render noble and agreeable.

The Castle of *Schleisheim* is a more regular Building than that of *Nymphenbourg*, and makes so grand an Appearance that I don't know any House in Germany that can compare with it. The great Stair-Case and the Salon in the large Apartment are the only Pieces in their kind. They are fac'd with Marble, and painted in a most correct and beautiful manner.

Taco, *Furstenriet* and *Starenberg* are Houses fit for the Solacement of a Great Prince, and will be-

Testimonies to Posterity of the Elector *Maximilian-Emanuel*'s grand and happy Taste.

Of all the Elector's Houses *Nymphenbourg* is that where the Court resides most. It is as well a Hunting-House as a Pleasure-House, by reason of a Park in the Neighbourhood which is eight Leagues in compass, and cut out into a great number of fine long Roads. Here the Elector comes to rouze the Stag; and there is a little Park adjoining to the Gardens, which, as well as the adjacent Fields, abounds with Pheasants, Partridges, and all other Game of that sort.

When the Court is at *Nymphenbourg* the Electress has a Drawing-Room there three times a Week where there is Gaming, and when that is over the Ladies sup with their Electoral Highnesses, who sometimes admit Gentlemen of their Court to their Table, but commonly all Foreigners. They who prefer taking the Air to Gaming, find open Calashes every Evening drawn by two Horses, at the bottom of the Steps on the side of the Garden: A Gentleman drives the Calash, two Ladies ride in it, and a Gentleman stands behind. And such as prefer the Water find very neat Gondolas finely gilt upon the Canal at their Service; so that there is no want of any thing to add to the Pleasures of all sorts in this inchanting Place.

Were I to enumerate to you all the various Pleasures of this Court I should never have done. For the present I shall confine myself to these already mentioned. I am resolved to set out in three or four days for *Stutgard*. I shall lie at *Augsbourg*, and at *Ulm*. A Frost which has held for a Month without ceasing has made the Roads so hard that I hope I shall roll along finely. I expect to hear from you at *Stutgard*. Pray take care that I be not disappointed, and believe that I am very sincerely, &c.

LETTER XV.

SIR, *Stutgard, Jan.* 14, 1730.

THERE is nothing remarkable between *Munich* and *Augsbourg* except it be the fine Abbey of FURSTENFELDT, which is in possession of the *Bernardin* Fryars. It was founded by *Lewis the Severe* Duke of *Bavaria* to attone for his Wickedness in putting *Joan* of *Brabant* his Wife unjustly to death. The History of *Bavaria* relates the Fact thus: *Joan* was a very beautiful Princess. Her Husband who was doatingly fond of her being obliged to take a Journey, put her under the Guard of one of his Aunts. While he was gone *Joan* wrote frequently to her Husband, and sometimes to his Prime Minister and Favourite. One day she put her Letters into the hands of a Domestic, charging him to deliver them as they were directed; but the Man made a Mistake, and gave the Letter which was for the Duke to his Favourite, and that which was for the Minister to the Duke. *Lewis* thought that his Wife's Style was too obliging to a Subject, and was even mad with Jealousy. He first kill'd his Favourite, and then taking horse posted to *Donawert* where his Wife was. He came to the Castle in the Night-time, murder'd the Porter with his own hand, put his Aunt and all with whom he had left his Wife in charge to Death; and then like another *Herod*, caused the unfortunate *Joan* to be beheaded. The Night after this barbarous Action, the Heirs of *Lewis*'s

Lewis's Head turn'd gray, tho' he was but twenty-eight Years old; which Accident made him sensible of his Guilt and of the Innocence of his Wife. As his Barbarity was great, so was his Repentance. He went on foot to *Rome* to beg the Pope's Absolution for his Sins, and obtain'd it on condition that he wou'd cause a Church to be built, and found a Monastery in his Dominions. *Lewis* returning from *Rome* founded the Abbey at *Furstenfeldt*. The first Establishment was only for eight Fryars; but the Piety of the Princes of *Bavaria* having wrought upon them to bestow their Favours upon this House, it now maintains thirty Fryars and an Abbot, whom the Monks have the Prerogative to chuse out of their own Body. These good Fathers are actually erecting a very stately Church, and they enjoy all the Conveniencies of Life.

The Country between *Munich* and *Augsbourg* is level and intermix'd with Woods and Plains. AUGSBOURG which is a Bishop's See, and an Imperial City, is the Capital of *Swabia*, and one of the biggest and handsomest Towns in *Germany*. A small Branch of the *Leck* passes thro' it, and supplies it with plenty of Water. The Streets of *Augsbourg* are broad, strait and lightsome; the Houses well built, and many of 'em full of Paintings. The Inhabitants look upon *Augustus* to be the Founder of their City. 'Tis true that Emperor sent a Colony thither, but the Town was founded before. It is not said what Name it went by before the Name of *Augusta Vindelicorum* was given it to distinguish it from the other Towns that bore the Name of *Augusta*. The clearing up of this difficulty is what I shall leave to the Antiquarians, and confine my self to the Transactions at *Augsbourg* for about two hundred Years past. What will render this City for ever famous is the Confession of Faith which the Protestant Princes presented here to the Emperor *Charles* V.

in the year 1530. Tho' the Protestants were at that time very powerful in *Augsbourg* they cou'd not keep their ground, for they were drove out by the *Bavarians*; but *Gustavus Adolphus* restored them in 1632, since which time they have kept their Footing there, and share the Government with the Roman Catholics. In 1687, the Emperor, *Spain*, the United Provinces, and the Electors of *Saxony*, *Brandenbourg*, and the Palatinate concluded that famous League at *Augsbourg* against *Lewis* XIV. who was beginning to inforce the Claim of the Duchess of *Orleans* his Sister-in-law to the Succession of the Elector Palatine *Charles-Lewis*, who was that Princess's Brother. In 1690, *Joseph* Archduke of *Austria* King of *Hungary*, the eldest Son of the Emperor *Leopold*, was consecrated and crown'd King of the *Romans* at *Augsbourg*, at which Ceremony the Emperor, the Empress, the Electors of *Mentz*, *Cologn*, *Triers*, *Bavaria*, and the Palatinate were personally present.

In 1703, the Elector *Maximilian of Bavaria*, made himself Master of *Augsbourg* in one Week's time. This City had demanded and obtained a Neutrality, but having afterwards received an Imperial Garrison the Elector made use of that Pretence to lay Siege to it. He caused the Fortifications to be demolish'd, foreseeing, no doubt, that he should not be able to keep the Place. *Augsbourg* was set free again by the Battle of *Hochstet*, and still enjoys its Freedom under its own Magistrates, the Bishop having no Authority in the City as to Temporals. The present Bishop is of the Family of *Neubourg*, and Brother to the Elector Palatine. This Prince has the same Goodness of Temper which is so natural to all his Family. As his Bishoprick is not one of the most considerable in *Germany*, so his Court is none of the biggest, but

his

his Houshold is well regulated, and every thing conducted in it with Order and Splendor.

The Chapter of the Cathedral consists of Persons of Quality who are oblig'd to make Proof of their Nobility. The Canons have the Prerogative of chusing their Bishop, who like all the Prelates of *Germany* is a Sovereign Prince. He dwells at *Augsbourg*, tho' he ought to reside at *Dillingen*. The Episcopal Palace is old, and not very commodious: It joins to the Cathedral, which is a *Gothic* gloomy unwieldy Fabric, but its Ornaments are very rich.

The most considerable Building is the Town-house, a very substantial Pile built all of Freestone except the Portico, which is of Marble. The Rooms are very fine, and the great Hall especially is to the last degree magnificent. The Walls are cover'd with Painting, being such Emblems and Devices as have relation to the Government. Nothing can be more beautiful than the Cieling which consists all of Compartments whose Frames are carv'd and gilt in an extraordinary manner, the whole enrich'd with Pictures and other Ornaments perfectly well dispos'd.

Before the Town-house there's a very stately Fountain, where, among other fine Figures of Brass, the Statue of *Augustus* which is represented in a most noble Attitude is highly esteem'd.

The City of *Augsbourg* is in my Opinion something like *Antwerp* with regard to the Spaciousness of the Streets and the Substantialness of its Buildings; and formerly when the *Venetians* were Masters of all the Commerce, it resembled it in Trade; for *Augsbourg* was then the Staple for Merchandize, which was from thence transported to a great part of *Europe*. But since *London* and *Amsterdam* are become the Warehouses of the whole World, and the Commerce of *Venice* decays, the greatest Trade of *Augsbourg* consists in Goldsmith's Wares, with which this City furnishes *Germany*, *Poland*, and in general almost

almost all the North. These Wares are much cheaper here than elsewhere, and when the Patterns are furnish'd People are well serv'd. Notwithstanding the Decay of its Commerce there are several very rich Families; but whether any can do what *Fugger* did to the Emperor *Charles* V. is a Question. That Monarch passing thro' *Augsbourg* lodg'd at *Fugger*'s House, who entertain'd him like an Emperor. The Fewel he burnt in every Chimney was Cedar, and after the Repast, which was extraordinary sumptuous, *Fugger* took a Bond for a very considerable Sum which the Emperor ow'd him, and threw it into the Fire.

The Nobility assemble commonly every Evening at the *Three Kings* Inn where I quarter. There's a very fine Hall well lighted, where they game, club for a Supper, and after Supper dance. Be not scandaliz'd that the Nobility have their Assembly at an Inn, it being one of the best Houses in *Germany* and the most superb Inn in *Europe*. There's very good Attendance. I have supp'd at it twice, and one cannot be better accommodated in any House whatsoever.

From *Augsbourg* I came to ULM another Imperial City. Tho' all the Country is even, yet 'tis very tiresome to Travellers because of the Pavement of the Causeys; but Thanks to the Snow which has levell'd the Ways, I have not been much incommoded; tho' on the other hand I had like to have been lost in the Snow, such a quantity of it having fallen for two Days that one could not distinguish the Roads. I found my self at a Post-Stage where my Guide, tho' he was a Man that had grown grey in the Business of Postilion upon the same Road, did not know the Way. I was in danger every Moment of tumbling into some Ditch, when just as we enter'd a certain Valley my Postilion sounded a Horn to give notice to any

Carriages or Horses that might happen to meet us to make way, when a Voice from the Hollow call'd out to the Postilion, *Who's that? Stephen? Oh!* cry'd the Postilion, *Is it you, Christopher? God be thank'd that I met with you!* Then turning towards me, he said with an Air of Satisfaction, *Now you are out of all Danger, for here's a blind Man that will conduct us to the Place we are going to.* I thought the Droll jok'd with me, but we had not gone many Yards farther before I really saw a poor Wretch who could not see, yet offer'd to be my Guide, and promis'd he wou'd conduct me very well. I abandon'd my self to him, and he walk'd so fast before my Chaise that the Horses follow'd him in a gentle Trot till we came safe to the Stage. There he told me that 'twas fifteen Years ago that he lost his Sight by the breaking of an Imposthume in his Eyes, after having suffer'd such horrible Pains for two Months that he bless'd himself for the Loss of his Sight; so that when I ask'd him if he was not very much concern'd at it, he said that at first it made him melancholy for some time, but that he always comforted himself by the Remembrance of the Torture he had undergone in the Loss of his Sight, and that he thought it were much better to be blind and to have his Health than to see, and suffer the Pains that he had endur'd; but that now he was so us'd to his Condition it gave him no Concern. Indeed, when I ask'd him, if he should not be very glad to recover his Sight? he said, Yes, if it were possible; but that if he must undergo the same Pains to recover it as he had felt in the Loss of it, he had rather by a thousand times continue blind. When I told him of my Surprize that he should find out the Way better than those who see, he told me that since he had been blind he came regularly on Sundays and Saints Days to the Place where we were to hear Mass, and that therefore the Road was become very familiar to him. He added, that he sometimes went alone to beg three or four Leagues from his Village, which was a quarter of a League from the hollow Way where I met with him. I sent the Man away, after giving him some Relief; and could not but admire the divine Providence, which tho' it had afflicted the poor Wretch with what to me seems more terrible than Death, gave him Strength to bear his Misfortune with Patience.

The City of *Ulm* is not above half as big as *Augsbourg*, but is much better fortify'd. The *Danube* which washes its Walls, becomes navigable at this Place, and a Boat goes from hence every Week for *Vienna*, which is a great Ease to People who are not in a Condition to lay out much Money; for it costs but a *Creutzer*, which is one Penny a *German* Mile. Tho' the City of *Ulm* maintains a very numerous Garison, and is very well fortify'd, and furnished with a good Arsenal, the Elector *Maximilian* of *Bavaria* took it by Surprize in 1702, it being a Place necessary for him to secure his Dominions on that side, and to facilitate the Passage of the *French* Troops that were to join his Army. General *Thungen* robb'd him of this Conquest the 10th of *Sept.* 1704, after about a Week's Siege.

Then it was that *Ulm* became again subject to its Magistrates who are all *Lutherans*. The Catholics cannot enjoy Offices, but have several Churches. This City drives a great Trade in Linnen, but few of the Gentry live here except the Patricians who are not more sociable than those of *Nuremberg* and *Augsbourg*. The Burghers and the Women in particular go dress'd like those at *Augsbourg*. To see them go to and come from Church is next kin to seeing a Masquerade, and 'tis certainly one of the most diverting Sights in this City, where really I did not give my self time to be tired, for I set out again

again the very next Day after I came, and arrived in this Town, where I have now rested my self a couple of Days.

STUTGARD lies in the middle of a Valley surrounded with Vineyards. 'Tis pretty large, has Streets broad and strait, but the Houses are of Timber. 'Tis the Capital of the Duchy of *Wirtemberg*, and was formerly the Residence of the Sovereigns of the Country; but *Eberhard-Lewis* the present Duke of *Wirtemberg* established his Seat some Years ago at * *Ludwigsbourg*, a new City and a new Palace of his own building.

The Duke's Castle is an old Structure of Freestone, compos'd of four Piles of Building, flank'd at each Angle by a Tower. The Walls of it are wash'd by Ditches which give it the disagreeable Air of a Prison. The Duchess who is the Duke's Wife, and Sister to the Margrave of *Baden-Dourlach*, has an Apartment in this Palace. You know that this Princess and her Husband don't live well together. The Prince † about twenty Years ago preferr'd a Mistress to her ‖, who certainly has neither the Beauty, nor the Merit of the Duchess. The Princess is remarkably patient under the Indifference of a Husband, and the Contempt of the most haughty Rival that ever was. The frequent Visits paid her by her only Son are all the Comfort she has. The Court neglects her, no body dares

---

* He died *An.* 1733, and leaving no Children, his Son and Grandson dying before him, was succeeded by *Charles-Alexander*, the eldest of his Cousin-Germans, the Son of Duke *Frederic-Charles*, who had been his Guardian till the Year 1693. The Duke *Eberhard-Lewis* was 57 Years of Age.

† The Duke was reconcil'd to her two Years before she died; and tho' she was no less than fifty Years of Age, it was reported for a good while that she was with Child.

‖ This was the Countess *de Gravenitz*. Since the Duke's Death the Duke Regent has commenc'd a Prosecution against her, and she traverses from one Court to another for that Protection which every one denies her.

to go near her, and whoever pays the Duchess the Respects that are naturally due to her, is sure to incur the merciless Hatred of the Mistress. I may be able perhaps to give you a farther Account of this Princess and her Rival when I have been at *Ludwigsbourg*, whither I propose to go to-morrow, and where I hope for a Line from you.

I am, &c.

LETTER XVI.

SIR, *Ludwigsbourg, Feb.* 2. 1730.

THE Duke of *Wirtemberg* is a Prince of a middling Size, and before he grew so fat was very well shap'd. He is genteel, affable, and well-belov'd, and few Princes treat their Courtiers with more Familiarity. He has been one of the best Dancers of his Time. He also sits perfectly well on horseback, and performs all bodily Exercises with infinite Gracefulness, and incomparable Dexterity. He takes pleasure sometimes in driving his own Coaches, and I have seen him drive eight Horses without a Postilion, and manage them with as much Ease as if there was but one Horse in the Harness. He is a Prince that loves Magnificence, is generous, gallant, and amorous. Tho' 'tis above twenty Years that he has kept one and the same Mistress, he is as passionately fond of her, and gives as shining Proofs of it as ever. During the last War his most Serene Highness commanded the Army of the Empire on the *Upper Rhine*. He has an only Son marry'd to *Henrietta* of *Prussia*, Daughter of the Margrave *Philip*, Brother to *Frederic* I. King of *Prussia*. This young Prince is called the hereditary Prince. He is short of Stature, but handsome. He has one of the best Tempers that can be desir'd in a Sovereign, being humane, good-natur'd, affable, and civil. It may be said that the Father and the Son are the two politest Men at the Court of *Wirtemberg*. The Father has spent several Years in *Holland*, *Lorrain*, *Geneva*, *Turin*, *Italy* and *France*. When he return'd from his Travels he went and marry'd at *Berlin*. He has an only Daughter who is very amiable. The hereditary Prince is vastly fond of Grandeur, Dancing, Plays and Music: He fatigues himself very much, and commonly rides seven or eight Horses in a Morning. His tender Constitution and the little Care he takes of it make me apprehensive he will not live to be an old Man*.

The hereditary Princess has an Air of Grandeur and Majesty suitable to her Rank. She is tall and handsome, has a noble Mien, and tho' she is not a regular Beauty, 'tis certain that she has a very good Look. She is extremely grave, and does not seem to take a great share in the Pleasures of the Court. She seems to be most of all taken with Dress, and her Apparel is not only splendid but well-fancy'd. Her Royal Highness, which is a Title given her because she is the Daughter of a King's Brother, is extremely gracious and civil to all Mankind, but particularly to those whom she knew at the Court of *Prussia*. She does me the honour to discourse with me sometimes. I find she thinks very justly, and that her Sentiments are very agreeable to her Birth. This Princess is of the *Calvinist* Religion, and she keeps a Chaplain who preaches to her in her own Apartment; so that now while the Prince

Alexan-

* He died at *Ludwigsbourg* the 23d of *Nov.* 1731.

Alexander de Wirtemberg is here, there are three Chapels in the Castles of as many different Religions.

The Countess *de Wurben* is the first Lady at Court next to her Royal Highness. She has been the Duke's sole Favourite for a long time. She is *Gravenitz* by Name, and is descended of a noble Family in *Mecklembourg*. The Duke first fell in love with her when she was but a Girl. She had the Assurance after she had been some Years in Favour to insist that the Duke should get a Divorce from the Duchess his Wife, by whom he had a Son, and marry her. When the Duchess was inform'd of her Rival's Demand she sued for the Emperor's Protection, and obtain'd it. That Monarch signified to the Duke that he would do well to remove his Favourite, who was therefore oblig'd to retire to *Swisserland*. The Duke who could not bear her out of his sight, followed her thither and stay'd there with her for some time, but at last being oblig'd to return to his Dominions, and not being able to take Madamoiselle *de Gravenitz* to him without reviving the just Suspicions of the Duchess, he look'd out for a Husband for his Mistress. The Count *de Wurben* a Gentleman of a good Family, and in mean Circumstances, but a very eager Stickler for the Favours of Fortune at any rate whatsoever, made an offer to marry Madamoiselle *de Gravenitz*. She was bestowed upon him with a Pension of 24000 Florins, and the Character of the Duke's Envoy Extraordinary to the Imperial Court. He engag'd never to make use of the Husband's Prerogative and never to require of his Wife to leave the Court. Upon this Condition he obtain'd even before he set out for *Vienna* the Office of *Landthoffmeister* or Lord Lieutenant of *Wirtemberg*, which is the highest Dignity in the Country. When the Marriage was concluded, Madam *de Wurben* returned to *Stutgard*, where she
had

had Lodgings in the Palace. All her Aim was to insult the Duchess, in hopes of provoking her to commit something so outragious as might embroil her with the Duke, and make him resolve never to forgive her; but this Princess equally virtuous and prudent, and always patient, bore all this Mortification without murmuring. The Mistress, who could not endure to see her in the Palace, obtain'd an Order from the Duke for her Retirement to the Estate which was settled on her for her Jointure; but the Duchess would never comply to it, saying, that if she had not been unfortunate enough in the Loss of her Husband she would not retire to her Jointure. This Refusal, how reasonable soever it was, affronted the Duke, who acquainted the Duchess that he did not look upon her any longer as his Wife, and gave orders that she should be treated no longer as a Sovereign. During this, Madam *de Wurben* became a Widow; whereupon all the Hopes reviv'd that she had presumed to entertain when a Maid. She persuaded the Duke to leave *Stutgard*, and to found *Ludwigsbourg*. As soon as this House was in a Condition to be occupy'd, the Duke and his Mistress came and liv'd in it. There's no sort of Intrigue which this Favourite has not try'd to put herself in the Duchess's Rank, but hitherto she has not been able to succeed. Mean while she enjoys all the Honours of a Sovereign. 'Tis at her Apartments that the Court is kept. Whenever the Duke plays 'tis there, and there it is he diets. In short she is treated in every thing upon a par with her Royal Highness. Her Excellency (which is the only Title given to this imperious Favourite since the Death of her Husband) is drawing on to fifty Years of Age, and yet carries a mighty Sway. She employs all the Remedies imaginable to cancel the Injuries which Time has done to her Complexion, and also to conceal her natural Temper; for Artifice

and

and Dissimulation are the Compounds of her Character. She is so eager in amassing of Riches that she makes it her chief Business. While she pretends a mighty Respect for the Duke, she expects like another *Astarte* that every Knee should bend and tremble before her. As she is the Reservoir of Favour, greater Court is made to her than to the Duke himself, and Woe be to those that dare to disoblige her! I must own however that she knows how to behave as well as any Woman in *Germany*, when she has a mind to shew her Politeness. The worst on't is, that she is not always so inclin'd; for she has been so long us'd to give herself great Airs that they are become habitual to her. The principal Offices of the Court are distributed among her Kindred or Creatures. Her Brother the Count *de Gravenitz* is Grand Marshal and Prime Minister. I hardly ever saw a handsomer Man: I must also do him the justice to declare that he is as civil as his Sister is haughty. Some Years ago the Duke obtain'd for him the Dignity of a Count of the Empire, in which Quality he was admitted also at the Dyet, and he has a Seat there on the Bench of the Counts of *Swabia*. His Authority is never oppos'd but by his Sister, to whom he will not always be obedient. 'Tis said their Divisions have sometimes gone so far that the Favourite has done all in her power to turn out her Brother, and he has try'd all Ways in his turn to remove his Sister, but the Duke has always been so good as to reconcile them. The Prime Minister and his eldest Son are honour'd with the Order of *Prussia*. There is no Court in *Europe* where there's such a Variety of Orders and Ribbons. The Duke bears alternatively the *Danish* Order of the *Elephant*, the *Prussian* Order of the *Black Eagle*, and his own Order which is that of St. *Hubert*.

The

The Hereditary Prince has the Order of *Prussia* and that of the Duke his Father.

The Prince *Charles-Alexander* wears the *Fleece*, and the Order of *Wirtemberg* *. Prince *Lewis* his Brother wears the *Polish* Order of the *White Eagle*.

The Baron *de Schunck* heretofore the Duke's Minister of State, and at present Great Bailiff of a Bailywic, is Knight of the Order of *Dannebrog*.

I should never have done were I to give you the Names of all the Knights of the Order of St. *Hubert*, and the many petty Sovereigns that have been the Grand Masters.

The Duke's particular or Cabinet-Council is compos'd of the Hereditary Prince and the Counts *de Gravenitz*, Father and Son, the Baron *de Schutz*, and M. *de Pollnitz* †. There are many other Counsellors of State, but not being admitted to the Cabinet-Council they are not in so much Esteem as the others.

His most Serene Highness keeps the Estimate of his Forces to himself. I think that he has now 4000 Men without reckoning his Life-Guards, which are two Companies, the finest of all the Guards in *Germany*. One of these Companies is commanded by the Lieutenant-General Baron *de Phul*, and the other by a Count of *Witgenstein*. They are dress'd in yellow, and are only distinguish'd by the Facing of their Clothes and their Bandeliers,

one

---

* He was Velt-Marshal of the Emperor's Forces, and Governor of *Servia* and *Belgrade*. He is one of the famous Generals of our Age, on whom Prince *Eugene* set a great Value. When he came to the Succession he obtain'd of the Diet of the Empire the Post of Velt-Marshal General jointly with the Duke of *Brunswic-Bevern* and the Prince of *Anhalt*. He married *Mary-Augusta* of *Tour Taxis*, by whom he has Children. He has two Brothers in the Emperor's Service, viz. Prince *Frederic*, and Prince *Lewis*, who distinguish'd themselves in the last War upon the *Rhine*.

† M. *de Pollnitz* left the Court in 1732, and is since retir'd to his Lands in *Saxony*.

one of which is Black and the other Red. Their Regimental Clothes are Yellow with Silver Lace. The Duke has also a Company of Cadets on Horseback, all Gentlemen. They are dress'd in Red, with black Velvet Facings and Silver Lace. They mount Guard at the Duke's Apartment only. Two of them always stand Centry before his Highness's Chamber-Door.

The Court of *Wirtemberg* is one of the most numerous in *Germany*.

There's a Grand Marshal, who as I have told you is the Count *de Gravenitz*, Brother to the Favourite.

A Marshal of the Court, who is second Son to the Grand Marshal.

A Travelling Marshal, who is Brother-in-law to the Prime Minister.

A Great Cup-bearer, who is the Baron *de Frankenberg*.

A Master of the Horse.

A Great Huntsman.

Four Chamberlains.

A Number of Gentlemen of the Bed-Chamber, and Gentlemen of the Court.

Two Captains of the Guards.

A considerable number of Counsellors of State and Aulic Counsellors.

Twenty Pages, all Men of good Families.

And finally a great many Footmen, and Officers of the Kitchen, Pantry, and Buttery.

The Duke's Stables are the best furnish'd of any in *Europe*. One shall not see finer Horses, or any that are better manag'd. The Hunting Equipage is also very magnificent; and I don't know one thing that is wanting. His Highness keeps a Company of *French* Comedians to whose Performance every body is admitted *gratis*. We have often Balls, Masquerades, and Concerts of Music. There is is an Assembly at the Favourite's House every day, where the Company plays at Piquet, Quadrille, and Pharo; so that here are all the Pleasures of a great Court. The Duke's Table is serv'd with very great Cost and Delicacy, and is commonly spread for sixteen Guests. The Duke sits at the upper end, between her Royal Highness and her Excellency. The Gentlemen are plac'd according to the Rank which they derive from their Employments, and the Ladies according to the Offices which are borne by their Husbands.

There's a Ceremonial observ'd here which is not known in any other Court, *viz.* the Duke's Ministers give place to no Foreigner, unless he be a Minister like themselves to some Prince, or unless he be a Count of the Empire. These have so distinguish'd a Rank at this Court that all who are not Counts must give place to them. A Count of the Empire, tho' he be a Cadet in the hundredth Generation, a Lieutenant or an Ensign, as it sometimes happens, in the Duke's Service, takes place of all Ministers and great Officers who are not Counts. This is a Regulation which her Excellency made after her Brother was created a Count, to the end that her Family might have the more Honour, and that the greater Respect might be paid to her own Dignity of Countess without a County.

I have told you that the Duke had transferr'd his Residence from *Stutgard* to *Ludwigsbourg*, and the reason which made him abandon the Capital of his Dominions; but why he preferr'd the Situation of his new Town to a hundred others that he might have chose more agreeable, is what I cannot account for.

LUDWIGSBOURG is remote from any River, great Roads and Forests. The Duke at first only built a small Mansion-House with two advanced Wings, so disposed that the Court lay between the House and the Garden; but he has since made great Additions

ditions to it, and is actually building a large Manſion between the Court and the Garden, to which the Wings of the former Building are to be joined. One *Friſoni*, an *Italian*, has the direction of theſe Works; in which it appears that he is a much better Maſon than an Architect. The new Building runs ſo far out that it diſcovers all the Effects of it. The Front of the Manſion conſiſts of three Stories, including the Ground-Floor; but on the Garden ſide there are only two of a moderate Height, ſo that one wou'd take this Building rather for an Orangerie than for the Palace of a Sovereign. The great Stair-Caſe is dark, the Apartments want Light, the Chambers are long and narrow, and have very few Out-lets. However, this ſingle Building was undertaken by *Friſoni* for 700000 Florins, excluſive of ſeveral ſorts of Materials with which he was furniſhed.

The old Manſion, which fronts the new, is not near ſo large, tho' it is three Stories high every way. The Apartments are ſmall and too inconvenient to live in, yet no Coſt has been ſpar'd to adorn them; Carving, Gilding, and Painting being employ'd in them with more Profuſion than Judgment. The Furniture is rich, but of a very odd Fancy. The beſt thing in all the Palace is the Chapel, which would every where be reckon'd a fine noble Structure. But notwithſtanding all the Faults which are obſerv'd in the Palace, it muſt be allow'd that whoever lives to ſee it finiſh'd will find it a magnificent Piece of Work. In the Gardens there are ſeveral Terraſſes, which riſing by degrees one above another, intirely bound the Proſpect of the Palace. 'Tis certain that when the Duke's Architects ſaw this Prince reſolutely determin'd to build at *Ludwigsbourg*, they ought at leaſt to have adviſ'd him to place his Palace at the very ſpot where his Gardens end: In this caſe it would have ſtood in the middle of a Plain, the Apartments would not have been cramp'd by the

But-

Buttresses, with which the Palace is encompass'd, and the Gardens wou'd have had a gentle Descent; and for a very little Expence there might have been a fine Piece of Water at one end, betwixt them and a Coppice, which is a Walk for Pheasants.

The City of *Ludwigsbourg* is as irregular as the Palace; and its Scituation, which is very disadvantageous, will always render it a very incommodious Town, because of the unevenness of the Ground. Most of the Houses are of Timber, and slightly built; for those who build them do it with an Ill-will, either out of Necessity, or to please the Duke who seems to be fond of building. This Prince has ruin'd *Stutgard*, and will never make a good Town of *Ludwigsbourg*; for if the Court was absent from it but one Year, 'twou'd be one of the meanest Villages in *Wirtemberg*. This Town is in no respect very agreeable. The Nobility here don't seem very fond of Strangers, and there are no Entertainments but what are made by the Duke. No body here, not even the Prime Minister keeps a Table; and all the Expence of the Courtiers is in their Dress, and their Horses. Yet there is not a Prince of the Empire who gives handsomer Salaries, except the Electors; so that the Case is the very reverse here to what it is at almost all other Courts, for here People grow rich, whereas elsewhere they are beggar'd. I have known Persons that came to this Court in mean Circumstances, and in a few Years got Estates. The Duke is by nature generous and beneficent, and wou'd be more so if his Liberality was not curb'd. He has given several Gentlemen Materials for building *gratis*; and the Houses were no sooner up but he purchas'd them, and paid as dear for 'em as if he had not contributed a Shilling towards raising them. I have been assur'd that his most Serene Highness's Revenues amounted to four Millions of Florins. 'Tis certain that he is

Master of one of the finest Countries in all *Germany*; a Country which has plenty of every thing, but Money is scarce by reason of the Fertility of the neighbouring Provinces, *viz.* the *Palatinate*, *Bavaria*, *Franconia*, and *Alsace*. The People are desirous of a War upon the Upper *Rhine*, in hopes of putting off their Commodities.

The *Lutheran* is the only Religion tolerated in the Duchy of *Wirtemberg*, tho' the Duke has permitted *Frisoni* the Director of his Buildings to erect a Chapel for the Use of the Catholic Workmen whom he has sent for from *Italy* to build the Palace; which Chapel however is design'd to be demolish'd as soon as the Works are finish'd: But I am rather inclin'd to think that the Court itself will one day have a Catholic Chapel; for if the hereditary Prince shou'd happen to die without Male-Issue, *Wirtemberg* will fall to the Share of Prince *Alexander*, (Cousin-german to the Duke) who has embraced our Religion; and who having Children by the Princess of *Tour* and *Taxis* whom he marry'd at *Brussels*, sees them brought up in the Catholic Faith.
I kiss your hand, and am, &c.

POSTSCRIPT.

Since I wrote the above, the Countess *de Wurben* is fallen under Disgrace, which I have been told happen'd by this means.

The Duke's Carriage to his Mistress had been cold for some time, when the King of *Prussia* came to *Ludwigsbourg* and exhorted him to be reconcil'd to his Wife, in order to get Heirs. The Duke cou'd not persuade himself to take the Duchess again; but however the King's Representations prevail'd so far, as to put him quite out of conceit with his Mistress. He just kept up a bare Acquaintance with her, and that was all; which she
per-

perceiv'd, and made no scruple to try the most extraordinary Methods to maintain herself in Favour. The Duke having been blooded in her Presence, she secreted a Napkin stain'd with his Blood. What Use she propos'd to make of it I know not, but she carry'd it to her Apartment. The Duke's *Valets de Chambre* missing the Napkin acquainted their Master of it. M. *de Roder*, a Gentleman of the Bed-Chamber, and a Favourite of his Highness, said that no body cou'd possibly take it but the Countess, and that to be sure she did it for no good. The Duke order'd M. *de Roder* to go to the Countess's Apartment and enquire into the Fact. *Roder* ask'd for the Napkin. The Countess deny'd her having it; but *Roder* affirm'd he saw her take it, upon which she was in a Passion with him, and told him she wou'd make him repent of his Ill-manners to her. *Roder* made answer, that all the Airs she gave herself were out of season, that her Reign was over, and that he wou'd oblige her to return the Napkin. The Countess not us'd to be talk'd to at such a rate, was frighten'd, and restor'd the fatal Napkin, which completed her Ruin. The Duke, when inform'd by his Favourite of what had pass'd, sent an Order to the Countess not to stir from her Apartment: And this Prince setting out soon after for *Berlin*, charg'd the hereditary Prince his Son to command Madamoiselle *de Wurben* to retire to her Estate. The Countess obey'd, and being indulg'd to carry what she had a mind to along with her, retir'd to a Territory of hers depending immediately on the Empire, not many Leagues from *Ludwigsbourg*. There it was that she heard of the Duke's Reconciliation with the Duchess, upon the Duke's return from *Berlin*. This News extremely shock'd her, because she always flatter'd herself that the Prince wou'd return to her: And perceiving now that she had no Hopes of being restor'd to Favour by the power of her own Charms, she had a mind to try what she cou'd do by I know not what Charm in the Magic Art. To carry her Point she was under a necessity of having a little of the Duke's Blood; and she wrote to his *Valet de Chambre*, promising him great Rewards if he cou'd procure her some. What does the Domestic but carry the Letter to the Duke? who immediately gave Orders to Colonel *Streitborst* to arrest the Countess, and carry her to some Place of Security. The Colonel taking a Detachment of Soldiers along with him, contriv'd it so that he came to the Countess's Seat at Night, and immediately surrounding the House, knock'd at the Gate, but no body making answer he thunder'd so hard at the Gate, that at length Madame *de Sultman* the Countess's Sister put her Head out at the Window, and ask'd who it was that dar'd to make such a Noise. *Streitborst* told her his Name, and said he came thither by Order of the Duke. Madame *de Sultman* made answer that the Countess was not well, and cou'd not be spoke with. The Colonel, who knew the contrary, said, that if they did not let him in he wou'd break open the Doors; upon which they thought fit to open them. During this the Countess was got to Bed; and *Streitborst* entring her Chamber found her there with her Sister and her two Brothers-in-law, the General *N. .* and *Sultman*, who was formerly at *Berlin* Equerry to the Countess of *Wartenberg*, and afterwards Privy-Counsellor to the Duke of *Wirtemberg*. The Colonel having signify'd his Order to the Countess, she affected to be in a dying Condition; but said that if she was able enough to get up she did not intend it, she being at home, and in a free House of the Circle of *Swabia*, from whence she did not think the Duke had Authority to remove her. The Colonel threaten'd that his Grenadiers shou'd pull her out of Bed; and the Lady seeing that she must obey,

thought

thought fit to rise. She fell on her Knees to *Streitborst*; but the hard-hearted Officer was deaf to her Cries, and conducted her to a place of Security where she is closely confin'd, and like to be a Prisoner as long as the Duke lives.

LETTER XVII.

SIR,   *Carlsroube, Feb.* 15, 1730.

I Deny that any Man can be happier than I am at this Juncture. You have wrote an excellent long Letter to me; you assure me that you are well, and that you have still an Affection for me; what more is there wanting to compleat my Joy? I am preparing to make you the best amends I can, and instead of a Letter to write you a Volume.

I came in one Day from *Ludwigsbourg* to CARLSROUHE, which is the Residence of the Margrave of *Baden-Dourlach*. The Name *Carlsroube* signifies *Charles*'s Rest. The present Margrave *Charles* of *Baden-Dourlach* was the very Man that laid both the Plan and Foundation of this City, and its Castle. Nothing is so pretty as the Disposition of the whole: I wish I were able to give you an Idea of it. Imagine the Margrave's House to be at the Entrance of a great Forest, in the Center of a Star form'd by thirty two Walks, the chief of which behind the Palace is three *German* Leagues in length. Two large Wings advance from the main

Body of the House, which deviating from each other in proportion as they lengthen, the whole together looks like a Theatre. Behind the principal Building there's a very high Octogon Tower which commands all the Walks. The Space between the two Wings forms the Court, and then come the Gardens and Parterres, at the end of which there's a Semi-Circle of Houses of an equal Height, built Arch-wise, and three Stories high including the Ground-Floor. Between these Houses there run five Streets, the middlemost of which fronts the Palace. At the end of the three chief Streets opposite to the Palace are three Churches; one belonging to the *Lutherans*, another to the *Calvinists*, and a third to the *Roman* Catholics; to which three prevailing Religions of the Empire the Margrave gave equal Liberty of Conscience when he founded the new Town.

The chief part of the Town lies behind the Houses that front the Palace. This properly speaking consists but of one Street, which is of a prodigious Length. All these Houses as well as the Margrave's are of Timber, so that you are not to look for fine or substantial Buildings at *Carlsroube*; but the Contrivance and Distribution of the whole taken together is really wonderful. I took the Freedom to tell the Margrave that I was surpriz'd that he had not at least employ'd Brick in the building of his Palace, and of the Houses which form the Half-Moon about his Gardens. ' I was
' wil'ing, *said the Prince*, to make myself a Place
' of Retirement, and to build without putting the
' Burthen on my Subjects. I chose moreover to
' have the Comfort of enjoying what I built. If I
' had us'd Bricks it wou'd have cost me a great deal
' more Money; and I cou'd not have finish'd my
' Buildings without laying an extraordinary Impost
' upon my Country. It wou'd have taken me up
' abun-

' abundance of Time too, and perhaps I shou'd never have had the Satisfaction of seeing an end to my Labours. Another Reason was, that my Country is so scituate as to be liable to be the Theatre of Wars, and I am not in a Condition to make this a strong Place, nor cou'd I encompass it with Walls. Do you think therefore that I shou'd have been justified in laying out a great deal of Money on a Place to see it burnt down before my Face, as I did my House at *Durlach*, and my other Houses which the *French* reduc'd to Ashes. I am but a petty Sovereign; I have built a House according to my Condition, and I had rather it shou'd be said of me that I have but a mean Habitation, and owe no Money, than that I have a stately Palace and am over Head and Ears in Debt.'

I have given you this account of what the Margrave said to me, because I thought it wou'd let you into an Idea of his Character. This Prince, to whom I was introduc'd on the very day of my Arrival here, took the trouble himself to shew me his Palace, and all about it. I thought the Apartments very well laid out, but there is not room enough to lodge the hereditary Prince, who lives in one of the Houses in the Semi-Circle fronting the Palace.

The Pheasant-Walk, which joins to the Castle, is the prettiest thing in the World. 'Tis a very large Inclosure, dispos'd in various Walks planted with Fir-Trees cut in the shape of a Fan. There's a great Basin in the Center always full of wild Ducks. 'Tis encompass'd with four Pavilions, made in the Form of *Turkish* Tents. Two of the Pavilions are Volarys, and the two others Summer-Houses, with Window-Curtains of Green Cloth. There are Sofas and Couches, after the manner of the Eastern Countries. In this Place of Retirement and Rest the Margrave spends some Hours every Day, and he is generally accompany'd by some young Ladies whom he teaches Music; so that they perform agreeable Concerts.

The Margrave was in the right to give his House the Name of *Charles's Rest*, for he leads the most tranquil Life here that can be. Far from being infatuated with vain Grandeur, he has the Charms of it, without the Check and Constraint of it. This Prince is of a very robust Constitution, and tho' he underwent a vast deal of Fatigue in his Youth, he is as fresh-colour'd and as vigorous as if he was but forty Years of Age. He travell'd when he was a young Man into the principal parts of *Europe*; and during his Father's Life-time was several Years in the Service of *Sweden*. When he return'd to his Dominions he serv'd in the Army of the Empire on the Upper *Rhine*, under his Cousin Prince *Lewis* of *Baden*. Tho' the Margrave is very fat, yet he uses a great deal of Exercise. He rises in Summer at five o'Clock in the Morning, and walks in his Gardens till the Heat of the Weather obliges him to retire within doors; then he does Business with his Counsellors, or else employs himself in Experiments of Chymistry, and sometimes he draws. He commonly dines at four o'clock, and is attended by Waiting-Women, of whom there are no less than threescore, tho' no more than eight wait upon one Day. These, when the Margrave goes abroad, attend him on horseback, dress'd like *Hussurs*. The Generality of these Damsels understand Music and Dancing; they also perform Operas at the Theatre of the Palace, and are Musicians of the Chappel. They have all Lodgings in the Palace. After Dinner is over the Margrave grants Audience to his Subjects; and upon particular Days of the Week hears all that come. Few Princes render Justice more speedily, and more punctually. Sometimes he goes a Hunting.

ing. He makes very light Suppers, and retires early to Bed. He delights in Agriculture, and is one of the greatest Florists living. This Prince is never unemploy'd. There are few things which he does not know, and very many which he understands to Perfection. His Conversation is as agreeable as any I know. He speaks several Languages well. His Behaviour is obliging and courteous. He loves Foreigners, treats them with Distinction, and loads them with Civilities. Upon Sundays and Holidays he eats with the Prince his Son, and the Princess his Daughter-in-law. His Table, which is then spread for sixteen Guests, is serv'd with more Delicacy than Profusion.

The hereditary Prince *, only Son to the Margrave, is pretty short, and has not the Life and Spirit of his Father. He is very complaisant and civil, and seems to me of a good-natur'd Disposition. He has been at *Paris*, in *England*, and in *Holland*, where he marry'd the Daughter of the unfortunate Prince of *Nassau*, who was drown'd in 1711, as he was passing the *Maerdyke* to the *Hague*, to adjust with *Frederic* I. King of *Prussia*, such Differences as related to the Succession of the late King *William* of *Great Britain*, to which they both laid Claim. The hereditary Princess seems to me to be well behav'd; and she makes very handsome Entertainments. The Court assembles at her House every day, *viz.* at Noon, and at five o'clock in the Evening; and there they dine, game, and sup. Foreigners are very well receiv'd there, and both the Ladies and Gentlemen are very civil and complaisant.

The Grand Marshal, and his Brother the Great Huntsman, are Persons capable of making a Figure with Distinction in the greatest Courts. The

* This Prince died the Beginning of the Year 1732, and left one Son.

The first marry'd a legitimated Daughter of the Margrave.

The Baron *d'Ixter*, President of the Regency, and Chief of the Council, is a Person of signal Merit, and capable of any Business, be it ever so great.

Generally speaking the Margrave's Court is extremely well regulated. This Prince is fond of the Nobility, and seeks to do them a Pleasure. He has none but Persons of Quality in his Service. 'Tis great pity that this Court does not come together again. The Margravine, who is Sister to the Duke of *Wirtemberg*, resides at *Dourlach*, and never comes to *Carlsroube* but when 'tis a Holiday, or when some foreign Prince is there. This Princess is actually very much indispos'd, so that I don't think I shall have the Honour of kissing her Hand. The Margrave also educates at his Court three young Princes his Nephews, the Sons of his Brother. They are under the Government of the Baron *de Gemming*, who takes very great Care of their Education.

As to the Margrave's Revenues, I cannot be positive what they are, because I found that People who ought to know best, vary in their Calculations not a little; some assur'd me they were 400,000, some 500,000 Florins, and others much more. Be it as it will, 'tis certain that the Margrave lives nobly, that every body is well paid, and that the Subjects are not over-burthen'd. Farewell, Sir, I set out to-morrow for *Rastadt*, and shall write to you as soon as I can, *&c.*

LETTER XVIII.

SIR, *Strasbourg, Feb. 28, 1730.*

IT took me up no more than four Hours to go from *Carlsroube* to RASTADT. As soon as I alighted there I notified my Arrival to the Grand Marshal, with a Request that he wou'd procure me the Honour of paying my Compliments to their Highnesses of *Baden-Baden*. I had for answer, that the Margrave was out a Hunting, and that therefore I cou'd not have an Audience before next day. I had patience to stay; and having by Good-luck some Books at hand, I spent all that day in Reading, and the next day too, but did not hear a Word from the Grand Marshal. Mean time as I did not come to *Rastadt* purely to read, and as 'tis a Town does not afford much Amusement, since a quarter of an hour is enough to know all the Streets, I was very chagrin. I sent a second Message to the Grand Marshal, but had the same Answer as before. I thought it improper to insist any farther, and gave over all hopes of seeing the Court of *Rastadt*. However I went to see the Margrave's Palace, which his Father the late Prince *Lewis* of *Baden* built from the ground. It is very much like to the Palace of *St. Cloud* near *Paris*, and seems to be a Building conducted with more Regularity than I observ'd in several new Houses in *Germany* left solely to the Direction of ignorant Masons, who without a Taste for Building have the Assurance to call themselves Architects.

The

The principal Stair-Case is large and lightsome. The Apartments have all the Conveniencies they can admit of. Those which are contiguous to the grand Stair-Case are distributed into several Partitions, for Shew and for Convenience. They are painted, gilt, and gaily furnish'd. The Margravine Dowager to Prince *Lewis* put them in this Condition against the Marriage of her Daughter to the Duke of *Orleans*; and the Furniture is indeed rich and well fancy'd. The Keeper shewed me the Closet in which Prince *Eugene* of *Savoy* and Marshal *Villars* sign'd the Peace in 1714. 'Tis pity that this truly magnificent Palace has no Gardens to it. There's Ground mark'd out for that purpose, and if Prince *Lewis* had liv'd they wou'd have been finish'd

After having seen the Apartments and the Chapel, which is small, but exceedingly adorn'd, not knowing what to do with myself I went to a Billiard-Table fronting the Palace, where I found some Gentlemen of the Court as idle as myself. They treated me as a Foreigner, and were complaisant to me. A young Fellow of a good Appearance, and who seem'd to have an Air of Politeness, having refus'd as well as myself to play, enter'd into a Conversation with me: And by degrees that Sympathy of our Tempers, which was a Stranger to the Laws of Reason, made us talk to one another with as much Freedom as if we had been old Acquaintance. I complain'd to him that tho' I had been three days at *Rastadt* I cou'd not get an Opportunity of paying my Duty to their Highnesses of *Baden*. He told me that I need not be surpriz'd at it; that since the Death of the late Prince *Lewis*, the Margravine his Dowager, who was hereditary Princess of *Saxe-Lawenbourg*, had introduc'd into her Court the Ceremonial of the Eastern Princes; that she never appear'd but in a full Divan, and

and that she did not permit any one whatsoever to come near to her Son except the Bashaws and Dervizes who were of the Council. The young Gentleman's manner of accounting for this matter made me smile, and put me upon asking him several Questions. 'How! *said I*, according to
' the Character I have had of the Margravine, she is
' very much of a Christian, and of that virtuous
' Heroine which the wise Man, if he had been still
' living, wou'd have propos'd to us for a Model.
' Indeed, *said the Gentleman*, the Character you
' have had of her is right enough: The Margravine
' has Piety and Virtues that render her valuable;
' but she has a Haughtiness, and a certain *Particu-*
' *larity* in her Temper, which is hardly to be pa-
' rallell'd. For instance, if she had receiv'd you it
' wou'd have been standing under a Canopy by an
' Arm-Chair, with as much State as the Empress.
' She wou'd have ask'd you two or three Questions,
' after which she wou'd have assur'd you of her
' Protection, and then have dismiss'd you without
' detaining you to dine with her, as is the manner
' of all the Princes of the Empire; but 'tis not the
' fashion here, *continued the Gentleman*. The Mar-
' gravine commonly dines in private, and we who
' are of her Court don't see her but at Mass. The
' young Margrave our Master wou'd like well
' enough to see Company, but his Mother giving
' him to understand that she does not care for it,
' he conforms to her Pleasure. The young Mar-
' gravine, who is the Daughter of the Prince *de*
' *Schwartzenbourg*, has no Authority, because tho'
' naturally obliging and civil she durst not put her
' good Qualities in practice, because the Margra-
' vine Dowager reproaches her that she does not
' know how to carry it like a Sovereign; by which
' means this poor Princess is oblig'd to be proud a-
' gainst her Inclination. If you were to see her

' you

' you wou'd be charm'd with her; for she is tall and
' handsome, of a lively fair Complexion, but not
' languid, and has a very noble Air. When
' the Margrave marry'd her she was an only
' Daughter, and the Princess of *Schwartzenbourg*
' her Mother, who had not lived with her Husband
' for near fifteen Years, was not like to have any
' more Children. But the Event has proved con-
' trary; for the Prince and Princess of *Schwartzen-*
' *bourg* are reconcil'd, and the Princess has had a
' Son, who has frustrated the Hopes of our young
' Margravine of being some day or other one of
' the richest Heiresses in the Empire. This has
' not advanc'd her in the Favour of her Mother-
' in-law, who often snaps at her; but there being
' no Remedy, the young Princess bears her Ill-hu-
' mours with Patience. As she is just brought to
' bed too of a Son, we hope she will have more In-
' terest; at least 'tis what we all wish, because she
' is a very good Princess. 'Tis not a Year, *con-*
' *tinued the Gentleman*, that our young Margrave
' has been of Age, nevertheless his Majority is so
' controll'd by the Ascendancy which the Dowager
' keeps over her Son, that it may be said 'tis she
' who governs still. This Prince accustom'd to
' obey knows not what is the Pleasure of com-
' manding. There's the same likelihood of his
' being a Dependant as long as his Mother lives;
' and indeed he ought to humour that Princess, as
' well because she was always a good Mother to
' him, as for the Advantages she is capable of doing
' him; for she is very rich, and has a noble Estate
' in *Bohemia*, which she wou'd perhaps give to her
' youngest Son, who is Canon of *Cologne* and *Augs-*
' *bourg*, if the Margrave disobliged her; tho' I be-
' lieve it must be a great Offence indeed that wou'd
' provoke her to disinherit him, because he was always
' her Darling, and perhaps too the most dutiful of
' all

' all her Children. Such is her Tenderness for this
' Son that when there was a Talk of his going
' abroad she wou'd needs go with him; and she
' actually accompany'd him all over *Italy*. Some
' People were indeed so ill-natur'd as to say that
' 'twas not out of Love to the Prince, but because
' she was afraid he wou'd wean himself from her
' Company, and break quite away from her. 'Tis
' said however that she is going to quit the Court, and
' to retire to *Etlingen*, which is the Place assign'd
' for her Jointure. We all wish it, not that we
' have any reason to complain of this Princess, but
' because we hope then to have a gayer Court.
' For the rest, to do the Margravine Dowager
' Justice, she has manag'd her Son's Finances with
' a great deal of Oeconomy. When the late Prince
' *Lewis* died he left a heavy Debt upon the Coun-
' try, which was also ruin'd by the late War. But
' the Margravine Regent has paid off all, and so
' happily retriev'd the Government and the Fi-
' nances, that when her Son came of Age she gave
' him considerable Sums, and the Country was in a
' better Condition than ever.'

There the Gentleman concluded. After putting several Questions to him I learnt that the Duchess of *Orleans* had been promis'd in Marriage to Prince *Alexander* of *Tour* and *Taxis**, that the Presents were made for the Wedding, and that the same was very soon to be celebrated: But when the Duke of *Orleans* actually sent M. *d'Argenson* his Chancellor to *Rastadt* to demand the Princess in Marriage, the Margravine her Mother thinking this a better Match beyond comparison, call'd back the Promise she had made to the Prince *de la Tour*, and concluded the Treaty with the Duke of *Orleans*. The young Margrave marry'd his Sister by Proxy, in pre-

* He has since marry'd a Princess of *Brandenbourg-Bareith*, who has embrac'd the Catholic Religion.

presence of M. *d'Argenson*, and the Princess was conducted to *Strasbourg*, where finding a Set of Domestics sent from *Paris* to receive her, she turn'd off all her *German* Servants and proceeded on her Journey to *Chalons*, whither the Duke of *Orleans* went to meet her.

The same Gentleman from whom I learnt all these Particulars told me likewise that the young Margrave, before he marry'd the Princess of *Schwartzenbourg*, was to have had the Daughter of King *Stanislaus*, but that the Margravine broke off the Marriage-Treaty which was very far advanc'd, because the King was not able to pay down a hundred thousand Crowns ready Money for his Daughter's Dowry. It was undoubtedly owing to that Princess's happy Star that the King could not raise the Sum, for in such case his Daughter would not now have worn one of the first Crowns in the World. The Gentleman told me moreover that the Margravine was mortify'd to the last degree when she heard that the Princess whom she had refus'd for her Daughter-in-law was become the Queen of *France*. She was apprehensive too that this Princess or the King her Father would take revenge for the Slight she had put upon their Alliance, and she wrote a Letter to King *Stanislaus* to congratulate him on an Event so glorious to him, and to recommend to him the Duchess of *Orleans* her Daughter. *I intreat you, Sir,* said she, *to prevail with the Queen your Daughter to honour my Daughter and all my Family with her Favour. I will presume to say that both I and Mine deserve it at your Hands for the Respect we have always had for you.* This Letter, which was as submissive as the Margravine's Conduct had been haughty, was receiv'd with very great Civility by King *Stanislaus*, who, after having read it to the Queen his Wife, could not help saying, *I am much oblig'd to the Mar-*

Margravine for this Letter, and he return'd her a very engaging Answer. 'Tis my Opinion that at that time, instead of bearing the Princess any Ill-will he took it very kindly of her that she had refus'd his Daughter for a Daughter-in-law. The officious Gentleman would perhaps have inform'd me of other Particulars concerning the Court of *Rastadt*, if the Margrave's Return from Hunting had not oblig'd him to go to the Castle. I thank'd him for the trouble he had given himself, and went and shut my self up at my Quarters.

I set out next day for *Strasbourg*, and in less than five Hours arrived at KEHL. 'Tis all an even Country, and admirable Roads. We travel thro' the Dominions of *Spire*, the Bishoprick of *Strasbourg*, and the County of *Hanau*. At *Kehl* I paid a Visit to the General Baron *de Roth*, the Governour of the Place, who entertain'd me at Dinner, and made me exceeding welcome, but so ply'd me with Liquor that I thought my self at *Fulde* or *Wurtzbourg*. After Dinner M. *de Roth* shewed me the Fortifications, which I found in a very bad State. The Commandant told me that he had taken a world of pains to represent it to the Dyet of the Empire at *Ratisbonne*, but that he might as well have talk'd to so many deaf Men. 'Tis certain that if Care be not taken, the *Rhine* will wash away the Fort one day or other, and carry it to *Holland*. The Marshal *de Bourg* said to me a while ago when we were talking of *Kehl*, that M. *de Roth* would do well to fasten his Fort with Chains to the Citadel of *Strasbourg*.

There's only a Bridge over the *Rhine* to pass from *Kehl* to STRASBOURG the Capital of *Alsace*, and formerly an Imperial City. The *French* made themselves Masters of it in *September* 1681, when they came to the very Gates of the Place before the Town had notice of their March, and when it was in no Condition to make refiftance; for whether they thought they had no need of being upon their guard, or whether the chief Burgomafters had been corrupted, the Town wanted but every thing. The Capitulation was figned on one fide by the Marquis *de Louvois*, and the Baron *de Monclar* Commandant in *Alface*; and on the other by eight Deputies of the City, which was fecured in all its Privileges, Prerogatives and Cuftoms, both ecclefiaftical and civil. The Bifhop was neverthelefs reftored to his See, and the Canons to the Cathedral, which had belonged for 152 Years to the *Lutherans*. *Lewis* XIV. made his entry into *Strasbourg* the 23d of *October* following, and immediately order'd a Citadel and other Works to be erected, which have fince been fo augmented that *Strasbourg* may now be rank'd among the moft important Places of *Europe*. The Marfhal Count *de Bourg* commands in it, and has one of the King's Lieutenants under him, who is always a General Officer. M. *Dangervilliers*[*] formerly Intendant of *Dauphiny*, is Intendant of the Province of *Alface* and the City of *Strasbourg*. Thefe Gentlemen, whom I have been to fee, receiv'd me with prodigious Civility, and very punctually return'd my Vifit.

The Marfhal Count *de Bourg* preferves a ftately Mien in an advanced Age, and one may eafily perceive he has been a very fine Man in his time. He was Page to *Philip* of *France* Duke of *Orleans*, Brother to *Lewis* the Great, and to that Duke's Favour his Advancement to Military Employments is very much owing, tho' 'tis true that he has diftinguifhed himfelf in the Service. On the 26th

---

[*] He was advanc'd to the Office of Secretary at War in the room of M. *le Blanc*, and was fucceeded as Intendant of *Alface* by M. *de Harlay*, formerly Intendant of *Metz*; and when the latter was made Intendant of *Paris* he was fucceeded by M. *de Brou*.

26th of *August* 1709, he defeated near *Rumersheim* the Count *de Mercy*, who commanded a flying Camp of 9000 Men detach'd from the Army of the Empire, then under Command of the Elector of *Hanover*, afterwards *George* I. King of *Great Britain*. This Victory gain'd M. *de Bourg* the blue Ribbon. King *Lewis* XV. gave him the Staff of a Marshal of *France*, and confirmed him in the Government of *Strasbourg*. The *French* Officers accuse this Marshal of Pride, but for my part, I have all the Reason that can be to love him for his Civility.

M. *Dangervilliers* is really more engaging than the Marshal, and is therefore more beloved by the Officers. He is affable and civil, complaisant to Foreigners, and lives with a vast deal of Splendor. The Princes of the Empire that border upon *Alsace* like him very well, and think he is more candid, and less haughty than his Predecessors.

There's not many of the Nobility settled in this City, and of these few that are wealthy; and therefore they live very much retir'd. The Canons of the Great Chapter who ought all to be Princes or Counts, are not of very great Service, because most of 'em holding other Benefices, only come to *Strasbourg* to pass away three Months there of their Residence, and by consequence they are here as Strangers. The best Houses therefore are the Intendant's and the King's Lieutenant's. There are always a great many Officers here who are indeed amiable Fellows, and know how to serve, and to be good Company too upon occasion. The Commandants of the Corps are in Years, and Officers of Experience, and the rest are clever smart Youths who long sadly to be fighting, and would fain make you believe the four Corners of the World will quickly be on fire. I have not seen finer Infantry than the *French* Infantry at this present time. There are very fine Gentlemen too in the Cavalry, but then they are not near so well mounted as ours. You know the Cry with us is that the *French* are ruin'd, and not able to do any thing more. How the Case stands with them, I really know not, but if one may judge of it by Appearances, it cannot be so. No Troops were ever better cloathed, better paid, more spruce, nor finer. The Officers are splendid; they game, divert themselves, and eat and drink well, which does not seem to me to be the Life of People in want. Upon these terms, I would be content to be in such want all my Life long.

The Garrison maintains a Company of Comedians who are paid by the Captains, and commanding Officers, for the Subalterns are admitted *gratis*. The Theatre, which is one of the prettiest in the Country, is maintain'd by the City.

A Man that has a Taste for a plain home-bred Girl may here find Amusement and good Blood. 'Tis observ'd that the *Lutheran* Women are the most beautiful, and the Sex at this Place is said to be very indulgent, and very tractable; so that I should be apt to think, a Man need not be very open-hearted to them.

Tho' *Strasbourg* may be reckon'd among the finest Towns in *France*, one can't say there's a single House in it that is magnificent, or makes a grand Appearance. The Cathedral is a very stately Building of *Gothic* Architecture; its famous Spire is one of the most lofty, and of the neatest Workmanship of any in *Europe*. *Misson*, who 'tis like always carried his Plummet and Foot-Rule in his Pocket, because he never fails to give the Length and Breadth and Height of a Thing, says that 'tis 574 Foot in height; and I believe he is not mistaken. *Erkivin de Stembach* who was the Architect, finish'd it in the Year 1449. 'Tis said that *Lewis* XIV. had a mind to have a Spire erected upon the second

Tower

Tower which seems to have been built with that View. He order'd M. *de Vauban* to draw a Model of it, and to compute the Cost, which he found would amount to several Millions of Livres. The King thinking that he could employ that Sum to a better purpose, contented himself with making a Present to the Cathedral of the Ornaments, and all the Priests Vestments for celebrating Mass upon the several annual Festivals; the whole of which is extraordinary sumptuous, and becoming the Magnificence of one of the greatest Kings in the World. 'Twas in the Cathedral of *Strasbourg* that the Duke of *Orleans* the first Prince of the Blood of *France* married as Proxy to *Lewis* XV. *Mary Lescinski*, the Daughter of King *Stanislaus*. This Ceremony, at which I was present, was more magnificent than what was observ'd at *Fontainbleau* at the Queen's Arrival; and the Concourse of *German* Noblemen and Princes hither upon the Occasion was prodigious. The Cardinal *de Rohan*, as Bishop of *Strasbourg*, gave the Nuptial Benediction. Nothing can be finer than the Speeches which his Eminency made upon that Solemnity: As they fell into my hands, I think I ought to communicate them to you. You will find them *verbatim* at the End of this Letter. *Poland* in this Instance, made a worthy Restitution to *France*, which many Years ago gave the *Poles* a King who was afterwards the unfortunate *Henry* III; and they have now in their turn given a Queen to *France*. But *Germany* may boast that the Queen derives from the Empire that Fund of Virtue which is the Source of her Happiness, and makes her admir'd by the Universe. *France* had for a long time left off sending to our Climates for her Queens. *Mary-Anne Victoria* of *Bavaria* was in a fair way to be one, but she died a Dauphiness*. *Lorrain, Scotland, Italy* and *Spain*, had

* The Wife of *Lewis* the Dauphin who was *Lewis* XIVth's only Son.

had as it were engross'd the Crown of *France* for their Princesses. But I hope the Virtues of the present Queen and the other *German* * Princesses who are now at the Court of *France* will oblige the *French* to confess that if our Princesses have not Crowns for their Dowries like the Infanta's of *Spain*, they have an Estate of more Value than all the Wealth in the World, *viz.* Piety, Charity, and Love for the People.

A great many young *German* Gentlemen come hither for the sake of learning *French*, and their Exercises, but I don't think they are a jot the better for it, because the Masters of their Exercises are not better Scholars here than they are in many Towns of *Germany*; and as to the *French*, they speak it very ill in this City; for the Inhabitants talk *High Dutch*, and our young Sparks are so pleas'd to hear their own Language spoke that they neglect to learn any other. Besides they always herd together, and too easily catch one another's Vices as well as Virtues. As they have not many Parts to shew, they spend their time at the Billiard-Table, the Coffee-House, and often at other Places not so honest, of which there are but too many here, this being a City as noted for Libertines as any in *Europe*.

I am, &c.

The Speech of Cardinal de Rohan *to the* QUEEN, *before the Celebration of the Marriage.*

MADAME,

'WHILE I see you in this sacred Temple approaching to our Altars to contract that illustrious Alliance which is to unite you to the greatest of Kings and the most amiable of Princes, I
' adore

---

* The Duchess of *Orleans* who is of the *Baden* Family, and the Duchess of *Bourbon*.

' adore what God designs you for, and admire with
' Transport the Course that Providence is steering
' to conduct you to the Throne which you are go-
' ing to ascend. You are descended, MADAME,
' from a Family illustrious for its Antiquity, for its
' Alliances, and for the eminent Employments which
' the great Men it has given to *Poland* have fill'd
' successively with so much Glory. You are the
' Daughter of a Father, who, thro' the various E-
' vents of a busy Life, chequer'd by good and bad
' Fortune, has always shewn himself the Gentleman,
' the Hero, and the Christian. You have for your
' Mother, and your Grand-mother, Princesses, who
' like to *Judith*, and to that virtuous Woman whose
' Character is drawn in the Scriptures, have attracted
' the Veneration and Respect of the whole World,
' by the Fidelity with which they always walk'd in
' the Fear of the Lord. In your Person, MA-
' DAME, are center'd all the Accomplishments that
' can be form'd by a happy Birth, and an admirable
' Education, supported by Examples equally strong
' and affecting. In you, that Goodness, that Mild-
' ness, and those Charms are predominant, which
' gain Love at the same time as they inforce Re-
' spect ; that Integrity of Heart which nothing can
' resist ; that Superiority of Understanding and
' Knowledge which are conspicuous, as it were in
' spite of you, and in spite of that Modesty and
' noble Simplicity which are natural to you ; and
' finally that which is the Crown of so much Merit,
' that Taste for Piety, and that Attachment to the
' true Principles of Religion, which animate your
' Actions, and regulate your Conduct. Adorn'd
' with all these Virtues, what Crown is there to which
' you might not reasonably aspire, exclusive of the
' Custom which in some measure obliges Kings to look
' no farther than round the Throne for Princesses
' that they have a mind should reign with them ?

' He

'He who disposes of Empires puts the Sceptre of
'Poland into the hands of a Prince to whom you
'owe your Being, and by giving the Father that
'Splendor conducts the Daughter insensibly to
'the sublime Station he is preparing for her. But,
'O God, how impenetrable are thy Designs, and
'how far above human Prudence are the Means
'thou makest use of to bring about thy wise Pur-
'poses! This Prince was scarce seated on the Throne
'in which the Choice of the Grandees, and the Af-
'fection of the People had plac'd him, but he was
'oblig'd to quit it: He is abandon'd, betray'd, per-
'secuted; one fatal Shot bereaves him of the Hero
'his Friend, and the chief Stay of his Hopes: He
'submits to the necessity of the Times without a-
'bating in his Courage: He seeks refuge in a Coun-
'try which is the common Shelter of unfortunate
'Kings: He comes to *France*, and thither, MA-
'DAME, you are following him. All that see you
'there, touch'd with your Misfortunes, admire
'your Virtue, the Odour of which spreads to the
'Throne of a young Monarch, who, such is
'the Lustre of his Crown, the Extent of his Power,
'and above all, the Charms of his Person, might
'have made his choice out of all the Princesses of
'the World: But being guided by wise Counsels,
'he fixes it upon You; and here the Finger of God
'is plainly visible in improving that very Misfor-
'tune which separates the King your Father from
'his Subjects, and takes you out of *Poland* to give
'Us in your Person, a Queen who shall be the Glory
'of a Father and of a Mother, of whom she is now
'the Comfort and Delight; a Queen, who shall
'render that Nation happy which most richly de-
'serves it, at least for its Respect and its Fidelity to
'its Sovereigns; a Queen, who being inviolably
'attach'd to her Duty, full of Tenderness and Re-
'spect for her Husband, and her King, and wisely
'em-

' employ'd in what is capable of procuring her solid
' Happiness, will revive to us the Reign of the
' Empress *Flaccilla*, of whom History says, that
' having always kept the Precepts of the Divine
' Law in her view, she conferr'd thereupon daily
' with the great *Theodosius*, and that her Words like
' a fruitful Rain, water'd with success those Seeds
' of Virtue which God had sown in the Heart of
' her Husband. Come then, MADAME, Come to
' the Altar. May the Engagements you are going
' to enter into, sacred of themselves, (since accord-
' ing to the Apostle, they are the Symbol of the
' Union of Jesus Christ with his Church) may they
' be also sanctify'd by your own Disposition. May
' you be so sensible of what you are going to be,
' that you may acknowledge that in crowning your
' Merits, he crowns his Gifts: And may you Chri-
' stians that hear me, when you see the shining Re-
' wards that are bestowed in this World upon true
' Virtue, learn to respect and love it.'

The Cardinal's Speech after the Celebration of the Marriage.

MADAME,

' NOW that august Ceremony is ended which
' crowns our Hopes and our Wishes; give
' me leave to desire your Majesty's Royal Protection
' for the Church of *Strasbourg*. This Church has
' not forgot and never will forget the signal Favours
' it has received from our former Kings. How great
' are its Obligations to our last Monarch! Being de-
' liver'd up by the Misfortunes of the Times to the
' Furys of Schism and Heresy, it would perhaps
' have perish'd as many others did, if that great
' Prince, by resuming the Rights of his Ancestors,
' had not undertaken its defence, and supported it
' with all his Power. To him it is oblig'd for the

' Ad-

'Advantage of being restored to the Possession of
'this sacred Temple from which it had been ba-
'nished. There's nothing here but what puts us
'in mind of his Pious and Royal Magnificence.
'Temples adorn'd, Pastors liberally maintain'd,
'Missions founded, new Converts protected and
'supported, are so many Monuments of the Zeal
'and Piety of a King whose Memory will never
'die. He had not the Comfort to finish the Work
'which he had undertaken; that is to say, the
'reuniting of all the Sheep of this illustrious Flock
'in one and the same Fold: This was reserv'd to
'the worthy Heir of his Zeal and Crown. It will
'be your part, MADAME, to represent to your Au-
'gust Spouse how much the Remembrance of his
'Great Grand-father, his own Glory, and our Ne-
'cessities, which are even those of Religion, require
'of him. You will not desire that Recourse shou'd
'be had to those Methods which exasperate, with-
'out persuading; such would not be to your Majesty's
'liking, and God forbid that we should suggest them
'to you. Those Children who disown us are your
'Subjects, MADAME, and the Church of *Strasbourg*
'confiding intirely in God's Mercy, still looks on
'itself as their Mother. We therefore conjure you
'by the Bowels of Jesus Christ, to employ, for the
'sake of uniting them, every Thing with which
'an active but sympathizing Charity may inspire
'you. God will bless your Majesty's Endeavours,
'and our Desires, and will employ the Instances of
'your Piety and your Faith to the total Confusion
'of Error, and the Triumph of the Truth. May your
'Reign be long over us, MADAME, for the Hap-
'piness of the King, and the Welfare of this great
'Kingdom. May God hear the Prayers which the
'Church has now offer'd up for your Majesty, and
'may you be so good as to place us in the Rank of
'your most zealous and most faithful Subjects.'

LET-

LETTER XIX.

SIR,   *Heidelberg, March* 12. 1730.

BEING in the Neighbourhood of SAVERNE where the Cardinal *de Rohan* lives, I had a mind to go thither. I have had the Honour to be known to that Prelate a long time, and was overjoy'd at the opportunity of paying my respects to him.

Armand Gaston Cardinal *de Rohan* was elected Bishop of *Strasbourg* the 10th of *April* 1704 *, and received the Cardinal's Cap from the Hands of *Lewis* XIV. the 18th of *May*, 1712. The Year following he succeeded the Cardinal *de Janson* as Great Almoner. The Emperor granted him the Temporal Investiture of the See of *Strasbourg* † on the

---

* The famous Cardinal *William Egon de Furstemberg* Bishop of *Strasbourg* died the 10th of *April* 1704, and was immediately succeeded by the Abbot *de Rohan*, who was chose Coadjutor *Jan.* 31, 1701.

† *Strasbourg* was an Episcopal See before the Year 376, for one *Arnaud* Bishop of *Strasbourg* was then present at the Council of *Cologne*. The Chapter is composed of 24 Members, *viz.* 12 Capitulars, and 12 Domicilairs, who must be all Princes or Counts. From 1592 the Canons were *Lutherans*, and Catholics till 1681, when *Lewis* XIV. having taken *Strasbourg*, established a Bishop there whose See was at *Molsheim*, and caused the Cathedral to be restored to the Catholic Canons; and notwithstanding the contrary Dispositions of the Treaty of *Westphalia*, in 1687, he turn'd the *Lutheran* Canons out of *Brudersdorff*, and the Prebends which they retain'd in the Chapter: Nevertheless the *Lutheran* Religion is tolerated in this City.

the 10th of *June* 1723, and in 1724, he obtain'd a Seat in the College of Princes at the Assembly of *Ratisbon*. This Prelate who is considerable for his Birth and Dignities, is much more so for his great Soul, his polite and obliging Behaviour, and for an Air of Grandeur which accompanies all his Actions. He is a comely Person, as are indeed all of his Family. Being noble and magnificent in every thing that he does, he lives wherever he is like a great Nobleman, but particularly at *Saverne*. I found at his Palace the Duke and Duchess of *Tallard*, the Duchess *de la Meilleraie*, Mademoiselle *de Melun*, the Prince and Princess of *Birkensfield*, M. *Dangervilliers*, the Intendant of *Strasbourg*, the Count and Princess of *Hanau*, and in short a great many Officers of Distinction. They had all convenient Lodgings and Accommodation in the Castle; and Gaming, taking the Air, Hunting, Music, and Good-Cheer were their constant Diversions.

The Bishops of *Strasbourg* have resided for a long time at the Palace of *Saverne*, which was always a convenient House; but the Cardinal *de Rohan* has made it very considerable. The outside of this Palace is not so magnificent as the inside. The Entry which leads to the chief Stair-Case is lighted to great advantage, and has several Outlets that have a convenient Communication with the lower Apartments, which are high, and very finely embellish'd. The principal Stair-Case is very grand, and leads to a stately Salon with most curious Decorations. It has a double Apartment which is render'd as commodious as possible; and the Furniture consists of Embroidery of Gold and Silver, which may be thought perhaps too rich. The Queen, who lodg'd at the Cardinal's House when she came to *Saverne*, was charm'd with the Splendor of it, and the extraordinary Respect with which she was attended here.

The

The Cardinal *de Rohan* designs that this rich Furniture shall remain annex'd to the See; for which his Successor will certainly have very great Obligations to him: But his Eminence was not so much oblig'd to his Predecessors; for when he was chose Bishop he found a House very much out of order, and scarce a Chair in it, whereas 'tis now fit for a King. His Eminency is about making very large fine Gardens, which are in very great forwardness, and perfectly answerable to the Grandeur and Beauty of the Palace; and at the end of them there is a stately Canal which cost infinite Labour and Expence. The whole of it is the more magnificent because *Saverne* stands at the foot of very high Mountains; and in digging the Canal the Workmen often met with Rocks which they were forc'd to blow up.

At the Cardinal's Table there's both Abundance and Elegance; and his Eminency entertains in such a manner as really charms his Guests. All his Domestics follow his example; and 'tis certain that they are all very diligent; and that there is not a House in *France*, or in *Europe*, where there's better Attendance. His Eminency's Houshold, and all his Temporal Affairs in general, are directed by the Abbot *de Ravanne*, Counsellor in the Parliament of *Paris*.

The Cardinal is one of the richest Noblemen in *France*, and without dispute the most expensive. He has built a Hotel at *Paris*, and furnish'd it sumptuously. He has made considerable Works at *Saverne*, and laid out a great deal of Money in Plate, Furniture, Pictures, antique Vessels, and Busts, Medals, and Books. Some time ago he purchas'd of the President *Menard* the famous Library of the illustrious Messieurs *de Thou*, formerly one of the most celebrated in *France*; and he daily inriches

riches it with all the most curious and uncommon Books and Manuscripts.

Besides all these Expences, the Cardinal intends also to build a new episcopal Palace at *Strasbourg* [*], where he is indeed but indifferently lodg'd at present. The Marquiss *de N...* talking of the Cardinal *de Rohan*'s Expence, said, *That, to be sure, his Eminency had found out the Philosopher's Stone*. I think so too, and that he has done it by procuring himself five or six hundred thousand Livres a-year in good Benefices.

From *Saverne* I went to HAGUENAU, and to WEISSENBOURG, formerly Imperial Cities, and now subject to *France*, but Places of little consequence. King *Stanislaus* after the Death of *Charles* XII. King of *Sweden*, being forc'd to quit *Deux-Ponts* to which he had retired with his Family, came and resided at *Weissenbourg*; and here it was that he receiv'd the first Proposals that were made to him for the Marriage of his Daughter with King *Lewis* XV. I came and took up my Quarters at LANDAU, one of the most scoundrel Places in the World, but the best fortify'd; and famous for having stood out several Sieges. The Emperor *Joseph* took it when he was King of the *Romans*. The *French* retook it a little before the signing of the Peace at *Rastadt*, by which Treaty it was left in their hands. They maintain a good Garison in it, and have added several Works to it.

From *Landau* I pass'd to BRHOUSEL, with an Intention to pay my respects to the Cardinal *de Schonborn* Bishop of *Spire* who resides there, but I did not succeed better there than at *Rastadt*; for his Eminency excus'd himself from seeing me because he was going a hunting, and put me off till next day; but I did not think it worth while to wait, what had happen'd to me at the Court of *Baden* being too fresh in my Memory. I was afraid of the same

[*] 'Tis already far advanc'd.

same Fate at *Brboufel*, where I lay at such sorry Quarters that I cou'd not avoid catching Cold, my Lodging-Room being without Glass, and be famish'd into the bargain, there being nothing to eat: Besides, my Landlord told me that the Cardinal made even those People who came to him upon Business dance attendance for three or four days. I said to my self therefore that he had much more reason to make me wait, who came to his Court out of meer Curiosity. I resolv'd therefore, as any Gentleman ought to have done in the like case, and took the opportunity of the Cardinal's Absence to go and view the outside of his Palace. 'Tis a great Structure not yet entirely finish'd, which the Cardinal has hitherto carry'd on from the very Foundation; but if I must be sincere with you, all these Works, considerable as they are, have been form'd upon pitiful Plans. It has cost a very large Sum of Money; and I fancy that in the time of the ancient *Teutonics*, it wou'd have been reckon'd a very fine Structure. The chief Beauty of it lies in its Situation; for a great Variety of agreeable Objects are discovered from the Apartments. The Gardens are also so new that one can scarce know the Plan of 'em; it seems to me that they are not of an extraordinary Taste, and that they wou'd be much more suitable for a private Man than for a Sovereign.

The Cardinal *de Schonborn* is a keen Sportsman. He has Game enough in his own Bishoprick, for the Country so abounds with all sorts that the Fields are ruin'd by the Deer. The Peasants are so hard put to it to preserve their Corn that they are oblig'd to watch it day and night. The Cardinal often makes Hunting-Matches for the Stag and wild Boar, in which they kill hundreds; at such times the Peasants are oblig'd to take a certain quantity of Meat, for which they pay so much a Pound,

Pound, according to a Price that is regulated. The Bishoprick of *Spire* is one of the fruitfullest Provinces in *Germany*, but the Inhabitants are extremely poor; for their Provisions lie on their hands, and they have scarce wherewithal to pay the great Taillies due to their Sovereigns.

The Dignity of the Bishop of *Spire* is elective, as are all the Bishopricks of *Germany* which are not in the hereditary Dominions of the House of *Austria*. The Bishop is Sovereign of the Country, but the City of *Spire* has particular Privileges, as have all the Imperial Cities. You know it was at *Spire* that the Emperor *Charles* V. establish'd the Imperial Chamber, which is as it were the Parliament of the Empire. The *French* having destroy'd *Spire* when they ravag'd the *Palatinate*, the Chamber or supreme Tribunal was transferred to *Wetzlar* in *Wetteravia*, where indeed it seem'd to be more in the Center of *Germany*, and secur'd from all manner of Insult.

Damien-Hugo Count *de Schonborn* Cardinal, is at this present Bishop of *Spire*, and Coadjutor of *Constance*. He is also grand Commander of the Teutonic-Order. He was heretofore a Member of the Emperor's Privy-Council, and his Plenipotentiary to the Circle of Lower *Saxony*. *Clement* XI. of the *Albani* Family honour'd him with the Purple. He is descended of a Family in which Merit has happen'd to be back'd by Fortune. The Cardinal's Father was the first Count of it. He was also one of the Emperor's Privy-Council, and Brother to *Lotharius-Francis* Elector of *Mentz* and Bishop of *Bamberg*. The Cardinal has actually a Brother who is Elector of *Triers*, another who is Bishop of *Wurtzbourg* and *Bamberg*, whom I have mention'd to you upon other occasions; and lastly, a third who is a Counsellor of State * to the Emperor,

---
* He was addmitted Kt. of the *Golden-Fleece* at the last Promotion.

HEIDELBERG.

peror, and is now the Head of the Family. Messieurs *de Schonborn* had formerly an Elector of *Mentz* in their Family, who was at the same time Bishop of *Wurtzbourg*, but that Prince left them no great Estate; so that they were not very rich when *Lotharius Francis*, Uncle to them all, was chose Elector of *Mentz*. But this Prince procur'd them both Wealth and Honours, and render'd the Count *de Schonborn*, who is Counsellor of State to the Emperor, one of the richest Noblemen in *Germany*.

From *Brhousel* to *Heidelberg* there's one of the finest Countries in the World, planted with Fruit, and especially Walnut-Trees, which bring in a great Revenue.

The City of HEIDELBERG, upon the *Necker*, is very much pent up by that River, and a Chain of Hills, so that 'tis not near so broad as 'tis long. This City is the Capital of the Lower *Palatinate*, and was formerly the Residence of the Electors. Here is a University which was founded in 1346, by *Robert* Prince *Palatine*, who was chose King of the *Romans*. No Town has smarted more by the Scourge of War. Since the Disgrace of *Frederic* Elector *Palatine*, whom the *Bohemians* chose for their King, it has been taken, plunder'd, or burnt four times. In 1622, the Emperor's General *Tilly* put 500 *Palatines* in it to the Sword, and at the same time the Emperor carry'd off the famous Library, which he gave in part to *Urban* VIII. who caused it to be placed in the *Vatican*, where 'tis still to be seen. In 1634, *Heidelberg* was besieg'd twice. *John de Werth* took it for *Lewis* XIV. but not being able to carry the Castle he retir'd. Not many days after, the Marshals *de Force* and *Brezé* forc'd the Quarters of the *Germans*, and took both the Town and Castle. The *French* took this City a third time in 1688, and again in 1693, which

VOL. I.   Y   was

was the last time, Sword in hand; at what time they committed Cruelties shocking to remember, and of which there are woful Marks still left in *Heidelberg*, and all the Towns in the *Palatinate*. This City was beginning to recover it self by the Elector's residing there, when it brought a more heavy Disgrace upon it self than all the Misfortunes it had suffer'd by the War. The Case was thus:

The great Church of *Heidelberg* since the Peace of *Westphalia* belongs half to *Roman* Catholics, and half to the *Calvinists*, of whom the former have the Choir, and the others the Body, and nothing but a thin Partition separates the two Communions. The Choir not being big enough to contain the Catholics when the Court resided at *Heidelberg*, the Elector propos'd to the *Calvinists* to yield him the Body of the Church, alledging that not only the Choir was too scanty, but that he shou'd be very glad that the Church in which the *Palatine* Princes lie interr'd were altogether Catholic. He promis'd at the same time that another Church should be built for them larger and finer than what they were to yield to him. The *Calvinists* said that the great Church had been granted to them by the Treaty of *Munster*; that all the Princes who were Guarantees of the Peace of *Westphalia* were engag'd to preserve them in the enjoyment of it; that therefore they could not give it up without violating that Treaty, which was their Security, and without rendring themselves unworthy of the Protection of the Protestant Powers. The Elector, in order to remove those Obstacles, consented that the Powers who were Guarantees of the *Westphalian* Treaty of Peace, in which the Church he desir'd was expresly mentioned, should be Guarantees of the Church which he promis'd should be built for them: But all these Offers how reasonable soever were not accepted by
the

the *Calvinists*. The Elector being thereby incens'd, made use of his Sovereign Authority, and took by force what they were not willing to yield to him; whereupon the *Calvinists* had recourse to the Protestant Princes of the Empire, the *Lutherans* as well as the *Calvinists*, who constituting but one Body and one Communion when the Catholics are to be oppos'd, united together, and engag'd in their Quarrel the Kings of *Great Britain*, *Denmark*, *Sweden*, and *Prussia*, and the *States-General*. These Powers caused the Catholic Churches in their Dominions to be shut up, sequester'd the Estates of the Convents, and made such Clamors and Menaces that the Elector was oblig'd to reinstate the *Calvinists* in the Nave of the Church; but he was so angry with the Inhabitants of *Heidelberg* for their Disrespect to him that he remov'd his Residence to *Manheim*. The Burghers were not very sorry at first for the Departure of the Court; for being accustom'd to its Absence, they flattered themselves that the Tribunals of the Regency, which, since the Accession of the *Newbourg* Family to the Electorate, had constantly been kept at *Heidelberg*, would remain there still. But they were soon thrown into the utmost Consternation when they saw those Tribunals follow the Elector. They went and cast themselves at the Feet of their angry Sovereign, and asking his Pardon for having affronted him, they offer'd him the Church which was the cause of his Displeasure, and conjur'd him to return to their City. But all their Supplications were fruitless; the Elector was stedfast in his Resolution to punish *Heidelberg*, and abandon'd it for ever. *Heidelberg* having no Trade, and subsisting only by the Court, or by the Tribunals of the Regency, of which it was totally depriv'd, falls now into decay, and will, no doubt, e'er 'tis long dwindle to little or nothing.

The Elector's Palace is higher than the City, and situate in such a manner that there's a Prospect from the great Apartments quite through the Opening between the Mountains, by which the *Necker* runs into the Plain. The Palace is built of Free-Stone, and is a magnificent Structure. The greatest part of it was burnt by the *French* when they destroy'd the *Palatinate:* The Lodging-Rooms that are subsisting are very substantial, tho' not built in the modern Taste. The Apartments are large, but want Ornament, especially since they have been stript of their Furniture. The Gardens were formerly reckon'd the finest in *Germany*; but there's scarce any thing left of them except the Place where they flourished. If one may judge of what they were by their Situation, they must have been very pleasant, by reason of the extensive Prospect they afforded into the Country.

I do not intend to detain you with an Account of the famous Tun, *Misson* having given a more exact Description of that than of many Towns which he treats of. You will in his *Travels* find a Cut of this Vessel, which will give you a more perfect Idea of it than any Narrative whatsoever. The Elector *John-William*, the Predecessor of the present Elector, gave a Companion to this Tun, which is not altogether so large, but much more adorn'd. They are both full of Wine. I remember that in 1719, when I was at the *Palatine* Court, the Elector ask'd me at Table whether I had seen the Great Tun; and upon my saying that I had not, that Prince, than whom there was not a more gracious Sovereign in the whole World, told me he would carry me to it. He made a Proposal to the Princess his Daughter, who was marry'd to the hereditary Prince of *Sultzbach*, to go thither after Dinner was over; which she accepted. The Trumpets led the way, and the Court followed in

great

great Ceremony. When we had mounted the Platform which is over the Tun, the Elector did me the honour to drink to me out of the *Wilkom*, which was a Silver gilt Cup, of a large dimension. He took it off clean at one Draught, and having caused it to be replenished, sent it to me by a Page. Good Manners, and the Respect I ow'd to the Elector's Commands, not permitting me to refuse the Chalice, I begg'd heartily that he would suffer me to drink it off at several Draughts; which was indulg'd me; and the Elector talking in the mean time with the Ladies, I took the opportunity of his Absence, and made no scruple to deceive him, for I return'd great part of the Wine to the bottom of the Tun, threw a part of it on the ground, and the rest, which was the least part of it, I drank. I thought my self well off that he did not perceive in what manner I bubbled him; for I saw he was very well pleased with me. Then several other great Glasses went round, and the very Ladies wet their Lips, which was the thing that effectually contributed to demolish us. I was one of the first that was overpower'd. I perceived those convulsive Motions that threaten'd me if I drank any more, therefore I sneak'd off and made the best of my way down from the Platform. I was endeavouring to get out of the Vault, but was stop'd at the Door by two Life-Guard Men, who with their Carabines crossing each other, cry'd, *Stand, there's no coming this way*. I conjur'd them to let me pass, and told them that I had very important Reasons for my departure; but I might as well have talk'd to the Wind. I found my self in a terrible Quandary: To get up again to the head of the Tun was Death: What would become of me I could not tell. In short I crept under the Tun, and there hoped to hide my self; but it was a fruitless Precaution: There's no avoiding a Man's Destiny. It was my

Fate to be carry'd out of the Vault, and to know nothing of the matter. For the Elector perceiv'd I was a Deserter, and I heard him say, *Where is he? What's become of him? Let him be look'd after, and brought up to me dead or alive.* The Guards at the Door being examin'd said that I came that way in order to get out, but that they sent me back again. All these Inquiries, which I heard from my Hole, made me burrow my self the more. I crept under the Covert of a couple of Boards I met with by chance, where nothing but a Cat, Devil, or Page could possibly find me out. But a little Page, who was indeed both Devil and Page too, ferreted me, and baul'd out like one that was mad, *Here he is! Here he is!* and then I was taken out of my Covert. You may imagine what a silly Figure I made. I was carry'd before my Judge, who was the Elector himself. But I took the liberty to challenge both him and all the Gentlemen in his Retinue, as being Parties in the Cause. *Alas! my little Gentleman*, said the Prince to me, *You refuse us for your Judges; I will appoint you others then, and we shall see whether you will come off any better.* He nominated the Princess his Daughter, and her Ladies to try me, and the Elector was my Accuser. After pleading my own Cause they put it to the Vote, and I was condemn'd unanimously to drink as long as I could swallow. The Elector said, that as he was the Sovereign he would mitigate my Sentence; that I should that day drink four Pint Glasses of Wine, and that for a Fortnight running I should tip off the like Glass to his Health immediately after Dinner. Every body admir'd the Elector's Clemency, and whether I did or not, I was fain to do as they did, and to return him Thanks. Then I underwent the heaviest part of my Sentence; I did not lose my Life indeed, but for some Hours I lost both my Speech and my Reason.

Reason. I was carry'd to a Bed, where when I came to myself I was told that my Accusers were in the same pickle as I was; and that none of them went out of the Vault in the same manner as they enter'd it. Next day the Elector was so good as to mitigate the remaining part of my Sentence, and excus'd me from the Penance to which I was condemn'd, upon my promising him that I wou'd make one at his Table for a Month to come.

I am, &c.

LETTER XX.

SIR, *Manheim, March 17. 1730.*

IN going from *Heidelberg* to MANHEIM we leave the *Necker* on the right hand, but keep almost all the way by the side of that River. 'Tis three Leagues from one City to the other, over a fruitful Plain. *Manheim* lies between the *Rhine* and the *Necker*, in a marshy Country, which has always been reckon'd very unwholesome. About fourscore Years ago this City was but a Village. *Frederic* Elector *Palatine*, who was chose King of *Bohemia*, caus'd it to be fortify'd, and built a Castle or Citadel there, which he call'd *Fredericsbourg*. At the same time a Town was built, of which all the Streets run parallel, the chief that passes thro' the middle of the Town was planted with Trees after the manner of *Holland*. But the *French* having taken *Manheim* in 1693, raz'd it to the ground, and

and by the Treaty of *Nimeguen* it was stipulated that *Manheim* should be demolished; which was done accordingly. *John-William* of *Newbourg*, the last Elector, began again to fortify *Manheim*, according to the Plans laid down by the famous *Coborn*; but those Works were suspended, so that no more than two Bastions and a Courtain were finish'd. When the present Elector *Charles-Philip* came to live at *Manheim* he caus'd those Works to be resumed which his Brother had discontinued, and to be carried on with such Diligence that in a few Years he put the Place in a state of Defence[*]. The Fortifications are all fac'd with Brick; and *Manheim* is now one of the best Places in all *Germany*.

This City has three fine Gates, of which that of the *Necker* is the most magnificent, and the best adorned; in which one sees beautiful Basso-relievos, after a Plan very happily executed. This Gate opens towards a long and spacious Street, at the end of which stands the Elector's Palace, one of the largest and most substantial Buildings in *Europe*. It were to be wish'd indeed that the Architecture had been more regular: Never had any Architect more Advantage, for he built it new from the Foundation, was not stinted for want of room, and as he set no Limits to his Expence, I should have thought that a masterly hand might have produc'd something curious. Nevertheless there are Faults in the Building which are shocking to such as have the least Skill in Architecture; insomuch that they who have a Taste for that Science are sorry that a Building which has been so expensive has been no better conducted. The Situation of this Palace is indeed very fine, at the end of the City, and of a very noble large Street, which like all the rest runs in a strait Line. The Palace, which has a great Square before

---

[*] This Fortress is now finish'd, and the Elector, who continues to keep his Court here, has a strong Garison in it.

before it, consists of a large number of Lodging-Rooms, with a great high Pavilion in the middle, and two advanc'd Wings, with ample Pavilions at the ends; where two other very extensive Wings rise on both sides that are likewise terminated by Pavilions, behind which there are other Lodging-Rooms. The inside of the Palace is form'd by two great Courts, which are to be separated by an open Gallery or Terrass, the Model of which is very much adorned with Architecture; but I can't think it will look well when 'tis done. The Apartments are adorn'd with fine noble Floors and Cielings, and have the finest Prospect in the World to *Spire*, *Franckendahl*, *Worms*, and all the Country in general, as far as the Mountains of *Alsace*, which consists wholly of Towns and Villages. All this fine fruitful Country is water'd by the *Rhine*, which passes behind the Palace of *Manheim*, and washes its Fortifications. Upon this beautiful Canal there are to be the Gardens of the Palace, for which there are intended two Courtains and a Bastion.

'Tis almost inconceivable how the Elector was able to get all the Works about *Manheim* finished in so few Years; for in short I remember to have seen Partridges where there are now Houses and Palaces. The whole Town is laid out in a most regular and charming manner; and 'tis without dispute one of the prettiest Towns in *Europe*. 'Tis pity the Houses are not higher: The reason they alledge for it is, that *Manheim* is a fortify'd Town, and that by consequence the Houses ought to be low. I know not what Authority there is for this, since *Strasbourg*, *Metz*, *Luxembourg*, and *Lisle*, are Places of much more Importance than *Manheim*, and yet the Houses are as high there as they are in other Towns.

The Palace is commodious, and yet, for what reason I know not, the Elector does not live

in

in it*. Some say that he has been told of so many Faults in it as have quite put him out of conceit with it, and others that 'tis because a certain Astrologer prophesy'd he would die there; but I am apt to believe that the latter Reason is no more than a Joke, and I dare to say that the Elector is too wise a Man to credit it. Mean time this Prince dwells in a House belonging to a *Jew*, to which several other private Houses are join'd; but for all that the Lodgings are very bad.

There can't be a better-natur'd Man than *Charles-Philip* of *Newbourg*, Elector *Palatine*. He is the best of Masters, and the most affable of Princes. He is reckoned extremely handsome, and one of the chief Dancers in his time; and he has a noble Aspect. His Behaviour and Conversation engage one to love him, and to pay one's court to him out of pure Inclination. He formerly was fond of Pomp and Pleasure, but since the loss of his only Daughter and his Son-in-law, who died within a few Years one of another, he seems to be no longer taken with what was heretofore his Amusement. The Elector has been twice marry'd, *viz.* first to *Louisa-Charlotte* Princess of *Radzevilie*, and secondly to *Theresa Lubomirski*, both *Polish* Ladies. The former left him a Daughter that was marry'd to *Joseph-Charles* Prince *Palatine* of *Sultzbach*, but died in 1728; as did her Husband the Year following. This Princess had such Beauty and Merit, that she was the Comfort of her Father and the Admiration of her Acquaintance. She left three young Princesses, whom the Elector causes to be educated at his Court, where they are now all that he has to delight him; but then they incessantly renew to him the sorrowful Remembrance of a Daughter who was extremely dear to him.

The

---

* He actually lodges there now.

The Death of that Princess has been a very great Affliction to the Elector, and chang'd the Face of the *Palatine* Court. Indeed as to Affability, and to the Goodness of his Temper, he is still the same Elector, but he has no longer that Gaiety of Humour which his Daughter's Company rais'd in him; for she had a thousand different Amusements for him, and Pleasures and Merriment every where accompany'd her. The Elector eats always in private, except on Holidays, and when there's any foreign Prince at his Court. After he has been in public at Mass, he commonly stops in one of his Apartments to chat with the Courtiers, or to play at Billiards till Dinner-time. After Dinner he goes to Bed, and lies there two Hours; then he rises, and after having caus'd himself to be dress'd, he gives Audience to his Ministers, and to such private Persons as want to talk with him. He is very attentive to those who speak to him, and answers them with Good-nature and Kindness. He seldom refuses what is in his power to grant; and when Reasons force him to a denial, 'tis visible that he is uneasy, and he refuses in so civil a manner, that People go away at least comforted, if not contented. At six o'clock in the Evening the whole Court meets in his Electoral Highness's Apartment, where there is Play till nine o'clock, and then the Elector retires, makes a very slight Supper, and goes to Bed in good time.

Tho' the Elector dines in private there's always a Table sumptuously serv'd for the hereditary Prince of *Sultzbach*, Brother to him who was the Elector's Son-in-law. This passes for the Elector's Table, is spread for eighteen Guests, and is serv'd by Pages.

The Prince *de Sultzbach* is look'd upon as the Elector's Heir, because 'tis not supposed that the Elector's Brother, the Elector of *Mentz*, would be be willing to quit the first Electorate of the Empire, and the great Benefices which he possesses, to become Elector *Palatine*, if he should happen to survive his Brother*. The Bishop of *Augsbourg*, the Elector's second Brother, being a Priest, cannot succeed. The Prince *de Sultzbach*'s Father is still living; but being as old as the Elector, he is not like to survive him very long†. The Prince *John-Christian* of *Sultzbach* was born in 1700. He is the Widower of the Princess *de la Tour* of *Auvergne*, who brought him for her Portion the Sovereignty of *Bergopzoom*; and left him a Son, who is educated at *Brussels* with his Great-Grandmother the Duchess Dowager of *Aremberg*. The Prince *John-Christian* is tall and extremely corpulent, insomuch that 'tis well if he has not the Dropsy. He spent the first Days of his Youth at the Court of *Lorrain* in *France*, and in the *Netherlands*, by which Travels he acquired a great deal of Politeness. He was lately betrothed to *Eleonora-Philippina* of *Hesse-Rhinfelds*, Sister to the Princess of *Piedmont*‖, and to the Duchess of *Bourbon*. This Princess is every day expected from *Turin*, to which Place she accompanied her Sister. Their Highnesses will then go and keep their Court at *Heidelberg*‡.

The

---

* This Prince died at *Breslau* in *April* 1732.

† His Name was *Theodore*. He was born in 1659, and died in 1732.

‖ The late Queen of *Sardinia*.

‡ The Prince *John-Christian* became Prince Regent of *Sultzbach* after his Father's Death, but did not long survive him, for he died suddenly *July* 20. 1733; so that Prince *Charles* his Son, born *December* 10. 1724, is now Prince *Palatine* of *Sultzbach*, Marquiss of *Bergopzoom*, and presumptive Heir to the Elector. He is a very forward hopeful Youth. The Elector has sent for him from *Brussels* to *Manheim*, notwithstanding the Intreaty of the Duchess *d'Aremberg* his Great Grandmother by the Mother's side, (who had the care of his Education,) that he might be permitted to stay with her. This young Prince's Grandmother

is

MANHEIM. 333

The Principal Noblemen of the *Palatine* Court are the following:

Francis-George Count of *Manderscheldt-Blanckenheim**, the Steward of the Houshold, Prime Minister, and Knight of the Order of St. *Hubert*. He is of illustrious Extraction; is a Man of Integrity and very great Probity, incapable of doing an ill thing, but not at all engaging in his Deportment; for he is reserved, with an Air of Haughtiness, which is a Defect that he was born with, and endeavours to conquer, but cannot. When one knows him intimately he proves a good Friend, and capable of doing one Service. He has very great Pensions from the Elector, and is the oldest of his Family, which being pretty numerous, he does not live in a very grand manner.

The Baron *de Sickingen* is Great Chamberlain, Minister of State, and Knight of the Order of St. *Hubert*. He is a Gentleman of a fine Presence, of an easy and engaging Access, with profound Learning, and Sentiments suitable to his Birth. He was Governor of the late Prince *de Sultzbach*, Son-in-law to the Elector; and he imprinted such Ideas of Men and Things in the Mind of that young Prince, as gave great hopes that his Government would be happy if ever he attain'd to it. M. *de Sickingen* was afterward the Elector's Envoy Extraordinary to the Imperial Court; and I knew him at *Vienna* where he was exceedingly beloved. At his return he succeeded his Brother in the Office of Great Chamberlain, which he exercises with the Approbation of the whole Court.

John-

is the Princess Dowager *d'Auvergne*, Sister to the Duke *d'Aremberg*, one of the toasted Beauties of her Time. She retir'd to a Nunnery, is a Lady of good Learning, and now one of the Heads of the *Jansenist* Party of *Holland*.

* He died soon after this was written, and his Place is not yet fill'd up.

John-Frederic Count *de Globe*, is Grand Marshal, Minister of State, and Knight of the Order of St. *Hubert*. He is very rich, and has a fine Estate in *Bohemia*. He was once the Elector's Page, who finding him at the bottom a Man of Integrity and Honour, took care of his Fortune, gave him the best Employments at his Court, and raised him to the Dignity of Count. M. *de Globe* has been seldom at *Manheim* for some Years past; which is a Loss both to Court and City, because he liv'd very nobly, and more than all, was very civil to Foreigners*.

The Baron *de Wohlin* is Master of the Horse †. He is one of those Men in whom we meet with that Candor and Probity so much boasted by our Fathers.

The Count *de la Tour* and *Taxis* is Captain of the Life-Guards, Lieutenant-General, and Knight of the Order of St. *Hubert*. His Carriage seems blunt and proud, yet he is familiar with those that are in his Confidence. He has considerable Credit at Court, owing to his Sister's being so long in favour with the Elector.

Julius Augustus Count *de la Marck*, Lieutenant-General, Captain of the hundred *Swissers*, and Knight of St. *Hubert*, is descended of an illustrious Family in the Empire. He spent part of his Youth in the Service of *France*, where his eldest Brother is now actually a Lieutenant-General, Colonel of a foreign Regiment, and a Commander of the Order of the *Holy Ghost*. He has learnt all the *French* Politeness; his

Be-

* I suppose M. *de Globe* is dead; at least he is no longer Grand Marshal, that Post being occupied by the Baron *de Beveren*, a Privy-Counsellor and President of the Ecclesiastic Administration at *Heidelberg*. This Minister does an Honour to the Elector's Choice of his Person.

† The Office of Master of the Horse is vacant; but the Count *de Nesselrod* does the Duties of it, in quality of Vice-Master of the Horse.

MANHEIM. 335

Behaviour resembles the Man of Quality; his Temper is gay, and he loves good Cheer, Joy and Pleasures.

The Count *Egmont de Hatzfeldt* Lieutenant-General, Minister of State, and Secretary at War, comes from one of the best Families in the Empire. This Nobleman is extraordinary civil; his House is open to all Persons of Distinction; he lives very nobly, and both his Lady and himself are very fond of entertaining Foreigners. They were both intrusted to conduct to *Piedmont* the Princess of *Sultzbach* first Wife to *Charles* Prince of *Piedmont**, and discharged their Employments in such a manner that they had the general Approbation of the *Sardinian* Court.

The Barons of *Hildesheim* and *Beveren* are both Ministers of State. The former acquired a very great Reputation in the Negociations that were carry'd on at *Heidelberg* in 1719, for the Church of the *Calvinists* which the Elector had a mind shou'd be Catholic. The second has been Envoy to the King of *Great Britain*. They are both to be valued for their Merit, live very honourably, and make Foreigners welcome.

I could tell you of many other Persons of Birth and Merit employ'd at this Court, but really my Letter would be too tedious. Nevertheless I cannot omit the mention of the Baron *d'Obsten*, whom you saw at *Breslau*, after he had quitted the Service of the *Czar*. He is settled here, but has no Character. He and all his Family are become of our Communion. He has a considerable Pension from the Elector, and is generally very well esteem'd. His Son, who is a Captain, is a young Gentleman of Merit, and his Daughters are young Ladies highly to be esteem'd for their good Behaviour and Politeness.

The

* The present King of *Sardinia*.

The Count *de Naſſau-Weilbourg* lives here alſo. His Birth would engage me to give you an Account of him tho' I were not induc'd to it by the Conſideration of his Merit. This Nobleman has an infinite ſhare of it; he is generous, magnificent, genteel, and civil, knowing what Family he is deſcended from; but knowing it for no other reaſon than to diſcharge all the Obligations of it. He is the Ornament of this Court, tho' he is not in the Service of the Elector. His Father was Velt-Marſhal, and Commander in Chief of the *Palatine* Troops during the Reign of the late Elector *John-William*. The Count I am ſpeaking of was Envoy Extraordinary from the Elector to the Court of *France* during the Minority of *Lewis* XV. He then went often to the Royal Palace to pay his court to the Regent's Mother, and there it was that I knew him; for that Lady and the whole Court of *France* had a very great Value for him. That Princeſs ſpeaking of him one day to me, ſaid ſhe was very glad that he was a Count of *Naſſau*; for indeed, ſaid ſhe, he deſerves to bear a great Name*.

There are amiable People here of both Sexes who are very ſociable, ſo that 'tis a Stranger's own fault if he miſſes of Amuſement here; for ſuch are generally treated very civilly. As for my own part, I have received ſo many Courteſies from the Elector, and ſo many Favours from his Court that I ſhall for ever acknowledge them.

The Nobility maintain a Company of *French* Comedians who act three times a Week upon a very little Theatre, but both the Townſmen and Foreigners pay. Tho' this Company, of which the Count *de la*

---

* General *Iſſelbach* Commander in Chief of the *Palatine* Troops, and Governor of *Manheim*, dying in *Auguſt* 1734, the Elector gave the Command of his Troops to the Count *de Naſſau-Weilbourg*, and the Government of *Manheim* to the Baron *de Zobel*.

la Marck has the Direction is not the beſt, yet 'tis a pleaſure to go to it for the ſake of ſeeing Company. In the time of the late Princeſs there were a thouſand Pleaſures which there are not now, ſo that her Death is ſtill lamented.

The Elector's Revenues are reckon'd at two Millions of Crowns. You may rate them more or leſs, 'tis no matter; for my own part, I affirm nothing, being not willing to imitate the Marquis *de Breton-Villiers*, who in his Memoirs of the Regency values the Revenues of all the Princes of the Univerſe with as much aſſurance as if he had been Superintendant of every one's Finances. The Elector has about 7 or 8000 Soldiers, excluſive of his Guards. His beſt Places are *Manheim*, *Juliers*, and *Duſſeldorp*. The three Religions tolerated in the Empire have Churches here, and the *Jews* a large Synagogue. They are very numerous at this Place, and two thirds of the Houſes belong to them, as being either built by them, or mortgag'd to 'em. Some of them are very rich, and drive a great Trade with the *Jews* at *Metz*, *Frankfort* and *Amſterdam*. 'Tis certain that they do a great injury to the Chriſtian Merchants, and that they are not honeſter here than elſewhere.

Don't write to me, if you pleaſe, before I have ſent you my Direction, becauſe I know not whether I ſhall ſtay long enough at *Frankfort*, to which ſome Affairs call me, to receive your Letters.

Juſt now we hear of the Death of Pope *Benedict* XIII. As I never ſaw a Conclave, and am in the Humour of Travelling, I have an inclination to take a tour to *Rome*. I ſhall not reſolve on it till I come to *Frankfort*. Which way ſoever I go you ſhall be inform'd, and I will not fail to deſire your Commands. Mean time I am always very ſincerely, *&c.*

LETTER XXI.

SIR,   *Frankfort, March* 21. 1730.

AT my Departure from *Manheim* I pass'd the *Rhine* over a Bridge of Boats, and in three Hours time arrived at FRANCKENDAHL, which was formerly fortified, but after having suffered by the general Conflagration in the *Palatinate*, was dismantled by the Peace of *Nimeguen*, and so it has remained ever since. It still bears the Marks of *French* Fury; and a great many Houses that were burn'd have not been rebuilt.

There's the finest Country in the World between *Franckendahl* and WORMS. I came hither at ten o' clock in the Morning, and spent the rest of the Forenoon in seeing what was most remarkable. *Worms* is not the Place now that it was before the *French* burn'd it. Its most wealthy Inhabitants instead of rebuilding their Houses, retir'd to *Frankfort* and *Holland*, so that the Chapter of *Worms*, which is wholly compos'd of Persons of Quality, is now the chief Glory of the Town. The Bishop of it is the Elector * of *Mentz*, who was chose *July* 12, 1694. This Prince has built a new Episcopal Palace, the Contrivance of which

---

* Since this was written the Elector of *Mentz* of the *Palatine* Family of *Newbourg* dying, the Chapter of *Worms* unanimously chose for its Bishop *Francis-George* Count *de Schonborn*, Archbishop and Elector of *Triers*.

which is beautiful. It joins to the Cathedral which is ancient, and built very substantially. The *Lutherans* have just built a fine Church, the Roof of which is painted. In several Compartments there's the History of *Luther*'s pretended Reformation. That Doctor is there represented as appearing before the Dyet of the Empire which met at *Worms An.* 1521. You know that he was cited to it by the Emperor *Charles* V. His Friends, to dissuade him from appearing, put him in mind of *John Huss*, who notwithstanding the Safe-Conduct that had been granted him by the Emperor *Sigismond*, was burnt by a Decree of the Council of *Constance*. *Luther*, without being intimidated, said, that *tho' he was sure to be engag'd with as many Devils as there were Tiles upon the Houses of* Worms, *he was resolv'd to go.* He went thither accordingly, and appear'd the 17th of *April* before the Dyet, where he offer'd, with a Courage deserving a better Cause, to maintain his Doctrine and his Writings against all that should go about to demolish them from the Holy Scriptures.

The City of *Worms* stands in the middle of a fine spacious Plain, abounding with Corn, Vineyards, and Fruit-Trees. A Wine is produced here which is call'd *Lieben-Frauen-Milch,* i. e. *Our Lady's Milk.* The *Rhine* is about three or four hundred Paces from the Town, but 'tis said it formerly ran close by the Walls of it. Which way soever one comes to *Worms,* one perceives at a great Distance the four Towers of the Cathedral which are all built of red Freestone. Two drunken Fellows mistook those Towers one day for Capuchin Fryars. Being in the Country at a pretty good Distance from the Town, as the Sun was going down, one of them said to his Comrade, *We have no Time to lose, the Gates are going to be shut.*——*No matter,* said the other, pointing to the Towers; *Don't you see those Capuchins there*

there before us? They are of the Town, and are going thither as well as we. You are in the right, reply'd the former, *let us drink the good Fryar's Health.* They had a Gourd Bottle full of Wine, of which they drank every Drop, so that they did not overtake the imaginary Capuchins till next Day.

There is not a finer Country than that between *Worms* and OPPENHEIM, a little Town upon an Eminence, on the left Side of the *Rhine*, to which we pass over a flying Bridge. The Road from *Oppenheim* is unpassable for near two Leagues, because 'tis commonly overflown by that River; but afterwards the Way is perfectly good to *Frankfort*. 'Twas very late when I came to this City, but by good luck the People of *Frankfort* who formerly shut their Gates at Sun-set have lately chose to keep them open till ten o'clock, so that for paying a Trifle one may enter the Town.

I know not whether I need give any Account of the City of FRANKFORT. It has been so often describ'd, and is so well known to the World, that I fancy every body knows what sort of Town it is, tho' they have not seen it. *Frankfort* is famous for its two yearly Fairs, *viz.* at *Easter* and *Michaelmas*. It suffer'd much by a great Fire in 1619, but the whole has been since rebuilt, and the Houses are finer than before. There are few Places upon the whole more disagreeable, and few Towns in *Germany* where the Common People are more unpolish'd. The Burghers are not to be match'd for Affectedness, and their Conversation is insupportable. The Magistrates are all *Lutherans*; nevertheless the principal Churches belong to the Catholics. The *Calvinists* may live in the Town, but cannot hold any Employments, and are oblig'd to go for Worship to *Bockenheim* in the County of *Hanau*, and to cause their Children to be baptiz'd in the *Lutheran* Churches. The great Church in which the Ceremony

mony of the Emperor's Coronation is perform'd is dark, and by no means proper for such an august Solemnity. You know that *Aix la Chapelle* is properly the Place set apart for the Coronation of our Emperors, and *Frankfort* for their Election. But since *Maximilian* I. no Emperor has been crown'd at *Aix*. *Frankfort* being situate in the Centre of the Empire is much more commodious for all the Princes, but particularly for the Spiritual Electors and for the Elector Palatine, who may send for their Equipages by Water and return them back by the same Convenience. When *Charles* VI. was crown'd at *Frankfort* in 1711, there was an extraordinary Concourse of Princes and Noblemen. Certain speculative Gentlemen made two Remarks on this Occasion, from which they presag'd two Things. The one was, that the Emperor made his Entrance into this City in close Mourning for the Emperor *Joseph* his Brother; whereupon they said that *Charles* wore Mourning because he foresaw that he should be the last Emperor of his Family. The second was, that as *Charles* return'd from the Church invested with all the Marks of Sovereignty, *Charlemain*'s Sword had like to have dropp'd out of the Scabbard; which the Elector of *Triers* of the *Lorrain* Family observing, catch'd hold of the Sword, and put it in again before it was quite fallen out of the Scabbard. Upon this, the same Calculators of Nativities said it was an Omen that the Emperor would never have a quiet Reign, and that he would always be in a Situation that would oblige him to draw his Sword for his Defence*.

---

* These sharp-sighted Gentlemen were not so happy as to foresee the Marriage which has lately united the Families of *Austria* and *Lorrain*, and brought the latter within View of the Imperial Crown, of which the Elector of *Triers* saving the Sword in the Scabbard seems to have been a remarkable Omen.

As to Persons of great Distinction at *Frankfort*, they are very few. The Chief are the Princess-Dowager of *Nassau-Ousingen*, born Princess of *Lovestein*; the Count *de Degenfeldt (Schomberg)* * Major-General of the King of *Prussia*'s Forces, and a Commander of the Order of the *Black Eagle*; and finally, Madame *la Raugrave* † Daughter of *Charles-Lewis* Elector Palatine: She is the last of the Blood of the Protestant *Palatine* Princes. The Senate of *Frankfort*, in consideration of her great Age, and in respect to her Birth, has granted her the Liberty of keeping a *Calvinist* Chaplain to preach in her own House. Sometimes the Prince *de la Tour* and *Taxis* ‖ Hereditary Post-Master of the Empire resides at *Frankfort*. His House is a great Relief to Foreigners. ** His Princess is a Lady of very great Merit, and has the Soul and Sentiments of a Queen. In the Houses of the Persons that I have mention'd there's an Assembly of both Sexes every Evening; but take them one with another they are very thin except at the Fairs, when there's a vast Resort of Nobility and Gentry. Most of the Electors and Princes of the Empire have their Agents at *Frankfort*, to whom they give the Title of Residents; but those Gentlemen are not a jot the more respected for it, most of them being Merchants of the City of *Frankfort* it self, who sollicit the Title in order to be exempt from the Authority of the Senate, and from the Payment of the Customs, and to qualify themselves

* He was the King of *Prussia*'s Plenipotentiary to the King of *Great Britain*, and is return'd to *Frankfort*, where he is Minister from the King of *Prussia* to the Circle of the *Rhine*.

† This Lady died *An.* 1733.

‖ Since the Author was at *Frankfort* the Prince *Alexander de la Tour* and *Taxis* who married a Princess of *Brandenbourg-Bareith*, resides in this City and is building a House there.

** She is *Louisa-Anne-Frances* of *Lobkowitz*, Daughter to the late Prince *Leopold* of *Lobkowitz*, who was the Empress's chief Steward till 1708.

selves to place over their Doors the Arms of the Princes to whom they send the News-papers.

The Count *de Degenfeldt* makes such a Figure here that he deserves a more particular mention. He is a Nobleman of good Extraction. He is a Native of the *Palatinate*, and spent his Youth in the Service of the Elector-Palatine. He was at that Time a *Calvinist*, but turn'd Catholic. Some Years after, he was reconcil'd to his former Communion, and married in *England* a Cousin of his, the Daughter of the Duke *de Schomberg*, with whom he had a very great Estate. He has also a considerable Expectancy from Madame *la Raugrave* a *Palatine*, his Aunt *. The Relation of M. *de Degenfeldt* to this Lady, brings to my Mind the History of the Mother of Madame *la Raugrave*, who as I have observ'd was a *Degenfeldt*. I have chose to give it you from what was told me by the late Madame of *France*, and from very good Memoirs that have been put into my hands. I have plac'd this History as a Transaction in the Time of the ancient *Germans*; and as I design'd to insert it in a Work which I have undertaken, for want of something else to employ my Time, I chuse to do it by way of a Discourse from Madame the late Electress of *Hanover* to her Daughter-in-law. I herewith send you the entire History, and at the End of it you will find the Key. As I fancy you are quite disengag'd in the Country, I don't apprehend that the reading of it will be Loss of your Time. I rather fear you won't like it; but in either case 'twill be your own Fault; I don't force you to read; you may if you please let *Gertrude* alone.

* This Lady died at *Frankfort* in *Feb.* 1733.

History of GERTRUDE a Marcoman Lady.

THE History of *Gertrude*, of which I propose to give you, my Princess, a Relation, is properly the History of the Extinction of my Family; for the fatal Passion of my Brother King *Malcolm* for that Lady, is in all appearance the Reason that there are no more left in my Family than three Princesses*, and my self.

There was such a Harmony in Sentiments betwixt my Brother and me, that it united us in the strictest Friendship. We had been brought up together in *Belgium* †, where the King my Father had been oblig'd to take refuge, that he might be nearer at hand to receive Succours from *Alfred* King of *Albion*, Father of the Queen my Mother, against the *Romans*, who after a long and bloody War had turn'd him out of his Dominions. That King amus'd him a long while with fair Promises; but the Misunderstanding which there was at that time between him and the States of his Kingdom, added to a certain Indolence in his natural Temper, hinder'd him from seeing the Effect of them; and the King my Father did not live long enough to be witness of the Peace which the *Romans* were at length oblig'd by his Allies to conclude. This was not an advantageous Peace for *Malcolm* my Brother, because in order to obtain it he was oblig'd to yield a part of his Dominions to the Prince of the ‖ *Boyens*, an Ally of the *Romans*, and upon these Terms he was left in quiet possession of the rest.

When

---

* Madame the Abbess of *Maubrisson*, Sister to Madame the Electress of *Hanover*, who is supposed to be the Person that speaks here; Madame the Duchess of *Hanover*, Mother to the Empress *Amelia*, and Madame the Princess of *Condé*.

† At *Rhenen*, a small Town in the Province of *Utrecht*.

‖ The *Upper Palatinate* yielded to the Elector of *Bavaria* by the Treaty of *Westphalia*.

When my Brother saw himself establish'd on the Throne, he thought of marrying. His Ministers propos'd the Princess of the *Catti* as the fittest Match for him, and assur'd him that besides her illustrious Extraction he could not marry a more beautiful Princess, or one of a better Temper. My Brother who only alter'd his Condition for Reasons of State, was willing enough to follow their Advice, and accordingly espous'd her. The Marriage at first prov'd very happy; the Queen his Wife had her share of Beauty, and tho' her Temper was very different from what it had been represented to my Brother, yet she so cunningly disguis'd it for some time that this Prince thought himself very happy in his Choice. But their Agreement was of a short Duration; the Queen's true Humour soon discover'd it self: It appear'd that she was ill-natur'd, and intolerably high-spirited; of an odd sullen Temper, always ready to contradict, and frequently subject to Chagrin, of which she herself knew not the Cause, and which she vented upon all that approach'd her without distinction. The King my Brother was of a Temper quite the reverse: He lov'd Diversions, was civil, affable, naturally gay, beneficent; and I don't speak it out of Partiality in favour of a Brother whose Memory is still dear to me, but I'll be bold to say, that if he had not been quite so choleric, he would have been the most accomplish'd Prince of his Time. Nevertheless he bore with his Wife's ill Humours very patiently at first, and endeavour'd to reclaim her by gentle Usage; but when he saw that all the Pains he took were to no purpose, he resolv'd at length to seek out some other Amusement.

The Beauty of *Gertrude*, Maid of Honour to the Queen his Wife, had for a long time smitten him, but hitherto he had only discover'd his Passion to her by his Glances, for fear of disgusting the Queen.

Gertrude

Gertrude who perceiv'd that my Brother did not look upon her with Indifference, affected to shun every Opportunity that Prince might take of revealing his Love to her. But Fortune favour'd my Brother, who being one day with his Queen in her Apartment, when the Discourse fell upon Jewels, perceiv'd that the Princess had left off wearing a certain Bracelet of which he had made her a Present, and asking her what she had done with it, the Queen told him that she believ'd she had laid it up in a Casket of which she had the Key in her Pocket. She made one of her Maids fetch it, and open'd it, but the Bracelet was not there, at which she seem'd uneasy. This my Brother observ'd, and taking a Pleasure in making her more uneasy, he said to her, tho' in a manner that shew'd he did not think as he spoke, that she had undoubtedly some Gallant in a Corner, to whom she had either given that Bracelet, or who had stole it from her. These Words, tho' deliver'd in jest, made a deep Impression upon the Queen, and as it was her Nature soon to take fire, she was stung to the quick at what he had said, and forgetting the Respect she ow'd to the King her Husband, was in such a Passion with him that she let fall some Words that were very affronting. My Brother who was naturally mettlesome and fiery, and far from expecting any such Treatment, made her answer, that if she continued to forget herself after that manner, he would find ways and means to humble her. Upon this he went out of the Room abruptly, and passing through the Antichamber, met the fair *Gertrude*. Such was his Disgust that instead of being upon the reserve as he had been, he had a long Conversation with her, and found her so sprightly and good-natur'd that he was compleatly charm'd with her. He declar'd his Love to her, and she was so artful that
tho'

tho' she gave him no Hopes, yet she did not rebuff him.

When my Brother was retir'd, *Gertrude* went into the Apartment of the Queen her Mistress, who plac'd her whole Confidence in her. That Princess no sooner saw her but she made a thousand Complaints of the King's Treatment of her. *Gertrude* seem'd to sympathize in her Resentment, and believing that the Queen could not fail to know that the King had talk'd with her in the Antichamber, she told her that the Prince having met her in her Passage gave her an angry Account of what had passed; and that she had done all she could to pacify him, but to no purpose: At the same time she blam'd the King's Proceeding; and encourag'd by the Liberty which the Queen gave her, told her that if she who was but a private Gentlewoman was so treated by any Husband, she would never pardon him tho' he were a King. She added several other Sayings which instead of pacifying this silly Queen, did but exasperate her the more.

In the mean time, *Malcolm*, who was impatient to know the Success of his Amour, wrote a Letter to *Gertrude* which he sent her by one of his chief Domestics, together with a rich Diamond Equipage. But the artful *Gertrude* whose Aim was to draw on his Passion, rather than to gratify it, was far from yielding to his first Attacks, and sent him back the Diamonds, tho' with a modest and respectful Answer, wherein she desir'd him to talk no more to her of Love. My Brother was too deeply smitten to be repuls'd; he doubled his Presents, was assiduous, and eager in his Courtship; and as 'tis very rare for a King of his amiable Personage to meet with long Resistance, *Gertrude* abated of her Shyness by degrees, and at length discovered that she was not insensible of Love. Their Correspondence which did not exceed the Bounds of Honour, was

kept

kept secret for a considerable time, but made the greater Blaze when it was known. *Malcolm* being one day with his Wife, happen'd, without perceiving it, to drop a Letter which the Queen took up, and found to be the Hand-writting of *Gertrude*. The Letter being written in *Latin* made the Queen the more curious to know what was in it; and she gave it to her Cousin, Prince *Valamir*, desiring him to unfold the Contents of it to her. This Prince was so unwise as to satisfy her Curiosity, and acquainted her that *Gertrude* by this Letter assur'd the King that he had gain'd her Heart. You will easily imagine how much the Queen was ruffled when she heard of this Intrigue: She could not contain herself; and without giving ear to the Arguments made use of by *Valamir*, she ran immediately to *Gertrude*'s Apartment in the Palace, who by good luck was gone abroad. The Queen thinking her Casket was in *Gertrude*'s Closet caused it to be broke open, and finding it there, open'd it, and took out all the Letters, of which several that appear'd to be from the King her Husband left her no room to doubt of that Prince's extraordinary Passion for *Gertrude*, and of the Intimacy there was between them. My Brother was quickly inform'd of what the Queen had been doing, but conceal'd his Uneasiness, shew'd his Wife no manner of Resentment, and only sent a Caution to *Gertrude* not to return to the Palace. *Malcolm*'s Silence deceiv'd the Queen, who indeed was not a Lady of very great Penetration, so that she flatter'd herself the King might possibly be ignorant of the Outrage she had committed; and upon this Supposition she thought it her best way to dissemble her Hatred and Wrath against *Gertrude*. She pretended therefore to be very uneasy for fear of what had happen'd to her, caus'd a Search to be made for her several days, and seem'd very much dejected at her

Absence.

Abfence. She hoped by all thefe Demonftrations of Friendfhip to decoy her back to the Palace, in order then to be compleatly reveng'd of her.

Thus Matters ftood when the King of the *Suevi*, the Brother-in-law of the Queen my Sifter-in-law, came to Court with the Queen his Wife. This Prince having obferv'd the Queen's Melancholy on feveral occafions, afk'd her the reafon of it one day as they fate at Table. 'You muft not be furpriz'd, 'faid *Malcolm*, to fee the Queen my Wife out of 'temper; 'tis her common Infirmity, and very of- 'ten fhe her felf knows not the caufe of it. My Ail- 'ment is but too real (reply'd the Queen in a great 'Pet;) and (then addreffing herfelf to her Hufband) 'faid fhe, it does not at all become you whofe dif- 'honourable Amours have been the only Caufe of 'my Diforder, to infinuate as if it were but imagi- 'nary.' This Anfwer made in fo public a manner, fo nettled my Brother that he turn'd pale for meer Vexation, and not being able to curb his Paffion, forgot his Dignity fo far as to ftrike her; upon which the unfortunate Princefs rofe from Table, and retir'd in Tears to her own Apartment. My Brother, whofe Paffion was always as foon over as it was eafily kindled, was forry in a very few moments after for what he had done, made his Excufes to the King and Queen of the *Suevi*, and rifing from Table, went with them to his Wife's Apartment, where he afk'd her pardon for what had pafs'd. This Atonement, which the Queen did not expect fo foon, touch'd her to the quick: The King and fhe embrac'd each other, and exchang'd their Promifes to forget as well as to forgive every Offence. But would you believe it? that fickle, fantaftical Creature my Sifter-in-law chang'd her mind all on a fudden, and when her Hufband came in the Evening with an intention to fpend the Night with her, fhe abfolutely refus'd to let him bed with her unlefs he

would

would resolve to deliver up *Gertrude* to her. *Malcolm*, who was still asham'd at what he had done in his last Fury, receiv'd so violent a Proposition with more Patience than he would have done upon another Occasion. He endeavour'd by fair Words to pacify his Wife, assuring her that nothing criminal had ever pass'd between him and *Gertrude*, and that tho' he had corresponded with the Girl by Letters, it was not out of any Love he had for her, so much as to know whether it was true that she wrote as good *Latin* as he had been told she did. Tho' this Speech of his was not very probable, yet as People are easily inclin'd to believe what they wish to be true, the Queen suffer'd herself to be at last persuaded, and was reconciled to her Husband without insisting any farther on the Sacrifice she at first demanded.

The Emperor being come to spend some Time at *Pluibourg*, summon'd an Assembly thither of the Princes of the Empire. My Brother went thither with the Queen his Wife; but the Consequence was that they were more embroil'd than ever; and my Sister-in-law was so unadvised as to let *Cæsar* and his Court be Witnesses of certain Brawls, which for her own Interest as well as her Husband's, she ought to have carefully confin'd within the Limits of her own Houshold. 'Tis true that my Brother had no very great Respect for her, and he lov'd *Gertrude* more than ever. Being hindred by a slight Indisposition from going to *Montpayen* where he kept her at one of his Houses, not a Day pass'd but he sent an Express to know how she did, and the Queen's ill Temper, who no doubt had better have try'd good-natur'd Methods to reclaim him, only incens'd him against her, and made him the fonder of *Gertrude*.

The Assembly of the Princes of *Germany* being over, and the Emperor return'd to *Rome*, my Brother

ther set out for *Montpayen* the Capital of his Kingdom, and gave orders for his Queen to follow him next Day. But for a Reason which I never could dive into, the Princess instead of obeying him stay'd a Month longer at *Pluibourg*, without vouchsafing to let the King her Husband know the Reason of her delay; and not only so, but when she came to *Montpayen*, she had the Assurance to go with a bold Face to her Husband's Apartment, without knowing how he would take it: But the Prince who had just Reason to be angry, foreseeing that she was like enough to take such a step, had given orders to refuse her Entrance; wherefore she was oblig'd to retire to her Apartment, whither a Captian of the Guards came in a Moment after, to tell her from the King that she was a Prisoner.

This unhappy Princess bore her Disgrace very weakly. She repented, but too late, of having been so imprudent as to contravene the Orders of the King her Husband; and hoping to work upon his Good-nature, she wrote him a most submissive Letter, begging his pardon for her Disobedience, and intreating him to restore her to her Liberty. My Brother sent her an Answer, wherein he only gave her the Title of the Princess of *Cattia*. He told her, 'that having consider'd the Disagreement there 'was betwixt his Temper and her's, he resolved to 'be divorc'd from her, and that she would do well 'herself to give her Consent to it; which if she did 'with a good Grace, he would restore her to her Liberty and settle a Revenue on her suitable to her 'Rank.'

This Answer was a Thunder-stroke to my Sister-in-law; she rav'd and tore like a mad Woman. She was for a long while like one out of her Senses, but recovering them at length by the help of her Women, and consulting with those that had the greatest share of her Confidence, she sent the King
word

word that he was Master, and might make use of his Authority, but that she would never consent to the Divorce.

My Brother who had fix'd his Resolution, and saw no other way to get possession of *Gertrude* than by marrying that Girl who had presum'd to set so high a Price upon her Favours, took off the Mask, notify'd his Design to the Court, and in a few days after, the Marriage was perform'd in the manner that you know is practis'd in *Germany* by Princes who marry beneath themselves, which excludes the Children by such *Venter* from succeeding to the Father's Estate. As soon as he was marry'd, he restor'd the Queen to her Liberty, and acquainted her, 'That by the Advice and Consent of the Priests 'of his Kingdom whom he had caused to be as- 'sembled, he had marry'd *Gertrude*. That the 'Thing being done and past remedy, he hoped she 'would resolve to make her self easy. That how- 'ever, he would always treat her as a Princess; 'that she should be welcome to continue in her A- 'partment at the Palace; that she should have her 'Guards to attend her, and that he had set apart a 'sufficient Fund for her Maintenance; but that he 'expected she would be so complaisant as to ac- 'knowledge *Gertrude* hereafter for the lawful 'Queen.'

My Sister-in-law who then saw that her Disgrace was infallible, gave her self up to Complaints and Tears, wrote to the King her Husband in the most moving Language, and implor'd the assistance of the King her Brother: But all was to no purpose; she was oblig'd to submit to her Misfortune, and to be patient under an Affliction which she had partly brought upon her self by her Folly.

While all this pass'd, my Brother was at one of his Seats not far * from his Capital, where he caus'd
Gertrude

---

* At *Schwetzingen*, a League from *Heidelberg*.

Gertrude to be treated as a Queen, and not long after carried her to *Montpayen* where the sight of her Royalty was a fresh Mortification to the Queen my Sister-in-law. However, the unfortunate Princess not yet despairing of the means of reclaiming her Husband, was resolv'd to make the last Attempt to turn that Prince's Heart. She dress'd herself in the most gay and rich Apparel that she could get, and taking her Children along with her, went to meet the King her Husband in the Room next to the Hall where he was at Table with *Gertrude*, and thro' which he must necessarily return. When he appear'd, she threw herself with her Children at his Feet, clasp'd his Knees, conjur'd him with Tears in her Eyes to look with Pity on an unhappy Princess whom he had formerly thought fit to make his Wife, and to consider that the Affront he put upon her by divorcing her, would be a Reproach to those very Children of whom he had been so fond. My Brother seem'd to be melted at so moving a Spectacle, look'd for some Moments on his Wife and Children with Tears in his Eyes, and he was just ready to raise her from the Ground, when *Gertrude* who was at his Heels, fearing what might be the Consequence of the Confusion that she saw him in, talk'd earnestly to him in the *Tuscan* Language, saying, *Remember*, my Lord, *what you promis'd me*. These few Words wrought so much on the unsteady Mind of my Brother that he only lifted up his Hands to Heaven and went on, shewing by the Trouble he was under, how little he was Master of his Reason upon this Occasion. The Queen my Sister-in-law remain'd for a while speechless, but Fury and Despair quickly seiz'd her Soul. She rose up and ran into her Closet, where snatching up a Dagger* she came back again with an Inten-

Vol. I.   A a   tion

* 'Twas a Pistol which the Count *de Hebenlo* snatch'd from her.

tion to stick it into her Rival's Heart. But the Rage she was in having so confounded her that she had not a Thought of concealing that Instrument of her Revenge, it was perceiv'd by one of the chief Courtiers who pluck'd it from her just as she was going into the Closet where my Brother was with *Gertrude*. That Prince hearing a Noise so near him ran out, and demanded what was the matter. ' 'Tis I, (said the Queen very couragiously) ' who was coming to ' revenge my self and you too on the Monster which ' disunites us; but that Traytor there (said she, ' pointing to the Man that had wrested the Dagger ' out of her Hands) has depriv'd me of the only ' Opportunity that I could call a Pleasure.——Prin' cess, (said the King to her very calmly) don't in' dulge your self any longer in such extravagant ' Passions, if you are unwilling that I should use ' you roughly.' Then he retir'd with *Gertrude*, and my Sister-in-law return'd to her Apartment in a Temper which you may easily imagine.

Clodius, who now governs the Empire, being at that time proclaim'd Emperor, this Princess made her Complaints to him, and desir'd him to reconcile *Malcolm* to her. But *Cæsar* having excus'd himself, my Sister-in-law who could no longer bear the Presence of her Rival, retir'd to the King her Brother, there to wait the End of her Misfortunes. My Brother liv'd afterwards very lovingly with his new Spouse, and had by her four Sons and as many Daughters. But Death having at last robb'd him of a Person so dear to him, the Prince was so afflicted for the Loss of her, that he spent two Years in continual Sorrow, and at length himself paid the same Tribute to Nature.

He

---

her, and shot into the Air from the Window. But here it was absolutely necessary to call it a Dagger, Fire-Arms being not known at the Time of which this History bears date.

He left but one Son and a Daughter by his lawful Spouse who surviv'd him some Years. The King my Nephew was marry'd, but he was of such a melancholy Temper, his Humour was so different from the Queen's, and there was so little Love betwixt them, that he died without Issue. With him I have seen my Family utterly extinct, its Dominions transferr'd to the Power of a Prince who is hardly related to us, and my Country abandon'd to the most dismal Desolation. For my Niece having marry'd *Meroveus*, Brother to *Ariovisto* King of the *Gauls*, the latter who is an ambitious Prince and goes to War upon every the least Pretence, asserted the Rights of his Sister-in-law without Delay, and pleading that she ought to succeed to the Inheritance of the King her Brother, notwithstanding the *Salic* Law establish'd in *Germany*, he sent a formidable Army into the Dominions of my deceased Nephew, where the *Gauls* at first meeting with no Resistance, committed enormous Cruelties, and extended their Fury even to the Violation of the Tomb of the Kings my Ancestors, whose dead Bodies were stripp'd and exposed to the Caprice of the unruly Soldiers: Calamities, which perhaps would never have happen'd, had it not been for my Brother's fatal Passion for *Gertrude*; because in all Appearance if he had liv'd in a good Understanding with his lawful Spouse, he would have had more Children by her, and I should not have had the Vexation to see the Throne of my Fathers posses'd by a foreign Family.

KEY to the History of GERTRUDE.

Albion, England.
Alfrede I. James I. *King of* England.
Ariovisto, Lewis XIV.
Belgium, Holland.

Boyens, (Prince of) the Elector of Bavaria.
Catti, (Princess of) the Princess of Hesse-Cassel.
Cæsar, the Emperor.
Clodius, the Emperor Leopold.
Germania, Germany.
Gertrude, the Baroness of Degenfeldt.
Malcolm, Charles-Lewis *Elector* Palatine.
Meroveus, Philip *of* France, *Duke of* Orleans, *Brother to* Lewis XIV.
Montpayen, Heidelberg.
Pluibourg, Ratisbon.
Romans, the Imperialists.
Rome, Vienna.
Suevi, (King of) the Margrave of Baden-Dourlach.

End of the History of Gertrude.

I have not scrupled to give you this History, because all the Persons who are Subjects of it are dead. I wrote it very much in haste, for the Diversion of the Princess d' A——, so that you must not be surpriz'd if you don't meet with all that Exactness which there ought to be in this little Narrative; tho' I must tell you again that every Tittle of it is true, so that you may read it as a History, and not as a Romance.

I have fix'd my Resolution, and now am setting out for *Rome*; therefore please to direct to me at *Venice*. I go to-morrow to a great Hunting-Match that is to be at *Darmstadt,* where I shall stay two Days: From thence I shall go and spend two more with the Count *de Hanau*; and then will I begin my Pilgrimage to the Holy Places. I am most entirely,

&c.

LETTER XXII.

SIR, *Munich, April 2. 1730.*

SINCE you received my last I have done and seen a great many Things. On the 23d of *March* I set out from *Frankfort* for DARMSTADT, the Capital of the upper County of *Catzenellenbogen*, and the Residence of *Ernest-Lewis* Landgrave of *Hesse-Darmstadt*[*].

This Town is extremely small, and only enclosed with Pallisadoes. If the Prince's Palace had been finish'd according to its Model, it would have been one of the greatest and most magnificent in *Europe*, and there might have been Lodgings for the Emperor, and all the nine Electors of the Empire. It would have been bigger than the Town, and have

[*] *Philip* the Magnanimous, Landgrave of *Hesse-Cassel*, was in 1518 Sovereign of all the Country of *Hesse*. He died in 1567, and left four Sons who shar'd his Dominions and form'd the four Branches of *Hesse-Cassel, Hesse-Marpurg, Hesse-Rheinfels* and *Hesse-Darmstadt*. The Landgraves *Lewis de Marpurg* and *Philip de Rheinfels* had no Issue, but their Nephew *Maurice* of *Cassel* having 18 Children, *Earnest* one of the Sons reviv'd a Branch of *Rheinfels* which was divided into those of *Rotenburg* and *Vanfried*, that are still subsisting. The Posterity of *George* I, Landgrave of *Darmstadt* was altogether as fruitful, and form'd the Branches of *Darmstadt, Butzbach, Hombourg,* and *Lauterbach*, some of which are extinct. The Landgrave-Regent is one of the sixteen Children of the Landgrave *Lewis* VI. Great-Grandson of *George* I. There are at present these six Branches of the Family of *Hesse*, viz. 1. *Hesse-Cassel*, 2. *Hesse-Philipstall*, 3. *Hesse-Rheinfels-Rotenbourg*, 4. *Hesse-Rheinfels-Vanfried*, 5 *Hesse-Darmstadt*, 6. *Hesse-Hombourg*.

cost immense Sums: That Part which is finish'd makes a very grand Appearance. But all those magnificent Works which the Landgrave Regent at first carried on with very great Vigour are entirely discontinu'd, and there's no Appearance that they will ever be taken in hand again. The old Palace is much more commodious than it seems to be; its Apartments being convenient, and richly furnish'd. The Landgrave does not live in the Palace, but leads a very retir'd Life in a little House upon the Square, where he is never seen but upon Sundays and Holidays. He amuses himself in turning of Ivory, making Chymical Experiments, and in Drawing. He loves Hunting above all things whatsoever. He delights in Agriculture, and in Music, and it may strictly be said that he is never unemploy'd. He has very great Knowledge natural and acquir'd. He has seen a great many Countries, and tho' sixty Years of Age he still looks well, and his grey Hairs, not to call them white, give him a venerable Air. He sits a Horse very well, walks well, and seems to enjoy perfect Health. His Wife was *Dorothy* of *Brandenbourg-Onoltzbach*, who died in 1705. They say that he lately married N—— *de Spiegel* the Widow of Count *Seibelsdorf* a Lieutenant-General in the Service of *Bavaria*. Be that as it will, the Marriage is not public, and the Lady still goes by the Name of her former Husband by whom she has Children. 'Tis true that the Landgrave pays her very great Distinction, and indeed she is very amiable.

This Prince commonly dines at a little Table spread only for four People; but on Sundays and Holidays he goes to the Palace, and dines with his Son at a Table cover'd for sixteen Guests, and sups with the Ladies who are never seen at Court but upon those Days. 'Tis a very hard matter to come at the Speech of the Landgrave, and much more to that of his only Son the hereditary Prince. The Hunting-Officers are the only Persons that have the Privilege of Access to them; for which reason this is not one of the most entertaining Courts; and a Man is under a necessity of throwing himself into the Town, where indeed there are a great many People of Merit who are civil to Foreigners.

The hereditary Prince *Lewis*, the only Son of the Landgrave, who was born the 5th of *April* 1691, is a handsome Man, has a noble Air, dances well, mounts a Horse well, has Vivacity, Spirit, and Politeness, but is often thoughtful, melancholy, and goes for Retirement to the Woods, where he is passionately fond of Hunting; but is apt to create himself Uneasiness, and does not know how to dissemble it. Tho' he has all the Qualities necessary to shine in Company, yet he sees but very little. He married *Charlotta-Christina* of *Hanau*, who dying in 1726, left him three Sons and two Daughters, the eldest of which was then seven Years of Age. By virtue of this Marriage the Prince is Heir to the Count of *Hanau*'s Estate in *Alsace*, and to all his Freeholds in general, which will be a very rich Succession.

Nevertheless the Court of *Darmstadt* is very numerous. The Landgrave has a great many Counsellors of State, Gentlemen of the Bedchamber and Court, and a greater Number still of Officers of the Venery, and Huntsmen. There is not a Province in *Germany* more proper for Hunting, nor in *Europe* where there are more Deer. 'Tis a flat even Country, and a gravelly Soil interspersed with Woods thro' which there are cut noble Roads. I have seen the Deer come up close to the Pallisadoes of the Town, and at their Rutting-time I have heard them cry as I lay in my Bed. This great plenty of Deer is extremely troublesome to the Peasants who are abroad day and night to watch their Fields. The

Landgrave and the hereditary Prince are so jealous of their Game that they reckon it as bad a Crime as Murder for any one to kill a Deer; and tho' 'tis an establish'd Custom among almost all Sovereigns to punish with Severity all those that kill a Creature which God however certainly created for the Use of all Mankind, yet there is no Prince who observes this Law more strictly than the Landgrave.

I cannot give you a more certain Account of the Revenues of this Prince than of those of all the other Sovereigns. 'Tis said that he has 5 or 600000 Florins *per Ann.* I am not very well inform'd of the number of his Troops, for I have only seen his Regiment of Guards which is in very compleat Order. His Horse-Guards are also very fine Troops, and commanded by the General *Miltitz*, who is at the same time Grand Marshal of the Court, the Honours of which he performs in a very handsome manner.

Tho' the Soil at *Darmstadt* is very gravelly, it produces excellent Pulse. I have seen Asparagus at the Landgrave's Table, three of which weigh'd a Pound, tho' indeed they were not altogether so nice. I remember that in a former Journey which I made hither in the Month of *December*, there were brought to the Landgrave in several Pots of Porcellain, a Dwarf Cherry-Tree laden with Cherries; Strawberry-Plants, an Almond-Tree, and in short, the Fruits of all the Seasons.

The intended Hunting-Match, for what reason I know not, was put off; and as I came hither only to see it, I staid but one Day and went to HANAU. The Count and the Princess of *Hanau* were but lately return'd from *Alsace*. The Town of *Hanau* is situate on a large Plain to the right of the *Main*. 'Tis divided into two Wards, the old and the new Town: The latter is much bigger than the former: It was built by the *Walloon* Protestants, who, during

ring the Duke of *Alva*'s Persecution under *Philip* II. King of *Spain*, quitted the *Netherlands* and came to settle at *Hanau*, which they fortify'd, and built in such a manner that all the Streets run parallel. The Count keeps several Companies in pay, from which he makes Detachments for the Quota he is oblig'd to furnish, as a Member of the Circle of of the *Upper Rhine*.

The *Walloons* who are settled at *Hanau* have established several Manufactures there, especially Woollen Stuffs. The *Calvinists*, the *Lutherans*, and the *Jews* are tolerated here, and as for us Catholics, we may go to Mass where we please.

The Count's Palace is in the old Town: 'Tis an ancient Building, and makes no great Appearance, but the Apartments are commodious, and very richly furnish'd. The Count has a very pretty Pleasure-House a quarter of a League from *Hanau*, call'd PHILIPSRUHE, *i. e.* (*Philip's Repose*) and built by the late Count *de Hanau*, Brother to the Count Regent[*]. 'Twas at this Seat that I found the Count of *Hanau*. There was a very numerous Attendance, and I heartily wish'd I could have staid there a few days. Few Princes in the Empire live more elegantly than the Count *de Hanau*. The Lady who directs the whole Houshold, and keeps all things in wonderful Order is the Princess [†] who is of the Family of *Brandenbourg-Anspach*, and Sister to the Queen of *England*. At this Court you have all the Liberty than can be desired. When you first come a Chamber is provided for your Lodging, and a Footman order'd to wait on you. Every Morning an Officer comes to know what you will please to have for Breakfast; and there's every Thing to be had that you call for. If afterwards you have a mind to go out a Hunting, you send to the Great Huntsman

---

[*] This Count died in 1736.
[†] She died at *Hanau* after a very long Illness.

man for a Guide and to the Count for Horses out of his Stables. If you come back too late for Dinner at Court, you are serv'd very elegantly in your own Apartment. In the Evening when you are retir'd from Company, a Butler takes care to provide you with Wine and Beer. The Servants of Foreigners diet with those of the Count. His own Table which is commonly for eighteen Guests is served as well as most, and a second Table is serv'd with the same Magnificence. The Count has a very great Family, and lives every way like a Prince; and indeed 'tis his own Fault that he is not one, for he has had the Imperial Diploma for it a long while, but he does not care to make use of it; saying, he had rather be the first Count than the lowest Prince. He is the last Male of his Family. After his Death the County of *Hanau* relapses to the Landgrave of *Hesse-Cassel*, according to the Treaty of Confraternity made between the several Families of *Saxony*, *Hesse*, and *Hanau*, which imports that the said Families shall succeed one another. The King of *Poland* as Elector of *Saxony* ought to have had his Share in the Succession to the County of *Hanau*, but his Majesty by a Treaty yielded his Rights to the Landgrave of *Cassel*. As to the Lands in *Alsace*, and the Freeholds, they revert, as I told you before, to the Children of the hereditary Prince of *Darmstadt*.

The Count of *Hanau* seems to be much older than he is in reality. He is a very civil Nobleman, and Hunting is a Diversion of which he is extremely fond, so that to kill a Deer upon his Lands is an unpardonable Crime; and the lesser Game, such as Rabbits, Hares, and Partridges, are equally his Care. All these Creatures spoil the Fields; but they serve for the Count's Amusement, while the poor Peasant is oblig'd to pay his Tax, and dares not speak a Word.

From

From *Hanau* to Munich I never made a stop; but after having travell'd thro' *Wurtzbourg, Nurembourg,* and *Augsbourg* arrived here last night, and propose to set out again to-morrow, and after two or three days stay at *Saltzbourg* shall proceed by the way of *Tirol* to *Venice,* where I beg you would not fail to let me hear from you.

I am just come from attending the Obsequies of *Theresa-Cunegunda Sobieski* Electoress of *Bavaria,* Mother to the Elector. This Princess died lately at *Venice,* to which City she retir'd eighteen Months ago, and her Corpse is forthwith expected to be interr'd in the Tomb of the Electoral Family. She has left, as 'tis said, near six millions of Florins, which, since she has made no Will, are to be equally shar'd between the four Princes her Sons. She has moreover left a Daughter who is a Nun in a Convent of this City. In 1719, when she took the Habit, I was present. She chose this retir'd Life against the Will of her Father the Elector, who did all he could to dissuade her from it; and she liv'd in great Reputation for her Piety. But to return to the Obsequies of the Electoress: The Elector and Electoress assisted at them, together with the Elector of *Cologne,* the Duke *Ferdinand,* the Bishop of *Freisingen,* the Duchess *Ferdinand,* and the two Princes her Sons. These Princes had Cowls upon their Heads, and great Cloaks, which is not one of the most becoming Dresses. The Family of *Bavaria* observes a very singular Custom, which is, never to give a black Livery, nor to line their Coaches. I think this reasonable enough, for it does not look very well in a pompous Funeral.

I am, &c.

LETTER XIII.

Saltzbourg, April 2, 1730.

SIR,

AT my Departure from *Munich* I went and din'd at *Eversberg*, a Village belonging to the Reverend Fathers the Jesuits, who have a House there which is a large one, and that's all 'tis good for. I went and lay at WASSERBOURG a Town of *Bavaria* built upon a Rock, so encompass'd with the River *Inn* that 'tis a perfect Peninsula. Mountains and Rocks hang over this Town as if they wou'd crush it, and indeed the Place is not worth much Description. It was settled as a Dowry on the Electoress *Theresa-Cunigunda Sobieski* who died last Month, but this Princess would never live in it, nor indeed do I know any other Prince that would.

After having pass'd the *Inn* * over a very slender wooden Bridge I climb'd a high Mountain, got down another, ascended a third, and so I travell'd all the way up Hill and down Hill till I came within two Leagues of *Saltzbourg*, where the Country becomes more passible.

The City of SALTZBOURG as well as the whole Archbishoprick takes its Name from the River *Saltz* which passes thro' the City and Country. It rises in *Tirol* and loses it self in the *Inn*. The Mountains that are about

---

* This River rises in *Tirol* a little above *Infpruc*, becomes navigable at *Halle*, and loses itself in the *Danube* near *Passau*.

about the Town make it not near so broad as 'tis long, tho' take it all together 'tis not a large Town. 'Tis very well fortify'd, and has a Castle which standing on an Eminence forms as it were a Citadel. 'Tis furnish'd with a good Arsenal, and all manner of Ammunition, and I have been assur'd that of Gunpowder alone there are no less than 20000 Quintals. Some Years ago when I was here, Lightning fell so near this Magazine that it wanted but half a Foot of penetrating to the Powder, which if it had touch'd I fancy I shou'd never have wrote to you more. There is always a Guard of fifty Men at the Castle, and the Garison of the Town consists of 600 Men who are lodg'd in the Caserns.

The City of *Saltzbourg* contains finer Edifices than many great Towns. It has a magnificent Cathedral which was consecrated the 24th of *September* 1628, by an Archbishop who was of the Family of the Counts *de Lodron*. 'Tis a vast Structure of Free stone, and has a stately Front which may be reckon'd the compleatest in *Germany*. The Italian Architect by whom it was directed has very much copy'd the Front of St. *Agnes*'s Church in the Square of *Navona* at *Rome*. It has four Marble Statues bigger than the Life, which represent St. *Peter*, St. *Paul*, St. *Rupert*, and St. *Virgilius*, of whom the two latter were the first Archbishops of this See. The whole Church is adorn'd in the inside with Pilastres of the *Corinthian* Order. 'Tis built in the Form of a Cross with a very high Dome which separates the Nave from the Choir. The high Altar which is at the bottom of the Choir is of Marble, as are the two Chapels that form the Cross: The Pavement of the Church is of great Squares of Marble of various Colours. 'Tis pity there was not more Inlet for Light, the Dome being the only lightsome Part of it. But as the Church is magnificent the

Orna-

Ornaments of the high Altar are more so. Upon the Grand Festivals it bears a Sun of Gold adorn'd with precious Stones to the Value of 100000 Crowns, a great Cross of massy Gold, and four golden Candlesticks. The Front of the Altar, and the Tabernacle are of massy Silver of excellent Workmanship.

St. *Rupert* surnam'd the Apostle of *Bavaria* was the first Bishop of *Saltzbourg* in 582. *Leo* III. whom the Church honour'd as a Saint, erected this Bishoprick into an Archbishoprick in favour of St. *Arnould*, in the Year 798. He had for Suffragans the Bishops of *Freisingen*, *Ratisbon*, *Passau*, *Briken*, *Gurck*, *Chiemsee*, *Seggau*, and *Lavant*.

The Archbishop has a Right of Nomination to the four last Bishopricks; only the Nomination to the Bishoprick of *Gurck* is alternative between this Prelate and the Emperor, as Archduke of *Austria*. The four Bishops bear the Title of Princes of the Empire, and enjoy all the Prerogatives annexed to that high Dignity. Notwithstanding this, the Archbishop never gives them the Preference, and when he talks to them, only compliments them with the Title of *Euer Freuntschaft*, i. e. *Your Friendship*. Service is perform'd in this Metropolis according to the Usage observ'd in St. *Peter*'s Church at *Rome*. The Chapter is compos'd of the Archbishop, a Provost, a Dean, and twenty four Canons, all Men of Quality, who are only oblig'd to four Months Residence, and the rest of the Time they may go where they please. Both the Provost and Dean have the Crosier and Mitre*. The Archbishop, as well as the Elector of *Cologn*, has the Privilege of dressing in the Habit of a Cardinal. This Prelate has the Directorship of the College of Princes at the Dyet of the Empire alternatively with the Archduke of *Austria*. He is moreover *Legatus natus*
&

---

* The Provost and Dean of *Passau* enjoy the same Prerogative.

& *perpetuus* of the Holy See, and Primate of *Germany*. His Titles are these, 'Leopold, by the
'Grace of God, Archbishop of *Saltzbourg*, and
'Prince of the Empire, perpetual Legate of the Holy
'Apostolic See of *Rome*, Primate of *Germany*, de-
'scended of the illustrious Family of the Barons of
'*Firmian*.'

The Archbishop at his coming to the See must pay 100000 Crowns to *Rome* for the Pall, but the Country generally raises it for him, besides making a free Gift of the like Sum to its new Prince. The Revenues of this Prelate are about 1500000 Florins a Year. The very Salt which is carried into *Bavaria* and *Swabia* brings him in 30000 Crowns. He is absolute Master of all his Revenues, and accountable to no body for what he lays out. The present Archbishop is of *Tirol*, of a distinguish'd Family, but not favour'd much by Fortune. He was born the 26th of *May* 1679, and succeeded *Francis-Anthony* the Count *de Harrach*. His Advancement was owing to the Division of the Chapter, who all wanted to be either Bishops themselves, or else to advance some one Friend or Cousin. After a great many Debates and Messages sent forwards and backwards, their Choice fell upon the Baron *de Firmian* who was at that time very infirm, which was the only Thing that procur'd him the Mitre; for the Parties that divided the Chapter united in his favour, because they thought him a Man not very long-liv'd; but they believ'd however he might live long enough to give each Party time to form its Cabals for advancing that Person to the Bishoprick who they thought would best serve their Purpose. But all those Gentlemen were mightily mistaken as to the Archbishop's Life. For this Prelate, like another Pope *Sixtus* V. lost all his Infirmities when he found the Mitre, and is very like to out-live many of his Electors.

This

This Prince is tall, has an auſtere haughty Air, ſeldom makes any Compliments, and talks much leſs, except when he is hunting, which is all the Pleaſure of his Life. He is almoſt always alone, and generally eats by himſelf. In the Summer-time he keeps altogether in the Country where he is of very difficult Acceſs, and keeps no Retinue, nor Company. He is accus'd of being too thrifty, and I don't know but there may be ſomething in it; but perhaps he would not appear to be quite ſo ſaving if he had ſucceeded any body elſe in the Biſhoprick but the Count *de Harrach*, the moſt generous, noble, and moſt magnificent Prelate of his Time. The Archbiſhop is naturally a Valetudinarian; and under God, he is oblig'd for the Preſervation of his Life to his Phyſician *Gerſner*, a Native of *Vienna*, a Man of great Skill in his Profeſſion, and of ſtrict Honour and Integrity, who has got ſo much the length of the Prelate's Foot that he is almoſt the only Perſon that dares to ſpeak to him with Freedom. The Count *d'Arco* Son to the Archbiſhop's Siſter is this Prelate's only Darling; for to the ſurprize of the whole Court, and Chapter, he prefers him before a Nephew of his own Name, a Canon of *Saltzbourg* and of *Trent*, a young Clergyman of great Hopes.

The Archbiſhop of the *Lodron* Family who caus'd the Metropolis to be built, likewiſe founded the Archiepiſcopal Palace, the Fortifications, and the Stables, which were all finiſh'd in the thirty two Years that he was Archbiſhop. The Apartments of the Palace being not laid out altogether in the modern Taſte, the deceaſed Archbiſhop *Anthony* Count *de Harrach*, made a thorough Change in them, and left little more than the Outſide ſtanding. The Palace at *Saltzbourg* is now more magnificent than many royal Houſes. It contains 173 Rooms all richly furniſh'd, without reckoning the Halls and Galleries. The Archbiſhop's Apartment is
ſtately:

stately: It has a great Marble Stair-case divided into three Flights, which leads into a spacious Guard-Chamber, from whence one enters into the Archbishop's Apartment consisting of several Rooms, where able *Italian* Masters have adorn'd the Cielings with very good Draughts. One is really surprized to see the Richness of the Furniture, and the infinite Variety of other things that are distributed up and down this vast Apartment; such as Marble Tables adorn'd with gilt Mouldings; old Porcellain of the most beautiful sort; Lustres of massy Silver, and Rock-Crystal of uncommon Workmanship; Chandeliers also of Silver or Crystal upon large gilded Stands, and a multitude of other things very well worth observation.

How magnificent soever this Apartment is, there's another made use of upon Days of Ceremony which infinitely surpasses it. I will only mention the principal Rooms of it. We first enter into a great Salon adorn'd with the Pictures of no less than fourscore Archbishops of *Saltzbourg*. Next to it there's another Salon ingeniously and magnificently decorated, which discovers Grandeur in every part of it. 'Tis furnish'd with a Suit of Hangings of Crimson-Damask with Gold Lace, forming a rich Architecture in Pilasters of the Composite Order, the Frize of which is adorn'd with a pair of Brackets, which is a vast Addition to the whole Decoration. The rich Gilding shines every where with profusion. At one end of the Room there stands in the Wall a sumptuous Beaufet of Silver gilt, and at the other there's a rich Canopy under which the Archbishop sits when he dines in State. There's a stately Lustre in the middle of the Room which consists of magnificent pieces of Rock Crystal. At the end of this grand Apartment there are two Galleries that deserve the attention of the Curious in Painting, who will certainly pass their time here very agreeably,

ably, and find a great many choice Pictures done by the best Masters. The Chimney-piece of the first of these Galleries is a great Ornament to it, being of the finest Marble adorn'd with Brass, gilt with Water-Gold. Over it there's a Statue of Brass as big as the Life representing *Antinous*. The second Gallery is as magnificent as the first. The Floor, Cieling, Door-Cases, and all the Ornaments in general are of fine Marble. The Walls are painted in Fresco, and exhibit Geographical Charts of the principal Dominions in *Europe* in divers Pictures, which are executed with very great Art and Exactness both as to the Painting and Disposition of the Things that are the Subjects of it.

A third Apartment which is over the Archbishop's is for lodging foreign Princes, and is not inferiour to the others in Grandeur and Magnificence. It consists of several Rooms all in a row. In one Room there are all the Pictures of the Emperors from *Charlemain* to *Charles* VI. The Rooms that follow it are hung with very rich Tapestry, particularly one Set representing the War between *Pompey* and *Cæsar*, which is so wonderfully well drawn that the Marshal *de Daun* Governour of *Milan* offer'd 40000 Florins for it to the late Archbishop. I shall say nothing of the other Apartments, having treated so much of the Archiepiscopal Palace; tho' if it had belong'd to a Temporal Prince I should have said much less of it, but I thought fit to give you an Idea of the Wealth of a Prelate.

Adjoining to the Palace there is a great Building which serves for lodging the Archbishop's Domestics. The Stables are fit for a King, and if a *Frenchman* was to see them he would be forc'd to own that as to the Inside they are more magnificent than the so much boasted Stables of *Versailles*. They hold 150 Horses in two Rows, with a broad Walk in the middle; and the Roof which is pretty high is supported by two Ranges of Stone-Pillars. Next to these Stables is a Riding-House cover'd, the Ceiling of which being painted in Fresco, represents a Tournament; and all round it there is a Gallery. 'Tis pity that this magnificent Riding-House is not broader. There's another Riding-House uncovered which has not its Fellow in the World. 'Tis a very great square Place, three Sides of which are lin'd by very high Rocks, in which three Rows of Seats are very artfully cut out for the Spectators, when there is any Carousal, or Combat of wild Beasts. The whole Work is really magnificent, and the old *Romans* would not have been ashamed to own it.

Trinity-College Church is extremely well adorned. The Floor is of Marble, and the Roof painted with a great deal of Art, representing the Assumption of the Virgin, and the Crown placing on her Head by God the Father and by Jesus Christ. The High-Altar is of a very singular Form, but very magnificent. Two Angels of Brass, exceeding human Stature, in a Posture of Humility and Adoration, support a Heart of Brass which serves for a Tabernacle. Over it is a Globe, between God the Father and the Redeemer. God the Father seems to rest his right hand upon the Globe, and presents the left to our Lord, who puts his left upon the Globe, and in the right holds a Cross. They are supported by very large Rays which shine with very rich Gilding. This stately Groupe is surmounted with a Glory, in the midst of which the Holy Ghost appears in form of a Dove, extending its Rays over God the Father, and God the Son. The whole is of Brass gilt with Gold, of a very curious Fancy.

Near this magnificent Church is the Palace of *Mirabel*, where the late Archbishop the Count *de Harrach*, used to spend the Summer. This Prince who is truly magnificent in every thing, caus'd this House to be built at a great Expence from the very

Foundation; but the Architect whom he employ'd has not answer'd his Intention, and it appears that he did not understand the proper Distribution of the Apartments. Every Part of it indeed taken distinctly, is beautiful, but there is not one in its proper Place. The grand Stair-Case is very fine, as well for its Contrivance as for its rich Ornaments, but 'tis placed in a Corner, and without a Guide 'tis no easy matter to find it. The Salon, which is the Master-piece of the Archbishop's Apartments, is worth the Observation of the Curious, with respect to the grand Manner in which 'tis painted: Marble, Brass, and Gilding, seem to have been bestowed on it with profusion. As to the Pilasters, the *Corinthian* Order is entirely observed; and there are Basso-Relievos imitating Brass which are well design'd, and make a very good appearance. 'Tis pity this fine Salon wants proportion, it being much too lofty for its Size; and 'tis still more to be lamented that it has not a Prospect over the Gardens, the River of *Saltz*, and the adjacent Country, which are the Objects that are discover'd from the Apartments next to the Salon.

The Chapel of *Mirabel* is also very magnificent; and though but of a middling Size, is not inferior to the finest Churches. This Palace is accompanied with Gardens finely adorn'd with Fountains and Statues; and there are several Orange-Trees planted in the Ground, which are cover'd up in the Winter in a wooden Box.

Thus, Sir, have I given you a very particular Account of the City of *Saltzbourg*: What remains for me is to speak of the Archbishop's Houshold, which will give you an Idea of his Wealth and Grandeur. This Prince has

A Steward,	A Grand Marshal,
A Great Chamberlain.	A Master of the Horse,

SALTZBOURG.

A Great Huntsman,
A Captain of the Guards,
A Master-Cook,
A Pay-Master,
Twenty-four Chamberlains,
Sixteen Gentlemen-Servants called *Truchsses*,
Sixteen Pages,
Fifteen Ushers of the Cabinet,
Eleven Ushers of the Chamber,
Forty-two Valets de Chambre,
Twenty-eight Footmen,
Eighteen Cooks.

How many Coachmen and Grooms he has I know not, but there must be a great number of 'em, the Archbishop having 750 Horses.

Besides the Officers that I have now mentioned, there are also the Great Hereditary Officers of the Archbishoprick, who are four.

The eldest of the *Lodron* Family is Hereditary Grand-Marshal.

The Count *de Kuenbourg* is Great-Cup-Bearer.

The Office of Master of the Pantry is vacant by the death of the Count *de Thanhausen*, the last of his Family.

The Count *de Torring* is Great Chamberlain.

All these Offices are executed by the eldest Sons of the Families above-mentioned.

The Archbishop confers the Order of St. *Hubert*, which was instituted the 25th of *November*, 1702, by the Archbishop *John-Ernest*, who has thereto annexed six Commanderies, or Prebends, of a considerable Revenue.

The Archbishops are obliged for most of their Wealth to the Princes of *Bavaria**. Mean time the Members of the Chapter of *Saltzbourg* admit of

---

* The Revenue of this Archbishoprick amounts to 600,000 Florins. The Archbishop has 60,000 Florins a-year for his private Expences, and 24,000 Crowns for officiating at three solemn Services, without reckoning the Deanery, which is worth 24,000 Florins to him.

no Princes, that they may have a Plea for refusing the Princes of *Bavaria*, of whose Power they are jealous; in which I think they shew more regard to the Rules of Policy than those of Gratitude.

The City of *Saltzbourg* is worth seeing, but does not afford Amusement. Every one lives here for his own sake, and except some Gentlemen of the Chapter, and the Master of the Horse, who is the Count *de Truchsses Zeil*, there's nobody to visit. The latter is a Nobleman whose Manners and Sentiments are intirely conformable to his Birth. I know nobody that is more polite; and I have abundant reason to praise his Civility to me. He is of a Family, one Branch of which is settled in *Prussia*, where it has for a long time held distinguished Employments, and produced Subjects of great Merit who have done the State good Service.

I forgot to mention two things to you that are worth seeing, *viz*. the Capuchins Convent, from whence there's a Prospect of a vast Tract of Country; and St. *Sebastian*'s Church-yard, in which is interr'd the celebrated *Paracelsus*; his Tomb lies in a Place very much neglected, behind a Door, where a *Latin* Epitaph says, 'There rests *Philip-Theophrastus Paracelsus*, the famous Physician, who with wonderful Art cured the Leprosy, Gout, Dropsy, and other incurable Distempers; and who after having given all his Estate to the Poor, died *September* 24, 1541.'

Paracelsus cured most of his Patients by Sympathy, which made the Vulgar, who are always apt to run into extremes, believe that he was a Magician. He wrote several Books, whereof one of the most curious is his *Treatise of Secret Philosophy*, which really contains such Passages as would make one believe that if *Paracelsus* was not a Conjurer himself, he was at least one of the Sect.

St.

St. *Sebastian*'s Church-yard is a square Place, encompassed with a Gallery supported by Arches: 'tis 119 Paces in length, and 96 in breadth.

The Neighbourhood of *Saltzbourg* is not disagreeable; and though the Valley in which the City lies is pretty much inclosed with Mountains, yet it presents several Objects that are pleasing to the Sight.

The Archbishop has two Pleasure-Houses, *viz. Cleisheim* and *Heilbron*, which are both of them beautiful and magnificent. *Heilbron* especially is worth seeing on account of its fine Waters and Cascades.

I hope to write to you speedily from *Venice*, and perhaps you will hear from me when I come to *Inspruc*; but this will depend on the Stay I shall make there, and on the Departure of the Post.

POSTSCRIPT.

Since the year 1730, that this Letter was wrote, great Revolutions have happened in the Archbishoprick of *Saltzbourg*, with regard to Religion; for about 22,000 Persons have abandoned this Country, together with their Estates and their Fortunes, and declared themselves of the *Lutheran* Communion; which is very strange, and almost inconceivable! For in short, those People never knew any Clergy but their own Priests, they lived in a Country where there was no Controversy about Religion, because all the Inhabitants were reckon'd staunch Catholics, by consequence those People could not be instructed; and even the greatest part of them could not read, but were bred up in such gross Ignorance that they scarce knew the Principles of Christianity. Therefore how could these poor People know that they were in an Error?

I am not ignorant that at the beginning of the pretended Reformation, there were *Saltzburghers* that followed the Doctrines of *Luther*, such as *Staupitz*, Abbot of *St. Peter*'s at *Saltzbourg*; *Paul Speratus*, a Preacher in the Cathedral of this City; and several others. But *Lutheranism* was thought to be quite suppressed in this Province, when it seem'd all on a sudden to take deeper Root than ever; tho', as I said before, I can't conceive how it should happen. Is it possible that the Archbishop, the Curates and Priests should take so little care of what ought to have been most dear to them, I mean the Salvation of Souls, as that so many Thousands of People should pass with them for good *Romans*, at the same time that they abhorred *Rome* and its Precepts? For in short, I suppose, and believe too, that there have ever been Protestants in this Country, since the pretended Reformation; it being not in the power of Man to destroy a Religion when once it has had Followers in a Country; but the Difficulty is, how those Sectaries should subsist there, without the Knowledge of an ecclesiastical Sovereign; and how it was possible for them, not only to subsist, but even to multiply, and the Priests and Archbishop not perceive it. Ought not the Curates to know the Sentiments of their Parishioners by Confession? Ought they not to acquaint the Archbishop their Head of it? and ought not this Prelate and his Priests to endeavour to reclaim those that go astray, by the Example of a lively Faith, and by charitable Exhortations, and from a Compassion for their Error, diligently to oppose the Propagation of it? But all this has been neglected: The Priests, and their Archbishop, knew not there was a Fire, 'till 'twas too late to put it out; and instead of the Good-nature, Compassion, and Charity, which like Water were necessary to extinguish it, they pour'd in the Oil of Hatred and Violence, and abandoned themselves to their furious Zeal. The haughty, rigid, and severe Archbishop, forgetting that he was both a Father and an Archbishop, and giving way to the Violence of his Temper, has for ever lost those Souls which he might have hoped to reclaim, by Instructions truly pastoral, and treating them as Children led astray; whereas this Prelate, by using the contrary Method, has caused a great many Persons to declare themselves Protestants, who would have died in the Bosom of the Church, if the proper Remedies had been employed, to bring them back to it.

But I am persuaded that among the Emigrants of *Saltzbourg*, there is a vast number who made Religion only a Cloak to leave their Country, in hopes of bettering their Fortunes elsewhere, and who were seduced by the ensnaring Temptation of throwing off the Yoak of Submission. Be this as it will, those unfortunate Subjects, like the *Jews*, are spread into divers Countries, as *Germany*, *Holland*, and *Prussia*, where the King, I must confess, (as much a Catholic as I am) has received them with a Charity and Generosity perfectly christian and royal; his Majesty having grudg'd neither Care nor Expence to convince the World that as *France* is the Asylum of unfortunate Kings, so the Dominions of *Prussia* are the Refuge of oppressed Subjects.

LETTER XXIV.

S I R,   *Infpruc, April* 9, 1730.

I Travelled hither all the way from *Saltzbourg*, with the fame Horfes, which is what I will never do again; for travelling by Poft is always beft; and though 'tis more expenfive, yet on the other hand 'tis lefs fatiguing.

Three Leagues from *Saltzbourg* ftands the little Town of HALLE, which belongs to the Elector of *Bavaria*, and is a Place confiderable for its Salt-Pits. It lies in a fmall Valley croffed by three Rivers, form'd by Torrents from the Mountains, which bring down a vaft quantity of floating Wood, that is ftopp'd at *Halle* by the Piles which either crofs or fhut up the Rivers. They lay the Wood up in ftore for the Salt-Works, which confume a great quantity of it.

After I had been all over the Salt-Works, I went and din'd at *Schneitzenrieth*, a forry Village, where, however, I far'd better than I have done at many good Towns.

When I had dined I purfued my Journey, and having travelled four Leagues, entred the Country of TIROL, the Paffage to which is very much ftraitened, fo that there's fcarce room for a Waggon, by two very high Rocks or Mountains, and two Forts between them, one belonging to the Archbifhoprick of *Saltzbourg*, and the other to the County of *Tirol*. Each Sovereign keeps a Garrifon in his Fort, and Officers to receive the Duties.

I

I lay that Evening at WAHTRINGEN, the first Village in the Dominions of *Tirol*, as one comes out of *Germany*. I here found a Parcel of Boys running about with lighted Touchwood in their hands, to the Houses, Woods, and Fields. Having ask'd an old Man the meaning of it, he told me that the Wood so lighted was confecrated by the Parfon of the Parish, and had the virtue of securing all Places to which it was carried, against Lightning. This Confecration of the Wood is always perform'd the *Saturday* before *Easter*, when a great Pile is erected before the Church, into which the Parfon throws Holy-water, and then fets fire to it. When the whole is well kindled, every one strives to snatch a Firebrand, with which they run to their Houfes and Lands, but with fo little care that I wonder they don't fet every place they come to in a Flame.

From *Halle* to *Wahtringen* the Country is every bit uncultivated. The Inhabitants live upon Milk, Pickled Cabbage, and Water-gruel. They have no Corn but what comes from *Bavaria*. All their Subftance and Trade is in Cattle, and their Mountains afford excellent Pafture.

Upon *Easter-day* I heard Mafs at *St. John's*, a great Village where there's a very pretty Church. I was very much pleafed with the Sermon that was preached by the Parfon, and with the Regularity with which the whole Divine Service was performed.

After Mafs I went and din'd at ELVAN, to which place I came through a Valley, which in the Summer time muft be very agreeable, but at the prefent Seafon is all covered with Snow. I was not more edified at *Wahtringen*, than I was fcandalized at *Elvan*, to catch my Landlord, a clever, merry Blade, engaged with one of his Maids in fomething else inftead of telling their Beads. My Prefence was so far from spoiling Sport that my Landlord invited me very civilly to do as he did, assuring me that his House was well furnish'd with Nymphs. In a very little time I was convinced that what he said was true, for being obliged by the Cold to stay in the common Room while one was aired for me, I saw half a score Lasses come in, who were all of them my Landlord's very humble Servants, and not in the least disposed to imitate the eleven thousand Virgins.

After Dinner, pursuing my way through Snows and Rocks, I went and lay at *Kundahl*. Next day I got beyond the Snow, and crossed a very pleasant Valley which brought me to RATENBERG, a Town on the Banks of the *Inn*, defended by a Castle built on a Rock, and stronger by its Situation than by its Works. The Elector *Maximilian-Emanuel* of *Bavaria* coming before this Castle on the 13th of *June*, 1703, obliged the Garrison, which was composed of the Militia, to surrender at Discretion. From this Fort to *Inspruc* I always kept along the River *Inn*, which runs through a fine Valley beween high Mountains that are much steeper on the right side of the River than the left; nevertheless there are Houses on them that are inhabited by the Miners. I can't imagine how it was possible for the good People to build in Places so inconvenient; for their Houses look as if they were stuck on to the Rocks, and as if nothing but a Goat or a Swallow could come at them. The whole Valley is very populous, and abounds with pretty Villages, Castles, and fine Country-Houses.

At the end of it stands the Town of SCHWATZ, which is very well built. The Parish Church is an ancient, fair, large Edifice; and wholly covered with Copper, as most of the Churches in *Tirol* are with Tin painted green, which has a very pretty look. The Houses at *Schwatz* are generally of Brick, so that 'tis very rare to see one of Timber. I observ'd

at

at the Inn where I din'd, and throughout the whole Country of *Tirol*, that when People came into any House, they said to the Master of it, *Hail, Jesus Christ!* to which he answered, *May Christ be praised, and the holy Virgin his Mother.* Then the Master of the House stepp'd forward, and took the Visitor by his hand. This method of saluting is practised among all the People throughout *Tirol*; and the Salutation is fix'd up in Print at all the Doors, with an Advertisement tack'd to it, importing, that Pope *Clement* XI. had granted an hundred Days of Indulgence, and plenary Absolution, in favour of those who should pronounce the Salutation and the Answer.

After having din'd at *Schwatz*, I continued to ride along the *Inn*; and three Leagues beyond that I pass'd the River, over a Bridge near *Fultishau*, a fine Convent of the Servite-Fryars, and went to HALLE, the second City of *Tirol*. The reverend Fathers the *Jesuits* have a fine House here, and a noble Church, with a great Garden to it. The Mint is also worth seeing, where they coin a great quantity of Species from the Silver and Copper taken out of the Mines of *Tirol*. The Water is brought to it by wooden Pipes. They drive a great Trade at *Halle* in Copper, Tin, and Salt, which is produced there in abundance, the Vent of it being promoted by means of the River *Inn*, which becomes navigable at *Halle*.

From this Town to *Inspruc* 'tis two Leagues, and a strait even Road which deserves to be planted on each side with Trees. INSPRUC, the Capital City of *Tirol*, stands in the middle of a Valley, on the Banks of the *Inn*, over which there's a wooden Bridge that leads to the Suburbs. *Inspruc* was heretofore the Residence of the Archdukes, the Sovereigns of *Tirol*; but since the august House of *Austria* has been reduced in *Germany* to the Imperial Branch,

Branch singly, this City has been only subject to Governors, who however were always great Noblemen. *Charles* Duke of *Lorrain*, who married the Queen Dowager of *Poland*, Sister to the Emperor *Leopold*, and who made himself famous by the Victories which he gain'd over the *Turks*, held this important Office. That Prince dying at *Inspruc*, was succeeded by *Charles* Prince Palatine of *Newbourg*, Brother to the Empress *Eleonora*, *Leopold*'s third Wife, but he renounced the Government of *Tirol*, on his Accession to the Electorate. He liv'd at *Inspruc*, with great Pomp, and his Absence is still very much lamented there. Since he went away, the Government of *Tirol* has remain'd vacant. They say 'tis designed for the Archduchess *Mary-Magdalen*, the Emperor's youngest Sister. This I know is what the Burghers of *Inspruc* wish for; but I don't think the Nobility do; because the Presence of the Archduchess would oblige the People of Quality to be at very great Expence; for they would be under a necessity of going to Court, as well as of carrying it more civilly to their Vassals.

The Count *de Konickel* is the Chief of the Regency: He has the Title of *Landshauptman*, which is much the same with Lieutenant-General of the Province, wherein he has the absolute Command, and all the Sovereign Courts depend on him. This Nobleman is a *Tirolese*, and lodges in a fine House which has been built by order of the States of *Tirol*, for the Residence of their *Landshauptman*. He conducts himself with Dignity, and is civil to Foreigners.

'Twas at *Inspruc* that the Emperor *Charles* V. received one of the greatest Shocks he had met with in all his Life. For he was surprized there with his Brother *Ferdinand*, King of the *Romans*, by *Maurice* Elector of *Saxony*, who, though his Creature, made War upon him nevertheless, on account of Religion.

Religion. The Emperor and his Brother were so near being taken that they had but just time to make their Escape to *Villaco*, a little Town upon the *Drave* in *Carinthia*. This was a terrible Reverse of Fortune for a Prince, who, but a few years before, had a Pope and a King of *France* too, his Prisoners.

Maximilian-Emanuel Elector of *Bavaria* was not more fortunate at *Inspruc* than *Charles* V. for though he made himself Master of it in *June* 1703, he was obliged to abandon it in *July* following, and to retire to *Bavaria*, after having tried in vain to force Passes which were in a manner inaccessible by Nature, and guarded not only by the Peasants but by regular Troops. His Design was to have joined M. *de Vendôme* in the County of *Trent*, and by that means to have opened a Communication with the *Milanese*. The Elector, whilst he was retreating, ran the hazard several times of losing his Life; and his Troops were for the most part knock'd o' th' head by Stones which the Peasants hurl'd at them in the Defiles which they were obliged to pass.

The City of *Inspruc* is absolutely defenceless, and were it not for its Suburbs, would be one of the least Cities in all *Germany*; but those Suburbs are very large, and the Residence of Persons of the greatest Distinction. The Houses are very commodious, well built of Brick, and for the most part with Piazzas, which is a great Conveniency to the Foot-passengers. There was heretofore great Store of Salt here, but for some years past the Pits are dry, which is a Loss to *Inspruc* of no less than 200,000 Florins a-year.

Though the City is small yet there are several very fine things to be seen in it. Such is the ancient Palace of the Archdukes, a vast large Structure, but without Architecture, or any manner of

Re-

Regularity. There are Pictures in it done by skilful Hands, particularly in that call'd the Giant's-Hall, where the Story of *Dejanira* is represented with very great Art and Perfection.

The Palace has very great Gardens belonging to it, but they are not well kept; yet there are the Remains of noble Fountains and brazen Statues. Among the latter is an Equestrian Statue of an Archduke of *Austria*, who is represented as large as the Life, in Armour, with Breeches after the Fashion of the Ancients, a Ruff, and little Boots. The Horse seems to rest upon his Haunches, in an Attitude as if he was just ready to leap off the Pedestal.

The Prince *Charles* of *Newbourg*, the present Elector Palatine, finding the old Castle not commodious enough, caused one to be built of Wood; which was some years ago burnt down to the ground by an accidental Fire.

The Parish Church is of modern Building, with a great Dome raised in the middle of the Cross. The whole Architecture of this Edifice is of the *Corinthian* Order. The Front is expos'd to an advantagious Point of View on a Square, and is adorned with three Orders, one above another, which makes the Fabric to rise in the whole to about 120 Foot height, exclusive of a great flight of Steps to it, after the manner of *Italy*. All the Parts of this Structure are charged with Ornaments of a clumsey Invention, and very ill executed; so that the Confusion resulting from it is infinitely shocking to those that have a nice Taste of Architecture. The Inside is more tolerable than the Outside, and is even magnificent. The whole Length from the Entrance to the Foot of the High-Altar, is 432 Feet. The Foundation of it was laid while *Charles de Newbourg* was Governor of *Tirol*, who plac'd the first Stone of it. The whole Decoration

of

of this Church confifts in Pilafters of red Marble, with a Vein of white, and the Chapiters are of Plaifter. The Roof is painted in Frefco by *Gofman-Daniel Offem*, a Native of *Munich*, who has fucceeded fo well as to give entire fatisfaction to fuch as have a Tafte for, and Skill in things that are curious. The High-Altar ftands under the Arch at the end oppofite to the Nave of the Church. 'Tis perfectly magnificent, adorned with four great Pillars of the Compofite Order, of green Marble with white Veins, whofe Chapiters and Bafons are of Marble of various Colours; and they fupport a Canopy, which is form'd by four Curves fill'd with a Glory.

The Tabernacle and the Front of the Altar are of maffy Silver, charged with feveral Mouldings, and Foliages of Silver gilt; and there are few Altars more fplendidly decorated. There is a miraculous Image of the holy Virgin, which the Archduke *Leopold*, the Sovereign of *Tirol*, brought hither from *Drefden*. That Prince made a Vifit to the Elector of *Saxony*, who fhewing him his Treafure, defir'd him to chufe any Piece that he lik'd beft; *Leopold* fingled out this Figure, becaufe he was told that in the early days of Lutheranifm, it had been caft three times in the Fire, and always taken out again without any damage. The Archduke on his return to his Dominions, made a Prefent of this Image to the Parifh, and it has ever fince been held in great veneration, and never fail'd of working great Miracles. Three great Lamps of maffy Silver are continually burning before it; and the other Chapels have each a Lamp of folid Silver whofe Light is always fhining. All this Plate was given to the Church by the Elector Palatine.

The famous golden Roof is near the Parifh-Church, and ferves to cover a Balcony of the Chancery which fronts the Square. They fay that *Frederic* of *Auftria*, the Sovereign of *Tirol*, caufed this Roof

Roof to be made, to let his Subjects see that he was not so bare of Money as they thought him, and that he did not deserve the Nick-name they had given him of the *Pennyless Prince*. There are many however who affirm that this Roof is not of Gold, while others say the contrary. As far as I can judge of it, I believe 'tis of Copper only covered with very thin Plates of Gold, and by consequence of no great Value. And supposing the whole Roof was of solid Gold, I don't believe the Expence was very extraordinary, though to be sure it was by much too great for so mean a purpose.

The House or College of the reverend Fathers the Jesuits, is a very great Building in which no Cost has been spared. Its principal Front is 166 Paces in length. These Fathers are the Directors of the University. Near to their College is the Church of the *Franciscans*, whose Convent was founded by the pious Legacies of the Emperor *Maximilian*, who on his Death-bed ordered his Successor to cause this House and Church to be built at *Inspruc*. His Grandson *Ferdinand* I. Son to *Philip* the Fair, perform'd his Will, and in honour of his Grandfather's Memory, raised him a Marble Tomb which may be rank'd among the most stately *Mausoleums* in *Europe*. The Emperor *Maximilian* is there represented on his Knees upon a Cushion, with his Hands lifted up to Heaven, and as it were prostrate in Prayer: He is adorned with the Crown, and the Imperial *Dalmatic*. This Figure is of a gigantic Size, and admirably well done in Brass. 'Tis plac'd on a great high Base of black Marble, forming an oblong Square, on an Ascent of three Steps of red Marble. The whole Base is divided into twenty-four Compartiments, or square Tables of white Marble, representing the memorable Actions of *Maximilian* in excellent Bas-Reliefs. The four cardinal Virtues in a mournful Attitude, are represented in Brass, as sitting on the Corners of the *Mausoleum*, and looking on *Maximilian*'s Statue. The entire *Mausoleum* stands by itself in the middle of the Church; and the following Inscription is engraved in Letters of Gold all round the Base of this Monument;

IMPERATORI CÆSARI MAXIMILIANO, PIO, FELICI, AUGUSTO, PRINCIPI TUM PACIS TUM BELLI ARTIBUS OMNIUM ÆTATIS SUÆ REGUM LONGE CLARISSIMO; SUB CUJUS FELICI IMPERIO INCLYTA GERMANIA, DULCISSIMA IPSIUS PATRIA, TAM ARMIS QUAM LITERARUM STUDIIS PLUS QUAM UNQUAM ANTEHAC FLORERE CAPUTQUE SUPER ALIAS NATIONES EXTOLLERE CŒPIT: CUJUS INSIGNIA FACTA TABELLIS INFERIORIBUS, QUAMVIS SUB COMPENDIO, EXPRESSA CONSPICIUNTUR. IMPERATOR CÆSAR FERDINANDUS, PIUS, FELIX, AUGUSTUS, AVO PATERNO PERQUAM COLENDO, AC BENE MERITO, PIETATIS ATQUE GRATITUDINIS ERGO POSUIT. NATUS EST DIE XXVII MARTII ANNO DOMINI M. CCCC. LIX. WELSÆ IN AUSTRIA DENATUS.

All this fine *Mausoleum* was executed with very great Care and Skill, by *Alexander Colin*, a Native of *Mechlin*; the Picture of which ingenious Painter, and that of his Wife, are kept in the Church, as an Acknowledgment due to that excellent Artist. This *Mausoleum* was mightily enriched by the Magnificence of *Frederic* Archduke of *Austria*, surnamed the *Pennyless Prince*, who caused to be placed in

the

the Nave of the Church twenty eight Statues of Brass seven Foot in height, representing so many Princes and Princesses that were related to the House of *Austria*. They are set up in two Rows from the great Gate to the Altar, and therefore separate the Nave from the two Wings on the Sides. 'Tis pity that those Statues are in the hands of Monks who neglect them very much, and suffer the Dust to eat into them. They would do much better in a Royal Palace: Some of them are in great perfection. I fancy you will be glad to know the Names of the Persons they represent.

I. The first, beginning on the right Side of the Altar, is the Figure of *Joan* of *Castile*, Mother to *Charles* V. and *Ferdinand* I. the Heads of the two Branches of the House of *Austria*; the first of which became extinct by the Death of *Charles* II. King of *Spain*, but the second still flourishes among us with Glory in the Person of the August *Charles* VI.

II. *Ferdinand* the Catholic, Father to *Joan*.

III. *Cunigonda* Archduchess, Daughter to the Emperor *Frederic* IV. and Wife to *Albert* of *Bavaria*, who died a Nun.

IV. *Margaret*, Daughter to *Henry* Duke of *Carinthia* and Count of *Tirol*, surnamed the *Pious*, because she founded and built several Convents. This Princess was nick-named *Margaret Wide-Mouth*: She was marry'd first to *John* Margrave of *Moravia*, Son to the Emperor *Charles* IV. whom she surviv'd, and marry'd to her second Husband *Lewis*, Margrave of *Brandenburg*, Son to the Emperor *Lewis* of *Bavaria*, whom she also surviv'd, and finding herself a Widow a second time, and without Issue to enjoy what she had, she made a Present of the County of *Tirol* whereof she was Sovereign, to her Cousins *Rodolph*, *Albert*, and *Leopold* of

Austria, which Grant was confirm'd by the Emperor *Charles* IV. in 1364.

V. *Mary* of *Burgundy*, Wife to the Emperor *Maximilian* I. the richest Heiress of her Time.

VI. *Elizabeth*, the Daughter of the Emperor *Sigismond*, and Wife to the Emperor *Albert* II. who carry'd the Duchy of *Luxembourg* to the House of *Austria*. She was Mother to the unfortunate King *Ladislaus*.

VII. *Godfrey* of *Bouillon*, Duke of *Lorrain*, King of *Jerusalem*, plac'd here among the Princes of the House of *Austria*, as being descended from the same Family as they.

VIII. *Albert* I. Emperor.

IX. *Frederic*, Archduke of *Austria*, he who was nick-named Prince *Pennyless*.

X. *Leopold* of *Austria*, surnamed the *Virtuous*, Son of *Albert* the *Wise*.

XI, and XII. Opinions are very much divided about the Persons who are represented by these two Statues; but 'tis generally thought they are the Emperors *Charles* V. and *Ferdinand* I.

XIII. The Emperor *Frederic* IV. Father to *Maximilian* I.

XIV. *Albert* II. Emperor, King of *Hungary* and *Bohemia*, and Father to the unfortunate King *Ladislaus*.

XV. *Clovis*, the first Christian King of *France*, who is plac'd among the Princes of the House of *Austria*, because their Genealogists derive them from the ancient *Franks* who subdued *France*.

XVI. *Philip* I. call'd the Fair, King of *Spain*.

XVII. The Emperor *Rodolph* I.

XVIII. The Archduke *Albert*, call'd the *Wise*.

XIX. *Theodoric* King of the *Goths*. I am not a Genealogist good enough to tell you in what Relation he stands to the House of *Austria*.

XX.

XX. *Ernest*, Archduke, Grandfather to *Maximilian* I.

XXI. *Theodebert* Count of *Provence*, from whom descended the Dukes of *Burgundy* and the Counts of *Hapsburg*.

XXII. *Arthur*, Prince of *Wales*, who marry'd *Catherine* of *Arragon*.

XXIII. *Sigismond*, Archduke and Count of *Tirol*, who adopted the Emperor *Maximilian* I.

XXIV. *Blanche Mary*, the second Wife of *Maximilian* I. which Princess was the Daughter of *John Galeas* Duke of *Milan*.

XXV. *Margaret*, Daughter of *Maximilian* I. who was marry'd first to *John* a Prince of *Spain*, and secondly to *Philibert* Duke of *Savoy*.

XXVI. *Cimburge*, Wife of *Ernest* the Archduke, and Mother to the Emperor *Frederic* IV.

XXVII. *Charles* the *Bold*, Duke of *Burgundy*, Father to *Mary* of *Burgundy* who was Wife to *Maximilian* I.

XXVIII. *Philip*, Duke of *Burgundy*, Father to *Charles* the Bold.

Besides these twenty eight Statues there are twenty three others plac'd upon the Cornish of the Portico which separates the Nave from the Choir: They are of Brass two Foot high, and represent those Kings and Princes whom the Church honours as Saints.

I am farther to acquaint you of the Chapel of this Church, call'd the Silver Chapel, because of the Image of the Virgin there of solid Silver as big as the Life in the middle of the Altar, with a great many Images of Saints all of the same Metal. The Ascent to this Chapel is by a winding Staircase. Here is to be seen the stately Tomb of *Ferdinand* Archduke of *Austria*, Count of *Tirol*, Son to the Emperor *Ferdinand* I. This Mausoleum is under an Arch which is pretty high. *Ferdinand*, whose Figure is of white Marble, seems to be asleep upon a Bed of black Marble rais'd one Foot from the Ground. The whole Arch is lin'd with Marble of various Colours, forming divers Compartments of very curious Workmanship, where you see the Arms of the Provinces reduc'd to the Obedience of the House of *Austria*: The different Colours are shewn by precious Stones enchas'd in Marble, and so curiously done that the Work seems to be enamel'd. Round the same Arch are plac'd five Bas-Reliefs, representing in as many Pictures the memorable Actions of *Ferdinand*. Five other Bas-Reliefs contain the Images of that Prince's Patrons, *viz.* Jesus Christ, St. *Anthony* of *Padua*, St. *George*, St. *Thomas*, and St. *Leopold*.

Near the said Tomb stands that of *Philippina* of *Welserin*, who was born at *Augsburg*, and the Wife of the Archduke *Ferdinand*, by whom she had two Sons, *Charles* the Margrave of *Burgau*, and *Andrew* Cardinal of *Austria*. This *Mausoleum* is of Free-stone and has nothing remarkable more than the following Epitaph:

Ferdinandus D. G. Archidux, Dux Burgundiæ, Comes Tirol, Philippinæ Conjugi Charissimæ fieri curavit. Obiit 24 Aprilis, 1580.

The Franciscan who shew'd me this Chapel assur'd me that it was one of the First-rate Chapels in the World, on account of the Indulgences which had been annex'd to it by the Beneficence of the Popes; that it was upon a par with the Chapel of the *Holy Sepulchre* at *Jerusalem*, with the Churches of *St. John de Lateran*, *St. Mary major*, and *St. Gregory* at *Rome*; and that, in fine, a Mass said in this Chapel for the Repose of a Soul departed, was enough to deliver it out of Purgatory.

These,

These, Sir, are the Remarks that I made in this City, from whence I am making ready to set out to-morrow. I expect to be well jolted all the way to *Venice*, where to make my self amends I will take my Pleasure in a *Gondola*. I wish with all my heart I had your Company there; we should then have the Satisfaction of seeing a great many fine Sights together. But for want of this Satisfaction I shall never cease to think of you; and pray don't forget me, but believe me to be for ever, *&c.*

LETTER XXV.

SIR, *Venice, April* 27. 1730.

I Wrote to you from *Inspruc* the very Day before I set out from thence for this Place, to which I arriv'd without any Misfortune. About three quarters of a League from *Inspruc* we came among very tiresome and disagreeable Mountains, the highest of which is call'd the *Brenner*, a Name that the Country People gave it when they clear'd it of the Wood, and burnt it. This Mountain is much more rugged on the side of *Trent* than 'tis towards *Inspruc*; 'tis for nine Months together cover'd with Snow, and I found a great deal remaining on it still; yet 'tis inhabited to the very Top. There is a Post-House, a Tavern, and a Chapel in which Mass is only said when the Snows are

are melted: It produces Corn and Hay in abundance. Near the Post-House there is a considerable Spring which at first forms a large Basin, and then divides into two Torrents which quickly change into Rivers, one whereof falls into the *Inn* above *Inspruc*, and the other, after becoming navigable two Leagues from *Bolsano*, loses itself in the *Adige* above *Trent*. The Passage of the *Brenner* is very painful, and sometimes impracticable when it snows or rains; so that Travellers are often oblig'd to stay several Days till the Return of fair Weather, which is the more inconvenient because the Inns on both Sides are of the worst sort.

Stertzingen a little Town four Post-Stages from *Inspruc*, has nothing remarkable; however I was well accommodated there. Next Day I went and din'd at BRIXEN an Episcopal City in an agreeable Valley, where I found the Season very forward. The Country between *Brixen* and *Bolsano* is extremely populous, and so manur'd that the steepest Mountains are cultivated.

BOLSANO is a pretty Town well inhabited, and drives a considerable Trade, having no less than four Fairs a Year. Its Situation is very agreeable, in the middle of a fine large Valley full of Villages and Vineyards. The Air here is much softer than in the rest of *Tirol*, and I found Trees here in full Verdure while in the Country they were but just budded. The Vines are very carefully watched by Men who keep Guard in Huts rais'd upon three Poles plac'd cross-wise, and high enough to command the Vineyards. *Misson* in his Voyage to *Italy* says, that these Huts or *Guerites* were for lodging the Guards that are posted to hinder the Bears from eating the Grapes. I know not who could tell him that there were any Bears in this Country, and if there are 'tis hardly probable they would venture into a Valley so populous as that of *Bolsano*. The
Wines

Wines of this Valley are the best in all *Tirol*; but they must be drank, as must all the Wines of this Country, the very Year of their Growth, or else they grow luscious, and then turn crabbed.

The Valley of *Bolsano* which extends to *Trent* is throughout equally agreeable; and is not incumber'd by those horrid Mountains that we were pester'd with in the Road from *Inspruc*.

TRENT is celebrated for the Council formerly held there. I went to see the Church of St. *Mary major*, where the Fathers of that Council held their Assembly. It has nothing remarkable besides its Organs which are of too enormous a Size for a Church, but are a very curious piece of Work; for they not only exhibit various Sounds, but imitate Vocal Music, the Notes of divers Birds, and the Noise of Kettle-Drums and Trumpets. The Bishop of *Trent* is a Prince of the Empire. The See is now vacant by the Death of the Count *de Wolckenstein* the last Bishop. The Chapter has fix'd the Election for next *May*. A great many Travellers highly extol the Bishop's Palace, but for my own part, I was not so fortunate as to observe any thing in it that was worthy of Attention.

Throughout all *Tirol* the Common People are very ill-favour'd: Most of the Women are disguis'd by Wens in their Throat*, and as if that was not enough they disfigure themselves by their Dress. The Country Women wear Stockings which have no Feet, and are gather'd into many little Folds from the Ancle to the Calf of the Leg: Their Shoes are exactly like those the Men wear. Their Petticoats are exceeding short, and ty'd up almost as high as their Breasts which are very large. With all this they have a Pair of Stays which reaches down to their

---

* The People about the *Alps* are very subject to those Swellings by drinking too much cold unwholesome Water.

their Waist, and renders them compleatly deform'd. Instead of other Head-dress they wear a green high-crown'd Hat, the Brims of which are let down, and is as unbecoming a part of their Dress as any of the rest. At *Brixen* the Blood mends, the Women are handsomer, the Men more genteel, and the People in general more civiliz'd; tho' take 'em all together the *Tirolese* are very honest People. They are staunch zealous Catholics, tho' they say that some of the Peasants, are *Lutherans*. The *Holy Virgin* and St. *Christopher* are the principal Objects of the People's Devotion: The latter is painted on all their Houses, and the Roads are full of little Chapels of the *Virgin* who is represented in all manner of ways. I have seen her painted in a Chapel standing with a great Veil over her Head which she extended with her Arms to cover the Pope, the Emperor, seven Kings, and as many Electors, who seem to be prostrate at her Knees.

As I left *Trent* I began to ascend a Mountain which does not become smooth till we reach to *Berschen* which is a Post-Stage and a half from *Trent*. This Mountain is exceeding steep, troublesome, and tiresome, and after 'tis pass'd, one is in a manner buried among Rocks and horrid Mountains which seem as if they would fall on the Heads of the Travallers; and I have been assur'd that this sometimes happens in rainy Weather, when so many Pieces crumble off of the Rock that it requires 4 or 500 Carts to clear the Roads. In short, all the Way till one comes within a League of *Bossagno* a City in the State of *Venice* is full of Rocks and Precipices; but from that Town to *Mestre* which is four Post-Stages from it, the Country is the finest in the World; and in short, every thing is good and pleasant except their Wine and their publick Houses. The Wine has naturally a musty Taste, and no Body, and the Colour is like that of the thick Wine of *Bourdeaux*.

This

This Country so abounds in Quails that the Post-Master of *Bossagno* assur'd me he had taken 720 in a Morning, that he drove a great Trade with 'em, and sent some of 'em to the State of *Venice*, and to *Lombardy*. Whether he said true, I know not, but he shew'd me 1100 live Quails which he kept in Wicker-Cages in a great Barn where he had hung all the Cages to Packthread to keep them from Rats and Cats.

At Mestre one embarks for *Venice* which is about seven Leagues from it; I made the Voyage in a Gondola in less than an Hour and half. As I travell'd post to *Mestre*, my Gondoliers, when I came to *Venice*, carry'd me to the Post-Office, where I was oblig'd to tell my Name, and the Business for which I came to *Venice*; but this is a Ceremony to which they who don't travel post are not subject. I went and took up my Lodging at the *White Lion*, highly rejoic'd that I could rest my self there after my Fatigue, and that I had lost sight of the *Alps*, those horrid Mountains which no body would chuse to live amongst but a *Swiss* or a *Tirolese*, who, as Cardinal *Bentivoglio* justly observes in his Voyage to *Swisserland*, are a People made for the *Alps*, and the *Alps* for them.

As I have been twice before at *Venice*, I serve as a * *Cicerone* to two *Bohemian* Counts whom I was acquainted with at *Prague*, and whom I happen'd to meet with at my Quarters. As 'tis customary to do to all Foreigners, I began with shewing them the Square of St. *Mark*, the chief Square of *Venice*, if not of the whole World. 'Tis adorn'd by the Palace of the *Doge*, the Church of St. *Mark*, and the *Procuraties*, or Houses of the Procurators, and has been pav'd within these few Years with
great

---

* This is the Name which they give in *Italy* to those who do the Office of Guides to shew Foreigners the Curiosities of any Town.

great Squares of Free-stone. We ascended the famous Tower of St. *Mark* which is a four-square Building, by a Stair without Steps. It was built by the Doge *Domingo Morosini*, to serve as a Watch-Tower to Ships at Sea; and that it might be seen a great way off he caus'd the Angel on the top of it to be gilt; but Time the Destroyer of all Things has stripp'd off the Gold. From this Tower one sees the whole City of *Venice*, the neighbouring Islands, and the *Terra Firma*, which all together makes a noble Prospect.

We afterwards enter'd St. *Mark*'s Church, which is an Edifice of *Grecian* Architecture, pretty dark and not very high, but after all, full of Curiosities worthy the Attention of a Traveller. As this Church has been describ'd with more Exactness than I can pretend to, I shall treat very succinctly of the chief Things which it contains. The grand Portico is so low that one must even go down some Steps to enter into the Church. There is a Platform over it on which are plac'd four brazen Horses brought from *Constantinople*, to which they were first carry'd from *Rome* by *Constantine* when that Prince transferr'd the Seat of the Empire from the one City to the other. Nothing is so magnificent and beautiful as those Horses. They were heretofore all over gilt, but People out of mere Avarice scrap'd off great part of the precious Metal, and all the rest is almost worn off by Time.

At the Entrance of the Church on the right-hand Side there is a square Stone which seem'd to me to be of white Marble, and is said to be a piece of the Rock which *Moses* struck in the Wilderness, whereupon there issued out Water. If this be really that Stone, what that Legislator did is so much the more to be admir'd, and may be reckon'd doubly miraculous; first in fetching Water to a Place where there was none before, and then the

bring-

bringing a quantity of it through four Holes no bigger than Pease sufficient to quench the Thirst of so numerous a Multitude. The Pavement of this Church is very grand, being of *Mosaic* Work exceedingly diversify'd with Stones of various Colours, Marble and Porphyry: But the stateliest Thing in all the Church are the Ornaments of the Altar for the great Holidays, of which that of St. *Mark* the Patron of the Republic is the most strictly kept. St. *Mark*'s Treasure is then all laid open, which consists in the rich Spoils taken from the Emperors of *Constantinople*. Every part shines with solid Gold, Pearls, and Diamonds; so that the Temple of *Jerusalem* excepted, I believe there's not a House devoted to God that could ever boast of so much Riches. All this Treasure is kept in St. *Mark*'s Tower, and none of it can be taken out but in presence of one of the Procurators, who must also be at the Altar when the Treasure is plac'd on it, and dare not stir from it till 'tis put up safe again.

St. *Mark*'s Church serves as a public Chapel to the Doge, who always is or at least ought to be attended thither by the Pope's Nuncio and the Ambassadors; but M. *de Gersi* the *French* Ambassador, from I know not what Punctilio of Honour, avoids being present at the same Functions with the Count *de Bolagnos* the Emperor's Ambassador*, whom he can't endure to see go before him. When the Doge goes to St. *Mark*'s Church 'tis always with great Ceremony: He walks between the Pope's Nuncio and the Emperor's Ambassador, and the other Ambassadors walk in the same Row according to the Rank of their Masters. They are preceded by six Trumpets, and six Banners are born before the Doge together with a Chair or Stool of State, there

---

* This Minister died at *Venice* in 1732, and was succeeded by Prince *Pio*.

there being no Back to it, and a Cushion of Gold Brocade. The Prince is dress'd in a long Robe of Gold Brocade also lin'd and fac'd with Ermin. The Senators follow him in Robes of red Damask, walking two and two. He is receiv'd at the Entrance of the Church by the Clergy of St. *Mark* who bring him Holy Water and Incense, which the Ambassadors receive after him. His Serenity and the Ambassadors fall on their Knees in the middle of the Nave, and then repeat the Prayers of *Domine salvum fac Principem nostrum*. Afterwards the Doge goes and places himself at the End of the Choir on the right Hand as we go in, and sits in the first upper Row of the Canons with the Pope's Nuncio on his Right and the Emperor's Ambassador on the Right of the Nuncio, and so on with the rest. The Doge does not sit down till the Senators are all enter'd, who, as they pass by his Serenity, make him a profound Obeisance; to which the Doge makes no manner of return. When every body is seated, the Doge accompany'd by the Ambassadors advances towards the Altar, the Nuncio strikes up High Mass and says the Overture, to which the Doge answers. After this, the Doge and the Ambassadors return to their Places, and the Prelate of St. *Mark* who is in waiting, continues the Office.

After the Mass is over, the Doge returns to his Palace attended by the same Train that accompanied him to Church. When he has ascended the grand Stair-case of his Palace he seats himself in an Arm-Chair which is plac'd over-against the Stair-case. After he has sate a few Moments, he dismisses the Ambassadors and the other Persons of his Retinue, and retires to his Apartment.

Next to St. *Mark*'s Church is the Doge's Palace, a vast Building, of which you will find a large Account in *Misson*'s Travels.

The

The present Doge is *Aloisio Mocenigo**, a Prince as much to be respected for his Merit as for his Dignity. He is a Gentleman of great Sagacity, talks well, is very polite, and has infinitely more Generosity than is ascribed to those of his Country. He is a handsome Man, and has a noble Aspect that is improv'd by his white Locks of Hair which render him venerable. Before he was advanc'd to be a Doge, which was in 1722, he serv'd the Republic with distinction in quality of Generalissimo. The vain Honours which this new Dignity has procur'd him have not puff'd him up, and he seems to think them rather a Burden than a Pleasure. Before he came to be Doge he was the most sociable Nobleman at *Venice*, and he now sees more Company than ever his Predecessors did. He masks himself at publick Rejoicings, goes out every Night in a common Gondola without Guard or Retinue, and diverts himself at his Brother's. He has sometimes too been upon *Terra Firma*, not valuing it tho' he lost for a while all the Honours annexed to his Dignity as Doge; for you know that this Character does not go beyond the Lakes. He is oblig'd to be present at all the public Ceremonies, tho' very much against his Inclination and Temper, which is far more uniform than that of the other *Italians*.

The Ceremony in which he shines with the greatest Lustre, is that of marrying the Sea, which without dispute is one of the finest Shews in all the World. 'Tis perform'd on *Ascension-Day*, when the Doge, the Ambassadors, and the Senate ride out into the *Adriatic* on board a Vessel call'd the *Bucentaur*, attended by the State-Gondolas of the Ambassadors gilded, with a vast number of other Gondolas and Galleasses which surround the *Bucentaur*, the most stately Vessel that was ever built, and more magnificent than all that History (or even

* He is dead, and succeeded by Don *Carlo Ruzzini*.

even Romance) tells us of the sumptuous Vessel of *Cleopatra*. When the Doge goes on board the *Bucentaur* he is saluted by the great Guns from the Galleys, the Men of War, and the Merchant-Ships in the Harbour; and while he performs the Ceremony of marrying the Sea by throwing in a Ring to denote the Sovereignty of the Republic over the Gulph, there's nothing heard but Kettle-Drums, Trumpets, and Concerts of Music, with the loud Acclamations of the People.

His Serene Highness marries two other Wives whom he maintains with as little Trouble as the Sea. They are the Abbesses of the Convents of the *Virgin* and St. *Daniel*. This Ceremony is perform'd upon St. *Philip*'s Day, when the Doge in a Galeass accompany'd by the Ambassadors and the Senate, repairs with a great Train to those Convents which are situate on the Shore behind the Arsenal. The Prelate who officiates for the Day receives him at the Entrance of the Church, brings him the Holy Water, and conducts him to a Place prepared for him in the Choir where he assists at High Mass. Then he repairs to the Grate, in which there's a large Opening where the Lady Abbess appears with her Nuns. The Abbess addressing herself to the Doge intreats him to continue the Favour of his Protection to herself and the Nuns; to which the Doge returns answer, that she and all the Convent may depend upon his Good-Will. Then he turns about and walks on foot to the Convent of St. *Daniel*, where his Reception and Transaction are the same as at the Convent of the *Virgin*. These two Convents have very singular Privileges. The Abbesses have the Crosier-Staff, and both they and their Nuns depend solely upon the Doge, and not at all upon the Pope or the Court of *Rome* either in Spirituals or Temporals. They have good Revenues and live as much as can be at their Ease. The
Dress

Dress of these Nuns is rather gay than modest. Like the Nuns at *Strasbourg* they wear their Hair in Tresses: Their Petticoats are so short that you may see their Ancles; and instead of Stays they wear Jackets with short Skirts, which are very becoming to those that are of a good Shape. Their Necks are quite bare, only when they go into the Choir they cover them with Veils of fine white Wool, which trail on the ground. These Nuns are the Daughters of the Nobles, and enjoy great Liberty, more than I believe they have under their Father's Roof.

The Festival of St. *Mark* is always celebrated with very great Solemnity. On the Day preceding, the Doge accompany'd by the Ambassadors repairs with a great Train to St. *Mark*'s Church, where he assists at the Vespers. Next Day the Confraternities, who are nine in number, meet at the Ducal Palace, accompany the Doge to Church in Procession, and are present at High Mass. After this the Doge returns to his Palace, and the Brotherhoods go round the Square. Each Society has magnificent Images, and two Canopies richly embroider'd with Gold and Silver; whose Poles or Supporters are of solid Silver. The Procession is clos'd by a Man dress'd in a Gown of red Damask, carrying a Pole with a moving Wheel at the end of it; which serves to support a gilt Lion surrounded with Laurel Branches, and little Standards of divers Colours. The Lion turns round incessantly, and the Man who carries it makes him leap, and play a hundred Gambols: He is surrounded with a Multitude of People, who cry out, God bless St. *Mark*. This Sight, how ridiculous soever, is nevertheless amusing, draws abundance of the Nobility to the Square, and on that Day every body is mask'd. After the Procession is over, the Maskers go to see the Doge's Table, who entertains

Vol. I.   D d   the

the Ambassadors and the Senate at Dinner, on a Table in form of a Horse-shoe; which is extravagantly adorn'd with Kickshaws, and Machines made of Starch, which are here call'd *Triumphs*. Nothing of the kind can be better executed, or more magnificent. As there is a great Apprehension of a Croud, all the Maskers are turn'd away at Dinner-time. They keep on their Masks all day long; and after Dinner all the Nobility, or to speak more properly, the whole City of *Venice* appears mask'd upon the Square of St. *Mark*; and indeed, for one who never saw it before, 'tis a remarkable fine Shew. What surpriz'd me, and if I may say it, made me laugh, was to see all the Maskers fall on their Knees at the Sound of the *Angelus*; you wou'd swear every body was in Rapture, yet every thing that goes before and that follows the Stroke of the Bell is not the most devout.

The Day after St. *Mark*'s we had another publick Shew, and by consequence a fresh occasion for the *Venetians* to masquerade it. That was the Election which the Fishermen, who are here call'd the *Nicolotti*, made of a Chief, who bears the Title of the Doge of the *Nicolotti*. Their Choice fell this Bout upon a Gondolier belonging to the noble *Giustiniani*. After the Election he was conducted to an Audience of the Doge of *Venice*, dress'd in a Robe of red Sattin, and otherwise accoutred like a Jackpudding. He was preceded by a great Mob of Pipers, Hautboys, and Fishermen. Just before him was carry'd a red Flag, with the Effigies of St. *Mark*. The Doge receiv'd him sitting on his Throne, and attended by the Council. The Complement of the Doge of the Fishermen was made with great Gravity, and answer'd by the Doge of the Republick in few Words; which done, he return'd in the same Order that he came.

came. This sham Doge has authority over all the Fishermen, is their Judge, gives them Licence to fish, and takes care that the City be well supplied with that sort of Provision. 'Tis said that this Office, which is for Life, is worth above 1000 Crowns *per Annum*. He had formerly the Privilege of commanding in a certain Quarter of the City, and assisted at all the Ceremonies where the Doge was present: He even accompany'd that Prince on board the *Bucentaur*, and had Precedency of all the Ambassadors; but they have lost that Right since, upon what occasion I know not, they gave up the Precedency to an Ambassador from the Emperor.

The Patriarch of *Venice* is the second Person in the State. The present Patriarch is of the Family of *Gradenigo*. The Authority of this Prelate is so stinted, that he only nominates to two or three Benefices. The Inhabitants of every Parish chuse their Parsons, which is always attended with Intriguing; for their Livings being very lucrative, have great Interest made for them. The Patriarch has a Privilege of having a Gondola painted Purple and Gold, with a Roof or Covering of Red Velvet; but this Gondola must not exceed a certain Degree of Magnificence. You know that the Gondolas of private Men must be black, and that none but Ambassadors have the Privilege of having theirs gilded.

Tho' the Churches of *Venice* have been sufficiently describ'd, I cannot help saying something of those that I thought the most remarkable. Without doubt the Front of the Church of the bare-footed *Carmelites*, situate upon the Great Canal, is the most magnificent, not only of *Venice*, but perhaps of *Europe*; as well with regard to the Proportions of Architecture that have been carefully observ'd, as with regard to the Fineness of the Marble, white as

Alabaster, with which this beautiful Front is wholly embellish'd. The Inside of this Church is extremely magnificent. The Roof is richly gilded, and curiously painted. The Walls are fac'd with Marble Pilasters; the Floor is of Stones inlaid with various Colours, and the Altars are exceeding stately: But of all these different things there seems to be too great a number, so that I could wish many of the Ornaments had been spar'd; for a noble Simplicity wou'd have look'd much better.

This sort of Simplicity is conspicuous in the Church of St. *George*, one of the biggest in *Venice*, the Architecture of which is surprizing. A Convent belongs to it, which for Magnificence and Regularity surpasses many Sovereign Palaces. The great Stair-Case is a fine piece of Architecture, and wou'd become a King's Palace much better than a Convent. This House has two noble Cloysters planted with Orange-Trees, a couple of spacious Courts, and two large Gardens well cultivated, which have Terrasses from whence there is a Prospect of the Sea, and the neighbouring Islands.

The Capuchins, whose Churches are very plain every where else, have a very noble one here, which is called *Al Redemptore*. It was built by order of the Republic to discharge a Vow they had made in the time of a Plague. The honest Capuchin who shew'd me the Church, made me take special notice of a Crucifix of Brass over the high Altar, whereon our Saviour is represented expiring, with his Head leaning on his right Shoulder. My Guide assur'd me that when the Crucifix was plac'd in the Church the Head of our Lord's Image was erect, but that it fell afterwards into its present Posture.

There are other Churches worth seeing, were it only for the stately Tombs of the most distinguish'd Families of the Republic. Such is the Tomb of the noble Family of *Cornaro*, in the Church of the

Cajetans, where are the Marble Effigies of eight Cardinals, and four Doges descended from that Family. In the Churches of St. *Paul* and St. *John* are Pictures very much esteem'd by the *Connoisseurs,* and there's the sumptuous Tomb of the *Valerios,* where the Father, the Mother, with the Son, are carv'd in their natural Proportion in Marble, apparell'd in the Habit of the Doge and Dogess.

Before I have done with the Churches, I think I ought to give you some account of that of the *Jesuits;* the Front whereof is of noble Architecture, well disposed, and the Ornaments not too much crouded; but the Decoration of the Inside is really grand. Nothing can be richer than the Choir, and the high Altar. The Choir consists of a spacious Dome supported by four large Pillars of white Marble, lin'd with great Flower-pieces of old green Marble. The Roof is painted and gilt. The high Altar, which is all of Marble, is a Pavilion or Dome supported by ten Columns wreath'd of the ancient *Greek* Marble. The Tabernacle is of Alabaster, incrustated with *Lapis-Lazuli.* To all this rich Work are added two Angels in their natural Proportion, over which are the Effigies of God the Father, and God the Son. The five Steps leading to the Altar are of green Marble, incrustated with old yellow Marble so artfully that this Work would easily be taken for a Piece of *Persian* Tapestry. The Pulpit and the Balustrade, which separates the Nave from the Choir, are of Marble, and perfectly answerable to the Magnificence of the whole Church.

I now proceed to the Arsenal, so much celebrated in *Europe,* perhaps more for what it has been than what it is at present. Three Nobles have the Management or Custody of it, who relieve one another every Week. He that is in waiting must visit the Posts in the Night-time; and the Centinels

tinels are oblig'd each to ring a Bell every Hour, that the Officer upon Guard may know they are at their Posts. No body can see the Arsenal without Leave of the Nobleman in waiting, who never refuses it to Persons of Rank. The first thing I was shew'd were four Rooms full of Arms necessary for the Marines, where are also kept the Cuirasses of those Generals who have most distinguish'd themselves in the Service of the Republic; but they are all full of Dust. Then I was shewed the Magazine of Anchors, and the Cellar to which the Workmen of the Arsenal go when they please to a Fountain of Wine and Water mix'd. As much diluted as this Wine is, 'tis said that there's no less spent here every Year than amounts to 74000 Crowns. This is an Endowment which was settled by one *Cornaro* Queen of *Cyprus*, for the Relief of the Workmen. Near this Cellar are the Forges, of which there are twelve; but there are only two actually at work. The Rope-Yard just by it, is 410 Paces in length, and serves at the same time for a Warehouse of Hemp, of which I did not see any great Quantity. In another Court there were a great many Cannon, both Iron and Brass, a Room full of Bullets, a Magazine of Cordage, a Timber-Yard, and three great Rooms full of Arms for the Foot Soldiers. There was another that serv'd as an Arsenal for the Horse, but 'twas lately burnt down by the Carelessness of a Centinel. The Dock for building and refitting of Ships forms a separate Court, in the midst of which there's a great Bason that communicates with the Sea, and is encompass'd with twenty six Sheds cover'd over, which contain as many Ships, Galleys, and Galleasses. The latter are Machines of a terrible Size, which have a sort of Battery at both ends. My Guide assur'd me that a *Venetian* Galleass was not afraid of twenty five *Turkish* Galleys: This may be; but I wou'd wou'd venture a Wager on the side of the Infidels. In this same Dock are the Prowes of twelve *Turkish* Galleys taken at the famous Battle of *Lepanto*. But the most noble thing in all this Dock, is the *Bucentaur*, which went out of Port for the first time in the Year 1728. This superb Vessel was built by *Antonio Corradini*; and is so well design'd, and the Ornaments of Sculpture, of which there's a great number, so well plac'd, that every thing is easily distinguish'd, and strikes with Amazement. 'Tis gilded down to the Water-edge, and 'tis said that the Expence of it amounted to 70000 Sequins. The Deck is cover'd from Head to Stern with Crimson-Velvet, bedaub'd with a broad Lace, and Gold Fringes. And the inside if possible is more magnificent than the Outside. There's a great Room the length of the Ship, where the Doge sits on a Throne, and the Ambassadors and Senators on Seats like those of the Canons in the Choir. The Cieling consists of Bas-reliefs in divers Compartments intirely gilt. The Floor is of Walnut-tree, incrusted with Ebony-Wood and Mother of Pearl. The Rowers who sit in the Hold of the Ship are all of one Livery, and their Oars gilt, which makes a very fine Sight when all hands strike together.

You know that the *Bucentaur* never goes out but once a-year, upon Ascension-day, when the Captain who then commands must take an Oath before he stirs out of the Harbour, that he will bring her back again into the Arsenal. He carries nothing aboard of his own, for unless the Weather be very fair indeed, the Ceremony is put off to another day. They build a new *Bucentaur* every hundred Years, and the old ones are laid up till they rot.

I just now hear that the Post is going off, so that I am oblig'd to defer what I have farther to say of *Venice* till the next. I shall be infinitely pleas'd if I can satisfy your Curiosity, and much more if I can prove to you that no body has a more profound Veneration for you than I, *Who am,* &c.

LETTER XXVI.

SIR, *Venice, May* 15, 1730.

THE Common-wealth keeps twelve Galleys in pay, and twenty Men of War. The *Capitana* Galley, call'd the *Fusta*, never goes out of the Great Canal, but is continually at Anchor before the Square of St. *Mark*. There's commonly four Galleys and as many Men of War in the *Levant*. Others lie at Anchor in the Canal of *Zueca*, which were lately drawn out of the Arsenal, because for want of Water the Ships receive Damage. The Power of the Republic consists chiefly in its Maritime Force. It maintains very few Land Forces, and those they have are all kept at *Corfou*, which is the Rampart of *Venice*, and the Defence of the Gulph; the Preservation of which is owing to the Count *de Schulemburg*, General in chief of the Republic; for in the last War when the *Turks* attempted to take it, 'twas he that oblig'd them to raise the Siege: And the Republic in acknowledgment of this important Service caus'd his Statue on Horseback to be erected in the Square of the Old Castle of *Corfou*; and settled a Pension upon him of 5000 Crowns a-year for his Life, besides his ordinary Salary.

'Tis certain that *Venice* has suffer'd a Decay both of Power and Commerce. The *Turks* have taken
the

the *Morea* from her; she has little or nothing left in the *Levant*; and as to her Places in the *Terra Firma* they are poor, depopulated, and meanly fortified. One of the main Securities of *Venice* is her Lakes; but for some Years past they begin to thicken so by the Mud and Dirt brought by the Rivers which fall into the Gulph, as in time must prove to the very great Detriment of *Venice*, because Ships which us'd formerly to go in or out with ease, can only go out now by the help of a Canal which has been cut for the purpose. This Inconvenience might have formerly been prevented for a trifle of Expence, whereas now 'tis past all remedy.

The Powers of which the *Venetians* ought to be most jealous, are the *Turks* and the Emperor, in whose Dominions they are in a manner inclos'd. The Great Duke of *Tuscany* and the Duke of *Parma* were formerly Powers which were of little or no Terror to the Republic; but if those Dominions shou'd ever come under the Sovereignty of *Don Carlos*, the political System of *Italy* will be very much alter'd, and the *Venetians* will in all probability be oblig'd to keep fair with him. The Republic has for a long time observ'd an exact Neutrality in the Quarrels among the Princes of Christendom, perhaps because it knows not for which side to determine itself; for tho' the Senate hates the *Spaniards*, and cannot forget the famous Conspiracy of the Marquis *de Bedmar* the Catholic King's Ambassador; they don't much like either the *Germans* or *French*, whose Power gives them Umbrage. And I believe, were it possible for the *Venetians* to hurt those three Powers at the same time, we shou'd quickly see their Republic rouze itself from that Lethargy in which it's profound State-Policy has doz'd it.

Since the *English* and *Dutch* became Masters of the Commerce of *Europe*, the Trade of *Venice* is as much de-

decay'd as its Power; and their Manufactures are sunk extremely. The *Venetians* heretofore furnished almost all *Europe* with Cloth; their Looking-Glasses, and those for Drinking, were also in great vogue, but those Manufactures are since transplanted into other Countries, so that *Venice* scarce furnishes any more than *Italy*. 'Tis worth while however to go and see the Glass-House where they work Night and Day, except in *August* and *September*, when the Heats are too violent. 'Tis certain the Drinking-Glasses made here are much stronger than any other, but as they are blown they are not near so substantial as the Glass that is run; however they require less Labour, and have the Advantage when they are broke of being melted again; the Matter of which they are composed being much more flexible than that of the run Glass.

The Nobles of *Venice* are Slaves to Policy, Diffidence, and Suspicion; and Ambassadors are much more so, whom every one shuns as suspected Persons, and whom a Foreigner can scarce talk to without renouncing his Correspondence with the Nobles. An Ambassador is oblig'd to confine himself to his own Family, or else to amuse himself in the Company of Foreigners, of whom there is always a good number in this City; for no Nobleman dare visit him without the express leave of the Senate, who now indeed grant it much more freely than they did formerly.

Customs are alter'd here in very many things. 'Twas formerly a Crime to see a Woman in private, and a Foreigner did not dare to run the Venture; but now the case is quite different, for there are several Houses of Quality where I am indulg'd, and am often *tête a tête* with the Mistress of the House, without any more notice taken of me than if I were in *France*, where Ease and Freedom are

so

so much boasted. The Ladies are great Visiters, and have Assemblies every Night, to which they repair alone in their Gondola's without any other Attendance but a Valet de Chambre, who serves as their Gentleman-Usher. They are mask'd at all public Performances, and go where they have a mind to it. This easy access to the Ladies contributes not a little to make my Stay in this City agreeable. I own to you that I am infinitely charm'd with it; there are a thousand Things here that please me, and were I to chuse any City in *Italy* to live in, 'twould certainly be this, where People enjoy entire Liberty, provided they don't meddle with the State and its Government, which after all too, I don't think a Foreigner has much to do with. Here one is in the Centre of civil Pleasures and Debauchery. God is as exemplarily serv'd here as in any Place whatsoever. Few Nations observe the Externals of Religion better than the *Italians* in general and the *Venetians* in particular, of whom it may be said that they spend one half of their time in committing Sin, and the other half in begging God's pardon.

Masquerades are more in fashion here than elsewhere. People go in Masks to take the Air, as well as to Plays and Balls; and 'tis the favourite Pleasure both of the Grandees and the Commonalty. This gives rise to many Adventures, and sometimes one makes Acquaintance under a Mask which would be impracticable perhaps, were not such Disguises in Fashion. I remember that the first time I was here I struck up an Acquaintance in the Square of St. *Mark* with two of the first-rate Ladies of this Country. They were mask'd, and I was in a Scarlet Domino embroider'd with Silver, which being a Habit that had been seldom seen here, drew the Eyes of all the Company in the Square upon me, and in particular of two Ladies, one of whom twitching

me

me by the Sleeve, said to me, 'Sir, I and the Lady
'here, my Friend, fancy by your Air which out-
'strips our Gentlemen, that you are a Foreigner,
'and we are inclin'd to think that you are no mean
'Person. We should be glad of your Conversation,
'and you will do us a Pleasure to take a turn with
'us round the Square.——You do me too much
'Honour, fair Lady (said I, walking on) and what
'you tell me of my Appearance pleases me the more
'because you are both the compleatest Ladies in the
'Place. As you guess by my Habit that I am not
'a common Person, your Air persuades me that I
'have the Honour to speak to Ladies of Quality.—
'You are not mistaken (said the same Lady to me)
'this Lady my Companion is Madame *M* . . . and
'I am the Wife of Mr. *C* . . . You find (continu'd
'she) that our Names are pretty well known in *Ve-*
'*nice*. Now, after having told you who we are,
'may we presume to ask who you are?' I gratify'd
their Curiosity by pulling off my Mask, which I
thought a Compliment due to their Quality. I had
scarce told my Name, when the Lady who had not
yet spoke one Word, said to me, 'You are not so
'much a Stranger among us as you imagine; your
'Name is very well known to me, and the late
'Madame *Duhamel*, your Aunt, whose * Husband
'was Commander in chief of our Forces, was one
'of my most intimate Friends, and she often told
'me how much she wish'd to see you here; but
''twas a Comfort she did not live to enjoy. She
'went with her Husband to *Corfou*, where he died
'not without Suspicion of Poison; for he was ac-
'cus'd of being too great a *Frenchman*; and your
'Aunt who was return'd from *Corfou* with a Design

---

* *Francis*, Count *Duhamel*, Lieutenant-General of the King of *Prussia*'s Army, Knight of the Order of the *Black Eagle*, and Colonel of a Regiment of Horse. The *Venetians* invited him to their Service in 1704, and gave him the chief Command of their Forces.

' sign to go and spend the Remainder of her Days
' at *Berlin*, died as she was performing Quarentine
' in our Port. You caus'd her Body to be remov'd
' to *Berlin*, and you was one of her Heirs ; and,
' tho' I don't mention it to make a Merit of it, I
' must tell you that you are oblig'd to me for it,
' since I pleaded for you against a very great num-
' ber of M. *Dubamel*'s Relations. My Love to your
' Aunt put me upon engaging Mr. *M* . . . to
' espouse your Interest, which he promoted with
' Success, and prevail'd on the Senate to prefer the
' Recommendations of the King of *Prussia* and the
' Elector of *Hanover* who both protected you, be-
' fore the Instances made by the *French* Ambassador
' in the Name of the King his Master, in favour of
' Messieurs *Dubamel*. I was infinitely pleas'd (con-
' tinu'd Madame *M* . . .) that I had an Oppor-
' tunity of serving you, and you may depend
' upon it that Mr. *M* . . . and I shall ever interest
' our selves heartily for all that belong to our de-
' ceased Friend.' I made answer to Madame *M* . . .
in Terms suitable to her obliging Expressions, and
crav'd her Permission to pay my respects to her at
her House. She answer'd me very civilly that she
would send her Husband to me, and that then she
should be glad to see me at her House. Next
Morning as I was ready to go out, and wait upon
Mr. *M* . . . to whom I thought I ow'd a Visit
after the Civilities I had receiv'd from his Wife, I
was told that he was at my Door and desir'd to
speak with me. I went and receiv'd him, and
found him every whit as polite as his Lady. He
offer'd to shew me the Curiosities of *Venice* till his
Wife was stirring. We went and saw several
Churches, after which he conducted me to his House
where I found Madame *M* . . . who receiv'd me
with all the Civility possible. She was a Woman
who tho' forty Years of Age shew'd that she had

been

been a very beautiful Lady in her time. Madame *C* .... happen'd to be in her Company, with whom she had been the Day before in the Square of St. *Mark*. I never saw a more beautiful Lady, or that had a nobler Carriage. She was not yet twenty Years of Age, but had been marry'd five Years to a Man, who tho' the most ill-favour'd of his Sex had a most amiable Behaviour. I fell in love with Madame *C* .... as soon as ever I saw her, and when I beheld her Husband, I had Presumption enough to believe that my Application to the Lady would not be disagreeable. But I soon perceiv'd that she was not a Woman for my turn; she quickly depriv'd me of all Hopes of Success; and I no sooner saw those Hopes vanish'd, which are the only Support of Lovers, but I dropp'd my Amour. I had another in view which was attended with better Success: M. *M* ... carry'd me to a Country-House of his towards *Padua*, and I don't know where I was ever more agreeably entertain'd in my whole Life. 'Tis at these Country Seats one sees the *Venetians* in Perfection, who are quite another sort of People here than in the City; for here they put off that grave serious Air which they affect in Town, and are quite sociable, civil, courteous, and live with more splendor. As these Country-Houses are near one another, the Gentlemen to whom they belong visit each other very much, and are almost always together; but at *Venice* they live with more Restraint.

I am in some doubt whether I should reckon the Music of the *Venetian* Churches in the number of its Pleasures; but upon the whole, I think I ought, because certainly their Churches are frequented more to please the Ear, than for real Devotion. The Church of *la Pieta* which belongs to the Nuns who know no other Father but Love, is most frequented. These Nuns are enter'd very young, and are taught Music,

Music, and to play on all sorts of Instruments, in which some of 'em are excellent Performers. *Apollonia* actually passes for the finest Singer, and *Anna-Maria*'s for the first Violin in *Italy*. The Concourse of People to this Church on Sundays and Holidays is extraordinary. 'Tis the Rendezvous of all the Coquettes in *Venice*, and such as are fond of Intrigues have here both their Hands and Hearts full. Not many Days after my Arrival in this City I was at this very Church, where was a vast Audience, and the finest of Music. As I was going out, a Woman who hid her Face accosted me, saying, there was a Lady in a Gondola who desir'd to speak with me. Tho' this smelt strong of an Adventure, which I was never very fond of, I however went along with the Woman; and really, not above ten Paces from the Spot I found a Gondola, in which was a Lady whom I knew to be the Daughter of the unfortunate Baron *de H*... of whose tragical Catastrophe you have heard. I own it mov'd my Compassion, as well as Sorrow, to see before my Eyes a young Lady of Rank in a strange Country and in such a Situation as made me surmise that she was in a bad Way. But it even touch'd me to the quick, when after having made her Apology to me for having sent for me, she said to me with a Voice interrupted with Sighs, ' For God's sake tell 'me what's become of my poor Father; is he still 'living? He has been the Cause of his own Unhappiness and mine too; he has plung'd me into an 'Abyss of Woe, but he is still my Father: Nothing 'can make me forget the Duty I owe him; I 'should be glad even to lay down my Life to re'lieve his Misfortunes.' I told her that I had not been at *Berlin* for a long time; that I had not kept up a Correspondence there with any body, and that consequently I could not tell her any News of her Father. I knew at the same time that he died in

Prison

Prison at *Spandaw*; but I was loth to be the Messenger of such bad News to a Person who seem'd to be already too much afflicted. 'I did not know
' you were at *Venice* (reply'd Madamoiselle *de H*...)
' or I should have sought an Opportunity to speak
' with you. I saw you at the Church of *la Pietà*,
' and the sight of you call'd my Misfortunes fresh
' to my Memory, as well as the sad Catastrophe of
' your old Friend my Father. I could not refrain
' shedding Tears, and the Remembrance of my
' Disgrace has eclips'd the Pleasure I take in seeing
' you.' I endeavour'd to assuage her Grief, and to calm her ruffled Soul; and therefore I went with her to her House, and when I saw her a little compos'd I ask'd her questions about her state of Life, and desir'd her to tell me how she had pass'd her time since she left *Berlin*. She answer'd me in every Point with a great deal of Honesty and Simplicity.
' After the Execution of that Sentence (said she)
' which degraded my Father from Nobility and
' Honour, and set him on a level with the basest
' Scoundrels, I had not the Courage to stay at *Berlin*. I went to *H*... to find out Madame *de*
' *B*... my Aunt from whom I hoped to meet
' with Protection; but I soon experienc'd that the
' Unfortunate have no Relations. My Aunt would
' not give me House-room, and sent a Confident of
' her's to tell me that she advis'd me to be gone from
' *H*... or else to change my Name and not to call
' me her Cousin, unless I had a Desire to be confin'd.
' But alas! I should then have taken it as a Favour
' if my Aunt had shut me up; for I was in extreme
' Want, and knew not what would become of me.
' I lodg'd at an Inn where I got my Living by mak-
' ing of Linnen and Washing, when a good likely
' young Man came and took up his Quarters in the
' very same House, who immediately struck up an
' Acquaintance with me. I know not what he saw
' in

'in me to charm him, for I did nothing but cry all
'the day long. Mean time he talk'd to me of
'Love, and gave me so many Demonstrations of
'his flaming Passion that I found he was really
'smitten with me. To tell you the whole Truth, I
'was not long insensible of the same Passion. He
'even offer'd to marry me, which, since he would
'not be deny'd, I consented to. He told me that
'he was an Officer in the Emperor's Service, and
'a Native of *Lubeck*, and that he was come hither
'to take possession of an Estate fallen to him
'by Inheritance. I took what he said to be true
'because he was handsomely equipp'd, and had his
'Pockets well lin'd. In short, I was smitten with
'him, and thought I should be very happy in taking
'him for my Husband. Not many Days after our
'Marriage, he told me that he must needs set out
'for *Hungary* where the Regiment was quarter'd,
'whereof he said he was a Lieutenant, and that
'consequently I must make ready to go with him.—
'We set out from H . . . and arriv'd happily at
'*Vienna*. It was in that very City that my Hus-
'band, who till then behav'd well towards me, and
'whose Conduct had been very regular, chang'd
'all on a sudden to the reverse. He spent the
'whole Day in Gaming-Houses, and the Night in
'Debauchery. Sometimes he never once came home
'for four or five Days together, and when he did,
''twas only to insult me, and to upbraid me with
'the misfortune of my Father, which I discover'd
'to him before Marriage, for fear he should reproach
'me one time or other with having deceiv'd him.
'He told me that I was a Disgrace to him, that
'his Colonel had broke him for marrying me, and
'that I was the Author of his Ruin. I try'd to
'pacify him, and spar'd no Pains nor Complaisance
'for it, but all to no purpose. I heard that my
'Husband was desperately in love with a common
'Prostitute,

' Prostitute, that he had ruin'd himself for her sake;
' and in a little time he was oblig'd to sell the very
' Clothes off his back. He had contracted Debts,
' and expecting every day to be arrested by his Credi-
' tors, he left *Vienna* privately, abandoning me to the
' most dreadful Despair.' Twas eight Months be-
' fore I heard a Word of him. At last I came to
' know that he was here at *Venice*, and I resolv'd to
' find him out. Madame the Countess of *W* . . .
' who had generously assisted me, fitted me out for
' the Journey, but when I came hither I did not
' find my Husband, who I heard was at *Padua*. I
' was making my self ready to follow him thither,
' when I heard the News that he was kill'd by a
' Student with whom he had a Quarrel at Gaming.
' His Death fill'd up the Measure of my Sorrow.
' I found my self quite a Stranger here without
' Friends or Subsistence. I endeavour'd, but in
' vain, to get my Living by my Labour, as I had
' done at *H* . . . but I found so little to do that 'twas
' impossible for me to hold out long; and I must un-
' doubtedly have sunk under my Misery if it had
' not been for the noble *D* . . . who out of Pity
' to my Condition reliev'd me six Years ago by
' granting me a Pension: But how happy should I
' be if I could live without it, and retire for ever to
' some religious Foundation!' Here the unfortunate *H* . . . concluded her Narrative. I sifted
her Sentiments about Religion: I knew she had
been educated in the *Lutheran*, but she express'd
her Inclination to embrace the Catholic Religion,
and also to turn Nun. I promis'd to serve her all
that lay in my power, and that same Evening I
spoke to Madame *M* . . . who promis'd me to
enter her into Orders as soon as she was turn'd Catholic. A Jesuit who has had the tutoring of her
for near a Month gives us Hopes that she will in-
stantly be qualify'd to take the Veil. She seems to
me

me to be very eager for it. A few days ago I acquainted her with her Father's Death, with which she seem'd very much affected, but at the same time she express'd her Submission to the Decrees of Providence, and told me her Misfortunes with so much Resignation, that I have Reason to think she will be very happy in the Retirement which she is about to embrace. If this be the Case, I shall think my self very fortunate in having contributed by my Advice to her Tranquillity. Heaven grant her Prayers may prevail that I my self may put those Lessons in practice which I have taught her, as to the Necessity of Conversion.

Pardon me, Sir, this long Digression. As you knew the unfortunate *H* . . . in his Prosperity, and as you are also inform'd of his Disgrace, I thought you would not be sorry to hear of the Fate of his Daughter. I now resume my Remarks on *Venice*.

Two Days ago I went to see the *Scuola St. Rocco*, which are Rooms where the Fraternities of that Saint meet, in which are Pictures done by the greatest Masters, particularly one in the great Room below, which is the Picture of the *Annunciation* done by *Tintoret*, a Piece highly esteem'd. This Picture is, without Contradiction, one of the finest and most affecting Paintings at *Venice*, because of the lively Expressions of Surprise, Admiration, and Joy which appear in the *Virgin's* Face. She is sitting in her Chamber, which the skilful Painter has represented as a plain mean Room in some Disorder with old and worn out Furniture. Upon the grand Stair-case there's another Picture representing the *Annunciation* in like manner, which is done by *Titian*, and is not one of the worst of his Performances. The upper Rooms are adorn'd with several Pictures done by *Tintoret*, in which he has described our Lord's Passion. Our Saviour appearing before *Pilate* is an admirable Piece; 'tis really moving to see the Modesty and Serenity of his Countenance. A second Picture represents our Lord carrying his Cross. In a third, we see him fasten'd on it, and expiring for the Salvation of Mankind. These are invaluable Pieces, and are reckon'd the compleatest that ever *Tintoret* painted.

I have also been to see the chief Palaces, which lie for the most part on the great Canal, and that call'd *Reggio*. They are very magnificent, but they are generally so like one another that he who has seen one may say he has seen them all. They have little Court-Yards, less Gardens, and no Stables. Nothing goes to form a Palace at *Venice* but the main Body of the Building, a great Salon in the middle, and Apartments on the Right and Left; and setting aside the Marble, there are Palaces as magnificent elsewhere which have only the name of a House.

The Square of St. *Mark* is the ordinary Rendezvous of all the Gentry at *Venice*. There are Nobles who keep their constant Circuits here as it were, and who never stir from the Place but to Bed, for they pass their whole Time in Gaming at the Coffee-Houses, or in the Peruke-Makers Shops. The number of their Nobles is not limited; and any body for paying down 100000 Ducats may purchase Nobility. These Gentlemen compliment each other with the Title of *Excellency*, and 'tis what they all challenge from Foreigners. Mean time, some of those *Excellencies* go to the Shambles, and to the Fish-Market, and carry home their Meat or their Fish under their Robes, and some are so very poor that they go a begging. This Title is so very common here that I had much ado to hinder a Lackey whom I hired from giving it to me. Tho' I told him that I was by no means *Excellent*, he made me answer that he knew full well what Obligations were due to my Excellency, and that he would not be thought to be wanting in Respect to my Excellency. A

French-

Frenchman lately come from *Constantinople* to whom I made my Complaints, how much this Title was prophan'd, assur'd me that the *Venetians* were still more lavish of it out of *Venice*, so that he heard the very Grooms belonging to the Baillo of the Republic at *Constantinople*, compliment one another with the Title of *Excellency*.

Among the *Venetian* Excellencies there are also *Petits-Maitres* who are known by their Doublets lin'd with Scarlet, their fine white Perukes, by their fantastical Step, and that Air of lolling which they give themselves in their Gondola's, which are much smaller and nimbler than the common sort. These *Petits-Maitres* are great Beaus, and have commonly more than one Mistress at a time, and indeed there are few Nobles but have one at least. These Creatures, excepting the little Liberty they enjoy, are as happy as Sultana's. Their Lovers treat them like Princesses, and the *Venetians* in general pay great respect to the whole Sex. I have seen *Faustina* the famous Singer, and *Stringuetta* the noted Courtezan come mask'd upon the Square of St. *Mark*, leaning on the Shoulders of Noblemen, and every Man paying them as much Obeisance as if they had been Ladies of great Importance. The same day that they appear'd on the Square there happen'd to be a Skirmish between two Women mask'd that were Rivals, who, as soon as they knew one another, fell out, went to Cuffs, tore off each other's Masks, and at last Knives were drawn, with which they cut one another so deeply that one of 'em was left dead on the Spot.

I now think it high time to finish my Letter which is already very long, and perhaps too full of Trifles. I have told you every Thing that came uppermost in my Mind, so that you have a perfect Farrago,

Farrago, which however is a Proof of the Pleasure I take in corresponding with you.

LETTER XXVII.

SIR,   *Ronciglione, May* 30. 1730.

AS it appears by all the Letters from *Rome* that they are on the point of chusing a new Pope, I set out sooner from *Venice* than I should otherways have done, and came post to this City without stopping much by the Way. I pass'd thro' PADUA, where I had the Honour to pay my Respects to the Prince *Emanuel* of *Portugal*, who is come to reside there for some time, and I was afterwards at the Comedy, which was indeed, a most wretched Performance, but the Assembly was gay and numerous: Among the rest there were a great number of Students and young Fellows, particularly one that made a very finical Appearance, who had ten or twelve Patches on his Face, a red Coat embroider'd with black Gawse, a Hat, a Shoulder-Knot, Stockings, &c. the whole trimm'd with Gawse. I took him at first for a Mountebank, but I plainly saw that the Whimsicalness of his Dress was the Humour of the Country. What gave me some Amusement was, to see a Hare which Harlequin had taught to play Tricks, to tumble Top over Tail, to leap over a Stick, and to beat a Drum with his two Fore-feet.

From

From *Padua* I went to FERRARA a City in the Ecclefiaftical State, where the Pope keeps a Legat who is always a Cardinal. It appear'd to me to be a large City with fpacious Streets, and fome fine Palaces, but it did not feem to be very populous, which is afcrib'd to the bad Air in this Country, otherwife one of the fineft in all *Italy*.

The Road from *Ferrara* to BOLOGNA is extremely level, and as good and agreeable in Summer as 'tis unpaffable in Winter. *Bologna* is the fecond City in the Ecclefiaftical State, and is a large fine Town. 'Tis in a moft charming Situation, all the Country round it being properly a Garden, and one of the moft fruitful and faireft flats in Nature. 'Tis faid this City contains near 80000 Inhabitants. The common People are civil and well bred, and none more polite to Foreigners than the Noblemen. There are ftately Palaces here, of which I will only mention that of the Marquis *Rinucci*, becaufe to me it feem'd to be one of the moft confiderable in the City. 'Tis very magnificent, and of a vaft extent. The Ground-Floor contains three large Apartments, the firft Story five, and the fecond as many. The Stair-cafe of this Palace is very much efteem'd for its Contrivance. In one of the Halls are two large Pictures: The firft is the Confecration of the Emperor *Charles* V. perform'd by the Pope at *Bologna*: The fecond reprefents *Frederic* IV. King of *Denmark* giving Audience to the Senate of *Bologna*: and their complimenting him on his Arrival. In another of thofe Halls are two other curious large Pictures; the one of Cardinal *Rinucci*, having Audience of the King of *Poland* when he was fent to him as Nuncio; and the fecond fhews the fame Cardinal receiving the Cap from *Lewis* XIV. King of *France*, at whofe Court he was Nuncio when he was promoted to the Purple. The Apartments adjoining to thefe Halls are alfo adorn'd adorn'd with excellent Paintings and very richly furnish'd.

The Churches of *Bologna* are not less magnificent than the finest Churches in *Italy*. I thought that of St. *Paul* the most worthy of Remark, which is serv'd by *Bernardine* Fryars. The Roof is adorn'd with Paintings representing the History of St. *Paul*. These Pictures which are highly esteem'd are the Performances of *Antonio Caccioli* and *Rolli* two Natives of *Bologna*, and they have both outdone themselves. The Painting of the Dome where St. *Paul* is represented on his Knees ready to have his Head struck off is admirably fine. The high Altar is of Marble of various Colours, finish'd with a great deal of Art. The Seats of the Monks are of Wallnut-Tree, and over them are several Pictures of the Life of St. *Paul* drawn by an able Hand, who was *Carache*'s Pupil. The Churches of St. *Catherine* of *Bologna*, and St. *Michael* in *Bosco* are well worth the Traveller's Observation, on account of the choice Pictures with which they are adorn'd. St. *Michael*'s in *Bosco* stands upon an Eminence three Miles from *Bologna*, to which there's an Entrance thro' a cover'd Gallery made like a Piazza. 'Twas a Work erected by the Citizens of *Bologna*, out of their Devotion to a miraculous Image of the *Holy Virgin* which is reverenc'd in this Church.

The Legate's Palace is very ancient, but grand and magnificent. 'Tis as strictly guarded during the Vacancy of the Holy See as if the Enemy were at the Gates of the City. All the Avenues to it are hung with Chains: The *Swiss* Guards are arm'd with Cuirasses: The Guard which consists of fifty Soldiers is barricaded with Pallisades and Chevaux de Frise, and the Palace-Gate is defended by eight Pieces of Cannon.

What

What remains for me to tell you of *Bologna* is, that 'tis one of the Cities in *Italy* where a Foreigner finds most Amusement. The Nobility not only strive to give him Pleasure, but he has fine Paintings to feast his Eye, and here are often excellent Concerts of Music, Operas, and Comedies, charming Walks, and genteel Country-Houses; which I take to be all that can be desir'd in Life.

From *Bologna* I travell'd in two days to *Florence*, after having been dragg'd in my Chaise thro' the *Apennines*, a prodigious Range of Mountains; which is a thing I shall never do again while I live; for I really suffer'd very much in this Road, and if ever you should have a fancy to come this way, I would advise you to carry Provisions or a Cook with you, for there is not one considerable Place in all the Road. *Fiorenzola*, which is almost half way, is a sorry little Town. From thence to *Scarperia* the Road is extremely rugged. One descends a high Mountain pav'd like a Stair-case, which to attempt in a Chaise, you are sure of being, if I may so call it, broke upon the Wheel, and therefore I chose to walk down. At *Scarperia* the Road becomes more passable, and it mends as you come near *Florence*. In our Way we pass'd thro' a Town call'd *Ponte* that stands at the Foot of a Hill, where the Great Duke has a Castle which appear'd to me to be very well fortify'd.

One perceives FLORENCE a great way off, and indeed it makes a fine point of View to see so great a City in a beautiful Valley between Hills which rise insensibly, and end at length in high Mountains, inhabited in such a manner that they may be reckon'd the Suburbs of *Florence*. The River *Arno* passes thro' both the City and the Valley. Among all the Cities of *Italy*, *Florence* may justly be surnamed the *Fair*, since it has all that can be desir'd in a great and wealthy Town, such as sacred and profane Edifices,

fices, Bridges, Monuments, and Fountains; yet 'tis not so large nor populous as *Bologna*. As I enter'd *Florence* I perceived over the Gate a Table of white Marble with a *Latin* Inscription on it, as follows:

FLORENTIA, ADVENTU FRIDERICI IV. DANIÆ ET NORVEGIÆ, AUGUSTI, FELICIS, QUOD EAM SUA PRÆSENTIA MAGNUS HOSPES IMPLEVERIT, AUGUSTA FELIX, AN. S. 1708. MENSE MARTIO.

'Twas the late Great Duke *Cosmo* who caus'd this to be engrav'd to the Honour of the King of *Denmark*.

The City of *Florence* has been so well describ'd that I shall pass very briefly over all that relates to the Buildings. The Square call'd *Piazza del Gran Duca* or the old Palace, contains Ornaments enough to embellish a great Town. Here you see a spacious Fountain which *Cosmo* I. caus'd to be built after the Designs of *Amminati* and *Philip Baldinucci*, two of the most famous Sculptors at that Time. Not far from this Fountain is the Equestrian Statue of *Cosmo* I. which is rais'd upon a great Pedestal of white Marble, with this Inscription engrav'd on the chief Front of it:

COSMO MEDICI, MAGNO ETRURIÆ DUCI PRIMO, PIO, FELICI, INVICTO, JUSTO, CLEMENTI, SACRÆ MILITIÆ PACISQUE IN ETRURIA AUTHORI, PATRI ET PRINCIPI OPTIMO, FERDINANDUS F. MAG. DUX III. EREXIT, AN. CIƆ IƆ LXXXXIIII.

On the other three Sides of the Pedestal are very fine Bas-Reliefs of Brass. The first represents *Cosmo* I. recogniz'd for Sovereign by the Senate of *Florence*;

Florence; the second the Ceremony of *Cosmo*'s Coronation, and the third the same *Cosmo* in an antique triumphant Car making his pompous Entry into *Sienna*, which was submitted to his Government. *Ferdinand* I. *de Medicis* when he erected this Statue to the Honour of his Father, employ'd in the Direction of it the famous *John Bologna*, who has very well answer'd the Opinion that had been conceiv'd of him.

In the Great Duke's Gallery near the Square, I saw the greatest Curiosities, both among the Antients and Moderns. A Busto of *Alexander* the Great, the famous Statue of *Venus*, cut by *Apollodorus*, with those of the Emperors and Empresses of *Rome*, and the greatest Personages of former Centuries; the best Originals of the greatest Painters; and a thousand uncommon things, such as Diamonds, Rubies, Pearls, Emeralds, Saphirs, Topazes, Amber, Porcellain, Crystal, Porphyry, Coral, Marble, and Granite, the Particulars of which wou'd form a Volume. They are actually engraving on Plates, and several Persons of Quality are contributing to the Expence of this fine Work, which is considerable, and for which excellent Designers are employ'd. This wou'd have been worthy of the Great Duke, and it seems to me that this Prince when he sees his Family extinct, and his Estate pass into the hands of Foreigners, ought at least to eternize the Glory of his Ancestors by publishing an Inventory of the immense Wealth which they have acquired, and transmitted to their Posterity.

Of all the Churches in *Italy* there are none more magnificent as to the outside than the Dome of *Milan*, and the Cathedral of *Florence*, both which are entirely lin'd with Marble of various Colours. A Citizen of *Florence*, who pretended to know the History of this City perfectly well, assur'd me that its Cathedral was built out of the Impost of

five

five *Sous* which had been laid upon every Piece of Cloth that was then sold at *Florence*; but I believe you may without Breach of Charity take this for a Story.

Over against the Cathedral is the magnificent Baptistery, to which there's an Entrance thro' three Gates of Brass, so artfully wrought that *Michael Angelo* said they were good enough to be the Gates of Paradise.

St. *Lawrence*'s Chapel, which is not yet finish'd, is the Admiration of all Connoisseurs, and is design'd to be the Place for the Burial of the Great Dukes, whose Remains are to be deposited in a Mausoleum of wonderful Workmanship, adorn'd with precious Stones. 'Tis 150 years ago that this Chapel has been building, and yet it wants two Thirds of being finish'd. If it were lawful to criticise the Conduct of Princes, I must say it again, that the Great Duke, who sees that his Greatness and his Family must end with him, ought to put the last hand to this Monument of the Magnificence of the *Medicis*: For can he hope, that if he himself neglects to transmit the Lustre of his Family to Posterity, his Successors will think to do it, who are nothing to him, or at least but very little? But such is the Humour of *John Gaston* Great Duke of *Tuscany*; he is so indifferent and unconcern'd about every thing, that he sees Foreigners dispose of his Dominions, and nominate his Successor, and the Courtiers ready to abandon him and to worship the said Successor; and yet the Prospect, how disagreeable soever it may be, does not seem to give him any Uneasiness: And he said some days ago, after he had sign'd his Last Will and Testament, declaring *Don Carlos* Infante of *Spain* his Successor, *that he had just got a Son and Heir by a Dash of his Pen, which he had not been able to get in thirty four years Marriage.*

Thus,

Thus, Sir, I have given all you will have of me this time touching *Florence*, where I cou'd stay but a few days, and then made no Acquaintance, having only been taken up in seeing the Curiosities of this City. At my Return from *Rome* I propose to come hither again, and make some stay in order to get a little Knowledge of the Court; and then you shall be inform'd of every Remark that I make.

From *Florence* I went and din'd at *Castilloncello*, and lay at Sienna a City in the Duchy of *Tuscany*, to which *Cosmo* I. *de Medicis* made it subject, not without great Resistance from the *Siennois*. The City which is both an Archbishoprick and an University, is very pleasantly situate, and enjoys a very good Air. 'Tis said that *Italian* is spoke here with more Purity than in any other Town in *Italy*. It seem'd to me to want Inhabitants, for I went thro' several Streets and did not meet a Soul. 'Tis said that a great many of the Nobility are settled in *Sienna*, and that Strangers are sure to meet with a civil Reception here, but as I staid no more than one day, I had only a cursory View of the Town. The Cathedral appear'd to me to be a great and noble Building lin'd with Marble. The Great Duke's Palace is ancient, but commodious. It has a Tower which is look'd upon as a singular piece of Architecture. The Great Princess * *Violante* of *Bavaria* is Governess of *Sienna*. She liv'd formerly in this City, and was mightily belov'd in it; but she has resided for some time at *Florence*. The Square which is before the Palace is oval, and hollow in the Middle, so that it may be laid under-water like the Square *Navona* at *Rome*.

From *Sienna* to *Viterbo* the Road is extremely bad, I passed the Mountain of *Radifocani*, situate in one of the vilest Countries in all *Italy*. At the top of the Mountain there's a Castle, where a Garison

---

* This Princess died in 1731, at *Florence*.

rison of fifteen Men is kept, with a Commanding Officer, whom I found at the House of Entertainment where I alighted. He had been a Lieutenant in *France* in the Royal *Italian* Regiment, and spoke very good *French*. He told me that the Inhabitants under his Government were as bad as the Country, of which some Moments after, I saw a Proof. A Mule-driver having a Quarrel with the Drawer, the latter stabb'd him with a Knife in the Rim of the Belly, with as much Sedateness as if he had been doing a good Action; and the Commandant never caus'd the Assassin to be apprehended: for which when I express'd my Surprize to him, he said he had nothing to do out of his Place; and that besides he did not dare to cause the Assassin to be apprehended, because he had three Brothers as wicked as himself, who wou'd not fail to take a Revenge if he was punish'd. And then, said he, I shou'd have enough to do if I were to cause all to be apprehended who give Wounds with Knives.

AQUAPENDENTE is a sorry little Town, and yet a Metropolis. BOLSENA is no better, and MONTEFIASCONE tho' a Bishoprick, wou'd not be worth mentioning, were it not for its Vineyards which produce excellent *Muscadine* Wine.

VITERBO, three Leagues from *Montefiascone*, seem'd to me to be a pretty Town. 'Tis adorn'd with three fine Fountains, and pav'd with great Flint Stones which are four foot long and two foot broad. This City has some fine Houses in it. 'Tis the See of a Bishop, and its Cathedral is a Structure which does not want for Grandeur. In this Church the Archbishop and Elector of *Cologn* was consecrated by Pope *Benedict* XIII. who came hither on purpose to save the Elector all manner of dispute about Precedency with the Cardinals; who were in their turn so disgruntled with the Pope, that none of them accompany'd him in this Journey.

MONTEROSO is a pretty Town, but RONCIGLIONE outdoes it; and indeed in all the Ecclesiastical State there is not a pleasanter. It drives a great Trade in Snuff. I came hither yesterday at Noon, and don't think of going away 'till this Evening, my Chaise being broke. I hope however to lie this Night at *Rome*, from whence I purpose to send you many good Stories forthwith. You will do me a Pleasure to let me hear from you; and to believe me in *Italy*, as well as elsewhere, yours, *&c.*

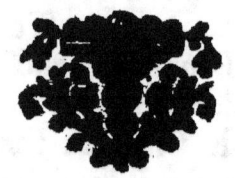

End of Volume I.

BOOKS of Voyages, and Travels, lately publish'd, printed for D. Browne, *without* Temple-Bar.

I. A COLLECTION of VOYAGES and TRAVELS; some now first printed from original Manuscripts, others now first publish'd in English; with a general Preface, giving an Account of the Progress of Navigation from its first Beginning. Illustrated with a great number of useful Maps and Cuts curiously engraven In 6 Volumes, Folio. Price 9 *l.*

N. B. Those Gentlemen who have the first four Volumes of this Collection, which were commonly call'd *Churchill's* Travels, may have the 5th and 6th Volumes to compleat their Setts.

II. Mr. LE BRUYN's TRAVELS into *Muscovy, Persia,* and the *East Indies:* containing an accurate Description of whatever is most remarkable in those Countries; and embellish'd with above 320 Copper-Plates, representing the finest Prospects, and most considerable Cities in those Parts; the different Habits of the People, the singular and extraordinary Birds, Fishes, and Plants, which are to be found: as likewise the Antiquities of those Countries, and particularly the noble Ruins of the famous Palace of *Persepolis,* call'd *Chelminar* by the *Persians:* the whole being delineated on the Spot from the respective Objects. To which is added, An Account of the Journey of Mr. *Isbrants,* Embassador from *Muscovy,* thro' *Russia* and *Tartary* to *China:* together with Remarks on the Travels of Sir *John Chardin* and Mr. *Kempfer,* and a Letter to the Author on that Subject. Translated from the French, with the original Copper-Plates. In two Volumes, Folio. Price 2*l.* 10 *s.*

III. REMARKS on several PARTS of EUROPE: relating chiefly to the History, Antiquities, and Geography of those Countries, thro' which the Author has travel'd; as *France,* the *Low-Countries. Lorrain. Alsatia, Germany, Savoy, Tyrol, Switzerland, Italy,* and *Spain.* Illustrated with several Maps, Plans, and above forty Copper-Plates. By J. BREVAL Esq; In two Volumes, Folio. Price 2 *l.* 2*s.*

IV. SIR HANS SLOANE's Voyage to the Islands of *Madera, Barbadoes, Nevis, St. Christopher's,* and JAMAICA; with the Natural History of the Herbs and Trees, Four-footed Beasts, Fishes, Birds, Insects, Reptiles, *&c.* of the last of those Islands. Illustrated with the Figures of the Things described, in above 300 large Copper-Plates, as big as the Life, in 2 vol. Folio. Price 5*l.* 10*s.* N. B. The second Volume may be had alone.

V. ITINERARIUM SEPTENTRIONALE; or a Journey thro' most of the Counties of *Scotland,* and those in the North of *England.* In two Parts. Illustrated with 66 Copper-Plates. By *Alexander Gordon* A. M. Folio. Price one Guinea.

VI. ROMA ILLUSTRATA: or a Description of the most beautiful Pieces of Painting, Sculpture, and Architecture, antique and modern, at and near ROME. In a neat Pocket Volume. Price 2*s.* 6*d.*

An Alphabetical INDEX

TO THE

FIRST VOLUME.

A

Abbesses of two Convents, the Ceremony of marrying them by every Doge of *Venice*, 400. Their Dress, 401.

Agrippina, Empress of *Rome*, 250.

Ahlen-Castle, in the Dutchy of *Zell*; the Retreat of the Duke's unfortunate Daughter, 62.

Aix-la-Chapelle, *t*. 199, 341.

Albert, Margrave of *Brandenbourg*, 82.

Albert I. Emperor, 388.

Albert II. Emperor, 388.

Aller, R. 61.

Alpes, for whom those Mountains were made, 395.

Altena, *t*. 53, 57. Distress of the Inhabitants, 58. Privileg'd Place for Bankrupts, 59.

Altenbourg, *t*. 167.

Altheim, Count and Countess, 255, 256.

Amelia, Empress of Germany, 228 to 230, &c. 344.

Amminati, Sculptor, 426.

Andrew, Cardinal of *Austria*, 390.

St. *Andrew*'s Order of *Muscovy*, 76.

Vol. I.

Angelo, Michael, his saying that certain Gates were good enough for Paradise, 428.

Anhalt-Cothen, Princess, 173.

Anhalt-Dessau Leopold, Pr. 37. His Amour and Marriage, and his Menace to shoot his Tutor, 38, 39. His Character by the late D. of *Savoy*, 39. His Valour, 39, 40. His Government, 82.

Augustus Lewis, Pr. his Wives and Issue, 83.

Anhalt-Zerbst, *Magdalen-Augusta*, Duchess of *Saxe-Gotha*, 181.

Anna-Maria's Violin, 415.

Anne, Princess-Royal of *Denmark*, and Electress-Dowager of *Saxony*, 100.

Anne-Frederica, of *Promnitz*, 83.

Anne-Sophia-Charlotte, of *Prussia*, Duchess of *Saxe-Eysenach*, 183.

Annunciation-Pictures, done by *Tintoret* and *Titian*, 419.

Anspach, 193, 204. See *Brandenbourg*.

Anthony Ulric, D. of *Brunswic-Lunenburg-Wolfembuttle*, 69, 71, 73, 75, 79.

Antinous's Statue, 370.

F f   An-

An Alphabetical INDEX

Antonietta-Amelia of *Brunswic-Blanckenbourg*, 72.
Apollodorus Statuary, 427.
Apollonia, the Singer, 415.
Appel, a Merchant at *Leipsic*, his House the Residence of the K. of *Poland*, 85.
Appennine Mountains, 425.
AQUAPENDENTE, *t.* 430.
Arch-duchesses, 232, 233. 381.
Architecture, the best Article that Princes can lay out their Money in, 10.
Aremberg, Duke and Duchess-Dowager, 332, 333.
Argenson, M. de, 303.
Arlington, Countess of, 67.
Arnheim, Marshal de, 40.
Arnim, *Sigismond* de, 146.
Arnould, St. 366.
Arthur, Prince of *Wales*, 389.
AUGSBOURG, *t.* 273. Its Comparison with *Antwerp*, 275. Its chief Trade, 275, 276.
Augusta, of *Saxe-Gotha*, Princess of *Wales*, 182.
Augustus III. K. of *Poland*, 97, 99. His Travels and Conversion to Popery, 101. His Marriage, 102, 165. His Love and Duty to his Father, 104. His Election and Coronation, 106. His Tutor, 126, 127. His Queen, 98. Their Children, 99.
Augustus William D. of *Brunswic-Lunenburg Wolfembuttle*, 69, 71, 73.
Augustus-Albert, Prince of *Prussia*, 113.
Augustus, Emperor, 273.
Aulic Council, at *Berlin*, 14. At *Vienna*, 244.
St. *Austin's* Tract of the City of God, 179.
Austria, House, of whom it now consists, 233. A Wish that it never may be extinct, 233. Its great Alliances, 250.

Austrian Princes, remarkable for an Air of Gravity, 112. Their People's Aversion to the *Bohemians*, 222. The scurvy Pun of a *French* Jester upon them, 228. Their Epicurism, 253. Pride, 254. Their Fondness for the Title of Count, 255.
Austrian and *Lorrain* Families united, 233, 341.
Auvergne, Princesses, 332, 333.

B.

Backover, M. Chancellor of *Saxe-Gotha*, 182.
Baden Baden, Margrave and Margravine, 213, 299, 300.
Baden-Dourlach, *Christian*, Margrave of, 183, 279. *Charles*, 293, 296, 298. Margravine, 298, 300, 301, 304.
Badiani, Count, 244.
Bahlberg, *Adolphus*, Baron of, 184.
Baldinucci, *Philip*, the Sculptor, 426.
Balls of *Bohemia*, compar'd with those in the *Hay-Market*, 223.
BAMBERG, *t.* 201, &c. the mighty Prerogative of its Bishop, 201.
BARBI, *t.* 82.
Bareith, Margraves. See *Brandenbourg*.
BAREITH, *t.* 204. Princess, 303.
Baron, the Title purchased in *Germany* by a Messenger, 256.
Basset, how a Lady made her Gallant's Fortune at it, 252.
Bass-Viols, a *German* Duke's Fondness for 'em, 168, to 171.
Bavaria, Electors of, 259, 262, 263. Its Division, 267. Riches and Revenue, 167, 168.

268. Electoress, 363, 364. Its Apostle, 366.
Baudiffin, M. Wolf, Henry de, 104, 127, 128.
Baumgarten, General, 84.
Beaufort, Marquis de, 135.
Beausobre, M. 15.
Bedmar, Marquis de, his Conspiracy, 409.
Beichling, M. Chancellor, 91.
Beichling, Countess Dowager, 141.
Belgrade, 248.
Belvedere-Palace, 4.
Benedict XIII. Pope, 337, 430.
Benedictines, a sort of Republic form'd in that Order, 190.
Benson, William, Esq; Director of the fine Waterworks at Herenhausen, 67.
Bentivoglio, Cardinal, his Remark upon the Alps and the neighbouring People, 395.
Bergenopzoom, 332.
BERLIN, t. 3. Its Obligation to the French Refugees, 3. Its Academy, 147.
Bernsdorff, John Hartwig Ernest, Baron of, 155.
Berschen, t. 394.
Beveren, Baron de, 334, 335.
Bevern, Brunswic Branch, 71. Charles, Prince of, 26, 72. Ferdinand-Albert, Prince of, 70, 71, 72. Elizabeth-Christina, Princess, 72.
Bilinski, Count and Countess, 118.
Bishoprick, which the first in Germany, 201.
Black Liveries, never given by a certain German Family, 363.
Blanc, M. de, 306.
Blanche, Mary, Wife to the Emperor Maximilian, 389.
Blanckenbourg, County, 79.
BLANCKENBOURG, t. 76, 78. Stupidity of the People, 78.

Blanckenbourg's Duke and Duchess, 71, 76, 78. The Duke's Treaty with the Elector of Hanover for a Vote and Seat in the Dyet, 79. His Accession to the Title of the D. of Wolfembuttle, 80.
Blanckenheim-Mandersheldt, Francis George, Count de, 333.
Bockenheim, t. 340.
Bohemia, 210, 211, &c. 244. Where and by whom its Kings and Queens are consecrated, 212. Its Saints, ib. The Wealth and Grandeur of its Nobility, and the Poverty and Slavery of the Peasants, 218, 219, 221. Its States, of whom compos'd, 222. Their Aversion to the Austrians, 222.
Bolagnos, Count de, 397.
Bologna, John, 427.
BOLOGNA, t. 423, 424.
BOLSANO, t. 392.
Bolsena, t. 430.
Bork, the Prussian Minister and General, 31, 42.
Bose, Countess of, 145.
Bossagno, t. 394.
Bot, the Architect, 10, 18. Compar'd to Bernini, 94.
Bothmar, Count de, 65.
Bouillon, Princes, why they had the Title of Domestic Highnesses, 210.
Bourbon and Austria, Houses, our Author's Wish that they might never be extinct, 233.
Bourbon, Duchess of, 310, 332.
Bourg, Marshal de, 306, 307.
Brandenbourg, Electors of, Joachim II. 196. John George, 204.
Brandenbourg, Lewis, Margrave of, 387.
Brandenbourg-Anspach, Margraves, &c. of, 193, &c. 195.

An Alphabetical INDEX

361. *Margravine*, 194. Her Present to our Author, 197. Death in this Family pretended to be always foretold by the Appearance of a Spirit, 196.

Brandenbourg - Bareith, Margraves, 200, &c. 205, &c. 303, 342.

BRANDENBOURG, t. 2.

Brandenbourg-Schwedt, Marquis of, 26. Margravine Dowager, 125.

Brandstein, Frederic-Augustus de, 145.

Brebentau, Mademoiselle de, 116, 157.

Brebentau, the Palatine of *Marienbourg*, 163.

Breitenbauch, Henry-Augustus de, 146.

Bremer, M. de, 195.

Brenner, Mountain, 391, 392.

Breslau, the Road from it to *Berlin*, 1.

Bretonvilliers, Marquis, Reflection on his Memoirs, 337.

Breze, Marshal de, 321.

BRHOUSEL, t. 318.

Brimstone, prescrib'd to the *Austrians* by a *French* Jester, 228.

BRIXEN, t. 392, 394.

Brocks, a *Hamburgher* and Poet, 53.

Brou, M. de, 306.

Bruhl, John and *Henry* de, 104, 129, 130, 131, 132, 140. *Adolphus* de, 140. Baron de, 174, 177.

Brunswic Hanover, John-Frederic, Duke of, 229.

Brunswic Family, 61, 69, 71. The Princes descended from it, 231.

BRUNSWIC, t. 69, 75.

Brunswic-Blanckenbourg, Lewis Rodolf, Duke of, 70, 231.

Brunswic - Lunenbourg - Wolfembuttle, Duke of, 231.

Bucentaur, a fine Venetian Galley, 399, 407.

Bulau, Baron de, 65, 66. Baroness, 66.

Burgau, Charles, Margrave of, 390.

Burgundy, Charles the Bold, Duke of, 389. *Philip* Duke, 389.

Buthler, Constantine, Baron of, 184.

C.

Cabinet Ministers, their Precedence at the Court of *Prussia*, 134.

Caccioli Antonio, Painter, 424.

Cadets Academies, 48.

Cæsar's War with *Pompey*, painted, 370.

Callenberg, Augustus-Henry Gottlob, Count de, 145.

Camke, Madame de, 25.

Camke, Messieurs de, 44.

Candi, a famous Painter, 261.

Carinthia, Henry Duke of, 387.

Carlowitz, John-George de, 145. Treaty, 238.

CARLSBAD, t. 208, &c. Virtue of its Baths, *ib.*

CARLSROUHE, t. 293.

Caroline, Princess of *Saxe-Eysenach*, 115.

Cassel, see *Hesse*.

Castel, Count de, 195.

Castilloncello, t. 429.

Catsch, M. a Minister of *Prussia*, 5, 17, 43.

Catzenellenbogen, upper County, 357.

Chains, that bound St. *Peter*, St. *Paul*, and St. *John*, three Links of them, 198.

Chalisac, M. 37.

Charlemain's Crown and Sword, 199. *Charles*, Margrave of *Burgau*, 390. *Charles* II.

K.

K. of *Spain*, 387. *Charles* IV. Emperor, 387.
Charles V. Emperor, 381, 387, 423.
Charles VI. Emperor, 70, 230, 341. His Diversions, 233. His Friendship and Gratitude, 256. His Love for the Empress, 257. Remarks on his Coronation, 341.
Charles-Christian, Prince of *Prussia*, 113.
Charles, K. of *Sardinia*, 335.
Charles XII. K. of *Sweden*, 55, 56, 123, 124.
Charles, Prince Palatine of *Sultzbach*, 332.
Charles, the Bold, Duke of *Burgundy*, 389.
Charles-Albert, Elector of *Bavaria*, 259. 262, 263. His Electoress, 263.
Charles-Lewis, Elector Palatine, 274, 342, 381, 383. *Philip* ditto, 328, 330, 331. His Revenues, 337.
Charlottemburg House, 35.
Child-bearing, ascrib'd to the Miracles of the two *Bohemian* Saints, 213, 214.
Christian, Margrave of *Brandenburg-Bareith*, 200.
Christian-Lewis, Margrave of *Brandenburg*. 28. *Ulric*, Duke of *Wirtemberg-Oels*, and *Bernstad*, 83. *William* of *Saxe-Gotha*, Prince, 182.
Christina-Louisa, of *Oetingen*, Duchess of *Blanckenbourg*, 70.
Christina, Princess of *Saxe-Weissenfels*, 114, 115.
Christopher, St. where most worshipped, 394.
Cicerone, the Meaning of that Word in *Italy*, 395.
Cinfuentes, Count de, 244.
Cleisheim, 375.
Clischoff, Battle, 163.

Clovis, K. of *France*, 388.
Coburg, t. 200.
Coborn, Engineer, 328.
Cohten, t. 83.
Colin, Alexander, Statuary, 386.
Collobradt, Count, 220.
Collonitz, the Count and the Cardinal, 248, 249.
Collowrat, Count and Countess, 133, 148.
Complimenters, nauseous, 199.
Conde, Princess of, 344.
Conferences, Counsellors of, 240, 244.
Constance, Council of, 15, 339.
Coquets, in *Venice*, the Place of their Rendezvous, 415.
Corfou, Island, 408.
Cornaro Family's Tomb, 404.
Cosel, Countess of, Mistress of the late K. of *Poland*, 90, 91, 117, 118, 120, 124. Her Menaces against him, 118. Count, 117, 136. Her Daughter, 142.
Cosmo I. Duke of *Florence*, 426, 427.
Costa, Count de, 101, 123.
Counts of the Empire, their Preheminence, 287.
Courland, Duchess Dowager, 200.
Craut, his surprising Rise from behind the Compter to the Ministry, 4.
Creutz, M. de, *Prussian* Minister, 5, 45.
Creutzar, Coin, 278.
Crossen, t. 1.
Culmbach-Brandenburg, Margraviate, 204. *George-Frederic-Charles*, the Margrave, 205. His Family and Revenues, 204, &c. 208.
Cunegonda, Empress, her Tomb, 202, 387.
Cup, which *Joseph* put in *Benjamin*'s Sack; the Reason our

An Alphabetical INDEX

Author had to remember that Passage, 204.
Customs, a remarkable Attachment to old ones, 78, 79.
Cyprianus, Dr. 179.
Cyprus, Cornaro, Q. of, 406.
Czarowitz, 70.

D.

Damnitz, M. de, Grand Marshal of Saxe-Gotha, 182.
Danckelman, Baron de, 15. He prophesies his own Fate, 16.
Dangervilliers, M. 306, 307.
Danneberg, Henry de, 71.
Danebrock Order, 74.
Dantzick, t. invested, 107. Reduc'd, 108, 109.
Danube, R. 278.
Darmstadt, t. 357. Landgraves, 357, 362.
Daun, Count and Marshal de, 246, 370.
Degenfeldt (Schomberg) Count de, 342, 343.
Dehn, Count de, 72, 73. A very fine Dancer, as well as Minister of State, 74.
Dejanira's Story painted, 383.
Delitz, Countess of, 66.
Denhoff, General, 7.
Denmark, Q. of, 208. The Prince Royal, 208.
Devos, Tapestry-maker at Brussels, 236.
Diedrichstein, Count, 147.
Doberginsky, M. 35.
Doges of Venice, their Marriage of the Sea, and of the Abbesses of two Convents, 399, 400.
Dohna, Count de, 6.
Dorffling, a Taylor, his Rise to be a General in the Army, 12.
Dorothea-Sophia, Princess of Prussia, 19.
Dorothy, Electress of Brandenburg, 19.
DRESDEN, t. 87, 157, &c.
Drinking hard, in Germany, our Author's humourous Account how it affected him, 184, 187, to 190, 204, 325, to 327. Where he reckons it an inseparable Function of the Ecclesiastical Courts, 204.
Duhamel, Francis, General, 7, 412 His Lady, 412.
Duvaine, General, 5.
Duval, a famous Soop-maker, 56.

E.

East-Friesland, George-Albert, Prince of, 208.
Eib, General, 191.
Einsiedel, John George de, 143.
Einsiedel, Curt de, 144. His Lady, 144.
Einsiedel Detler, Henry de, 146.
Eleonora, Empress, 240, 381.
Eleonora, Princess of Neubourg, 230.
Eleonora-Philippina, Princess of Hesse-Rhinfels, 332.
Elizabeth, Empress of Germany, 232, &c. Her Abjuration of the Lutheran Religion, 232.
Elizabeth-Sophia of Brandenbourg, Duchess Dowager of Courland, 200.
Elizabeth-Christina of Oetingen, Duchess of Blanckenbourg, 76.
Elvan, t. 378.
Emanuel, Prince of Savoy, 238.
Emigrants, of Saltzbourg, 375, 376.
Emperors of Germany, the Ceremony of their Audiences, 225. Their Dining, 225. Suppers, 227. Pictures, 370.
Empresses, the Respect paid to them, 228 to 230, &c.

Em-

Empress Dowager, 229.
Eosander, the Architect, 10.
Erdmansdorff, *Ernest-Ferdinand* de, 144.
ERFURT, t. 178.
ERLANGEN, *Christian*, t. 200.
Ernest-Augustus, the first Elector of *Hanover*, 63, 67. How he obtain'd that Dignity, 68.
Ernest, Arch-Duke, and his Wife, 389.
Ernest-Augustus, Duke of *Saxe-Weimar*, 173.
Ernest the *Pious*, Duke of *Gotha*, 178.
Etiquette, in foreign Courts, what, 224.
Eslingen, t. 303.
Eversberg, t. 364.
Eugene of *Savoy*, Prince, his Palace. 236. His Character, 237, 241. His Regiment of Dragoons, 237. His Sickness, Death, and Interment, 238. His Employments and Estate, 238, 240. His last Will, 239. His Library, 239. His Nephew, 239.
Excellency, the *Venetians* Fondness for the Title, 420, 421.
EYSENACH, t. 183. See *Saxe*.

F.

Fatima, a *Turkish* Lady, 115, 116.
Favourita, the Emperor's Palace, 234.
Faustina, the Singer, 421.
Ferbellin, t. 50.
Ferdinand I. *de Medicis*, 427.
Ferdinand, K. of *Castille*, 387.
Ferdinand, K. of the *Romans*, 381.
Ferdinand I. Emperor, 385, 387. His Son's Tomb, 389, and Wife, 390.
Ferdinand-Albert, D. of *Brunswic-Lunenbourg* and *Bevern*, 70, 71, 72. His Merit and Preferment, 72.
Ferdinand-Mary, Elector of *Bavaria*, 259. His Wife, 260.
Ferdinand, Duke of *Bavaria*, 263, 264. His Duchess, 263.
FERRARA, t. 423.
Finck, of *Finckenstein*, Count, 25.
Fiorenzola, t. 425.
Fermian, Barons of, 367.
Fishermen, at *Venice*, their Election of their Doge or Chief, 402.
Fitztuhm, Count de, 91, 142. His Daughter, 150.
Fleming, *James-Henry*, Count de, Prime Minister of *Poland*, 73, 74, 89, 90, 92, 102, 125, 144, 152, 155, 162. His Reason for employing Foreigners before *Saxons*, 155. The Origin of his Family and his Education, 162. His Preferments from first to last, 162, &c. His Marriage and his Duels, 163, 165. His Conduct with regard to *Patkul*, 164. His Estate, 165, 166. His general Character, 166.
Fleming, Mademoiselle de, 116.
Fleury, Marquis de, 135. Cardinal de, 241.
FLORENCE, t. 425.
Fohsen, Mademoiselle de, 38.
Forbenius, how he saved the Life of the Elector of *Brandenbourg*, 51.
Force, Marshal de, 321.
Forchs, the *Starost* assassinated, 155.
Francfort, on the *Rhine*, 340. Privilege of those here called Residents, 342.
Francfort, on the *Oder*, t. 2.
Francis I. K. of *France*, his solemn Affirmation, 215.
Franconia, Duke, 185, 191.

An Alphabetical INDEX

Frankenberg, Baron de, 236.
FRANKENDAHL, t. 338.
Frauenstad, Battle, 163.
Frederic, of *Austria*, nick-nam'd the *Pennyless* Prince, 385, 386, 388.
Frederic, Elector Palatine, who was chose K. of *Bohemia*, 210.
Frederic IV. Emperor, 387, 388. His Mother, 389.
Frederic, Electoral Prince of *Saxony*, 99, 112.
Frederic II. Duke of *Gotha*, 180, 181. III. the present Duke, 181, 182. His Brother *William*, 181. His other Brothers and Sisters, and his Revenues and Guards, &c. 182.
Frederic-Augustus II. K. of *Poland*, 94, 101. His Nativity calculated at *Venice*, 95, 96. His Death, 96. His Queen, and her Death, 97. His Change of Religion, 100. The Method he took to convert his Son, 101. His Natural Issue, 115, &c. His Generosity, 164.
FREDERIC IV. K. of *Denmark*'s Compassion to the *Altenois*, 58, 59. His Queen's Retirement, 59. His giving Audience to the Senate at *Bologna*, 423, 426.
Frederic, the *Fair*, 230.
Frederic-William, Elector of *Brandenbourg*, his Statue, 9. His remarkable Speech to his Soldiers, 50. His Daughter, 200.
Frederic I. K. of *Prussia*, his Statue, 8, 297.
Frederic, Prince Royal of *Prussia*, 25.
Frederica-Sophia, Princess of *Prussia*, 25, 26.
Frederica-Louisa, Princess of *Prussia*, 26. Of *Saxe-Gotha*, Princess, 182.
Fredericsfeld, House, 27.
Friesberg, Baron de, 61.
Friesland, *Henry-Frederic*, Count of, 123, 139, 142.
Frisoni, an Architect, 288, 290.
Fuchs, Baron de, the *Prussian* Minister, 4, 29, 41.
Fuchs, Countess de, 254.
Fugger, Maximilian, Count, 266. His generous Entertainment of the Emperor *Charles* V. 276.
Fuhl, de, Great Marshal, 90.
FULDE, t. 184. Magnificence of its Abbot, 184.
Fultishau, Convent, 380.
Furstemberg, Prince, 165. Cardinal, 315.
Furstenfeldt, Abbey, 272, 273.

G.

Gala, Days of, what, 226, 227, 228.
Galeas, *John* Duke of *Milan*, 389.
Gallasch, Count de, 211.
Gardeners, the best in all *Germany*, 85.
Garment, Christ's, a Relique of it, 198.
Gaston, *John*, Great Duke of *Tuscany*, 428.
Gates, thought by *Michael Angelo* to be good enough for Paradise, 428.
Gemblours, Abbot of, his sole Privilege of celebrating Mass booted and spurr'd, 191.
Gemming, Baron de, 208.
Gentleman, two *French* Kings fond of the Title, 215.
GEORGE I. K. of *Great-Britain*, his Wife, 61, 62. His Administration, 61, 64, 68.
George II. King, 64, 69.
George-William, Margrave of *Brandenbourg-Bareith*, 205.
George

George (*St.*) Pobess of, 212. Order Bavarian, 260.
George I. Landgrave of *Darmstad*, 357.
German Language, its Excellency, 93, 195. Vanity of the *Germans*, 198.
Gerss, the *French* Ambassador, 397.
Gersner, Physician, 368.
Gerstorf, *Gotlob-Frederic*, Baron de, 47.
Gertrude, a *Marcoman* Lady, History of her, an entertaining Novel, 343, &c. Its Key, 355.
Gilles (*St.*) Count de, 92.
Glass Manufacture of *Venice*, 410.
Globe, *John-Frederic* Count de, 334.
Goblet of Gold, the Pleasure with which our Author drank out of it; and how he wish'd to carry it off, 204.
Godfrey of *Bouillon*, K. of *Jerusalem*, 388.
Gobren, Baron de, 45.
Gortz (*Henry*) Baron de, 54. His famous Copper Coin, 56. His Execution, 57.
Gortz, the *Hanoverian*, 64.
Gotha, see *Saxe*, and *Frederic*, and *Ernest*.
GOTHA, t. 178. Its Dukes, 178, 179, &c. Duchesses, 181. The noble Library here, 179. Their Revenues, 182.
Gravenitz, Count de, 284, 285, 286.
Gravenitz, Countess de, Mistress of the D. of *Wirtemberg*, 279, 282, to 284.
Gravity, an Air peculiar to the *Austrian* Princes, 112.
Grosh, the Value of that Coin, 85.
Grumkau, the *Prussian* Minister, 5, 31, 43.

Grunberg, the Architect, 6.
Guide, a remarkable one that was blind, 277.
Guides, the Name given to them in *Italy*, 305.
Guldenstein - Huguetan, Count de, 35.
Gundacker de Staremberg, Count, 241.
Gustavus-Adolphus, 259, 274.

H.

Hacke, M. de, 46.
Hagen, Baron de, 75, 101.
HAGUENAU, 381, t.
Hall, the largest next to *Westminster*, 215.
Halle, t. 82, 377, 380. University, 85.
HAMBURGH, t. 51, 199. Its Dispute with *Denmark*, 52. Its Opera, 52. Its Mob, 54. Vindication of its Citizens from the Charge of Cruelty to the *Altenois*, 58. Their Respect to the *Jews*, 53, 59.
Hamelen, t. 68.
Hanau, Count of, 359, 361, 362.
Hanau, *Charlotta-Christina* of, 359.
HANAU, t. 360, 362.
HANOVER, 63, 68. *Roman* Catholics there, 63. Revenues of the Electorate, 68. —— Electoress of, 343, 344.
HARBOURG, t. 60, 68.
Hardenberg, M. Grand Marshal of *Hanover*, 64, 65.
Harlay, M. de, 306.
Harrach, Count de, 242, 367, 368, 371.
Hattorsi, Ministers compar'd to *Louvois* and *Barbesieux*, 65, 66.
Hatzfeld, *Egmont* Count, 335.
Haugwitz, *John-Adolphus* de, 142.

HEIDEL-

An Alphabetical INDEX

HEIDELBERG, t. 321, 322. Its Decay to what owing, 323. Its famous Tun, 324.
Heilbron, 375.
Henrietta-Benedictine, the Princess Palatine, 229.
Henry II. Emperor, his Tomb, 202.
Henry IV. Emperor, the pompous Interment he wish'd his Enemies, 168.
Henry III. K. of France, 309.
Henry IV. K. of France, his Ambition to be called the first Gentleman in his Kingdom, 215.
Herenhausen Palace, 67.
Herford Abbey, 27.
Hering, M. de, Vice-Chancellor of Saxe-Gotha, 177, 182.
Hermitage, a Seat near Bareith, 207.
Herzan, Maximilian Count de, 146.
Hesler, M. de, 108.
Hesse Princes, 357.
Hesse-Cassel, Philip the Landgrave of, 357, 362.
Hesse-Darmstadt, Ernest-Lewis Landgrave of, 357. His Wife, 358. His Son and his Wife, 359. His Revenues and Troops, 360.
Hesse-Rhinfels, Princess of, 332.
Hildesheim, Baron, 335.
Hochstet Battle, 262.
Hoffman, Professor of Physic at Halle, 208.
Hohenlo, Count de, 353.
Holstein-Beck, Lewis-Frederic Pr. of, 150.
————— Charles-Lewis Pr. of, 120, 150. Dorothy, Princess of, 205.
Housten, Christopher-Francis de, Pr. and Bp. of Wurtzbourgh, 185.
Hoym, Count de, 91, 92, 117, 118. His Catastrophe, 136, 137.

Hubert (St.) his Legacy, 190. Noted for killing Rats, 196.
HUBERTSBOURGH, t. 86, 103, 157.
Huss, John, 339.
Hussites, the Remains of 'em, 216.

I

Jacobi, the Statuary, 9.
Jacquelot, M. 15.
Janson, Cardinal, 315.
Jews, the Respect shewed them at Hamburg, 53, 59. Not tolerated at Anspach, and why, 198. Their Punishment for crucifying an Infant of Christian Parents on Christmass-day, 216. Vast number of 'em in Bohemia, 216. and the Palatinate, 337.
Ilgen, Baron, Prussian Minister, 31, 41.
Ilten, Messieurs de, of Hanover, 66, 67.
Inn River, 364, 379, 380.
INSPRUC, t. 380.
Joan of Castille, 387.
John's (St.) Village in Tirol, 378.
John (St.) of Jerusalem, Kts. of, 28.
John (St.) Nepomucene, 212, 213.
John-Ernest ABp. of Saltzbourg, 373.
John-Adolphus of Saxe-Weissenfels, 99, 114.
John-George I. Elector of Saxony, 114.
John-George III. Elector of Saxony, 94.
John-George IV. Elector, 94.
John-Augustus of Saxe-Gotha, Pr. 182.
————— Adolphus, ditto, 182.

John-

John William, D. of *Saxe-Eisenach*, 183. Elector Palatine, 324, 328.
Jonas, the tall Grenadier, 35.
Joseph, Emperor, 274.
Iser R. 258.
Isselbach, General, 336.
Judas's Lanthorn to be seen in two Places, 81.
Ixter, Baron de, 298.

K.

Kalestein, Baron de, 25.
Kara-Mustapha, Grand Vizier, 247, 248.
KEHL, t. 305.
Kendal, Duchess, 66.
Kevenhuller, Count de, 246.
Keyserling - Hermann - Charles, 154.
Kilmanseck, Madame de, 67.
Kinsberg, Baron de, 195.
Kinski, Counts, 154, 220, 221, 244.
Kinski, Countess of, 154.
Klenzek, Mademoiselle de, 55.
Kniphausen, Baron, the *Prussian* Minister, 31, 44.
Kokersowitz, Countess, 148.
Konickel, Count de, 381.
Konigsegg, Count de, 147, 239, 242, 243. His Marriage, 243. His Nephew, 243, 244.
Konigstern Castle, 87.
Koningsmark, *Aurora* Countess of, 115.
Kuenbourgh, Count de, 373.
Kundahl, t. 379.
Kurtzrok, Baron, 54.

L.

Lactantius's Works, 179.
Ladies, *Venetian*, in Masks, pick'd up by our Author, 411. and himself pick'd up by a Lady in Distress who knew him, 416.
Ladislaus, King, 388.

Lagnasco, Count, and *Josepha* Countess of, 151, 152, 157, 158.
LANDAU, t. 318.
Lands, how entail'd, and how secur'd in *Bohemia*, 218, 219.
Larks, where they most abound, 85.
Laxembourg, the Emperor's Palace, 234.
Leibnitz, the Philosopher, 156.
Leine, r. 63.
LEIPSICK, t. 83. Why 'tis called the Jewel of *Saxony*, 84. Its Fairs frequented by a great number of Princes and Princesses, 85.
Lenfant, M. Author of the Council of *Constance*, 15.
Leopold of *Austria*, surnam'd *the Virtuous*, 388.
Leopold, Archduke, 210.
———Emperor, 230.
———Bp. of *Saltzbourgh*, his Houshold and his Revenues, 367, 373. Why compared to Pope *Sixtus* V. 367.
Levant Women, their great Confinement within doors, 52.
Leubnitz, *Charles*, 140.
Lewis VI. Landgrave of *Darmstad*, 357.
Lewis, the Hereditary Prince, 359.
Lewis of *Bavaria*, Emperor, 260, 387.
———of *Baden*, Pr. 299, 303.
———*Ernest* of *Saxe-Gotha*, P. 182.
———*the Severe*, Duke of *Bavaria*, his Murder of his Minister and his Wife, 272. His Repentance, 273.
———*Rodolph*, D. of *Brunswic-Lunenburg*, and *Blanckenbourg*, 70, 231.
———Margrave of *Brandenburg*, 387.

Lewis

An Alphabetical INDEX

Lewis XV. K. of *France*, his Marriage, 304, 309. Cardinal *Rohan*'s Speeches upon it, 310, 313.
Lichtenstein Palace, 236.
Lieutenant of the Police at *Paris*, 246.
Linange, Mary-Christina-Felicite, Countess of, her Husbands, 183.
Linar, Maurice-Charles, Count de, 143.
LINTZ t. 258.
Lipski, John-Alexander, Bp. of *Cracow*, 149.
Lobkowitz, Pr. and Princess, 342.
Lodron, Counts of, 365, 373.
Lopol, General de, 30.
Lorrain, Francis Duke of, his Marriage to the Archduchess, 233, 341.
———— *Charles*, Pr. 239, 385.
Losenstein, Eleonora Countess of, 151.
Loval, Baron de, kill'd in a Duel with Count *Flemming*, 163.
Lovestein, Princess, 342.
Louisa - Dorothea Duchess of *Saxe-Gotha*, 181.
Louvois, Marquis, 306.
Lowendahl, Waldemar Baron of, 121. His Service to six Kings, 121. His Wives and Issue, 122. His Son *Waldemar*, 122, 139.
Lewenitz, Henry - Rodolph de Schonfeld, Lord of, 145.
Lubomirski-Theresa, Electoress Palatine, 330.
Lubomirski, Madame de, Rival to *Fatima* a *Turkish* Lady, Mistress to the late K. of *Poland*, 116, 117.
Lubomirski, George-Ignatius Pr. of, 150, 151.
Ludo, Count de, his wise Reason for marrying a Tradesman's Daughter, 45.
Ludwigsbourg t. 279, 287.

LUNENBURG t. 68.
Lunenburg-Zell and *Lunenburg-Hanover* Families united, 61.
Luther, Martin, his resolute Expression when dissuaded to go to the Dyet, 339.
Lutzelbourg, Anthony Count de, 123.

M.

Magdebourg Duchy yielded to the House of *Brandenbourg*, 80. Character of it, 81.
MAGDEBOURG t. 48, 80.
Maintenon, Madame de, Mistress of *Lewis* XIV. her Fortune told by a Mason, 96.
Malchau House near *Berlin*, 29.
Manger, a Relique of our Saviour's, 198.
MANHEIM t. 327.
Manteuffel, Ernest Count de, 134.
Marck, Julius-Augustus, Count de la, 334, 337.
Marcoman Lady, the History of one, 344, &c.
Margaret of *Tyrol* surnam'd *the Fious*, and nicknam'd *Wide-Mouth*, 387.
Maria-Anne-Caroline of *Newbourgh*, 263.
Maria-Magdalena, Archduchess, 233, 381.
Maria Elizabetha, Archduchess and Governess of the *Netherlands*, 233.
Maria-Amelia Princess of *Prussia*, 113.
Maria-Anne-Sophia Princess of *Prussia*, 113.
Maria-Josepha Princess of *Prussia*, 113.
Maria - Theresa Archduchess, 232, &c. Her Marriage to the D. of *Lorrain*, 233.
Maria-Josepha Q. of *Poland*, 98, 102, 110, 111, 112.

Maria-

Maria-Anne-Victoria of *Bavaria*, 309.

Maria Empress of *Germany*, her illustrious Relations, 250, 388.

Maria-Adelaide of *Savoy*, 260, 268.

Maria-Lescinski Q. of *France*, 304, 309.

Mark's, St. Festival, how celebrated at *Venice*, 401.

Marriage of the Sea, 399, 400.

Marriage of Princes how limited by the Laws of *Germany*, 60, 352. A Princess charg'd with abusing that Sacrament of the Church of *Rome*, 202.

Martinitz, Count of, 213, 214.

Masquerades at *Venice*, 412.

Mass, by whom alone celebrated with Boots and Spurs on, 192.

Matthias Emperor of *Germany*, 210.

Maubuisson, Abbess of, 344.

Maurice, William, Pr. of *Saxe-Zeitz*, 99.

―――――― Elector of *Saxony*, 381.

―――――― Count of *Saxony*, 115.

―――――― of *Saxe-Gotha* Pr. 182.

Maximilian, Emperor, 385, 388. His Statue, 386. Wife, 388, 389. His Daughter, 389. Father-in-law, 389.

Maximilian-Emanuel, Elector of *Bavaria*, 262, 263. 268, 274, 278, 379, 382. *Joseph* the Electoral Pr. 263.

Meinders, M. de, the *Prussian* Minister, 41.

MEISSEN *t*. 86.

Melvil, M. 65.

Menard, President, 317.

Mentz, Lotharius-Francis de Schonborn Elector, 201, 203, 310, 321, 338. His Severity to Robbers, 202.

Mercy, Count de, 244. His Defeat, 307.

MERSEBOURG *t*. 167, 168. Its Duke's Fondness for Bass-Viols, 168, 170, 171. His Duchess, 169.

MESTRE, *t*. 394, 395.

Metsch, Count de, 54, 242, 245.

Mile-posts in *Saxony*, 84.

Milk of our Lady, a Wine so called, 339.

Miltitz, General, *Alexander de*, 78, 100, 105, 107, 360.

Minckwitz, Charles-Christian de, 146.

Miracles ascrib'd to the two Saints of *Bohemia*, 213, 214.

Misson, Maximilian, criticized, 308, 392.

Mobs of *Amsterdam* and *Hamburg* compar'd, 54.

Mocenigo-Aloisio, Doge of *Venice*, 399.

Modena, Renaud d'Este Duke of, 230.

Molard, Count de, 255.

Molsheim t. 315.

Monclar, Baron de, 306.

Montbijou Palace, 3.

MONTEFIASCONE *t*. 430.

MONTEROSO *t*. 430.

Monte-Sancto, Count of, 244.

Montmorency, Francis Count de, 152. His Countess, 152.

Moravia, John Margrave of, 387.

Moschinski, Anthony, Count and Countess, 117, 120, 142.

Moses, a Piece of his Rock, 396.

Motteris, Mademoiselle, 243.

Mountpleasant, a fine Seat near *Hanover*, 67.

Muchlberg, the strong Lines cast up there by the Prince of *Beveren*, 72.

Munchausen, M. 65, 77.

Munchenbourg t. 2.

MUNICH *t*. 258, 268, 363.

Muscovy, Anne Czarina of, her Marriage, 200.

N.

An Alphabetical INDEX

N.

Nassau-Friesland, Prince, his untimely end, 297. His Daughter, who is Sister to the Pr. of *Orange*, 297.
Nassau, *Idstein*, Pr. 169.
────── *Weilbourg*, Count, 336.
────── *Ousingen* Princess, 342.
Nativities, Calculators of 'em refuted, 341.
Natzmer, Marshal de, 33, 40.
NAUMBOURG, t. 171, 172.
Neitsch, Mademoiselle de, 145.
Nepomucene (St.) *John*, 212, to 215.
Nosselrod, Count de, 334.
Neukirch, *Benjamin*, a Poet, 195.
NEUSTADT, t. 200.
Nicolotti, Fishermen at *Venice* so call'd, their Election of a Doge of their own, 402.
Nightingales, a Multitude of 'em, 86.
Nobility at *Venice*, the Purchase of it, 420.
Noyelles, Count de, 152.
NUREMBERG, t. 196, 197. Its Government compar'd to the *Venetian*, 197.
NYMPHENBOURG Palace, 268, 270, 271.

O.

Occo the Antiquary, 179.
Oder, River, 2.
Oetingen, t. 80. Princesses, 70, 76, 231.
Obsten, Baron de, 335.
Olbreuse, Madamoiselle de, 60, 62. Her Daughter, 62.
OPPENHEIM, t. 340.
Oranjebourg, t. 49.
Orders of Knighthood, the *Prussian*, 29. The *Bavarian*, 260. Of St. *Hubert*, 373.
Orleans, Duke of, 243, 306. Duchess, 274, 303, 304, 310.
Orselska, *Anne* Countess of, 119, 150.

Ossem, *Gosman-Daniel*, the Painter, 384.

P.

PADUA, t. 422.
Palatinate, Upper, 344.
Palatine, Electors, 274, 322, 323, &c. 328, 381. Revenues, 337. Who the last of the Protestant Princes of this Title, 342.
Paracelsus, where bury'd, 374. How he wrought most of his Cures, 374.
Passau, t. 366.
Patkul, Count, 164.
Patriarch of *Venice*, 403.
Patricians in *Germany*, who they are, 197, 198, 200.
Pechtelsheim, Baron de, 188, 189.
Peine, Painter, 11, 83.
Pennyless-Prince, the Nickname of an *Austrian*, 385, 386, 388.
Petits Maitres, at *Venice*, 421.
Philibert D. of *Savoy*, 389.
Philip IV. of *Spain*, his Reverence to the Viaticum, 249.
────── D. of *Burgundy*, 389.
────── Margrave of *Brandenburg*, 19, 20, 281. His Dowager, 20, 26. His Sons, 27. His Uncle *Albert*, 27. *Albert's* Sons, 27.
Philippina Charlotte, Princess of *Prussia*, 16, 72.
Philippina of *Welserin*, Archduchess, 390.
Philipsruhe, a Pleasure-House, 361.
Phul, Baron de, 285.
Pilate's Basin, 81.
Piosas, Count, 261.
Plassenberg Castle, 208.
Platen, Count de, 66. Countess, 67.
Pleasure-Houses, who has the finest in *Europe*, 268.
Plesk, *Helmnich* de, 145.

Plu-

to the First Volume.

Pludowska, Baroness, 135.
Poddewitz, the *Prussian* Minister, 31.
Poland, the Equivalent it has given to *France* of a Queen for a King, 309.
Polentz, M. de. 78.
Pollnitz, M. de, Cabinet-Counsellor to the D. of *Wirtemberg,* 285.
——— Baron, (our Author) his Conference with a *Lutheran* Doctor after he had turn'd *Papist* from a *Calvinist,* 160.
——— *Henrietta,* 7.
Pomerania. Hither, yielded to *Sweden.* 80.
POMMERSFELDEN, t. Seat of the Elector of *Mentz,* 203, 204.
Pompey's War with *Cæsar* painted, 370.
Ponte. t. 425.
Porcellane, finer in *Germany* than in *Japan,* 87, 88.
Portugal, Mary-Anne Queen of, 233.
——— *Emanuel* Pr. of, 422.
Pose, a Merchant at *Leipsic,* his fine Garden, 85.
Potschin, Madame de, 152.
Potzdam Castle, 34.
PRAGUE, *t.* 210.
Preysing, Maximilian Count de, 266, 267.
Princes, petty, more inaccessible than great ones, 83.
Privy-Counsellor's Preferment owing to a Present of a Bass-Viol, 171.
Profusion of Princes in what Article 'tis most justifiable, 10, 103.
Promnitz, Erdmann Count de, 135.
Proselytes, by what means they are soonest made among the Gentry, 161.
Provence, Theodebert Count of, 389.

Prussia, K. 21, 31, *&c.* 376. His Queen, 24. His Soldiery, 21, to 24, 34. His Children, 25, *&c.* 30, 72. Princess Royal's Marriage, 205.
Pruth Battle, 123.
Pultowa Battle, 123, 164.

Q.

*Q*Uails, abundance of 'em, where, 395.
Quilian, St. 191.

R.

*R*Abutin, Marshal de, 240.
Radifocani, M. 429.
Radjowski, Cardinal, 116, 150.
Radzevil, Louisa-Charlotte Pss. of, 330.
Radzevil, 2d Wife of Marshal *Flemming,* 92, 165.
RASTADT, *t.* 299. Prince of *Baden's* Palace here compar'd to *St. Cloud* near *Paris,* 299. Treaty sign'd there, 300.
Ratenau, t. 50.
RATENBERG, *t.* 379.
Rats; a Saint that was famous for killing them, 196.
Ravanne, Abbot de, 317.
Raugrave, Madame la, 342, 343.
Rechberg, Gaudentz Count de, 166
Reinbabe, Baron de, 176.
Religion, the Externals of it, where best observ'd, 412.
Residents for the *German* Princes at *Franckfort,* their Privileges, 342.
Rheden, M. de, 64, 66.
Rhenen, t. 344.
Riga Siege, 163.
Rinucci, the Cardinal and the Marquiss, 423.
Robert, Prince Palatine, K. of the *Romans,* 321.
Rock, Moses's, a piece of it, 396.
Rocoule, Madam de, 25.

Roder,

Roder, M. ..., 261.
Rodolph, Emperor, the Speech he made after he had one of his Hands cut off in Battle, 168.
Rohan, Cardinal *Arm. and Gaston*, 309. His Speeches on the Marriage of the Queen of France, 310, 315. His Election and Death, 315. Character, 316.
Rohr, Baroness Dowager of, 148.
Rolle, the *Brandenburg* Minister, 4.
Rolli, the Painter, 414.
ROME, t. the *German* Emperor's Right to live there, 201.
Ronaw, Count de, Envoy of *Saxe-Gotha*, 181, 182.
RONCIGLIONE, t. 430.
Rossing, M. de, 78.
Roth, Baron de, 305.
Rotofski Count, 115, 119.
Rupert, St. 365, 366.
Rutowski, Count, 115, 116, 118.
Ruzzini Carlo, Doge of *Venice*, 399.

S.

SAltz, R. 364.
Saltzbourg, t. 364. Its Revenues, and Houshold of its Archbishop, 367, 373. A great Revolution in this Country, 375.
Saltzdahl Seat near *Brunswic*, 75.
Sapieha, *Benedict*, 163.
Sardinia, King and Queen, 332, 335.
SAVERNE, t. 315.
Savoy, see *Eugene* and *Emanuel*.
Saxe-Lawenburg, Princess, 300.
———*Weissenfels, John-Adolphus* Prince of, 99, 114. *Sophia* Princess of, 200. *Christina* Princess of, 114, 115.
———*Weymar* Dukes, 172, 173, 174, 175.

——— ..., ...-*William* ..., 99, 171. ———Cardinal ...
———Duchy, 167. Wealth of its Peasants, 167.
———Coton Dukes, 173, &c. Duchesses, 181.
———Forbi Duke, 82, 83.
———*Meynungen* Princess, 181, 200.
———Chevalier de, 116.
———*Eysenach* Dukes, 173, 182.
Saxony ill provided with Ordinaries, 86. Present State of its Court, 99, to 155. Character of the Men, 155. of the Women, 156. of the Clergy, 159.
Scarperia, t. 425.
Schindler's Lace Manufactory, 7.
Schleisheim Palace, 270.
Schluter the Architect, 10.
Schmiedel, Baron de, 176.
Schneitzenrieth, t. 377.
Schomberg, Marshal, 17.
Schonborn, *Francis George*, Count, 338.
———*John-Philip-Francis*, Count, 54, 185, 186. *Damian-Hugo* the Cardinal, 318, 319, 320.
———*Frederic-Charles*, Bp. of *Bamberg*, 185, 190, 191, 202, 242. *Lotharius-Francis*, another of its Bishops, 201.
Schoning, General, 116.
Schorrer, the Pope's Vicar at *Hanover*, 64.
Schulemburg, Count de, 408.
Schulenbourg, General, 61. His Duel with Count *Fleming*, 163.
Schwabach, t. 196.
Schwartzenberg, Pr. 213, 223, 301, 302, 304.
Schwetzingen, t. 352.
Schwizinski, *Nicholas*, 147.
SCHWATZ, t. 379.

Sea,

Schenck and *Schutz*, Barons de, 285.

Sea, the Ceremony of marrying it, 399, 400.

Seckendorf, Baron and Count, 54, 195.

Seefeldt-Torring, *Maximilian*, Count de, 265.

Sebgutt, Counts of, 147.

Seibelsdorff, General, 358.

Seiffertitz, *Adolphus* Baron de, 141.

Sickengen, Baron de, 333.

SIENNA t. 429.

Sigismond, Emperor, 339, 388.

Sigismond, Archduke and Count of *Tirol*, 389.

Silenus's Legacy, 190.

Sobieski, *John* K. of *Poland*, 247. His Daughter, 262.

Soissons, Countess of, 238, 239.

Soliman, the Sultan, 248.

Solkeofski, *Alexander Joseph*, Count de, 98, 103, 104, 128, 133, 139, 143.

Sophia-Wilhelmina, Princess of *East-Friesland*, 83.

——— *Christiana-Louisa*, Princess of *Bareith*, 205.

Spain, Council of, at *Vienna*, 244.

Span, Baron de, 162, 163.

Speratus, *Paul*, 375.

Spiegel, Madame de, 116, 358.

Spiga, the Pope's Vicar at *Hanover*, 63.

SPIRE t. 310.

Sporcke, M. de, 77.

Spree, River, 3.

Staden, Siege, 57.

Stadtholder at *Vienna*, 246.

Stanislaus, K. 318. His Daughter's March on foot with the Prince of *Baden*, 304. Marriage to *Lewis* XV. 309.

Stanisiawski, N N. de *Sobgutt*, 147.

Staremberg, *Maximilian*, 246.

VOL. I.

Staremberg, *Ernest-Rudiger*, Count de, 239, 247.

Staremberg, *Guido*, Marshal, 239.

Staremberg, *Gundacker*, Count, 241.

STARGARD, t. 162.

Staupitz, Abbat, 375.

Stein, Baron, 72. Baroness, 130, 148.

Steinbeck, General, prov'd a cruel Incendiary, 57.

Stein Wein, a sort of Wine so called, 190.

Steinbach, the Architect, 308.

Sternberg, Count, 211.

STERTZINGEN, t. 392.

Stetin, t. its Sequestration, by whom obtain'd, 164.

Stotterheim, M. de, Cup-bearer to the D. of *Saxe-Gotha*, 183.

Strada, *James* de, 179.

Strahlsund, Siege, 124.

STRASBOURG, t. 305, 315. Noted for Libertines, 310.

Streitborst, Colonel, 292.

Stringuetta, the *Venetian* Courtezan, 421.

Studenitz, Baron de, 176.

STUTGARD, t. 179, 289.

Sulkowski. See *Solkeofski*.

Sulteman, M. and Madame de, 292.

Sulzbach, *Joseph-Charles*, Pr. and Princess of, 324, 330, 331.

——— *Theodore*, Prince, 332.

——— *John-Christian*, Prince, 332, 333.

——— *Charles*, Prince, 332.

Sympathy, its Power, 374.

T.

Tartary Women, what they say to their Husbands when they come home without Booty, 247.

Gg   *Tele-*

An Alphabetical INDEX

Telemachus, translated into *German* Verse, 195.
Teschen, George, Prince of, 116, 117. Princess of, 117, 150.
Thanhausen, Count de, 373.
Thaun, Count and Countess, 151.
Theodebert, Count of *Provence*, 389.
Thirheim, Sigismond, Count de, 258. 265, 266.
Thomasius, the Civilian, 156.
Thorn of our Saviour's Crown, 81.
Thou, Messieurs, their Library, by whom purchased, 317.
Thungen, General, 278.
Tilly, Count, his Massacre of the *Swedes* at *Brandenburgh*, 2. Of the *Palatines* at *Heidelberg*, 321.
Tintoret, the Painter, 419, 420.
Tirol, Country, 377. Manner of Salutation here, 380. Dress of the People, 393. Their Saints, 394.
Titian, the Painter, 419.
Torring, Ignatius-Joseph, Count de, 265. 267, 373.
Tour of *Auvergne*, Princess, 332.
Tour and *Taxis, Alexander*, Pr. of, 205, 303, 342.
——— *Mary-Augusta*, Princess of, 285, 290.
Tournay, Siege, 124.
Towers, mistaken for *Capuchin* Friars, 339.
TRENT, *t.* 393.
Truchsses, Zeil, Count de, 374.
Tschernin, Count, 211, 222.
Tuhlmeier, Secretary, *Prussian*, 43.
Tun, at *Heidelberg*, 324.
Turks, where they have reason to laugh at the Christians, 54.
Tuscany, John Gaston, the Great Duke, 428. His Saying when he declared Don *Carlos* his Successor, 418.

Tutors, or Governors, a mercenary sort, 217, 218.

V.

Valerio's Tomb at *Venice*, 405.
Vatican Library, 321.
Vauban, M. Engineer, 309.
VENICE, *t.* 395, 396, &c. Its Doges, 389, 390. Patriarch, 403. Churches, 403, &c. Arsenal, 405, &c. Bucentaur, 399, 407. Forces, 408. Lakes, 409. Its political Interest, 409. Trade, 410. Nobles and Ambassadors, 410. Ladies, 411. Music, 414. 415. Palaces and Gentry, 420.
Vernesobre, Baron de, his Gains by *Mississippi*, 8.
Viaticum, the Homage paid to it in Popish Countries, 249.
Vicardel, Francis, Marquis of *Fleuri* and *Beaufort*, 135.
Vieban, M. de, *Prussian* Minister, 43.
VIENNA, *t.* 224. Sieges, 237, 239, 247, 248. Its Police, 246. Its Governour how still'd, 246. Its Garrison, 247. Fortifications, 249. Women, 251, &c.
Vierec. M. de, 46.
Villaco, t. 382.
Violante, of *Bavaria*, Princess, 429.
Violin, the first in *Italy*, 415.
Virgilius, St. 365.
Virgin Mary's miraculous Image at *Inspruc*, 384. The Adoration paid to her in the Countries of *Trent* and *Tirol*, 394.
VITERBO, *t.* 430.
ULM, *t.* 276.
Unertel, M. de, 267.
Voltaire's Life of *Charles* XII, King of *Sweden*, Reflection on it, 32.

W.

W.

Wackerbarth, *Augustus-Christopher,* Marshal *de,* 91, 99, 102, 124.
Wackerbarth, *Salmour-Gabaleon-Joseph,* Count *de,* 104, 112, 124, 126, 165. His Countess, 125.
Wagenhelm, M. *de,* of *Hanover,* 66.
WAHTRINGEN, t. 377.
Walbourg de Truchsses, Count *de,* 27.
Waldstein, Count and Countess *de,* 147, 148.
Wales, FREDERIC, Prince of, 26, 64. AUGUSTA, Princess of, 182.
Wallenstein, Count and Countess of, 151, 153.
Walrave, M. Engineer, 82.
Walstein, the great Soldier, 210.
Wartemberg, Count and Countess, 3, 5, 6, 7. The King of *Prussia*'s Tears at his Funeral, 7. His Administration, 36, 42, 44, 134.
Wartensleben, Count, 17, 36.
Wasserbourg, t. 364.
Water works, at *Herenhausen,* 67.
Wederkopf, M. *de,* 80.
Weiller, a *Prussian* Colonel, 20.
Weimar, t. 172. Its Dukes, 172 to 176.
Weissenberg Battle, 210.
WEISSENBOURG, t. 318.
Wenceslaus (St.) K. of *Bohemia,* 212, 213.
Wens in Throats, 393.
Wensen, M. Marshal of the *Prussian* Court, 7, 8.
WERMSTORF, t. 86, 103, 157.
Werth, John de, 321.
Wetzlar Tribunal, 245, 320.
Whim, a fine Seat so called near *Hanover,* 67.
William of *Saxe-Gotha,* Prince, 182.
William-Henry, Duke of *Saxe-Eysenach,* 183.
Willigise, ABp of *Mentz,* 179.

Wirtemberg, **Lewis** Prince of, 151, 285. *Charles-Alexander* Duke, 279, 285, 290. His Duchess, 285. His Brother *Frederic,* 285.
Wirtemberg, Eberhard-Lewis D. 279, 280, 289. His Duchess, ib. 280. His Son, 281. Daughter, *ib.*
Wirtemberg-Oels, Augusta-Louisa, Princess of, 83. *Christian-Ulric,* Duke of, 83.
Witgenstein, Count, 285.
Woad, three sorts of it, 179.
Wohlin, Baron *de,* 334.
Wolckenstein, Count *de,* 393.
Wolfembuttle Family and Court, 69 to 72. Its Inhabitants compared to the Hogs of *Westphalia,* 75. The Duchess Dowager, 80.
WOLFEMBUTTLE, t. 75.
Wolffenstein, Sophia-Christina, Countess of, 208.
Women, of the *Levant* and *Hamburg,* their great Confinement, 52.
WORMS, t. 338.
Wratislaw, Francis-Charles, Co. *de,* 147, 148, 153. His Countess, 154.
Wreech, de, Colonel, 30.
Wurben, Countess *de,* Mistress to the D. of *Wirtemberg,* 279, 282, 283, 284. Her Disgrace, 290, &c.
Wurm, M. *de,* Master of the Horse to the D. of *Saxe-Gotha,* 183.
Wurmbrandt, Count *de,* 245.
Wurtemberg, Christina-Charlotta de, Margravine of *Brandenburg-Anspach,* 194.
WURTZBOURG, t. 185. Power and Splendor of its Bishop, 190.

Z.

ZECH, Bernard, Baron *de,* 138.

Zell,

An Alphabetical INDEX.

Zell, Duke and Duchess, 60, 61, 62.
Zell, t. 61, 68.
Zenta, Prince Eugene's Victory there, 237.

Zinzendorf, Lewis, Count de, 240. The Dignity hereditary in his Family, ib.
Zobel, Baron de, 188, 189, 336.
Zochau, Baron de, 193, 195.

FINIS.

ERRATA.

IN the first Col. of Letter M, in the Index, Line 6 from the Bottom, for p. 113, read 114. Line 7, 9, and 11, for *Prussia* r. *Poland*. In the 3d. Column of the same Letter, read lines 34, 35, 36, thus;

Moschinski, *Anthony*, Count and Countess, 117, 120, 142.
Moses, a Piece of his Rock, 396.

www.ingramcontent.com/pod-product-compliance
Lightning Source LLC
Chambersburg PA
CBHW072114220426
43664CB00013B/2111